LIVING AND WORKING IN WARTIME CHINA

LIVING AND WORKING IN WARTIME CHINA

Edited by Brett Sheehan and Wen-hsin Yeh

University of Hawai'i Press
Honolulu

Paperback edition 2023
Printed in the United States of America

Library of Congress Cataloging-in-Publication Data

Names: Sheehan, Brett, editor. | Yeh, Wen-hsin, editor.
Title: Living and working in wartime China / edited by Brett Sheehan and Wen-hsin Yeh.
Description: Honolulu : University of Hawaiʻi Press, [2022] | Includes bibliographical references and index.
Identifiers: LCCN 2022025040 | ISBN 9780824888824 (hardback) | ISBN 9780824892159 (pdf) | ISBN 9780824892166 (epub) | ISBN 9780824893163 (kindle edition)
Subjects: LCSH: War and society—China—History—20th century. | World War, 1939–1945—Social aspects—China. | China—History—1937–1945.
Classification: LCC DS777.518 .L585 2022 | DDC 951.04/2—dc23/eng/20220622
LC record available at https://lccn.loc.gov/2022025040

ISBN 9780824893156 (paperback)

Cover art: Policewoman searching female passengers and their belongings at Qianmen Station (June 1938). North China Railway Archive.

University of Hawaiʻi Press books are printed on acid-free paper and meet the guidelines for permanence and durability of the Council on Library Resources.

Contents

Acknowledgments

The editors and contributors would like to thank the Li Ka-shing Foundation Program in Modern Chinese History at the University of California at Berkeley for funding the initial conference that led to this volume. This is a better volume for the many useful suggestions made by two anonymous readers. Any remaining faults are our own. Finally, this manuscript could not have come to fruition without the support and help of the editors and staff of the University of Hawai‘i Press, with special thanks to Masako Ikeda, Grace Wen, and Bojana Ristich.

Introduction

Living and Working with War

BRETT SHEEHAN

This volume reflects on the variety and detail of Chinese experiences under conditions of war during the period of Japanese invasion from 1937 to 1945 (China's World War II), a defining event in China's modern history. In regard to the war, scholars have productively studied mobilization, state building, regional variations, the less than black-and-white nature of collaboration, gender, soldiers, and the experiences of businesspeople caught with divided loyalties among other topics.[1] Here we change the focus from high-level politicians to individual, often anonymous, experience; from politics and diplomacy to culture and economy; and from war planning and fighting to living and working. The focus on culture and economy brings into sharp relief, on the one hand, the enormous gap between elite demands for mobilization and the reality of everyday life, and, on the other hand, the role of mid-level bureaucrats and professionals caught in the web of war planning and charged with carrying out mobilization for total war. Through these professionals, we will also see experiences of people at lower levels of society, and together they will show new contours in our conception of World War II in China and total war in general.

Although many scholars now agree that it is important to pay to attention to the varieties of experience of the war, this period of tremendous upheaval is still often referred to in totalizing terms. For example, Diana Lary, who elsewhere emphasizes disparate regional experiences, describes the war as a time when "The natural trust between individuals and groups that had been the glue of traditional society was gone, broken by the war, eroded, undermined, and betrayed in myriad ways."[2] Lary sees the violence and chaos of World War II as "sweeping away one society without producing a new one."[3] Likewise, the Chinese-language literature on the war often accepts its total nature uncritically, even enthusiastically. For example, in the words of a history of World War II, published in China in 2000, "Salvation of the nation from destruction became the responsibility that could not be shirked by any Chinese. . . . [Expelling the Japanese] was a test of every circle and every Chinese person, and this is the only standard [to determine] loyalty to the motherland."[4] These post-hoc totalizing conceptions of the war echo the ideas of elites from the period of the war itself who stressed the totality of people's commitment to the war effort. Leaders on all sides of the conflict spoke in terms of the totality of the war, especially in the sense of requiring the loyalty, obedience, and sacrifice of the people. In reality, however—to paraphrase Rebecca Walker's work on extended conflict in Sri Lanka—total war in China was a time when people suffered, survived, resisted, and collaborated within the endurance of the everyday.[5]

The elite call on the spiritual and military power of the Chinese people during World War II dated back to the crises of the late nineteenth and early twentieth centuries. The intellectual Liang Qichao picked up the ideas of German and Japanese thinkers in a 1902 essay where he advocated "what Stanislav Andreski calls 'militolatry,' or civic militarism, as a solution to China's chronic weakness."[6] The idea of a militarized route to modernity had had a major impact on the early development of Chiang Kai-shek, the leader of China's Nationalist Party.[7] The idea of militarization as state building fused with the concept of total war when in the twentieth century wars became, "in Michael Howard's words, 'a conflict not of armies, but of populations.'"[8] Scholars have criticized the total war concept on several grounds, not least because it overstates "limits" placed on wars prior to the twentieth century and because it elides varieties of experiences.[9] Thus, rather than a description of reality, "total war" is a useful concept because it is an unrealizable ideal held by military and civilian planners.[10] At its heart, the total war ideal demanded control of the economy and the productive resources of entire societies.[11] Control of the economy, in turn, required the active commitment of the populace, the hearts and minds of the people. It is in this dual mobilization, economic and cultural, that we see individuals living and working with war in this volume.

As Japanese aggression intensified in the 1930s, Chinese political and intellectual elites discussed total war mobilization more and more frequently. In 1935 the military officer Xu Tingyao "argued that the First World War demonstrated conclusively that modern warfare demands huge reserves of manpower."[12] Chiang Kai-shek himself acknowledged the industrial aspect of modern warfare when he said, "The coming international war before our eyes can only be a three-dimensional war of pure science," and he anticipated the use of electrical devices, chemicals, machines, and poisons. Even before the outbreak of war in 1937, Chiang called for general mobilization, economic as well as spiritual, against Japan: "So-called military strength now includes all the people of a country. Everyone should participate in the war and give their efforts for national defense. All material, even each straw and each log, are all needed for national defense."[13]

The expectations of support and sacrifice—"each straw and each log"—were magnified by a lack of the material bases for total war. In the years leading up to the war, Chinese industrialization lagged behind Japan's, and the gaze of most Chinese leaders remained on internal conflict rather than external threats. Even highly industrialized Japan was not fully prepared for total war.[14] Because of inadequate material resources, Chiang and other elites fell back on the idea of the "strength of the people" as a tool of war. In writings and speeches before and throughout the war with Japan, Chiang reiterated this theme of spiritual strength, which had great resonance with earlier ideas about militarization as a route to modernity. In a prewar text he wrote, "With military valor [*wude* 武德] we need not rely on weapons. With military valor we can develop a kind of strength of spirit. Not only will the weapons of our enemies not be able to destroy the strength of this spirit, but with this strength of spirit we can have victory over our enemies!"[15] For Chiang, the idea of war was intimately linked to the idea of a disciplined and modern people. "Chiang used the constant threat of violence to promote the citizen-soldier as a 'missionary' of the New Life Movement, to forge new models of citizens through the conversion of untrained and undisciplined soldiers."[16] Mao Zedong, leader of the Chinese Communist Party, echoed similar sentiments in his concept of people's war (*renmin zhanzheng* 人民戰爭), which relied on the power of the people for victory.[17] Likewise, Zou Taofen, a leftist critic of the Nationalist regime, used the journal he edited to advocate active participation of the whole of the Chinese people in the war against Japan.[18] For their part, the Japanese occupiers too looked for cooperation from the Chinese people. Thus, the competing regimes of World War II China were locked in a battle not just for the resources to wage total war (or at least something conceived as total war), but also, given the limited nature of resources, for spiritual support.

"Spiritual mobilization," "people's war," "general mobilization," and all such concepts show elite views of the total war ideal derived from ideas of military discipline as a route to modernity, combined with the exigencies of total war based on assumptions of the commitment and participation of entire populations and the full resources of nations. Elite perceptions of war made no allowance for civilian life separate from war mobilization and modern discipline, thus day-to-day activities of living and working became, in theory, subordinate to the exigencies of war, and it is this idea of the war that has become enshrined in some later portrayals. As the war proceeded for eight long years, realities showed the unrealistic nature of elite ideals. For leaders, this meant ad hoc adaptation to the mobilization of economic and human resources, combined with advocacy of a war of spirit to supplement the lack of resources. For the Chinese people, called on by Nationalist and Communist leaders, as well as Japanese occupiers, to commit fully to the war, it meant a variety of experiences within the "endurance of the everyday," ranging from stoic adaptation to profiteering to humor to tragedy.

The essays here try to leave romantic views of war aside and mine new primary sources to bring fresh perspectives on the complexities of living and working in wartime China. We see individuals living and working under regimes attempting to simultaneously mobilize material resources and harness the spiritual power of the people, with mixed results on all counts, with continuity and creation, as well as disruption and destruction. Because elite ideals of total war stressed spiritual and human mobilization in the absence of huge economic and industrial resources, the chapters here focus as much on culture as economy; thus the mobilization and control of cultural resources plays as prominent a role in this volume as the mobilization and control of material goods. The chapters here sample experience under all of the regimes of World War II China: the Nationalists in the southwest, the Communists in their base areas in the north, the Japanese occupation regimes in both North and South China, and the foreign concession "islands" in Tianjin and Shanghai. As such, this book provides a valuable opportunity to compare the disparate experiences of living and working under those regimes, a topic for which details and texture still remain sparse.[19] The chapters are divided into four parts: "Living and Working in Urban Daily Life," "Living and Working with Culture," "Living and Working with Provisioning," and "Living and Working on the New Frontiers." Inevitably, the realms of these divisions often cross. In addition, the mid-level officials and managers at the center of many of the activities of "working with war" also had to live with war, and their lives can illustrate much.

Part I examines the experiences of living and working in wartime urban China through the lenses of housing and women's work. Glosser's account of housing in Shanghai questions the romance that pervades many histories of the war and concludes that the vast majority of Shanghainese had neither the time nor the leisure to aid the war or perhaps to even think about it very deeply. For many, it was "something to endure." If so many people had only peripheral involvement, she asks, "Who, or what, won the war?" Glosser's stories of grit and ingenuity in Shanghai are echoed in the experiences of women looking for work in wartime Beijing. Sophia Lee's account of occupied Beijing portrays a situation where women subverted conventional social norms by finding, and sometimes creating, income-producing opportunities.

Part II shows how bureaucracies in all of China's competing wartime regimes struggled with the perceived need to control culture and use it to mobilize for the war effort. Di Wang's essay about teahouse culture in Chengdu shows a part of daily life that, on the surface, had only peripheral relations to the war. Conflicts about teahouses reflected many of the divisions that characterized Nationalist-controlled China at the time: coastal versus inland culture, elites versus commoners, elite culture versus popular culture, local versus national culture, and local places versus the nation. As a way of trying to paper over these fault lines, the state tried to insert the priorities of total war by using teahouses as venues to shape culture and promote patriotic education. Comparing film censorship in the Nationalist and Japanese-occupation governments, Chaoguang Wang shows similar propensities for cultural control among both the Nationalists and the Japanese occupiers. Both wanted ideological conformity with government goals, but both also had general moral concerns about romance, nudity, and frivolous content not appropriate in wartime and not appropriate to state visions of disciplined modernity. Within this shared predilection for control and moral approbation, many differences existed in the details of each regime's censorship. In particular, central censorship authorities and local officials were often at loggerheads over what constituted proper content. In his chapter, Maruta Takashi shows how regimes across China used the regulation of calendars and the celebration of holidays for newly formed political purposes. The regimes shared a modern commitment to close regulation of time and promulgation of the Western calendar, but each regime had its own peculiarities in regard to the celebration of holidays. Variation was the norm even within regimes. In the end, all of China's regimes straddled the line between promoting modern and patriotic holidays in sync with the newly adopted Western calendar and in appropriating traditional dates from the lunar calendar tradition. With tea, film, and calendars we see governments that often considered customs and cultural practices a hindrance to both mobilization for war and modernity.

Part III shows mostly mid-level state and private functionaries working under wartime conditions to provision both the state and private markets. Parks Coble sets the stage for the most important context of China's political economy during the war by examining the causes and effects of wartime inflation. Coble shows how warring regimes in China competed with their currencies, as well as with their military forces. To keep the upper hand in this "currency war," the Nationalists maintained the convertibility of their currency into foreign exchange. The end result was runaway inflation, alienation of China's allies, and increased resentments within China as people perceived others, especially those living in the foreign concessions in Shanghai, as having special privileges and better lives. The constant erosion of living standards in both Chinese- and Japanese-controlled areas eroded the governments' legitimacy among both the Chinese people and the world at large. Sheehan studies attempts of the North China occupation regime to encourage jute cultivation for the manufacture of the gunny sacks vital to wartime supply lines. He concludes that the Japanese-occupation regime proved unable to link the supply lines of rural development and urban production in North China. The process of provisioning relied on an army of Japanese and Chinese technocrats whose careful plans "coexisted with the reality of a messy, venal, and often violent political and military process." For Kwan, the provisioning and supply of salt provided the Nationalists, Communists, and Japanese-occupation regimes with an opportunity for state building, portending a large state role in commerce for postwar regimes. Salt famine, rationing, blockades, smuggling, black markets, rising prices amid supply gluts, and exports to Japan and Korea reigned. In the end, as with managing the currency and the provisioning of jute, none of the parties' plans bore full fruition.

Finally, the book returns to both culture and wartime production, but this time on China's newly important frontiers. Matthew Johnson brings us the story of Sun Mingjing, a film educator for the Nationalists. His work shows that provincial development and mass education efforts to acculturate ethnic minorities on the margins of the Nationalist state continued throughout the war. For many of the border officials with whom Sun came into contact, "experience of war" referred to civil conflict, frontier security, and cycles of ethnic violence—all of which had emerged prior to 1937 amid the ruins of the Qing empire. Sovereignty and territorial control, rather than total war per se, were the goals that drove these local, or sub-national, developmental initiatives. Control was an issue with soil conservation projects in Gansu Province as well, as Micah Muscolino shows, but in this case he shows a centralizing and modernizing state in conflict with local landholders and land rights. Concerned about grain supplies, the Nationalist government dispatched a group of experts with international educations and connections to devise soil conservation methods for a province where food production had not previously been a national priority. Objecting to technocratic plans, local landholders stymied these efforts by drawing on a repertoire of strategies, including invoking the language of war mobilization, claiming the need to preserve tradition, and using Nationalist legal statutes.

Much of the value of these chapters comes from the specificity of their detail, bringing new texture to our picture of wartime China and new evidence for the large diversity of experiences. The government dispatched experts to the frontier to conserve soil and document local conditions; control of salt derived from ad hoc decisions and local market forces; housing supply in Shanghai changed based on the ability to construct temporary walls and floors; the value of various currencies was subject to the success or failure of distant battles; women's work in Beijing expanded to include professions like policing. War affected the holidays one celebrated, the kinds of movies one was allowed to see, the stories told in teahouses, or the operations of a business. Crowded housing in Shanghai dictated the ability of families to live together, women's work in Beijing subverted family norms, and war needs brought urban technocrats into contact with rural and frontier China. Likewise, living in one part of China or another meant using one type of currency or having to choose between competing types. Together, all of these localized perspectives provide a less universalized picture of the experiences of living and working in wartime China than allowed for by either elite conceptions of total war at the time or by more recent totalizing characterizations. At the same time, however, several themes do appear frequently in the research presented here. Four of those themes stand out.

First, although the idea of total war assumes a kind of totalizing commitment that would entail a sharp divide between the war and what came before, in reality there existed many significant continuities with the prewar period. Surprisingly, many of these continuities took place at the policy level. Film censorship rules grew out of prewar practice, in terms of both institutional structure and content analysis. Holidays too often utilized prewar, and often pre-twentieth-century, precedents. The Nationalist assumption of control of the money supply in 1935 led to both the currency war and the wartime inflation. Many of these continuities involved the practices of daily life and cultural production. For example, Chengdu teahouse culture remained strong, even under the onslaught of criticism that time spent at teahouses detracted from commitment to the war. Elsewhere, even local Communist officials often celebrated holidays in a traditional manner in spite of policy directives to do otherwise. Border conflicts and development projects had roots in the nineteenth-century decline in the Qing empire. At the same time, government influence on filmmaking, official holidays, and even teahouse culture shows continuities in the state as a paternalistic moral force, although these forms of cultural production and practice became imbued with new content as the need for discipline and sacrifice for the war effort brought new content to old forms.

Second, the war exposed many of the rifts and fault lines of Chinese society, in contrast to elite calls for unity. Women in Beijing went to work in spite of family and societal pressures to conform to traditional roles. Shanghai residents lived within a hierarchy of housing based on differences in square inches and access to windows. Movie production companies and their audiences maintained their preferences for romance and sword-fighting movies in resistance to state calls for art in support of war. Teahouse users defended their leisure against accusations of frivolity. Inconsistent and ever-changing government policies resulted in a revolving door of new and old holidays established in the interest of shoring up state legitimacy. The currency war created chaos and economic instability. The production of gunny sacks for the war effort resulted in an uneasy collaboration fraught with danger, incompetence, and the propensity for parties on all sides to milk the project for self-interest rather than state goals. The control of salt production remained a goal of all the wartime regimes, but trade across borders was common and often encouraged. Frontier elites and peoples had only tenuous connections to central government priorities, including the war. Soil conservation efforts resulted in a clash between scientific practice and local interests.

One of the primary fault lines involved conflict between technocratic elites and the local people with whom they dealt. Soil conservation specialists felt that local farmers failed to understand scientific principles. Managers of the jute cultivation research station felt that Chinese peasants and Japanese teachers both tried to turn the station's goals to personal advantage. The documentary filmmaker Sun Mingjing saw the vast chasm that separated minority peoples on the frontier from mainstream Chinese society. Elites of all sorts felt that the war was misunderstood by China's populace; politicians and bureaucrats alike felt the need to forge a nation of common interest and tried to do so by regulating everything from production to teahouse conversation and movie content to calendars.

Third, the essays here bring to light the odd paradox between professional conduct and commitment on behalf of mid-level technocrats and the chaos and poor organization that characterized all the governments of the wartime period. Bureaucratization made the exceptional routine while at the same time allowing for venality, waste, and incompetence on all sides. The flip side of the modernizing state-building and cultural control efforts of these regimes was the difficulty of realizing any of them fully. Showing the contradictions inherent in living and working with war, several of the essays stress state weaknesses and the inability of the state to access adequate resources. Incompetency in government, a split between rural supply and urban demand, local opposition, distractions of the need to find housing or a job, unstable currency, and corruption all hindered abilities of the wartime regimes to build the states they imagined or mobilize the resources needed for "total war."

Fourth, the existence of mutually hostile and ideologically opposed regimes would normally point to significant and unbridgeable gaps among implacable enemies, but the essays here show some remarkable similarities across regimes. A short list of similarities would include forms of film censorship, control of commodities such as salt, use of holidays to promote state legitimacy, continuation of the functioning of international networks, and corporatist organization. In fact, the regimes shown in these essays shared a commitment to state building in modes each considered modern. Regimes adopted foreign calendars and holidays to support state ideologies; built salt tax bureaucracies and modernized salt-producing equipment as an important means of raising revenue; professionalized police forces, even with the inclusion of women officers; continued prewar development programs in peripheral and border regions; and promoted cultural production to bring those regions into the state discourse.

One of the greatest similarities across regimes was the prominent role of technocrats in the war effort. For Communists, Nationalists, and Japanese occupiers alike, mid-level bureaucrats proved indispensable in helping regimes reach their goals. To do so, many of them called on international networks forged before the war began, and some of those networks involved contact between Chinese and Japanese. In the chapters that follow, readers will see technocrats at work trying to regulate calendars, conserve soil, control the money supply, provide housing, suggest employment opportunities for women in need, cultivate jute, make educational films, control teahouse conversations, and control salt production. These bureaucrats provided continuity with the prewar period, set up much of the organizational capabilities regimes would use in the postwar period, and brought the ordinary to the extraordinary job of war mobilization.

The importance of these mid-level functionaries echoes in some ways Janis Mimura's study of Japan's wartime technocrats. In her work, Mimura borrows James Burnham's idea of "managerial revolution," where "the capitalist class was being replaced not by the proletariat, but by a new quasi-class of 'managers.'"[20] In looking at the Japanese occupation regime in Manchuria, Mimura argues that the leaders of Manchukuo "were highly rational and conscientious public servants who promoted a vision of an ultramodern Japan." In their work, Mimura sees the roots of postwar Japan based on "a new technocratic mindset," when "defeat laid the grounds for the transition from techno-fascism to postwar managerialism."[21] Thus, although Mimura makes a link between managerialism and Japanese fascism, she allows for a transformation to align with other political systems. The essays in this volume show a similarly important role for technocrats with ties to a common view of modernity, though without the Fascist political overtones studied by Mimura and with greater latitude for error, failure, and corruption than her model allows. The common ingredient is a vision of technocratic and managerial modernity that could accommodate all the ideologically opposed regimes in China during World War II.

Of course this was war, and the similarities shared by the regimes, including this technocratic managerial approach, did not change the fact that the various sides were implacable enemies locked in combat. The essays in this volume expand our view of that conflict by showing that some lives were completely overturned by the war while for others life went on, though with adaptations to turmoil. Survival often meant adapting to constantly changing conditions in the political regimes, the availability of housing, work, cultural production, and the provisioning of resources. Above all, these stories question categories of normal and abnormal times. To return to the conceptualization provided by Rebecca Walker, "There are forms of everyday life in violent contexts, which cannot be understood through the juxtaposed categories of the ordinary and extraordinary."[22] In living and working during war, one adapted to a new kind of wartime "normalcy," all the more significant for not always being extraordinary. These stories about living and working in wartime China serve as a reminder that in many places then, and in the world today, wartime is, and has been, "normal."

Notes

1. For work on wartime state building, mobilization, and extraction, see Duara, *Culture, Power, and the State;* Duus et al., *The Japanese Wartime Empire;* Eastman, *Seeds of Destruction;* Strauss, *Strong Institutions in Weak Polities;* and Young, *China's Wartime Finance and Inflation.* For more recent interpretations, see Henriot and Yeh, *In the Shadow of the Rising Sun;* Hsiung and Levine, *China's Bitter Victory;* MacKinnon, Lary, and Vogel, *China at War;* Wakeman, *The Shanghai Badlands;* and Yeh, *Wartime Shanghai.* For collaboration, see Barrett and Shyu, *China in the Anti-Japanese War;* Boyle, *China and Japan at War;* Brook, *Collaboration;* and Fu, *Passivity, Resistance, and Collaboration.* On business, see Bian, *The Making of the State Enterprise System in Modern China;* Coble, *Chinese Capitalists in Japan's New Order;* Cochran, *Chinese Medicine Men;* Frazier, *The Making of the Chinese Industrial Workplace;* Howard, *Workers at War;* and Sheehan, *Industrial Eden.* On women, see Li, *Echoes of Chongqing.*

2. Lary, *The Chinese People at War,* 196.

3. Ibid., 195.

4. Zhang, *Zhongguo kangri zhanzheng shi,* 1. Unless otherwise noted, translations are mine.

5. Walker, "Violence, the Everyday and the Question of the Ordinary," 9.

6. Green, "Turning Bad Iron into Polished Steel," 156.

7. Ibid., 157.

8. Chickering, "Total War," 26.

9. Ibid.

10. Mieszkowski, "Great War, Cold War, Total War"; Beckett, "Total War," 29 and 214.

11. Ibid., 33.

12. Landdeck, "Under the Gun," 68.

13. Quoted in Zhong, "1931–1937 JiangJieshi yingdui riben qinhua de junshi sixiang," 39 and 41.

14. Barnhart, *Japan Prepares for Total War,* 18, 20. See also Dower, "The Structures and Ideologies of Conquest," 17–22, and Levine, "Introduction," xxi.

15. Quoted in Landdeck, "Under the Gun," 40.

16. Flath and Smith, *Beyond Suffering,* 7.

17. "Mao Zedong de renmin zhanzheng lilun"; Liu and Liu, "Mao Zedong dui Wang Chuanshan quanmin zhanzheng sixiang de jicheng he fazhan."

18. Zou, however, complicated the picture of a top-down, state-led total mobilization by declaring that the journal he edited also wanted to provide a means by which the government could hear the voice of the people. Zou, "Quanmin Kangzhan de shiming." *Quanmin Kangzhan* resulted from the merger of two other periodicals: *Anti-Japanese War* (*Kangzhan* 抗戰) and *All the People* (*Quanmin* 全民).

19. Lary, "Introduction," 7–13.

20. Mimura, *Planning for Empire*, 7.

21. Ibid., 1, 3, 6.

22. Walker, "Violence, the Everyday and the Question of the Ordinary," 13.

Bibliography

Barnhart, Michael A. *Japan Prepares for Total War: The Search for Economic Security, 1919–1941*. Ithaca, N.Y.: Cornell University Press, 1987.

Barrett, David P., and Lawrence N. Shyu. *China in the Anti-Japanese War, 1937–1945: Politics, Culture and Society*. New York: Peter Lang, 2001.

Beckett, Ian F. "Total War." In *Total War and Historical Change: Europe, 1914–1955*, edited by Arthur Marwick, Wendy Simpson, and Clive Emsley, 24–41. Buckingham: Open University Press, 2001.

Bian, Morris L. *The Making of the State Enterprise System in Modern China: The Dynamics of Institutional Change*. Cambridge, Mass.: Harvard University Press, 2005.

Boyle, John Hunter. *China and Japan at War, 1937–1945: The Politics of Collaboration*. Stanford, Calif.: Stanford University Press, 1972.

Brook, Timothy. *Collaboration: Japanese Agents and Local Elites in Wartime China*. Cambridge, Mass.: Harvard University Press, 2005.

Chickering, Roger. "Total War: The Use and Abuse of a Concept." In *Anticipating Total War: The German and American Experiences, 1871–1914*, edited by Roger Chickering, Stig Förster, and Manfred F. Boemeke, 13–28. Cambridge: Cambridge University Press, 1999.

Coble, Parks M. *Chinese Capitalists in Japan's New Order: The Occupied Lower Yangzi, 1937–1945*. Berkeley: University of California Press, 2003.

Cochran, Sherman. *Chinese Medicine Men: Consumer Culture in China and Southeast Asia*. Cambridge, Mass.: Harvard University Press, 2006.

Dower, John W. "The Structures and Ideologies of Conquest." In MacKinnon, Lary, and Vogel, *China at War*, 17–22. Stanford, Calif.: Stanford University Press, 2007.

Duara, Prasenjit. *Culture, Power, and the State: Rural North China, 1900–1942*. Stanford, Calif.: Stanford University Press, 1988.

Duus, Peter, Ramon Hawley Myers, Mark R. Peattie, Wan-yao Chou, and Japan–United States Friendship Commission. *The Japanese Wartime Empire, 1931–1945*. Princeton, N.J.: Princeton University Press, 1996.

Eastman, Lloyd E. *Seeds of Destruction: Nationalist China in War and Revolution, 1937–1949*. Stanford, Calif.: Stanford University Press, 1984.

Flath, James, and Norman Smith, eds. *Beyond Suffering: Recounting War in Modern China*. Vancouver: UBC Press, 2011.

Flath, James, and Norman Smith. "Introduction." In Flath and Smith, *Beyond Suffering*, 1–10.

Frazier, Mark W. *The Making of the Chinese Industrial Workplace: State, Revolution, and Labor Management*. Cambridge: Cambridge University Press, 2002.

Fu, Poshek. *Passivity, Resistance, and Collaboration: Intellectual Choices in Occupied Shanghai, 1937–1945*. Stanford, Calif.: Stanford University Press, 1993.

Green, Colin. "Turning Bad Iron into Polished Steel: Whampoa and the Rehabilitation of the Chinese Soldier." In Flath and Smith, *Beyond Suffering*, 153–185.

Henriot, Christian, and Wen-Hsin Yeh, eds. *In the Shadow of the Rising Sun: Shanghai under Japanese Occupation*. Cambridge: Cambridge University Press, 2004. Cambridge Modern China Series.

Howard, Joshua H. *Workers at War: Labor in China's Arsenals, 1937–1953*. Stanford, Calif.: Stanford University Press, 2004.

Hsiung, James Chieh, and Steven I. Levine, eds. *China's Bitter Victory: The War with Japan, 1937–1945*. Armonk, N.Y.: M. E. Sharpe, 1992.

Landdeck, Kevin Paul. "Under the Gun: National Military Service and Society in Wartime Sichuan, 1938–1945." PhD dissertation, University of California at Berkeley, 2011.

Lary, Diana. *The Chinese People at War: Human Suffering and Social Transformation, 1937–1945*. New York: Cambridge University Press, 2010.

———. "Introduction: The Context of the War." In MacKinnon, Lary, and Vogel, *China at War*, 7–13.

Levine, Steven I. "Introduction." In Hsiung and Levine, *China's Bitter Victory*, xvii–xxv.

Li, Danke. *Echoes of Chongqing: Women in Wartime China*. Urbana and Chicago: University of Illinois Press, 2010.

Liu Huaming 劉華明 and Liu Bolan 劉伯蘭. "Mao Zedong dui Wang Chuanshan quanmin zhanzheng sixiang de jicheng he fazhan 毛澤東對王船山全民戰爭思想的繼承和發展" (Mao Zedong's inheritance and development of the total war thought of Wang Chuanshan). *Zhumadian shizhuan xuebao* 駐馬店 9, no. 1 (February 1994); http://china.eastview.com.libproxy.usc.edu/kns50/detail.aspx?QueryID=285&CurRec=13; accessed October 17, 2018.

MacKinnon, Stephen R., Diana Lary, and Ezra F. Vogel, eds. *China at War: Regions of China, 1937–1945*. Stanford, Calif.: Stanford University Press, 2007.

"Mao Zedong de renmin zhanzheng lilun" 毛澤東的人民戰爭理論 (Mao Zedong's theory of people's war). http://www.cetin.net.cn/storage/cetin2/js/jswz/jsll/mzddrmzzll.htm; accessed October 17, 2018.

Mieszkowski, Jan. "Great War, Cold War, Total War," *Modernism/Modernity* 16, no. 2 (2009): 211–228.

Mimura, Janis. *Planning for Empire: Reform Bureaucrats and the Japanese Wartime State*. Ithaca, N.Y.: Cornell University Press, 2011.

Quanmin Kangzhan 全民抗戰. http://www.cmic.zju.edu.cn/cmkj/web-zgxwsys/9/images/406.jpg; accessed October 17, 2018.

Sheehan, Brett. *Industrial Eden: A Chinese Capitalist Vision*. Cambridge, Mass.: Harvard University Press, 2015.

Strauss, Julia C. *Strong Institutions in Weak Polities: State Building in Republican China, 1927–1940*. Oxford: Oxford University Press, 1988.

Wakeman, Frederic, Jr. *The Shanghai Badlands: Wartime Terrorism and Urban Crime*. Cambridge: Cambridge University Press, 1996.

Walker, Rebecca. "Violence, the Everyday and the Question of the Ordinary" *Contemporary South Asia* 18, no. 1 (March 2010): 9–24.

Yeh, Wen-Hsin, ed. *Wartime Shanghai*. London: Routledge, 1998.

Young, Arthur N. *China's Wartime Finance and Inflation, 1937–1945*. Cambridge, Mass.: Harvard University Press, 1965.

Zhang Xianwen 張憲文, ed. *Zhongguo kangri zhanzheng shi* 中國抗日戰爭史 (1931–1945) (History of China's Anti-Japanese War [1931–1945]). Nanjing: Nanjing daxue chubanshe, 2001.

Zhong Hua 仲華. "1931–1937 Jiang Jieshi yingdui riben qinhua de junshi sixiang 1931–1937 蔣介石應對日本侵華的軍事思想" (Jiang Jieshi's military thought about responding to the Japanese invasion of China, 1931–1937). *Lishixue Yanjiu* 歷史研究, no. 10 (October 2003): 40–41.

Zou Taofen 鄒韜奮. "'Quanmin Kangzhan' de shiming '全民抗戰' 的使命" (The mission of all the people's Anti-Japanese War), *Quanmin Kangzhan,* no. 1 (July 7, 1938). Accessed in Zhongguo xinwenshi 中國新聞史; http://www.cmic.zju.edu.cn/cmkj/web-zgxwsys/fujia/9-23.html; accessed October 17, 2018.

PART I

Living and Working in Urban Daily Life

Housing and Women's Work

CHAPTER 1

Managing War

Eleanor Hinder and Shanghai's White-Collar Chinese Workers

SUSAN GLOSSER

On August 13, 1937, Japan launched its attack on Shanghai by intentionally bombing civilian neighborhoods and the factories where these civilians worked. The assault laid waste to the homes and factories of Zhabei (閘北) and Hongkou (虹口), a Chinese-governed district of Shanghai north of the Huangpu (黃浦) River. When the bombing started, Huangpu residents grabbed what they could—their children, suitcases of belongings, pans—and fled over the Garden Bridge in hopes of finding refuge in the International and French Concessions. The 300,000 survivors overwhelmed the concessions; in the days before refugees found housing or a refugee center, they wandered the city, feeding their families on the side of the street and sleeping in doorways, on sidewalks, in cars, or on car roofs. The influx of people overtaxed public latrines, and refugees were forced to use lanes and alcoves as toilets.

In total, a million people fled into the foreign concessions from the southern section of the city, Huangpu, Zhabei, and the rural surrounds as far as fifty miles out. As refugees scrambled for shelter, vacant apartments and offices filled to bursting.[1] The flood of people overwhelmed a city already packed to capacity and altered the atmosphere and depressed the quality of life in nearly every neighborhood. By December 1937, city officials returned about 375,000 refugees to the countryside—even when they had no homes or villages left to go to. Another 140,000 entered refugee camps, and as many as 250,000 took refuge in the Jacquinot Safety Zone, established in November 1937 in the southern, Chinese-run section of the city.[2] The rest sheltered with family or found housing of their own in the concessions.

This essay on wartime housing in Shanghai during the early years of the Japanese occupation (1937–1945) reconstructs how agents of the Shanghai Municipal Council (SMC) and the workers they studied "managed" the war. It is also part of the growing historiography on daily life in Republican China. Historians' interest in the topic was, in part, prompted by the opening of the People's Republic of China (PRC) archives to foreign scholars in the 1980s and the discovery of the rich materials they contained. At about the same historical moment, the abundant information that emerged in the United States in the early 1980s about the ravages of the Great Leap Forward and the Cultural Revolution led many college students and young historians to reject the romance of Mao's revolution. Many in this cohort followed their professors' examples and began to explore the population that had all but disappeared from the modern history of China. Shanghai, in particular, became the object of intense study, in part because its municipal archives were comparatively open. Because of limitations of space, my overview is brief and does not cover every relevant book or essay.

Wen-hsin Yeh was the first historian to call our attention to petty urbanites (*xiao shimin* 小市民) as such. Her scholarship has introduced us to the landscape of their personal and professional aspirations and their previously disregarded role in Republican urban culture. Through his study of Shanghai street peddlers, Lu Hanchao acquainted us with the consumer and food culture that entertained and sustained Shanghai's petty urbanites. Christian Henriot, who has worked extensively on what visual culture can tell us about the past, also explored the role of peddlers in street culture through visual sources. Shanghai was not the only city studied. Wang Di added depth to our knowledge of urban leisure in Chengdu.[3]

The search for information on the lives of ordinary urbanites has been particularly intense in studies on the War of Resistance, 1937–1945. Knowledge of the experiences of a people that survived eight years of invasion, occupation, and resistance is reason enough to research them. But most books that focus on ordinary urbanites in wartime also explore the implications of wartime experience for state-society connections and for the civil war that followed. In *Shanghai Splendor,* Yeh argues that when the economic downturn of the 1930s and the impoverishment of war crushed petty urbanites' hopes for personal fulfillment and economic success, they turned their backs on the Nationalists and looked to communism for solutions. Zhao Ma's *Runaway Wives* examines how some poor women survived war and poverty by taking advantage of state-sponsored transportation systems and new marriage legislation. Alison Rottman's research bridges the gap between war and home by examining the reasons why women left home to join the Fourth Route Army and what their lives were like after they joined. Chang Jui-te, Gang Tan, Danke Li, and Nicole Barnes open our eyes to life in Chongqing during the war. In the process, these scholars illuminate wartime connections between the personal and the political and their implications for the civil war that followed in 1946. Finally, there are scholars who have integrated the stories of ordinary people into narratives of war and revolution. Among them are Steve MacKinnon and Diana Lary. Gail Hershatter's *Women and China's Revolutions* is one of the latest additions to this group.[4]

Despite many decades of studies on the rise and victory of the Chinese Communist state, we are still compelled to explain it. Like my predecessors, I have been drawn to research how ordinary people experienced the war and to contemplate how those experiences shaped China's future. I hope what follows raises as many questions as it answers.

Eleanor Hinder

At the forefront of Shanghai's effort to deal with the turmoil of war was an Australian woman named Eleanor Hinder. Born in 1893, Hinder earned a Bachelor of Science degree at the University of Sydney in 1914. Upon graduation she began a lifelong career in worker education and advocacy. Hinder belonged to the generation of women from the United States and the British Commonwealth who came of age in the early twentieth century and found purpose and employment in the Progressive effort to improve standards of living for the poor working classes at home and abroad. She first visited China in 1923. At the outbreak of the war she had already lived in Shanghai for a decade and been serving as the chief of the Industrial and Social Division of the SMC for nearly five years. She held this position until August 1942, when she fled China to escape internment. Hinder was a strong presence in the administration of the International Settlement; she made it her job to push for better wages and working conditions for laborers and white-collar workers. She also contributed to the prominent English-language papers, the *North China Daily News,* the *Chinese Recorder,* and the YWCA organ *Green Year.*[5]

Hinder's studies and reports have rarely, if ever, been used before. I make extensive use of them—to good advantage, I hope. I have also drawn on contemporaries' accounts in memoirs and the popular journal *Shanghai Life* (*Shanghai shenghuo* 上海生活). Most of the information here covers the isolated island (*gudao* 孤島) period, when the Japanese occupied the Chinese-governed sections of the city and its own concession in Hongkou but left the International Settlement and French Concession in control of their respective foreign governments.

Housing

In the first years of the war, Hinder used her own observations and those of SMC investigators to report on housing. Even before the war, people lived like sardines. In 1935 the most crowded area of Shanghai held 547 people per acre. In this area 41,160 houses held 113,286 families. The mode was four families—twenty-four people—per house. Just prior to the war, most Shanghainese lived in neighborhoods with densities above three hundred people per acre.[6] In 1938 a textile mill manager in the International Concession commissioned a study of his employees' living conditions; he found that the modal number of families in the sixty houses he surveyed was 7.22 and the median was 5.81.[7] In one report

Hinder provided a schematic, "non-scientific but revealing," picture of the typical urbanite's housing in Shanghai's characteristic row house, or *shikumen* (石庫門). The typical row house measured ten to twelve feet wide, twenty-four to forty feet deep, and two or three ten-foot stories high. A "single bay" house had a living room at the front, a kitchen in the back, and two bedrooms upstairs.[8]

> The typical Shanghai "Chinese house" was entered from the small courtyard in the front. One stepped into the main downstairs room which was often the residence of the principal tenant, who may have cut a narrow passageway to provide other tenants with access to their own quarters, or allowed his own room to be the passageway. As a rule he built a vertical partition toward the back of the room thus making a second room that lacked a window. This room in turn may have had a horizontal partition, creating an upper room, access to which could be obtained halfway up the stairway. This dark loft could be the only home that many a family knew. The kitchen, at the rear of the house was used sometimes for its original purpose; more likely it was the residence of yet another family, while portable coal-briquette stoves of firebrick were placed anywhere for cooking purposes. In the same way the upper front room could have both vertical and horizontal partitions, making space for other families; and the room above the kitchen would house yet another household. The area for each family was very small.[9]

In this fashion, up to forty people could be jammed into houses intended for a single family of three to six people.

As demand for housing rose, so did rent. Although landlords could legally increase rent by no more than 20 percent a year, by 1942 rents were five times what they had been in 1936. Other expenses rose apace. In 1942 the cost of water equaled the legal rent.[10] Other practices made renting decent quarters even more difficult. Prewar landlords might let renters fall behind by as much as two or three years, and some were even reluctant to let their houses because the trouble of collecting rent was not worth the small profit. By contrast, wartime landlords were eager to rent and wanted their money on time.[11] This situation was dramatized in the 1937 film *Gudao tiantang* (孤島天堂 Heaven in the isolated island), in which a hard-hearted landlord throws a bedridden widow and her several small children out onto the street.[12]

Skyrocketing rents drove almost everyone into smaller quarters. Families who had occupied a small row house or apartment before the war found themselves vying with thousands of others for "dovecotes," the popular term for single "rooms" that had been carved out of a single-family house. In April 1941 ratepayers expressed their concern about overcrowding by passing a byelaw that required rentals to provide 30 square feet of floor space and 400 cubic feet of "clean and unobstructed internal air space per person"—a space of about 6 by 5 feet and a little over 13 feet high.[13] But most renters lived in spaces that fell below this minimum standard. In fact, the ratepayers passed the measure with the understanding that "the Commissioner of Public Health would apply the byelaw with discretion, at first only in the most flagrant cases, because of the housing shortage."[14] The relatively small fine—no more than twenty dollars—underscores the SMC's reluctance to hold landlords to a standard that scarcity made impossible to uphold.

Many of these houses lacked toilets and running water, and the public latrines built for prewar residents could not accommodate the wartime population. As a result, residents usually kept lidded chamber pots in their crowded rooms. In such close quarters, tuberculosis, typhus, smallpox, and cholera became common, though the city never faced the epidemics it feared.[15]

The Pavilion Room

One of the many terms the Shanghainese used to describe the consequences of overcrowding was "pavilion room" (*tingzijian* 亭子間), a romantic description of a room built out from the back of a house over the kitchen. It opened onto the landing between one floor and another and was originally intended as a maid's room. Perhaps the biggest advantage of the pavilion room was its location at the back of the house, its many windows, and the fact that it was the only sublet room to have its own entrance. (Other tenants usually had to cut through other renters' rooms to reach their own.) Somewhat secluded from the rest of the house and with its own entrance, the pavilion room could feel like a tiny house. It could be sufficient and even comfortable for a single person.[16] By the SMC's own wartime standards, a ten-foot square pavilion room could fit three people without qualifying as overcrowded, though most fell short of the 400 cubic feet of internal air space.

A rental's location and the size of one's family determined the tenants' comfort or misery. A pavilion room in a Western-style house probably had a small yard or garden below. Those who rented one in a free-standing house in the International Settlement might even hear birds sing. A pavilion room in a poor and crowded neighborhood would have looked out on a narrow lane and faced another pavilion room as little as six feet away. Those in busy commercial districts were immersed day and night in the noise of car motors and beeping horns, the rumble of trolleys, the call of vendors, and a cacophony of popular songs and local operas blasting from shop radios.[17]

Pavilion rooms attracted the attention of city officials and residents in part because they were one of the first rooms a family rented out when it decided to take in subletters.[18] They were also magnets for gossip and fantasy. The literary minded often imbued these tiny rooms with a romanticism that resembles our fantasies about artists' garrets. In fact, most who rented pavilion rooms were poor students, starving artists, desperate prostitutes, and poor families. The privacy of these rooms also appealed to those who wanted to elude some of the surveillance that went on in such crowded quarters. This privacy gave the pavilion room a reputation as a refuge for illicit love and a shelter for prostitution. Because of its reputation and low rent, some residents were reluctant to let others know they rented a pavilion room.[19]

Because of their size, occupants of pavilion rooms made do with only the necessities: a bed, a table, a chair or two, a few bowls, a chamber pot, perhaps a tiny cook stove, a lamp or single bare electric bulb hanging from the ceiling, and maybe an advertising poster for decoration. When an entire family occupied a pavilion room, basic standards of neatness and hygiene were difficult if not impossible to maintain. One essayist for *Shanghai Life*, Duo Jiugong, described with horror the difficulties of rearing children in such a tiny space:

> Mid-level pavilion rooms are generally occupied by petty urbanites. A single person's place is still clean and tidy. But if there are children . . . then it's really a mess. Pavilion rooms are not large, so one needs to arrange the furniture like crack troops. If one can arrange a twin bed, a desk, and a sofa in opposite corners and hang a painting on the wall, a person can lie on the sofa and feel quite peaceful. In this little paradise, one has room to breathe. But if the furniture is all over the place or there is that heavy red Ningbo furniture, a chamber pot, a crate, an urn, and spoons all thrown together with everything in the universe, the pavilion room feels like a warehouse.[20]

Duo's ideal of the pavilion room and the rarified modern lifestyle vanishes in the face of the realities with which most Shanghainese contended.

The Dovecote

Another common sublet was the *gelou* (閣樓 dovecote), a term that could refer to a garret, an attic, or a loft created by a platform of boards placed between the floor and ceiling or on the underside of the stairs.[21] The front of a loft might be boarded shut, except for an entry "door" to provide some privacy. A ladder allowed occupants to crawl up into it. Some were even built over a stairway. Lofts were sometimes nicknamed "ups and downs" because renters had to leave the cramped loft for nearly every need.[22] Dovecotes were the rooms that most grievously violated the SMC's minimum standards for space. Most were too low for occupants to stand upright and were so shoddily built that dirt, light, and noise drifted into the room below. Sometimes residents could even see their "upstairs" or "downstairs" neighbors through the floorboards. Unlike the pavilion room, all lofts were miserable. All were cramped. They rarely had windows, and the noise was constant. Attics sometimes had windows, but they were bitterly cold in winter and stifling in Shanghai's steamy summers. The dovecote's low monthly rent, generally less than ten dollars, was its only redeeming feature.

Incredibly, even such cramped quarters as dovecotes could be further subdivided. In December 1940, *Shanghai Life* carried an account of the living conditions of a writer who had fallen on hard times because he had put off leaving Shanghai until escape was impossible. Like most everyone else, his wartime expenses outstripped his income, and three years into the war the once successful writer had slipped into desperate poverty. The author of the account found the writer living in a house on a dirty little lane. To reach the writer's quarters, the author climbed two pitch dark flights of stairs to a newly built third-floor garret.

> The door was partially open, and I glanced inside. All I saw was a chaos of curtains. It turned out that [the writer] shared his little room with three other families. They had put up curtains so that each could have a separate space at night. Because the curtains were blocking the door, I was uncomfortable just walking in, so I called quietly and out came a familiar face. . . . His hair was disheveled and he blushed. He said, "Elder brother, it's hard to welcome you here; it's such a tiny place and filthy. Do you want to come in . . . ?" I followed him, boring through the curtains. We went by two families' rooms in this little dovecote. I could see that males and females lived in very intimate circumstances; entire families slept together. His room was the left cubicle. In this place, so little that it was difficult to turn around, he sat, slept, ate, and spent his time. His wife and child were still sleeping soundly. . . . He liked to let them sleep as long as possible because that way they might manage on just two meals a day. . . . He usually got up at dawn to write for his living. We whispered for fear of waking his neighbors. . . .
>
> He and his wife had cut their expenses to a minimum. Their one-third of the loft, though it was so tiny, cost a relatively expensive eight yuan a month because it was in a safe neighborhood.[23]

The SMC had the authority to take down illegal structures like dovecotes, but because it recognized that people in subdivided row houses simply could not afford larger spaces, it often did not enforce the codes. In fact, before the war, a committee on housing appointed by the SMC in 1936 recommended that further construction of lofts be banned in order to reduce the number of families living in a single house. The SMC rejected the recommendation, however, because it knew that at less than ten yuan a month, a crowded loft was a shelter of last resort and a better home than the street.[24]

Early in the war, one resident of a loft wrote an essay that described what it was like to live in a subdivided row house. It was a three-story house, and "because the subletting landlord [was] calculating and resourceful," he had managed to rent to ten households, a total of twenty-three–twenty-four people; there was so much coming and going in one room upstairs that the author couldn't quite tell how many lived there. This house probably originally had six rooms: a living room, a kitchen, a room off the kitchen that usually served as the cook's bedroom or a storeroom, a large bedroom on the first floor, a pavilion room off the landing, and two or three small bedrooms on the second floor. There was also a drying porch, either on the third floor or on the roof. This was a house designed for a family of four or five people. The landlord almost quintupled this number with the usual innovations. He and his wife lived in the storeroom off the kitchen. He added two lofts, one between the first and second floors over the living room and one between the second and third floors. Two people lived in the lower loft, and five people lived in the second. He divided the living room and rented each half to a family of four. Three women rented the second floor, and three men rented the second-floor pavilion room. A woman and her maid rented the third-floor room, and a couple occupied the third-floor pavilion room. Finally, to a single man he rented the drying porch, a flat area of the roof that usually had a very small brick or cement structure on it for storage. Having created his cash cow, the landlord, who was in his fifties, spent his days wandering around book stores. His wife, a young woman from Suzhou in her twenties, took care of all the household's business.[25]

The essay writer provided a piteous account of his own experience in this crowded household. After August 13, he had left Hongkou and lived for a month in a shelter in Wangjiasha. After a month of looking, he finally found a loft between the second and third floors for five yuan a month. "So," he said, "I squeezed my family of four into a tiny loft and became 'Mr. Dovecote.'" When an in-law showed up, he took him in too, and they were so cramped that they absolutely could not fit another person into the room.

> There's no way to express the suffering of the common people during the war. . . . Everything is down to bare bones. I put a mat on the floor to sleep. At night it is so hot, like being an ant on a hot rock, and there's nowhere to go. Then bugs come out of the floor and bite me all over. I try to put up with it, but I can't stand it. I'm up several times trying to kill them. So I always sleep late. But the cop who occupies the living room downstairs gets up at seven or eight and makes a lot of noise, going on and on in his Shandong accent, often waking me from sweet dreams. On the second floor there's a taxi dancer. Lascivious men visit her several times in the middle of the night. She returns at five or six in the morning, and the *pengpeng* of her heels always wakes me up.[26]

This account brings home the noise, heat, and filth of the loft. The author asserted, "These ten views from a loft describe a typical house. We live in a bird cage."[27] Many other sources confirm his descriptions.

The Cost of Living

So far, we have looked at housing from two perspectives. In her capacity as chief of the Industrial and Social Division, Hinder provides observations and statistics from which we can build a general view of population density, housing types, and costs. The *Shanghai Life* essays bring to life popular perceptions of housing conditions. Fortunately, Hinder's search for reliable information takes us even closer to the realities of wartime housing. In the fall of 1941, just before the Japanese invasion of the International Settlement and the end of SMC independence, Hinder conducted a study of Shanghai's white-collar Chinese salaried employees.[28] Her primary objective was to create a standard of living index comparable to those available for Chinese laborers and Western salaried employees. In the process, she asked all kinds of questions about housing, family composition, household composition, spending habits, income, and possessions. Her expansive vision and relatively rigorous methodology provide an intimate view of the daily life of Shanghai's petty urbanites.[29]

Hinder began by writing to seven hundred enterprises to explain the project and call for participants. Those who complied included the Borden Company, Shanghai Electric Construction Company, National Committee of the Young Men's Christian Associations of China, Lester Chinese Hospital, China General Edison Company, the Chinese Post Office, the China General Omnibus Company, Ltd., the Municipal Police, the Shanghai Power Company, the Public Works Department, the SMC, Chase Bank, the National Carbon Company,

Eastman Kodak, the French Municipal Council, the Inspectorate General of Customs, the Shanghai Telephone Company, the National City Bank, Arnhold and Company, and the China Soap Company.[30]

Hinder placed advertisements in the leading newspapers—the *New China Daily News, Sin Shun Pao, Central China Daily News, China Press, Shanghai Evening Post and Mercury, National Herald, Cheng Yien Pao*, and the *Chinese American Daily News*—and asked the editors to support the survey in editorials. We know that *Sin Shun Pao* agreed to her request.[31] Given the number of respondents, it is likely other newspapers cooperated too. Hinder also asked radio stations to broadcast a ten-minute explanation of the project by Mr. T. Y. Tsha, the study's statistician. At the time, radio stations frequently adopted a public service role, and it seems likely that some stations participated.[32] As Hinder explained in a letter to the radio station HMXC, she had met with representatives of companies, municipal departments, voluntary organizations, and educational institutions "[in order] that there may be understanding and goodwill toward the project."[33]

Hinder also hoped the project would boost appreciation for SMC contributions to life in Shanghai:

> I should be glad if the public welfare aspect of the matter could be stressed [in the radio broadcasts]: that those who can conform with the criteria . . . should be willing to keep records in a spirit of service to society. I should appreciate it also if there would be some expression of approval of the Council's continued interest in the livelihood of the residents at the present time. Its importation of rice is an important contribution but administrative functions such as the making available of accurate information on living costs are also important. I would like the public to become cognizant of this.[34]

Employees responded enthusiastically. Hinder wanted 500 families to survey; 1,038 volunteered to participate.[35]

In late summer Hinder wrote to all the families who had volunteered to participate. She welcomed them and detailed their task:

> In writing you for the first time, I extend to you a hearty welcome and an appreciation of your generous assistance in the study. I am enclosing herewith (i) a Direction Book, (ii) a Record Book, and (iii) a return envelope. Please note the following: (1) Read carefully the direction book, and the Forms in the Record book before you start record keeping. (2) As soon as you complete October records, mail the Record Book on November 1.

Use the return envelope. No postage needed. Simply mail it. Our delay in mailing back the records would result in delay in progress of the study. (3) Keep truthful records. Do not leave out any items of income and expenditure. Record everyday [*sic*]. Do not delay.

Yours faithfully, E. M. H.[36]

Hinder set six criteria for choosing eligible subjects. The "principal householder"—i.e., the head of household—could be a salaried employee of any kind. Farmers, laborers, and owners of any kind of enterprise were explicitly excluded. The family could not derive its support from an inheritance or an allowance from the family. Families were to have a husband and a wife present and no more than ten members, "excluding boarders and servants." Hinder included only renters in her survey, excluding thereby both homeowners and those who lived at their place of employment. Finally, Hinder's subjects were to eat meals prepared at home by housewives or cooks, with the exception of lunch or "outside tiffin."[37] Hinder had originally planned to limit her subjects to those making less than 1,000 Chinese National Currency a month, but because so many police wanted to participate in the survey, she agreed to extend the limit to 2,000 *fabi* per month.[38] Hinder conceded but made sure to break down her analyses into three groups: households making less than 500 *fabi* per month; those making between 500 and 999.99 per month, and those making 1,000–2,000 per month.

Hinder assumed the Western conjugal family ideal as her model of the family, an ideal to which many of Shanghai's petty urbanites aspired.[39] In restricting her subjects to married couples with children, she left out widows, widowers, and single men and women, some of whom had not married because they could not afford to support a family. In her reports she never explained why she chose to do this. With her knowledge of Shanghai, Hinder must have known that many of the city's families were not organized according to her model. Perhaps this was a methodological choice intended to regularize her sample as much as possible in order to make generalizations about the population. Hinder's choice of sample may also have been ideological. Letters between Hinder and some members of the SMC suggest she wanted to examine married couples with children because she was pushing employers to pay employees a family wage—that is, one that would allow a man to support his family without drawing his wife or children into the workforce. It took Hinder almost a year and a half to get her project approved because some members of the SMC believed that she was trying to prevent the "inevitable" fall of living standards during the war or even to raise them. The dispute led to several meetings and forceful letters in the spring of 1940 (March–May) about whether Hinder's cost-of-living indexes were crafted to support her economic agenda or an accurate reflection of workers' living conditions. One Mr. Powell vociferously opposed her belief that "the wage of a principal householder should meet at least minimum family subsistence costs."[40] He argued this was a Western view, and the West might in the future itself go to the "Eastern" system, in which several family members worked to cover the family's expenses.[41] Her efforts to secure a family wage for white-collar employees were cut short by the war. However, her close attention to the persistent problem of debt suggests she was interested in tracking the information that could support such an argument.

The subjects of Hinder's survey were not representative of Shanghai's Chinese population. They were white-collar workers for foreign and Chinese firms and municipal services—the most stable enterprises in the city. Among the 418 households that Hinder used in her calculations, there was only one widower and three concubines.[42] (Three heads of household had a wife and a concubine.) We can, however, use their atypicality to our advantage. Presumably these were, by and large, among the most prosperous Chinese households in the city. Yet we will see that even these people had a difficult time making ends meet. And if even these families found it hard to piece together a living during the isolated island period, how much more difficult it must have been for laborers and the thousands of families bereft of a mother or father.

Hinder knew her job. Her directions were precise and the questionnaire was clearly laid out. She asked each family to detail the composition of its household, the size of its living quarters, whether it had access to a kitchen or bathroom, the number of windows, the number of common rooms if any, goods on hand, and every penny spent or earned each day from October 1, 1941, to December 31, 1941. Hinder was exacting. Of the 1,038 respondents, she threw out over half; 167 families quit the survey early, and 448 provided inadequate documentation. Only 423 households made the cut.[43] In her numerical analyses of these cost-of-living studies, Hinder usually provided a profile of the average household calculated on the basis of all 423 families and then, when possible, gave a breakdown of how the average varied by income group.

The Shape of Households

Households most commonly ranged in size from four to seven members. In addition to the required mother and father, the average household contained two or three children and either a relative, a boarder, or a servant. Fewer than 10 percent of households reported a paying guest; the vast majority of houses literally had no room to spare. (Hinder's precise figures were as follows: 6.55 people with 5.83

family members, .08 "paying guests," and .065 servants.)[44] Households were a little more than twice as likely to include a female relative as a male relative. These figures also suggest that when households included relatives, they tended toward the traditional practice of housing the husband's relatives. For example, 121 households included the husband's mother and forty-two his father, while only twenty-six households included the wife's mother and three included the wife's father. There were seventy-nine husbands' siblings living among these households and at most eight of the wives' siblings. The fact that only one household contained a daughter-in-law suggests that either married couples lived on their own or sons could not afford to marry—a common complaint in late Republican Shanghai.[45] Hinder found no sons-in-law lodged with their wives' natal families.[46]

Nevertheless, most households did not contain a relative. Although these households were structured as conjugal families, we cannot assume they preferred this family form. Because the survey did not address informants' preferences for family organization, we cannot know whether choice, necessity, or obligation had the upper hand in their households' organization. The statistics do indicate that the higher the household income, the larger the family; it may be that families housed as many relatives as they could. We know from many accounts that those living in Shanghai were under intense pressure to take in relatives who had fled to the city. Households with income below 500 *fabi* averaged 5.3 members. Those in the middle group (500–999.99 *fabi*) averaged 6.83 members, and those in the highest income group (1,000–2,000 *fabi*) averaged 7.86 members—though this average may have been affected by the fact that Hinder did not include families with more than ten members in the study.[47]

One other area in which traditional values may have exerted their influence is suggested by an uneven gender ratio of daughters to sons. The ratio, .87, is skewed in favor of males among children aged 2–13.9 but favors females in older age groups with a ratio of 108.3.[48] Infanticide, abandonment, or a tendency to provide better food and medical care to sons may explain the gender imbalance in the younger group. Individual household survey books suggest that the gender ratio favored females in the older groups because single daughters lived at home and helped their mothers with housework while some sons lived at their place of work or at their school or college. The slightly higher average age of daughters, 9.63, compared to sons, 9.05, also supports this hypothesis.

The husband, or "householder" as Hinder called him, was the breadwinner in these families, and on average he supported five (4.97) other people in the household, including servants.[49] The husbands worked in a wide range of occupations that Hinder categorized as either manufacturing or service. In the former she included woodworking, furniture manufacture, the metal industry, earthenware, construction, gas, water, electricity, chemicals, textiles, leather and rubber, food and drink, paper and printing, and "other." In the later she grouped transport and communication, brokerages, real estate, money, banking, insurance, wholesaling and retailing, professional firms, public service, teaching, and mission work. Nearly a quarter (101) of the 418 husbands worked in manufacturing. The other 317 worked in service.[50]

Almost all the wives worked in the home; they routinely described their occupation as "housework" (*jiawu* 家務). Only nineteen wives reported working for wages. Fifteen of these wives were teachers; one was in "transport and communication;" two were in the fields of money, banking, or insurance; and one was in "other." Compared to the Beijing women studied by Sophia Lee in this volume, they had a much narrower range of occupations, but this might be an artifact of the way Hinder selected her sample. Only nine sons and thirteen daughters living at home worked for wages outside the home. Two daughters worked in manufacturing, and all the other children worked in service industries. Unlike mothers, most of the children did not give their wages to the family.[51]

A fair number of these households were able to educate their children. Of the 2,162 family members of these households, 512 attended school. If we subtract husbands, wives, those aged sixty and above, and those aged two and below (418 husbands, 420 wives, 139 aged sixty and up, and 75 below two years old) from the family member total of 2,162, we find that 37 percent of family members attended school. In fact, the percentage of school-age children was higher than that because children did not attend school until the age of five or six.[52] In the forty-three individual survey records that I reviewed, most families who sent boys to school sent girls too.

A quick note on native place: Hinder took account of the husbands' and wives' home province, though only in aggregate. Until we have access to all the surveys, we cannot know whether and how frequently husbands and wives came from different provinces. Most respondents came from Shanghai (ninety-nine), Jiangsu (321), or Zhejiang (171). There were thirty-two from Anhui and twenty-three from Fujian. The rest came from the provinces of Henan, Hebei, Yunan, Hubei, Shandong, Sichuan, Liaoning, and Helongjiang, with somewhere between two and twelve for each.[53]

The low numbers of wage-earning wives and children seem to suggest that husbands/fathers earned enough to support their families, yet that was not the case. In fact, most households spent much more than they took in. The earnings and income of an average family of 6.55 persons totaled ¥554, but the expenditures came to ¥680.[54] In other words, the average family overspent its income by ¥126, or 23 percent, even though most of the employees regularly received rice and/or supplementary income from their employers to help them meet the ever-rising cost of living. Hinder included these employer subsidies in the category of "other income." Those with salaries under ¥500 could cover less than half of their expenses on their salaries alone. These families struggled even with augmented earnings. Those who earned between ¥500 and ¥999.99 spent between 11 and 22 percent over their augmented earnings, while those in the highest bracket of ¥1,000–¥2,000 exceeded their augmented earnings by 6–12 percent.[55]

To cover their deficits, families either drew down their savings or borrowed money. A few sold things, received payments on loans they had made, or borrowed from their native place associations (*tongxianghui* 同鄉會).[56] Pawning, which figured large in the Republican-era literary imagination, was of little use to these families, probably because they owned few superfluous things. Pawning items covered only .90 *fabi*, or 0.21 percent, of the monthly deficit of the poorest families.[57] It is also possible that people sold their possessions rather than pawned them.

The average household of 6.55 people spent 99.77 percent of its income on consumption. Interest on debts, taxes, and the like accounted for the remaining fraction of a percent. On average, food accounted for 49 percent of monthly expenditures, housing for 16 percent, clothing for 11 percent, and miscellaneous for 24 percent. The percentages for food, clothing, and miscellaneous varied somewhat by income group. However, the percentage of income spent on housing remained within half a percentage point for all three income groups—15.3 percent for the lowest and 15.8 percent for the highest.[58] This suggests that families rented the best rooms they could possibly afford.

Hinder was an ardent proponent of improved conditions for all of Shanghai's working classes. Consequently, although she likely participated in the SMC committee that had established minimum square footage and cubic space per person in rentals, she meticulously crunched the numbers that revealed the disparity between legal and actual living conditions. She began by calculating the average size of families (excluding servants) by income group. Family size averaged 5.3 in the lowest income bracket, 6.8 in the middle bracket, and 7.8 in the highest. Most families in the lower- and middle-income groups crammed themselves into one room: 99 of 124 families in the lowest group and 116 of 223 families in the mid-level group. The average number of rooms per family in these two groups was 1.3 and 1.96, respectively. The average number of rooms per family for the highest income group was 2.01. This was bleak enough, but Hinder brings home the severity of crowding by also tabulating the number of standard rooms, thirty square feet per person, per family. This approach dramatically underscores the overcrowding people endured. Fifty-three of the ninety-nine families in the lowest income bracket lived in one substandard room. The "devaluation" of the informants' housing situation in the middle group was significant but smaller; in this group twenty-nine families lived in one substandard room. No families in the highest income group lived in a substandard room.[59]

Life in a Dovecote

Statistics provide a general outline of living conditions, but it is the cost-of-living survey books that provide the raw material for images we can hold in our minds. These laconic reports of household composition, accommodations, occupations, income, and expenses speak eloquently to the details of daily life and provide an intimate picture of life in Shanghai's "dovecotes." Below I relate the housing conditions of several respondents. I have tried to locate at least one example for each kind of room described above. (To my knowledge, no respondent family had an entire house to itself.) Despite Hinder's request, respondents seem to have named their room only when it was somewhat marginal—a pavilion room or a dovecote—or one that was not normally used for sleeping—a living room, kitchen, or alcove. They seem to have used the term "bedroom" only when they rented multiple rooms. When they did not name the room they occupied, it is impossible to know for sure where they were in the house. But my working assumption is that they lived in a bedroom. Information on income and consumption fills out our picture of families' circumstances. All names are pseudonyms.

The Chens occupied a pavilion room, and their living conditions must have approached some of the worst. Five people—a husband and wife, aged fifty-nine and fifty-three respectively; a son and daughter, aged twenty-six and fourteen respectively; and a forty-three-year-old female servant—lived in a room that measured eleven by eight feet, with an eight-foot ceiling. The room probably had windows—most pavilion rooms did—but the family had no kitchen or bathroom. The husband worked as a secretary at the Yingshang Water Company, and the son worked as a factory apprentice. This is one of the very few families in which the wife worked—and it may explain why a family in such straitened circumstances kept a servant. It is also possible that the woman had worked for the family prior to the war, and the family felt obligated to keep her. The room must have felt crowded during the day, with just the servant and the daughter, who listed no occupation, but it would have been positively claustrophobic with everyone home. Each person had only eighteen square feet of space. Simply creating places for everyone to sleep must have been a challenge. No matter how they arranged it, only a few inches separated one person from another when they slept. They likely had few possessions—a couple of changes of clothes, perhaps some books and magazines, some cooking utensils, a chamber pot, and bedding. We know they had very few consumable goods at hand—only seven *dou* of rice, one and a half *jin* of salt, and one *fabi*'s worth of kindling.[60] Their meager stores were matched by a frugal and monotonous diet of vegetables, pickles, flat bread, and tofu. A typical day's groceries cost between 2.5 and 3.5 *fabi.* With a monthly income of just 366 *fabi,* this family occupied the very bottom rung of salaried employees. The family did not supplement its income by drawing on savings, borrowing money, or pawning its belongings. Either the family lived within its means, or it had already exhausted its savings, was unable to borrow, and had pawned all it could.[61]

Some families lived in spaces so small that it must have been nearly impossible for them all to be at home at one time. The Zhang family—a mother and father, aged forty-three and forty-five respectively; a four-month-old infant; three boys, aged eight, eleven, and seventeen; and three daughters, aged thirteen, eighteen, and twenty-three—squeezed into a single room eleven feet square. (A twenty-one-year-old son attended Hujiang College and probably lived in the dormitory.) Given that there was barely enough room for all of them to lie down at night, the Zhangs probably installed a sleeping loft. The family counted itself lucky for the room's four windows, but it had no courtyard—most likely the courtyard had been turned into shelter for another family or given over to a small business. The Zhangs had no access to a kitchen and would have cooked their spartan meals on a small coal stove in their room. They had no bathroom but depended instead on the night soil carrier, who emptied their chamber pots every morning. His "wine fee" of .50 *fabi* appears on their list of expenditures on October 6, 1941. The importance of remaining on good terms with this provider of a necessary service was evident later in the month at the Harvest Moon Festival. Although the family purchased no moon cakes or other special foods for the festival, it gave the night soil carrier a .50 *fabi* "Harvest Moon Festival tip."

The Zhangs' reserves were slim but better than the Chens'. At the beginning of October 1941, they listed quite a few unused consumables—a *dou* and a half of millet, thirty *jin* of coal briquettes, a washcloth, a tooth brush, two packs of toilet paper, five *jin* of charcoal, two tubes of toothpaste, a half *jin* of salt, a half jin of sugar, a bar of soap, and a half *jin* of oil. The Zhangs ate a little better than the Chens did; they bought an average of three kinds of vegetables and a fish or half a *jin* of meat most days of the month.[62]

Some families lived in much better circumstances than the Zhangs did. The Qians' quarters were roomy by comparison. The husband and wife shared a sixteen-by-fourteen-foot room with their five-year-old son and rented half of a room that ran along one side of the courtyard for the husband's mother. The fifty-eight-year-old woman had a luxurious 120 square feet to herself, though her small grandson probably had the run of the place. The family had running water and electricity, as well as a kitchen and living room it shared with other tenants. There was no bathroom, so the family's expenses included 1 *fabi* a month to the night soil collector. The family was well off compared to most of Shanghai's Chinese residents; nevertheless, it must have pinched when the family's prewar rent almost doubled from 35 to 65 *fabi* per month.[63]

Couples with no children or parents to care for still lived in straitened circumstances. The Lins were both twenty-two years old. They lived alone in a third-floor attic room only ten feet square. Huddled beneath the roof, they stifled in summer and froze in winter. They lived without a kitchen or bathroom. By the SMC's standards, the two had plenty of room in terms of square feet—fifty square feet each—but it is likely they could stand up straight only in the center of the room. They did have two windows, a rare amenity in October 1941; although they managed to buy a light bulb on the fourteenth of the month (at 1.25 *fabi*, it cost a tenth of the husband's monthly income), they did not come up with the 3 *fabi* for the electricity until the very last day of the month. Many days of the month they bought only a small portion of cheap vegetables or tofu and paid a trolley fare. To their income of 127 *fabi* they added 3 *fabi* when a friend repaid his loan and 1.2 *fabi* from selling old bottles. The husband's father also gave them 10 *fabi*. Even so, they overspent their monthly income by 58.5 *fabi*.[64]

The Yang family must have been among the poorest of Hinder's informants. It was one of only two families in which the wife had died. The widower, aged twenty, lived with his forty-nine-year-old father and nine-year-old sister. The young man worked in a framing shop, and his father was a driver for a sand and gravel yard. Between them they earned 125 *fabi* a month, though they brought home only 115 *fabi* because one of their employers supplied two *dou* of grain but charged the discounted rate of 10 *fabi* per *dou*. One of the men received rice, but no vegetables, at work for lunch. The Yangs economized by spending only 6 *fabi* a month on a windowless garret that was only six and a half feet long, four feet ten inches wide, and six feet nine inches high. In such tiny quarters the men likely could not raise their arms above their heads or stretch them to either side without scraping their knuckles. With only 10.4 square feet and 70.2 cubic feet per person, their room fell far below the per capita minimums of 30 square feet of floor space and 400 cubic feet of air space.

The Yangs' consumption was as restricted as their living quarters. They began the month of January 1942 with two *sheng* of millet, some salt, and .20 fabi of tobacco for a hookah.[65] They purchased small amounts of meat only three times that month—three small fish, four ounces of pork, and another eight ounces of fish. In that entire month the Yangs bought only a few items—two bars of soap, one pencil, two trolley fares, one haircut, some cigarettes, and hookah tobacco, for a total of 6.3 *fabi*—in addition to food, fuel, and boiled water. The little girl did not bring in any income or go to school. Under the circumstances, all the housekeeping chores must have fallen to her. Her brother and father bought no candy, clothes, or toys. Even so, the Yangs overspent their income by 37 *fabi*. In mid-month they borrowed 12 *fabi*. Although they repaid the sum three days later, at month's end they borrowed another twenty.[66]

Conclusion

In an earlier essay on the images of women in resistance, I suggested that the valorization of housewives' work in the home by resistance organizers both created a role in the war for a population under strict surveillance and recognized the importance of reproductive labor in wartime. I also argued that propaganda aimed at Shanghai's population, especially women, provided important psychological support to a people enduring a long occupation. But as I look more closely at the parameters of daily life in occupied Shanghai, I have begun to reconsider this hypothesis and question my assumptions about the general population.

Most of Hinder's subjects were among the most comfortable Chinese workers in Shanghai—or perhaps in the country for that matter. She also took this snapshot long before conditions hit their nadir. The hard facts of their lives prompt me to reconsider my earlier beliefs about citizens' roles in the war. It seems likely that most Shanghainese had neither the time nor the leisure to aid the war or perhaps to think about it very deeply. It was something to endure. In the rest of China conditions were usually even worse. It seems possible then, even likely, that most Chinese, like their compatriots in Shanghai, managed only to live from day to day and had no role in China's victory in the War of Resistance. This possibility forces us in turn to reexamine our assumptions and to reconsider late Republican state-society relations, the logistics of the war, and the relationship between Guomindang (GMD) and Chinese Communist Party (CCP) resistance efforts and propaganda. Ultimately, we must continue to ask who, or what, won the war.

Notes

I would like to thank my fellow conference participants for their comments and conversations. I am particularly grateful to organizers Wen-hsin Yeh and Brett Sheehan for their suggestion that we consider whether our subjects dealt with the war by treating it as something to manage. It is a useful tool for moving our focus from the heroics of resistance to the mundane daily struggle for survival. Many thanks also to Gail Hershatter. I deeply appreciate her thoughts on the challenge of articulating historiographical issues for which we have not yet developed a vocabulary.

1. Chen, *Kangzhan shidai shenghuo shi,* 47–48.
2. Henriot, "Shanghai and the Experience of War," 224.
3. Yeh: "Progressive Journalism and Shanghai's Petty Urbanites," 186–238 and *Shanghai Splendor;* Lu, *Beyond the Neon Lights;* Henriot, "Street Culture"; and Wang, *The Teahouse.*
4. Yeh, *Shanghai Splendor;* Ma, *Runaway Wives;* Rottmann, "Resistance, Urban Style"; Chang, "Bombs Do Not Discriminate?"; Gang, "Living Underground"; Li, *Echoes of Chongqing;* Barnes, *Intimate Communities;* MacKinnon, *Wuhan, 1938;* Lary, *The Chinese People at War;* Lary and Mackinnon, *The Scars of War.*
5. From 1913 to 1923 Hinder joined various efforts to improve workers' education and living conditions. She first traveled to China when she received a stipend from a Christian women's group interested in workers' living conditions. In 1926 she received a Rockefeller Foundation award through the YWCA of China to spend two years in Shanghai. Hinder left Shanghai in 1928 but returned in 1930, when the YWCA invited her to work in education. In 1931 she was appointed adviser to the Special Committee of the Employers Federation in Shanghai, established to investigate the international and economic problems that might be created by the Nationalists' Factory Law of 1931. From 1946 to 1948 she worked for the United Nations Relief and Rehabilitation Association on projects associated with postwar China. She continued to work for a variety of international organizations until her death in 1963. Wheelhouse, *Eleanor Mary Hinder,* 31–35, 80, 82, 88–89.
6. Hinder, *Life and Labour in Shanghai,* 82.
7. Ibid., 83.
8. Ibid., 82.
9. Ibid., 27. Hinder's description closely resembles the layout of the house featured in the popular play *Shanghai under the Eaves* (*Shanghai wuyan xia* 上海屋簷下) by the popular playwright and screen writer Xia Yan 夏衍.
10. Hinder, *Life and Labour in Shanghai,* 88.
11. Chen, *Kangzhan shidai shenghuo shi,* 47.
12. The most disturbing aspect of this scene is the widow's joy at finding that her neighborhood friends have built her a "two-story" lean-to not five feet high just outside her former courtyard. She crawls into the ground level through a square opening in the wall, and the children clamber up a few rickety steps into their "garret."
13. Hinder, *Life and Labour in Shanghai,* 90n6.
14. Ibid., 90.
15. Ibid.
16. Duo, "Shanghai tingzijian poujie tu," 67–69.
17. Benson, "The Manipulation of Tanci in Radio Shanghai during the 1930s," 118.
18. Duo, "Shanghai tingzijian poujie tu," 67.
19. Ibid.
20. Ibid. Unless otherwise noted, translations are my own.
21. *Gelou* can also be translated as attic, garret, or loft. "Dovecote," puns "pigeon" (ge 鴿) with the first syllable "pavilion" (ge 閣) of *gelou.*
22. Chen, *Kangzhan shidai shenghuo shi,* 49.
23. Qian, "Gelou zuojia fangwen ji," 78–82.

24. Hinder, *Life and Labour in Shanghai,* 84–85.

25. Xiang, "Gelou shi jing," 76.

26. Ibid., 73–74.

27. Ibid., 77.

28. Early in 1941, the SMC membership, which had consisted almost entirely of British nationals, was redistributed. The Americans, British, and Japanese took three seats each. Four seats were given to the Chinese and one each to the Dutch, Swiss, and Germans. This gave the Japanese a majority influence on the council. On December 8, 1941, the Japanese consul general asked the SMC to carry on and promised that Japan would interfere only as necessary. But within a few weeks, the Japanese forced the British, Americans, and Dutch to resign. By the end of 1942, the Japanese had taken control of nearly all the SMC's divisions—the police, public works, public health, finance, judiciary, and fire. Hinder, "Japan Moves In," 36–37.

29. From 1936 through 1942, the Industrial and Social Division of the SMC maintained cost-of-living indices on Chinese workers. With the advent of the war and rapid inflation, many employers and employees pressured the SMC to create a cost-of-living index for salaried Chinese employees too. Approval of the study was delayed at first because informants were to report their own expenses, and some on the SMC feared employees would exaggerate their expenditures. Hinder overcame this criticism by pointing out that because informants had been pulled from many organizations, "there [could] be no collusion to agree to increase consumption or prices of the same items." She could also have pointed out that the prices of everyday purchases were well known. In fact, Hinder and her division tracked them. Hinder letter to G. Godfrey Phillips, secretary and commissioner general of the SMC, September 15, 1941; in Hinder, letters and memos, SMA.

30. Hinder, letters and memos, 1941, SMA.

31. Hinder, letters to newspaper editors; Hinder to *Sin Shun Pao* editor, August 15, 1941; in SMA.

32. Benson, "The Manipulation of Tanci in Radio Shanghai during the 1930s," 117–146.

33. Hinder, letter to radio station HMXC, August 15, 1941; in SMA.

34. Hinder, likely spring or early summer 1941; in Hinder, letters and memos, SMA.

35. Participants likely saw the survey as an excellent opportunity to plead their case to their employers. For some reason, the police responded with special fervor; four times as many police volunteered to participate as were needed. Hinder balked at including such an excess of respondents from one occupation but conceded when Captain Smyth, deputy commissioner of police, wrote that "consideration has been given to the subject of curtailing the number of men supplying figures to you but it is the considered opinion of senior officers that it would be unwise to do so at the present time and therefore no alteration to the original scheme will be made." Perhaps he feared for his corps' morale. Hinder to Captain Smyth, and Smyth to Hinder, no dates, but the exchange likely took place mid-summer to early September 1941. In Hinder, letters and memos, SMA.

36. Hinder, letters and memos, likely August 1941, SMA.

37. Hinder, letter to radio station HMXC, likely August 1941; in Hinder, letters and memos, SMA.

38. On the *fabi* and other currencies that circulated in wartime China, see Parks Coble's chapter in this volume.

39. Glosser, *Chinese Visions of Family and State;* Yeh: "Progressive Journalism," and *Shanghai Splendor.*

40. Hinder, memo to SMC, spring 1940; in Hinder, letters and memos, SMA. The SMC suspended publication of the indexes until the issue was resolved. Some SMC members vociferously rejected her claim that as of March 1940, workers needed a 368 percent pay increase to maintain the standards of living they had achieved in 1936.

41. "Minutes on Meeting of Committee on Cost-of-Living Index Figures" (May 21, 1940). They disputed her assertion that "to maintain the 1929–1936 standard, workers would have to pay in March 1940, 3.68 times as much as in 1936." In Hinder, letters and memos, SMA.

42. Hinder, "The Standard and Cost of Living of Chinese Salaried Employees in Shanghai," 3. Prices rose drastically after the Japanese attack on Pearl Harbor on December 8, 1941, and the subsequent Japanese occupation of the International Concession. Hinder tried to respond by providing a provisional index in June 1942 based on just 100 families from her study.

43. Hinder, "The Standard and Cost of Living of Chinese Salaried Employees in Shanghai," table 14, 4; in Hinder, letters and memos, SMA. The full report, based on all 423 families, was finished in July 1943 and published in 1945. I use the later, full report.

44. Hinder, "The Standard and Cost of Living of Chinese Salaried Employees in Shanghai," 3–4. The numbers provided are Hinder's. I calculated most of the percentages.

45. Yeh, *Shanghai Splendor.*

46. Hinder, "The Standard and Cost of Living of Chinese Salaried Employees in Shanghai," 6.

47. Ibid., 4.

48. Ibid., 3–4.

49. This is a good example of how the very structure of Hinder's survey supported an argument in favor of the family wage.

50. Hinder, "The Standard and Cost of Living of Chinese Salaried Employees in Shanghai," 7.

51. Ibid., 6–7.

52. Ibid., 3, 6–7

53. Ibid., 8.

54. Respondents completed the survey in 1941 using the *fabi* currency, but when Hinder wrote her report in 1945, she used yuan for aggregated statistics. It is possible she drafted her report before the Japanese surrender and used a more neutral term. In any case, when data come from the surveys, I use *fabi* but keep Hinder's yuan when citing her report.

55. Hinder, "The Standard and Cost of Living," 3–4.

56. Ibid., 10, 18.

57. Ibid., 18.

58. Ibid., 10.

59. Hinder, *Life and Labour in Shanghai,* 764; Hinder, "The Standard and Cost of Living of Chinese Salaried Employees in Shanghai," table 14.

60. *A dou* 兜 is a dry measure used for grain, roughly equivalent to a peck, which equals about 2.3 gallons or 8.7 liters. These employees received 16 gallons or 61 liters of rice. The *jin* 斤, a unit of weight, was roughly equivalent to a pound.

61. Hinder, Cost of Living Questionnaire #890; in Hinder, letters and memos, SMA.

62. Hinder, Cost of Living Questionnaire #365; in Hinder, letters and memos, SMA.

63. Hinder, Cost of Living Questionnaires #30 and 415; in Hinder, letters and memos, SMA.

64. Hinder, Cost of Living Questionnaire #415; in Hinder, letters and memos, SMA.

65. A *sheng* 升 equals roughly one liter or two pints of grain.

66. Hinder, Cost of Living Questionnaire #973; in Hinder, letters and memos, SMA.

Bibliography

Manuscript Collections and Archives

Hinder, Eleanor. Letters and memos. Shanghai Municipal Archives (SMA).

Newspapers and Periodicals Cited as Primary Sources

Shanghai shenghuo 上海生活 (Shanghai life). As reprinted in *Shanghai shenghuo, 1937–1941,* edited by Shanghai Shehui Kexue Huan 上海社會科學院 (Shanghai Academy of Social Sciences). Shanghai: Shanghai shehui kexue yuan, 2006.

References

Barnes, Nicole Elizabeth. *Intimate Communities: Wartime Healthcare and the Birth of Modern China, 1937–1945*. Berkeley: University of California Press, 2018.

Benson, Carlton. "The Manipulation of Tanci in Radio Shanghai during the 1930s." *Republican China* 20, no. 2 (April 1995): 117–146.

Chang, Jui-te. "Bombs Do Not Discriminate? Class, Gender and Ethnicity in the Air-Raid Shelter Experiences of the Wartime Chongqing Population." In *Beyond Suffering: Recounting War in Modern China*, edited by James Flath and Norman Smith. Vancouver: UBC Press, 2011.

Chen Cunren 陳存仁. *Kangzhan shidai shenghuo shi* 抗戰時代生活史 (History of life during the Anti-Japanese War). Shanghai: Shanghai renmin chuban she, 2001.

Duo Jiugong 多九公 (pen name for Jiang Donglang 江楝良). "Shanghai tingzijian poujie tu" 上海亭子間剖截圖 (A sketch of Shanghai's pavilion rooms). *Shanghai shenghuo,* 1938:67–69.

Gang, Tan. "Living Underground: Bomb Shelters and Daily Lives in Wartime Chongqing (1937–1945)." *Journal of Urban History* 43, no. 3 (2017): 383–399.

Glosser, Susan. Chinese Visions of Family and State, 1915–1953. Berkeley: University of California Press, 2003.

Henriot, Christian. "Shanghai and the Experience of War: The Fate of Refugees." *European Journal of East Asian Studies* 5, no. 2 (January 1, 2006): 215–245.

———. "Street Culture, Visual Fragments and Everyday Life: Narrating Peddlers in Shanghai Modern." In *Visualising China, 1845–1965: Moving and Still Images in Historical Narratives,* edited by Christian Henriot and Wen-hsin Yeh, 93–128. Leiden: Brill, 2012.

Hershatter, Gail. *Women and China's Revolutions.* Lanham, Md.: Rowman and Littlefield, 2019. Critical Issues in World and International History.

Hinder, Eleanor. "Japan Moves In." *Far Eastern Survey* 12, no. 4 (February 22, 1943): 36–37.

———. *Life and Labour in Shanghai: A Decade of Labour and Social Administration in the International Settlement.* New York: Institute of Pacific Relations, 1944.

———. "The Standard and Cost of Living of Chinese Salaried Employees in Shanghai." In Shanghai Municipal Council, Industrial and Social Division, October 1941–July 1943, 1945. In SMA.

Lary, Diana. *The Chinese People at War: Human Suffering and Social Transformation, 1937–1945.* New York: Cambridge University Press, 2010.
Lary, Diana, and Stephen R. Mackinnon, eds. *The Scars of War: The Impact of Warfare on Modern China.* Vancouver: UBC Press, 2001.
Li, Danke. *Echoes of Chongqing: Women in Wartime China.* Urbana: University of Illinois Press, 2010.
Lu, Hanchao. *Beyond the Neon Lights: Everyday Shanghai in the Early Twentieth Century.* Berkeley: University of California Press, 1999.
Ma, Zhao. *Runaway Wives, Urban Crimes, and Survival Tactics in Wartime Beijing, 1937–1949.* Cambridge, Mass.: Harvard University Asia Center, 2015. Distributed by Harvard University Press.
MacKinnon, Stephen R. *Wuhan, 1938—War, Refugees, and the Making of Modern China.* Berkeley: University of California Press, 2008.
Qian Yiming 錢一鳴. "Gelou zuojia fangwen ji" 閣樓作家訪問記 (My visit to a writer in a garret). *Shanghai shenghuo*, no. 12 (1940): 78–82.
Rottmann, Allison. "Resistance, Urban Style: The New Fourth Army and Shanghai, 1937–1945." PhD dissertation, University of California at Berkeley, 2007.
Wang, Di. *The Teahouse: Small Business, Everyday Culture, and Public Politics in Chengdu, 1900–1950.* Stanford, Calif.: Stanford University Press, 2008.
Wheelhouse, Francis. *Eleanor Mary Hinder: An Australian Woman's Social Welfare Work in China between the Wars.* Sydney: Wentworth Books Pty, Ltd., 1978.
Xiang Yu 湘雨. "Gelou shi jing" 閣樓十景 (Ten views of a loft). *Shanghai shenghuo*, no. 3 (1938): 73–77.
Yeh, Wen-hsin. "Progressive Journalism and Shanghai's Petty Urbanites: Zou Taofen and the Shenghuo Weekly, 1926–1945." In *Shanghai Sojourners*, edited by Frederic Wakeman, Jr., and Wen-hsin Yeh, 186–238. Berkeley: Institute of East Asian Studies, University of California at Berkeley, 1992.
———. *Shanghai Splendor: Economic Sentiments and the Making of Modern China, 1843–1949.* Berkeley: University of California Press, 2007.

CHAPTER 2

Women at Work in Wartime Beijing

SOPHIA LEE

To Mr. Q & A: I don't know if you also feel this way: with today's high cost of living, supporting a family on ¥100 a month is so difficult. Since the suicide of that elementary school teacher, I have started to wonder about the end of the road in my own future. To be sure, the authorities are quite solicitous of our welfare, but I still cannot make it. We are a big family of thirteen, the type of "four generations under one roof" people exalt. Except for me, a wage earner, members of my family are all strictly consumers. And because of our bannermen heritage, they are set on maintaining a certain lifestyle. In short, they are completely unwilling just to make do with whatever is available and economical. I have suggested that my two older sisters go out to find some proper employment. They are the only two in the family able to work at this time. But my elders insist that we are a scholarly family of long standing, and no daughter from this family should ever go out to work. They feel such a move would ruin the family's reputation. I really do not know what to do with this stubborn attitude. I am afraid that defying my elders would bring them heartache, but without land or house and with no other income, I really cannot support my family any longer. Please give me some guidance.

Respectfully,
Ran
Qingdao Telephone Company

Mr. Ran: Living in this extraordinary time, everyone should make do and persevere. Everyone should stiffen his spine and learn to accept innovation. You are the backbone of this old, traditional family. You should fly the standard of reform. Why shouldn't women have jobs? During this transformative time, everyone has an obligation to serve society. You can explain to your elders that modern women working outside the home is an honorable phenomenon—definitely not something that would ruin a family's reputation. Wait until your sisters find work and can show your elders some concrete achievements; then their old-fashioned thinking

> may spontaneously evaporate. With three people working to support the family, many difficulties can be eliminated. Mr. Ran, please pluck up your courage and proceed.

Appearing in the March 1943 issue of an in-house publication of the North China Telegraph and Telephone Company, the above exchange carried a headline asserting that at a time of fast-rising prices, the clamor for "women to return home" had quieted down. Certain aspects of Ran's dilemma, such as his family's refusal to economize, might not have been a common problem, but his family's economic hardship, his wish to have his two sisters working, and perhaps even his elders' reluctance to allow young women into the workplace were issues quite familiar to many urban residents in occupied North China.[1]

As noted by Parks Coble in this volume, war and occupation triggered hyperinflation throughout China from 1937 to 1945. The general price index in Beijing, pegged at 100 in April 1937, reached 147.56 one year after the war began and hovered around 300 three years later. Repercussions from Japan's attack on Pearl Harbor led to even higher prices and worse shortages of daily necessities. By the spring of 1943, when the exchange cited above appeared in print, the general price index registered at more than eight times that of April 1937, and grain prices had increased more than twenty-sixfold.[2] Arguably, wartime economic stress was the single most powerful force that, in both overt and subtle ways, reshaped the attitudes and practices of Beijing's Chinese residents. One consequence of economic distress was an increase in the number of Chinese female wage earners. This development was different from state-directed wartime mobilization of women to perform tasks normally expected to be done by men had they not been conscripted. Driven by pressing economic needs but without systematic support from the authorities, women in wartime Beijing, longtime residents as well as recent arrivals, entered a labor market that was also full of men seeking work. Finding and sometimes creating income-producing opportunities, many of these women subverted not just conventional social and cultural norms, but also familiar tropes about life under the occupation. Despite—and perhaps because of—the difficulties of the occupation, women individually and in groups helped to transform opinions and conventions about a woman's place both within and outside the home.

The challenges these working women encountered and the strategies they deployed were randomly recorded without elaboration in contemporary print sources because readers of these sources did not need background or details: they were either witnessing or experiencing the phenomenon first hand.[3] For complicated reasons, postwar sources have all but ignored this facet of the occupation. As a result, we know very little about who were the women searching for employment, the kinds of work they were able to find, and the ramifications of this wartime development beyond meeting immediate, urgent financial needs. *Funü zazhi* 婦女雜誌 (Women's journal), a monthly published in Beijing from September 1940 to the end of the war, offers rare albeit fragmentary glimpses of women at work, especially in jobs that were byproducts of the occupation. Using commentaries and personal accounts from the magazine, in this chapter I attempt to look for some answers to the questions raised above. Relying on this publication as the principal source inevitably means that although the magazine's editorials and reports about women's work cover a broad range of white- and blue-collar occupations, the narrative voices mostly reflect the evolving concerns and perceptions of the journal's readers—literate women—rather than a cross section of the city's adult female population as a whole.

Women and Work in Wartime, in Discourse

Although the *Women's Journal* was endorsed by the occupation authorities and received supplemental funding from the regime, it would be a mistake to assume that the publication was nothing more than cover-to-cover propaganda bolstering a regime lacking legitimacy. Product advertisements and reader subscription fees also contributed to its operation, thus exerting some influence over editorial decisions on the magazine's contents, consisting mainly of opinions, reports, profiles, advice, and readers' submissions—all centering on gender, sexuality, and family issues.[4]

The occupation regime never treated the welfare of women as a high priority. To be sure, Chinese women, often as mother figures, were used as a "gendered archetype" in propaganda posters promoting Sino-Japanese common cause, but the slogans on these posters, as well as many other text-only exhortations placed on public walls and in the margins of dailies, did not directly address women and the myriad challenges they faced during wartime.[5] The regime's avowed political and ethical compass, *xinmin* 新民 (people's renovation) ideology, was based on the Confucian classic *Daxue* 大學 (Great learning), which, at its core, extolled the inextricable linkage between personal cultivation and the ordering of the family and the state. This is not the place to consider the relevance of *xinmin* precepts to North China in the 1930s and 1940s. Suffice it to say that the Confucian text also made no explicit reference to women. This neglect of women in both policy and ideology actually gave commentators and editors of *Women's Journal* a tacit exemption from the obligatory but often tortuous attempts by ideologues and officials of the occupation regime to shoehorn all manner of issues into a haphazardly designated *xinmin* niche, as was prevalent in several newspapers and periodicals. Instead, mindful of the conservative bent of the regime, the journal's female and male pundits writing about women's status and responsibilities found safe haven in the concept of *xianqi liangmu* 賢妻良母 (virtuous wife and good mother), a protean notion applicable to a broad range of settings and activities.[6]

In their varied explications of a virtuous wife and good mother, commentators all agreed that managing a household and taking care of the needs of everyone in that household was a woman's natural calling (*tianzhi* 天職). However, they differed on whether working outside the home was an asset or liability for a virtuous wife and good mother. Although no pundit deemed education and experiences outside the home innately harmful to women, many frowned upon the lifestyle of urban women, whether working or not, as the epitome of undisciplined, self-centered, if not outright profligate, liberties sanctioned by the May Fourth and New Culture movements. In earlier issues of the magazine, pundits tended to stress the primacy of a stay-at-home woman fulfilling her natural calling of caring for everyone in her family. However, worsening economic conditions, especially during the last years of the war, all but rendered moot the debate whether a virtuous wife and good mother, or a single woman, ought to work for a wage—as the exchange cited at the start of this chapter suggests. Ultimately, *shidai nüxing* 時代女性 (contemporary women); *xinshidai funü* 新時代婦女 (women of a new era), embodying both domestic skills and occupational expertise; and even on occasion a term that originated in the Nanjing regime, *xinguomin funü* 新國民婦女 (new citizen-women, who integrated familial, societal, and national responsibilities), began to overshadow *xianqi liangmu* in status, and women were urged, once and for all, to leave the ranks of "unproductive parasites" 寄生蟲 (*jishengchong*).[7]

One overarching conundrum that commentators were never able or willing to clarify was the role that occupied Beijing's Chinese women—and men—ought to play in support of the ongoing war. Unlike most newspapers and periodicals published in the city, *Women's Journal* did not devote much space to battlefield reports or the regime's policies purportedly aimed at contributing to the war effort. The occupation was basically treated as a given, requiring minimal elaboration. The war that had triggered the occupation was referred to in a variety of oblique, coded ways that clumsily avoided the explicit label of "war"—until Wang Jingwei's regime in Nanjing officially declared war on the Allied nations in January 1943. Subsequently, the expression *juezhan* 決戰 (decisive war) acquired currency throughout occupied China. This belated change in nomenclature conveniently dovetailed with the North China regime's explicit call for mobilization of civilian women and men in support of the war. But when the authorities in Beijing urged women to redouble their economizing efforts to maintain hearth and home while contributing toward increased production and air raid preparedness, their willing response probably had nothing to do with extending the life of the regime but everything to do with protecting themselves and their families from starvation and American bombers. In short, these women worked under a foreign military occupation—and in some cases for the occupiers—out of personal necessity above all other concerns.[8]

In a process explored more fully by Maruta Takashi in this volume, true to their avowed conservatism, the occupation authorities did not include International Women's Day, March 8, in their official calendar of important dates. (That date retained significance in both Nationalist- and Communist-controlled areas.) Despite this symbolic severance of ties with a global female community, *Women's Journal*'s reports and photo essays continued to provide a window onto women's wartime activities in both the Axis and Allied nations, with special focus on—and praise for—their willingness to add to their own tasks what had been done by men now on the battlefield. Occasionally, these reports touched upon state or community social services, such as child care, aimed to help married women mobilize for the war effort. A few Chinese commentators registered approval for such support. Japanese women's forbearance, perseverance, and frugality as they engaged in a wide array of home-front activities were singled out as exemplary behavior worthy of emulation by Chinese women.[9] It is unclear how such exhortations were received by Chinese readers of the magazine, who themselves had to face their own wartime challenges with forbearance, perseverance, and frugality.

The contents of *Women's Journal* reflected the precipitous decline of living standards in occupied North China. The earlier issues (published in 1940 and 1941 when the general price index registered at about three to four times that of April 1937) regularly offered women beauty tips and comments on seasonal fashion; Chinese and Western recipes called for meat, fish, eggs, flour, and sugar. By 1944 and 1945, when the general price index had risen more than twelvefold from its prewar numbers, readers were urged to stop using cosmetics as an austerity measure and given tips on using substitutes for ordinary food items no longer available in markets and stores. Time and again the magazine offered advice on how to circumvent a severe shortage of soap; one month before Japan's surrender, an article instructed readers to do laundry in water in which ash from incense or certain plants had been steeping for a day.[10] Since its inception, the magazine served as a forum for women not just to discuss the intrinsic value of wage-earning work, but also to give advice on how and where to find work.

Moreover, on its pages women shared individual work experiences. Thus, in many ways, *Women's Journal* created a vital network through which readers were able to empathize with other women's wartime challenges—and in some instances learn from uplifting accounts of how they had overcome difficulties.[11]

Women and Work in Occupied Beijing, in Practice

The Chinese population in wartime Beijing, which eventually topped 1.8 million, represented about a 13 percent increase from its prewar level. As before, men outnumbered women by a wide margin, but the disparity became less pronounced. More research is needed to explain this change, though it is obvious that an influx of women from war zones and the departure of men for unoccupied areas contributed to this demographic shift, however modest.[12] The city before the war did not have a sizable female workforce. According to one set of statistics compiled by the municipal government, in 1936, only about 7.6 percent (or forty-five thousand) of Beijing's Chinese female population were wage earners. Of this number, about 40 percent were employed in "personal services" (*renshi fuwu* 人事服務), ranging from domestic service to waitressing to prostitution; 36 percent were in "professional occupations" (*ziyou zhiye* 自由職業), covering a wide assortment of work including doctors, nurses, teachers, and store and office clerks; and 22 percent worked in factories, commerce, and agriculture.[13] These job classifications tally with what Republican-period reformist and bureaucratic writings had designated as *zhiye* 職業—that is, a "regular paying job requiring skill and professional training" and normally performed at a place outside one's own home. Extant data from the municipal job placement office (*zhiye jieshao chu* 職業介紹處) during the first half of the occupation show that approximately 10–15 percent of inquiries about employment came from women, but in percentages more women than men got hired (usually as servants, family tutors, and store clerks). Unmarried women far outnumbered married ones among those seeking and finding work; the pattern was reversed among men: more married men sought and found work. On average, each month fewer than two hundred individuals used the municipal job placement service to look for work, and under fifty found employment.[14] They represented but a small fraction of Beijing's job seekers, urgently devising ways to earn a wage in an economy crippled by skyrocketing prices.

As Zhao Ma notes, the above-mentioned concept of *zhiye* overlooked the exchange of labor for wages in the informal economy: part-time, informally arranged work performed either within or outside the worker's home.[15] A frequently discussed topic in *Women's Journal*, this type of part-time work was called *fuye* 副業. (Depending on context, this can mean sideline work, part-time work, or casual labor.) Wartime statistics for working women comparable to the 1936 data cited above are not readily available, but extant sources strongly suggest that various kinds of *fuye* made the difference between starvation and survival for many women and their families, even if they also had income from employment commonly associated with *zhiye*. In short, the job market for Chinese women and the kinds of women seeking work in the wartime city contained both familiar and new features.

Wartime Beijing was a premier political and cultural center, not an industrial hub. The occupation regime was never flush with funds, and with the exception of the police force, those working for government institutions, including schools, saw their wages essentially frozen, falling increasingly behind inflation. The handicraft industries that had employed women, both in small-scale workshops and factories, as well as sideline work done at the women's homes, suffered a precipitous decline, especially after the start of the Pacific War, when their major customers, Western markets and Western tourists in the city, vanished. No doubt some who had lost their jobs in these handicraft industries vied for a chance to enter the factory established by the city's Social Affairs Bureau in 1940 that offered bare-bones room and board up to a year to about two hundred females aged 15–35 who either had been forced to leave school or had become unemployed. In exchange for room and board, these women learned to produce handmade and machine-made apparel and toys that were sold at moderate prices in stores in the city and beyond. In addition, municipal records counted, on average, two or three hundred women as regular factory workers (men numbered over five thousand); they worked ten-hour days making matches, paper, and medicine, among other items.[16] Arguably, the city's economy during the occupation was propped up mainly by its service sector, meeting the needs of not just an expanding Chinese population, but also those of an unprecedented influx of Japanese civilians. The number of civilian Japanese residents exploded from slightly over two thousand on the eve of the war to about ninety thousand near its end. A large contingent of white-collar employees of "government-policy companies" (*kokusaku gaisha* 國策會社), with families in tow, contributed to that sharp increase.[17] Wartime Beijing's Japanese community did not have the benefit of the infrastructure that had developed for decades at the various Japanese concessions and probably needed more ad hoc local support. On the whole, the Japanese in Beijing were more white-collar and prosperous than the Chinese, and their presence created both white- and blue-collar employment for Chinese men and women. This remains a subject difficult to research because of its sensitive nature and the paucity of accessible documentation.

Japanese official organizations and companies that arrived in wartime Beijing employed a mixture of Japanese and Chinese staff. It should be noted that many Japanese offices had their own Japanese female staff. For example, as of October 1940 (shortly after *Women's Journal* debuted), about 37.5 percent of Japanese living in Beijing were female, and about 48 percent of them (11,191) had occupations. The Japanese women's top five employers were (1) companies, banks, and stores (3,163 female workers); (2) the railway (i.e., the North China Transportation Company [J. Kahoku Kōtsū Kabushikigaisha 華北交通株式会社; Ch. Huabei Jiaotong Gufen Youxian Gongsi 華北交通股份有限公司], a government-policy company) (2,991 female workers); (3) businesses with geisha, prostitutes, and waitresses (1,258 female workers); (4) government offices (966 female workers); and (5) medical institutions (392 female workers).[18] Some of the women were spouses of men working in Beijing; others were single, and a number of them were recruited through newspaper advertisements in Japan.[19] It is difficult to gauge how many Japanese women worked alongside Chinese women and men and what kinds of interactions they had both within and outside the workplace. Many contemporary accounts point to language as a barrier to meaningful association. Wartime wages for female white-collar Japanese on the continent were generally higher than back home, and rationing of goods was considerably less stringent. In other words, most Japanese women in occupied Beijing had a more comfortable life than their counterparts on the home islands. Some male Chinese employees of Japanese organizations in Beijing earned good salaries but seldom in parity with their Japanese colleagues, who usually received additional compensations in money and kind for working abroad and had fewer dependents than their Chinese colleagues. The same disparity likely existed between female Japanese and Chinese employees in Japanese organizations. At the North China Telegraph and Telephone Company, for example, both Chinese and Japanese employees were allowed to become members of the company cooperative, but many items at the cooperative store, such as refined sugar and certain kinds of rice, were available only to Japanese employees. During the second half of the war, the company did provide Chinese employees with flour and other necessaries at subsidized prices.[20]

An article in the November 1942 issue of *Women's Journal* offered brief descriptions and commentaries on eighteen occupations presumably deemed most suitable for Chinese women, at least in the opinion of the magazine. The list began with lawyer, secretary-assistant, editor, journalist, writer, and musician; it followed with schoolteacher (especially at the elementary level), artist, physician, pharmacist, police, bureaucrat, office worker, and typist; the list concluded with photographer, film actor, theatrical actor, and singer. Appearing one year after the start of the Pacific War, which had begun to affect the living standards even of the elite, this list, on the whole, represented a fantasy bearing little resemblance to the reality of the contemporary job market. However, probably because wartime Beijing's job market was full of male job seekers, established notions of gender appropriateness remained central in this and all other discussions about women's work.[21]

Curiously, a normally indispensable wartime female occupation, nursing, was absent from the list, which did include physicians and pharmacists. The magazine did publish a few articles about nursing, depicted as satisfying though with low wages, but never linked the profession to war casualties, civilian or military. It is not clear how or where wounded Chinese soldiers fighting for the regime were treated. Japanese medical personnel tended to wounded Japanese soldiers. The regime's public health officials oversaw vaccination campaigns against a variety of communicable diseases but made no attempt to recruit a large number of nurses and doctors to carry out those duties. In short, Chinese women in occupied Beijing were deprived of the opportunity to "heal bodies and build the nation," pivotal roles ascribed by Nicole Barnes to female providers of civilian and military medicine in the Nationalist area.[22]

Of the eighteen occupations on that list, police and typist were the two that became more conspicuous after the war began. Beijing's municipal government started to recruit female police in 1933 as part of a national move directed by the Nationalist government. This represented both an acknowledgment of an expanding female presence in public space and simultaneously a wish by the authorities to regulate that presence for the sake of public probity. Those in favor of adding women to Beijing's police force also believed that because policemen could not as a matter of course investigate and conduct body searches on women, male criminals often used them as decoys in kidnapping, smuggling, and other nefarious schemes. Thus, having policewomen ready and able to stop and frisk suspicious females in public places would likely reduce the crime rate in the unsettling time of the early 1930s.[23] Initially, about a third of Beijing's policewomen were assigned to patrol railroad stations. When the city came under Japanese occupation in August 1937, this particular kind of socially accepted intrusion of the state—in the form of a policewoman conducting body searches on women—facilitated the implementation of heightened security measures mandated by the new regime. In fact, frisking all women and children and checking their luggage at city gates and railroad stations became the primary duty of the city's female police force (though the degree of enforcement varied according to the alert level).[24] In this way, Beijing's policewomen gained much greater visibility as they took up positions, together with male Chinese and Japanese police forces, at checkpoints at city gates and train stations (see figure 2.1).

Figure 2.1. Policewoman searching female passengers and their belongings at Qianmen Station (June 1938). Source: North China Railway Archive (North China Railway Archive Committee), photo ID 3601-002940-0.

Paradoxically, that high visibility, sanctioned by social and gender norms, did not elevate the status of women within the police force—and most likely diminished their status in the public mind.

To qualify for the police force, a woman had to be above eighteen years of age and unmarried, with at least an elementary school education and in good health. After six months of training, a recruit was assigned to duties around the city. *Women's Journal* did a short profile of the city's female police force in its March 1941 issue. Their monthly pay, according to the article, started at a modest sum of ¥30 (close to half of an elementary school teacher's monthly salary). Although the police force was the only government agency that regularly handed out small salary boosts to its rank and file during the occupation, it is difficult to ascertain whether policewomen were accorded the same increases as their male counterparts. Up at 5:30 a.m. and to bed at 9:30 p.m., these women spent six to seven hours each day on duty, six days a week. They lived in a specially designated dormitory, ate their subsidized meals at the canteen, and wore government-issued uniforms (the same as men during the cooler months but black skirts in warmer weather). The women were praised for their dedication, working alongside their male colleagues without any trace of coquetry or timidity. However, the profile also pointed out that for physiological reasons policewomen were not dispatched to nighttime or dangerous duties. When this profile was published, Beijing's female police had grown to ninety-one (including three patrol chiefs and six captains) from its first class of eighteen in 1933. Nonetheless, that was still a tiny fraction of the city's police force, numbering over eight thousand men in its rank and file (a fact not mentioned in the profile). Although policewomen and policemen worked at the same locations, the women were segregated within the organization in many ways. Even in the police personnel statistics compiled monthly by the municipal government, the category of policewomen was placed near the end of the roster, appearing after the police band.[25]

Young women—and men—interested in jobs as security guards could also apply at the North China Transportation Company, a Japanese national-policy company that oversaw the operation of land and water transportation systems throughout occupied North China. A small number of Chinese women were hired to maintain order at train stations and to guard rail lines in the countryside against sabotage. From its establishment in 1938, the company always had more Chinese than Japanese employees; the overall ratio was 76:24 in March 1939, though Japanese outnumbered the Chinese in upper management. Near the end of the war, when fewer Japanese men were available to work in the company, 83 percent of its security force was Chinese, totaling 18,362 men and women. Additional research may reveal the number of Chinese women working as railway security guards (especially in the last years of the war) and the precise nature of their duties at train stations where Chinese policewomen were also posted. The image crafted by the North China Transportation Company for its uniformed female guards was one of modernity: in photographs some sported permed hair, a style not seen on Beijing's Chinese policewomen.[26]

For more sedentary jobs, women could become typists; they were in demand, as readers of help-wanted ads in Beijing's dailies knew well. This occupation required training on the machine and, for many jobs, at least a basic command of Japanese.[27] As Thomas Mullaney shows, despite discursive representations of typing as "women's work," typing schools were attended by both men and women. However, fragmentary evidence from Beijing's typing schools does indicate a slight edge of female over male enrollment. Mullaney suggests that typing schools could be "spaces of possibility, and social mobility." But as individual accounts in *Women's Journal* revealed, they also served as a holding zone, a temporary stop for people losing their place on the social ladder. That would be one likely explanation for the presence of normal school and college students (or even graduates) on the rosters of typing schools: such students either had had to stop their formal education because of financial reasons or were unable to find work after graduation. Similarly, lack of employment could very well be the reason that some typing school students stayed on for advanced training after completing a course.[28]

Besides typing, Chinese-language tutoring (*Huayu jiaoshi* 華語教師) was the other "growth industry" in the female job market.[29] It is interesting that this occupation was excluded from the list of eighteen presumably "suitable" female occupations noted above. Chinese-language tutoring was basically one type of part-time work (*fuye*) that emerged with the occupation. On rare occasions readers of dailies did see advertisements for such instructors or students, but normally lessons were arranged through a third party known to both the instructor and the student. A common setup would have the tutor meet with her student(s), either an individual or a small group (sometimes members of a family), and provide Chinese lessons for a few hours each week. Some competency in Japanese—and an ability to speak "standard Beijing dialect"—ensured good pay at these jobs. The informal nature of this employment makes it difficult to find details on the number of women engaged in this line of work or the amount or range of pay they received. Presumably if a woman had a number of these part-time jobs, she could earn an adequate income.[30]

Another type of work missing from that list of eighteen was telephone switchboard operator. Beijing's telephone company, founded in 1904, expanded considerably once the occupation began. During the war, the number of telephones installed in the city's offices, stores, and individual homes increased 34 percent, from 13,362 in June 1937 to 17,970 four years later. The volume of long-distance calls expanded more than twofold. Although two of the city's four telephone exchanges were converted to automatic dialing, increased volume in both local and long-distance calls required a larger work force.[31] Before the war, operators

Figure 2.2. Chinese switchboard operators (March 1939). Source: North China Railway Archive (North China Railway Archive Committee), photo ID 3605-013522-0.

appeared to be exclusively male, with a mandatory retirement age of forty because of the physical dexterity and mental acuity required for the task.[32] When a Japanese government-policy company took control of the telecommunications agencies in the city, it followed the practice on the Japanese home islands and began to recruit and train young Chinese women in both the technical and linguistic skills essential to serving Chinese and Japanese customers (see figure 2.2). Male Chinese operators continue to work for Chinese customers, and Japanese female operators were also added to the staff to facilitate services for Japanese customers. As individual accounts below illustrate, young Chinese women took on the challenge of switchboard operation for varying reasons.

Policewoman, railroad security guard, typist, Chinese language tutor, and telephone switchboard operator were all employment opportunities that either emerged or expanded because of the Japanese presence. Other opportunities that are even more difficult to explore because of the lack of accessible sources belong to the category of "personal services." *Women's Journal* was mostly reticent about this entire sector of female employment—not just about the impact of the expanding Japanese population, but also about wartime continuity and change from the perspective of both Chinese workers and clients. As mentioned above, over a thousand Japanese geisha, prostitutes, and waitresses worked in wartime Beijing. It is well known that some Chinese women were forced into working as prostitutes for the Japanese military, but the magazine never mentioned those euphemistically called "comfort women."

It is beyond the scope of this chapter to delve into the large and complicated subject of domestic service in the occupied city, but some numbers from the 1940 Japanese Foreign Ministry data cited above permit a few tentative remarks. As of October 1940, among 62,159 Japanese residing in Beijing, only 207 men and 177 women were engaged in domestic service, presumably for other Japanese.[33] For a relatively well-off foreign community at that particular time period, the low numbers of Japanese servants undoubtedly meant the employment of local Chinese domestic workers. Wealthy Japanese households often brought at least one Japanese servant with them to Beijing and then added local hires to their household staff. Many Japanese households with no Japanese help hired at least one Chinese female servant; if they could afford another, they would also hire a male servant. Some of the domestic workers lived in their employers' homes (one interviewee, a teenager during the war, told me his family's Chinese female servant lived with her young daughter at his home). Other female Chinese domestics worked on an hourly basis and lived elsewhere. The Japanese generally paid higher wages than the Chinese. A March 1941 article claimed that higher pay and hourly work were creating a shortage of domestic help for the Chinese population.[34] This shortage might have been somewhat offset later by the dismissal of servants by Chinese households as economic deterioration dictated belt tightening. In fact, starting in 1943, the authorities paid considerable attention to an austerity campaign that urged Beijing residents to grow food in their own yards (or wherever possible), walk or use their bicycles instead of public or private vehicles, and conduct daily life without relying on others, which in part meant to do without servants.

Hoping to stave off a total economic collapse of the family, a sizable number of Chinese women from all walks of life resorted to one or more part-time jobs to cobble together much needed income that became an integral and, in some cases, substantial contribution to the family income. Family tutor (*jiating jiaoshi*

家庭教師) in wealthy Chinese households, long held as a respectable female occupation, was one common part-time employment undertaken by well-educated Chinese women. But such opportunities, like joining the police force, barely made a ripple on the overall demand by women for work. With ingenuity and grit, many more capitalized on the special needs of an especially trying time and created an impressive array of income-generating ventures. In early 1941, one contributor in *Women's Journal* suggested no fewer than eighteen ways a woman could use her sewing, embroidery, and cooking skills—female pursuits sanctioned by tradition—to start a business from her own home. Perhaps as a nod to the pressing contemporary need for work, this how-to article counseled assertive marketing. For example, a maker of children's clothing should routinely send mimeographed advertisements to friends and neighbors and follow those up with personal visits when she could show potential customers an assortment of samples. A strategically timed visit to an expectant mother, a few months before the birth, could lead to orders for many years to come.[35] It is impossible to know just how many women engaged in activities similar to those suggested in this article. But it is easy to imagine in the later years of the war, when material shortages became acute, that enterprising women earned money by doing alterations or repurposing usable parts of worn adult clothes for children. Women willing and able to travel devised ways to make the most of regional shortages. Zhao Ma presents a memorable vignette of Beijing women donning ten pairs of pants and then boarding a Chengde-bound train to exchange the pants for grain. Perhaps other Beijing women emulated Shandong women by engaging in *paomaimai* 跑買賣 (literally, running trade)—that is, using the railways to transport inexpensive items to sell to Anhui customers. Reportedly it was hard work but quite profitable. In the final years of the war, tending to one's victory garden also came to be regarded as part-time work. Such efforts usually filled the hungry stomachs of family members, but sometimes these small harvests were probably traded for other foods or sold outright.[36]

"My Work Experience": A Sampling

From time to time, *Women's Journal* put out calls for essays detailing women's lives and contemporary experiences. According to the editors, the response was enthusiastic. A handful of these submissions were chosen to appear in print, and their authors received modest payments.[37] These essays represent rare individual voices from a period for which personal experiences that were made public, especially those reconstructed after the war, were often hewed to fit prescribed molds. Granted, these women's accounts, appearing in an officially sanctioned publication, successfully met at least the minimum requirements set by censors. Nevertheless, their nuanced narratives reveal a surprising degree of immediacy and candor that broaden and deepen our understanding of how ordinary women coped with extraordinary difficulties during the occupation. They also remind us that even as women, individually and collectively, were charting new courses for themselves, prevalent notions about gender and work still left plenty of imprints on these new courses. These essays, plus cartoons, also offer insights into both the explicit limitations and implicit liberties guiding the publishing industry, supposedly monitored with unrelenting vigilance by the regime. Below are summaries of a few essays, including occasional partial verbatim translations (within quotation marks).

Policewoman

Five months after the matter-of-fact, positive profile of policewomen described above, the August 1941 issue presented an ensemble of an artist's sketches of five working women in summertime: a switchboard operator, typist, binder, policewoman, and singer, accompanied by interior monologues. The monologue by a policewoman on duty at a train station begins with an exchange between her and a few rural women, probably bringing produce to the city's market:

> "What's that?"
> "Cucumbers."
> "And what's that?"
> "Millet pancakes."
> "What else?"
> "Two cloves of garlic."

Then the policewoman reveals her own feelings: "Though appreciative of the importance of my job—and even my sharp-looking uniform—I am tired of the excessive ordinariness and stress of a monotonous life: the unfulfilling, endless back-and-forth with exhausted, malnourished people giving off the stench of suffocating heat mixed with sweat in a third-class train compartment. I imagine a change to something different."

The policewoman's musings offered a different perspective of policing than what had been presented in the magazine's positive profile only five months earlier. Although extant records are too meager to form any generalizations, two police logs of contraband confiscated at city gates and rail stations throughout the city suggest that a policewoman's day was not filled with suspenseful encounters with female lawbreakers, thus perhaps contributing to the monotony that irked the policewoman sketched above. For example, during June 1939, three women entering the city were discovered to be carrying opiates, four with moonshine, and one with banned currency plus opiates; one leaving the city was caught carrying an opiate. In an eighteen-day period in April 1940, eight women were found to be carrying various kinds of opiates, and one, moonshine.

A cartoon in the August 1941 issue could be taken as a lampoon of the practice of body searches. It shows a young policewoman at a city gate explaining to a plainly dressed elderly woman, probably returning from a visit to the countryside, that everyone entering the city has to be searched. The old woman's retort—"But am I from the countryside?"—implies that in her mind, the purpose of a body search is to prevent subversive country bumpkins from entering the walled city and that she, not from the countryside, should be exempted from such a nuisance. Whether intentional or not, in two different genres in a single issue of *Women's Journal*, an utterly bored policewoman on duty at a train station and an annoyed Beijing resident at a city gate subtly but unambiguously expressed their feelings toward the mandated body search.[38]

Switchboard Operator

In the same ensemble piece published in the August 1941 issue, a switchboard operator and a typist stress the drudgery of their tasks. Overhearing a conversation between two young people arranging a rendezvous, the switchboard operator imagines them enjoying a moonlit boat ride at Beihai Park while she herself toils away in stifling heat.

Recounting the hectic pace of her job, one switchboard operator explains that the day shift lasted from nine in the morning to six in the evening, and the night shift, from five to ten-thirty. For each hour of work, she was allowed a twenty-minute break. After every eight days of work (each averaging six hours), she had a day off. This operator had been a normal school student. She does not say precisely why she had left school but hints at an abrupt and involuntary departure. Even though she avoided wearing the company insignia in public, her company uniform readily identified her occupation. The novelty of female telephone operators—and possibly their special role as operators for the Japanese—generated unwanted public attention. On the street some people poked fun at her and called her *nüsiji* 女司機 (loosely translated as a female mechanic; male telephone operators were called *siji*), which she found quite demeaning (see below). She was resigned to forsaking her own future because her family needed her income.

Another operator began working for the telephone company in 1939, also after quitting school because of a downturn in her family's financial situation. She reports receiving a monthly salary of ¥25, of which she sent ¥10 home to her mother. For a while, she supplemented her telephone company salary with a

Chinese-language tutoring job (a *fuye*, according to her), which she took on with great reluctance, but it brought in an additional ¥15 each month, thus "¥10 more for home."

Not all operators went to work with such reluctance. One middle school student became so taken with the telephone exchange room during a visit to the telephone company that she took the company's recruitment examination against her family's wishes. Among the forty chosen from more than three hundred applicants, she dropped out of school to work as an operator. In addition to becoming proficient at the switchboard, she also acquired enough Japanese to handle calls from Japanese customers, but Korean customers remained a problem because she had difficulty understanding them when they spoke. She liked the camaraderie of her coworkers but not the behavior of rude customers. She was still living at home and relied on her family for a considerable portion of her living expenses because her earnings were minuscule. She thought about returning to school but realized that her family would not be able to finance that. In fact, she indicated that her family would not be able to support her if she just quit her job and stayed at home.[39]

At a roundtable discussion organized by the in-house publication, several female operators in Beijing grumbled about the tedium of the work and the low pay. A few even thought about asking their superiors for a raise but, worried about their displeasure, they gave up on the idea. One speculated that impatient and dissatisfied customers, who routinely blamed operators for a slow connection, a busy line, and many other problems, had succeeded in creating a negative public image of switchboard operators. Another, who had been on the job for more than two years, complained that people, unfamiliar with the technical complexities of the telephone, treated the operators as uneducated laborers with no special skills. She grumbled that disgruntled male customers frequently seemed to revel in lodging sexist criticisms against the work done by female operators; some declared outright that telephone service had deteriorated since women had become operators. When she first began to work at the telephone company, she told relatives and friends about her work. Now when she left her office after work, she dreaded running into people she knew. If asked about her work, she would rather say that she was not employed. Nonetheless, she was staying on because she preferred the anonymity of her workplace to the office intrigues at other possible places of employment.[40]

Typist

One young woman began to learn typing in the summer of 1938, when her older brother left home for an undisclosed location and her family's fortunes took a downturn. By then, she had already stopped attending school for a year. Her family needed her support, and she thought typing suited her quiet personality. Moreover, tuition for the typing school was affordable, so she took up typing. After some initial anxiety about her own ability, she became adept at using the machine in the three-month course. However, upon completing the course at a reputable school, she was not able to find a job (and hinted at the endemic practice of using personal connections to obtain employment). Finally, in the summer of 1939 she got a job as a Chinese-language typist at a (presumably Japanese) cultural organization. She found the work challenging, especially since not all the forms and styles used in the office were covered in the three-month course, but she was glad to receive a salary for her toil. Although she married in 1940, she continued to work, with the encouragement of her husband. Married life meant additional tasks at home, but she had help. She also raised the seemingly inevitable question of having children and was in favor of the establishment of well-organized child-care facilities for the benefit of both the children and working parents.[41]

Office Worker

Office work had not been a common female occupation in Beijing before the war. Women working in offices in the wartime city unanimously agreed on the difficulties of often finding themselves being not just the only female (or at least the only single female), but also the youngest at their workplace. Their advice stressed working extra hard to prove one's worth and navigating with great care the complex office personnel maze. In addition, they strongly urged current and aspiring female office workers to do everything possible to avoid being viewed as a mere "vase" (*huaping* 花瓶)—that is, a decorative ornament at work. Several related incidents of sexual harassment by male colleagues and bosses.[42]

Social Hierarchy in Disarray

The individual work experiences presented above are varied, but one common thread linking several personal histories was the issue of *shixue* 失學 (basically, involuntary withdrawal from school), an enormous concern with numerous ramifications in occupied Beijing. As shown above, these young women stopped their schooling because their families were no longer able to afford the tuition, or their families needed extra income that they could provide by working. They helped to preserve their natal families, but they also had to rearrange their own future plans. Their experiences were but a few examples of how economic insecurities triggered by war and occupation caused not only deep dismay over thwarted personal goals, but also simmering anxieties over permanent loss of status for oneself and one's family. One young woman went to work because her widowed mother demanded her support. With an elementary school education, she could find employment only as a hostess at a Chinese restaurant. She was very unhappy about her predicament: "Anyone who knew my late father's position in society would appreciate that no daughter of his should be doing this kind of work." A few days after she began to work there, she was sexually assaulted by a customer, so she quit that job. Still needing to earn money, she found work at a famous upscale café but still had to fend off lecherous customers and an unsavory boss.[43]

Women's Journal frequently touted teaching, especially in elementary schools, as one of the most suitable—and honorable—occupations for women. In its January 1945 issue, a teacher (older than the young women profiled above) described, with palpable poignancy, a day in her life; her account brought into sharp relief many serious problems facing white-collar workers—both women and men—near the end of the war and how they tried to scrape by:

Getting up at the crack of dawn in a frigid room, the teacher graded student papers while trying to nurse her three-month-old infant, a task made difficult because she was malnourished. When she went to work, she left her baby at home alone. Standing in front of her students, she "heard the baby's cry" and worried that the infant might tumble out of bed. The baby's father had left the city six months ago, and she had not heard from him since. During a break between classes, colleagues in the teachers' lounge grumbled about the continuing upsurge in the prices of millet, coal, and cloth. At lunch time, she dashed home to feed her baby, who was exhausted from crying, while she ate her own lunch of a sorghum bun and salted vegetables. She also ran into the rent collector and had to explain, once again, why she still needed a few more days to come up with rent money.

After she finished teaching at 4:30, she went home to nurse her child again before hurrying to her second job: ostensibly, two hours of tutoring two children in a wealthy home. But she often also had to run errands for the pampered wife and fend off the husband's advances. The silver lining of this woeful account: this was her payday at the wealthy household. Using the "reward for thirty days of torture," she quickly bought milk, food, and fabric for her child and went home. After the baby went to sleep, she fingered the sweater she was knitting for someone. "Only half a sleeve left to do; maybe tomorrow she will finish the job; perhaps the customer will pay ¥50, she hopes." As she was falling asleep, her thoughts turned to "tomorrow, rent, rice, fuel." Reaching under her pillow for the money that remained, she knew she was still ¥80–90 short.[44]

This schoolteacher did not mention the amount of her salary. But her story helps to illustrate in stark terms a 1943 cause célèbre in the news: an elementary school teacher with a family to support had died from an illness attributed to malnutrition (an average elementary school teacher earned about ¥70 monthly). Ensuing reports and editorials following that tragic death not only bemoaned the fate of civil servants, but also used another familiar phrase that meant rickshaw pullers (who could earn ¥5–6 yuan each day) were doing better than low-level office workers (*xiao zhiyuan buru yangchefu* 小職員不如洋車夫). These comments were not so much intended to begrudge the hard-earned income of rickshaw pullers, but rather they telegraphed deep anxieties about a social hierarchy in disarray. Readers of *Women's Journal* no doubt also felt great unease when they saw, in one issue, instructions on how to unravel worn-out socks in order to reuse the thread for other urgently needed personal or household items, and then, a few issues later, an official rebuke toward a group of women indulging in a new fad of folding bills of both small and large denominations into butterfly hair ornaments (presumably because they had money to flaunt and also because hyperinflation was fast discounting the worth of those bills).[45] We have no idea how Ran fared after the exchange noted at the start of this chapter. Even if his sisters were able to overcome family objections, thus breaking their familial norm, actually finding work probably would have been an equally great, if not greater, challenge to overcome.

Conclusion

The War of Resistance was both a national crisis and a personal crisis, and the two were fused tightly together. A cartoon in the May 1943 issue of *Women's Journal* depicted a multitasking woman (see figure 2.3): she was simultaneously reading (perhaps preparing a lesson plan for school), knitting (possibly a sideline job), and rocking a baby in a crib tethered to something that looked like a spinning wheel, which she was keeping in motion with her foot. The accompanying caption may be loosely translated as "Now that we are in wartime mode, women should make contributions on many fronts." Readers would have readily recognized the mockery in that caption because the war had been roiling their lives long before Wang Jingwei's official declaration.

Commenting on gender and the two world wars in Europe, one scholar notes that "the organic discourse of wartime patriotism, with its emphasis on national solidarity, discouraged expressions of women's rights and needs, labeling them selfish, divisive, or even treasonous."[46] But this observation is directed at combatant nations, not nations or territories under foreign military occupation. In

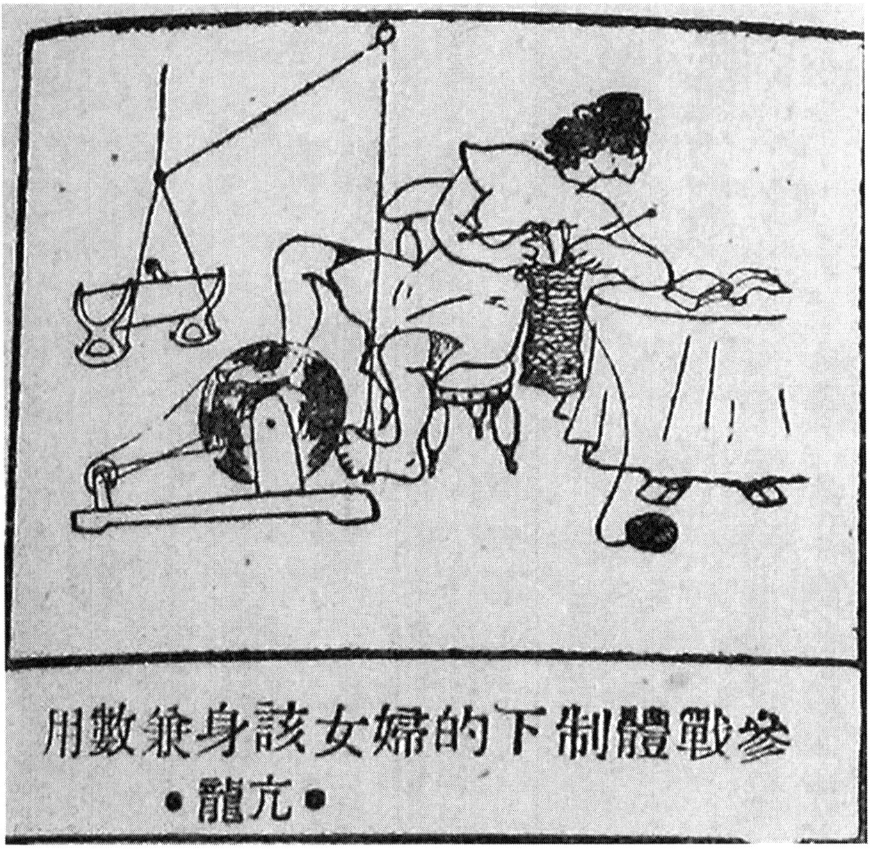

Figure 2.3. Multitasking woman. Source: *Funü zazhi* 4, no. 5 (May 1943): 30.

studying women at work in occupied Beijing, we should be constantly mindful of the constraints placed on the freedom of expression during the occupation, but we must also fully acknowledge that after Japan's defeat, a much more powerful imperative—namely, a postwar Chinese "discourse of patriotism, with its emphasis on national solidarity"—has seriously hampered attempts to understand women's—and men's—experiences under occupation. We have at our disposal only fragmentary evidence, usually in the form of print sources from the occupation years, to piece together the stories of working women in Beijing. But even the few sources cited in this chapter amply illustrate how women in Beijing, with ingenuity and grit, employed all manner of strategies to navigate the difficult circumstances resulting from war and occupation. Examined in economic, social, and cultural contexts rather than the familiar political and nationalistic framework, their wartime experiences unfold in several directions that add nuance to our understanding of life for both the occupiers and the occupied. These women's ventures into the job market seldom led to financial independence and personal autonomy, and in fact not a few worried about downward mobility. Perhaps more research will be able to determine whether their work experiences, however grueling and unpleasant, might have translated into some form of symbolic autonomy and professional pride—even if that meant working for or with those who belonged to the occupying nation. Maybe it was not a coincidence, as recorded in the transcript of the switchboard operators' roundtable discussion mentioned above, that after offering ample complaints highlighting the drudgery and low pay of their job, three operators who responded to the moderator's question, "Would you like to work after marriage?," said "Yes"—though they gave no indication that they would like to remain at the same job. After all, less than ideal working conditions and occasional public derision notwithstanding, switchboard operators were the select 15 percent who had passed the telephone company's competitive recruitment tests. Also requiring more detailed study are the possible shifts in personal dynamics within the family when female labor, albeit deployed often as a last resort, brought in proportionately more earnings than before the war.[47]

Writing in *Women's Journal*, many working women—perhaps indifferent to, if not contemptuous of, the mission of the occupation regime—subverted their assigned social and political places and brought into the open an array of issues challenging working women: gender discrimination, pay gaps, sexual harassment in the workplace, and work-home conflict, just to name a few. Under very trying circumstances, working women of wartime Beijing helped to amplify the female presence in public space. As a result, the very notion of working women, with all its ramifications in economic, social, cultural, and political realms, was refashioned.

Notes

I would like to thank Wen-hsin Yeh and Brett Sheehan for their encouragement and help in writing this article. I am also indebted to Susan Mann, Gail Hershatter, Linda Grove, Karen Turner, Joshua Howard, David Serfass, Ernest P. Young, and Robert Borgen for reading earlier versions of this article. Their comments and questions have helped to clarify my argument and presentation.

1. The North China Telegraph and Telephone Company (J. Kahoku Denshin Denwa Kabushikigaisha 華北電信電話株式会社; Ch. Huabei Dianxin Dianhua Gufen Youxian Gongsi 華北電信電話股份有限公司) was a Japanese government policy organization that during the war absorbed the telecommunications agencies of Beijing and other cities in

occupied North China. *Huawen beidian* 華文北電 (hereafter *HWBD*) 3, no. 3 (March 1943): 34. The idea that women ought to return home was promoted in the print media, especially women's periodicals, to convey conservative Chinese notions about gender roles. On rare occasions expressions conveying this idea were also used in Chinese reports to illustrate at least one facet of Nazi policies toward women. See, for example, Bock, "Nazi Gender Policies and Women's History." For examples of discussions of women and work in unoccupied China, see Li, *Echoes of Chongqing;* Howard, "The Politicization of Women Workers at War"; Barnes, *Intimate Communities;* and Hershatter, *Women and China's Revolutions,* 165–218. Unless otherwise noted, all translations are mine.

2. These figures were compiled monthly by the Social Affairs Bureau of the Beijing municipal government and published, on an irregular basis, in the city's dailies such as *Shibao* and *Peking Chronicle.*

3. See, for example, *Funü zazhi* (hereafter *FNZZ*) 1, no. 1 (September 1940): 32–39; 1, no. 3 (November 1940): 7–11; 2, no. 1 (January 1942): 17, 23; 2, no. 2 (February 1942): 9, 10–11; 3, no. 3 (March 1942): 45–47; 4, no. 8 (August 1943): 22–23; and *Zhiye funü yuekan* 2, no. 4 (May 1946): 19. In wartime Shanghai, "economic pressures pushed more married women into the workforce . . . and caused single women to delay marriage in order to continue working," notes Hershatter in *Women and China's Revolutions,* 185.

4. Kōain Kahoku Renrakubu, *Hi Kahoku ni okeru shinbun zasshi, tsūshinsha chōsa,* 101–102. Although this report indicates that *FNZZ* was distributed gratis, the publication itself is filled with evidence that at least some readers paid for subscriptions and others purchased single issues at newsstands and bookstores. In order to conserve diminishing resources, the authorities merged several Beijing daily newspapers into one in May 1944. *FNZZ* was one among a handful of periodicals that continued to publish until July 1945, but its size was reduced and production quality declined. The circumstances of prewar periodical publishing that gravitated toward Shanghai above all other cities, plus the quirks of publishing under the occupation, made *FNZZ* the longest-running women's magazine published in Republican-period Beijing. See Jiang and Liu, *Beijing funü baokan kao,* 25. Using two newspapers as his principal sources, Wu Jen-shu (Wu Renshu), "Jiehou funü: Kangzhan shiqi Suzhou lunxianhou de funü shenghuo," analyzes employment opportunities for women in the service sector, plus other changes in women's lives, in occupied Suzhou.

5. Taylor, "Gendered Archetypes of Wartime Occupation," notes the difference between visual and textual propaganda, and the "ideological cleavage" between the "traditional" and the "new" in the regime's propaganda.

6. The term has had a long history in the Chinese lexicon. It was appropriated by the Japanese and then subsequently found its way back to China. See Glosser, *Chinese Visions of Family and State,* 203n13.

7. See, for example, *FNZZ* 1, no. 1 (September 1940): 24–25; 1, no. 3 (November 1940): 7–11; 1, no. 4 (December 1940): 1–3; 2, no. 2 (February 1941): 6–7, 10–11; 2, nos. 4/5 (May 1941): 25–27; 2, no. 8 (August 1941): 93; 3, no. 2 (February 1942): 8–11; 5, no. 2 (February 1944): 10–12; 5, no. 12 (December 1944): 3; 6, no. 2 (February 1945): 11.

8. U.S. fighter planes carried out a few sorties on military targets outside Beijing starting in January 1945 but did not inflict serious damage. More than a year before these sorties, the threat of such attacks prompted mandatory construction of air raid shelters, monthly drills, and instructions to men and women to prepare proper clothing and emergency kits in the event of an air raid.

9. *FNZZ* 1, no. 1 (September 1940): 54–55; 1, no. 3 (November 1940): 71–72; 2, no. 2 (February 1941): 67–71; 2, no. 3 (March 1941): 47–51; 2, no. 9 (September 1941): 50–51; 2, no. 11 (November 1941): 32–33; 3, no. 5 (May 1942): 4–15; 4, no. 6 (June 1943): 2–3.

10. *FNZZ* 4, no. 2 (February 1943): 44–45; 4, no. 3 (March 1943): 26–27; 6, no. 2 (February 1945): 38; 6, no. 7 (July 1945): 32–33.

11. See Joan Judge's analysis of the notion and shaping of "experience" in *Funü shibao,* an early Republican-period publication, in Judge, *Republican Lens,* ch. 3.

12. According to Bernhardt ("Women and the Law," 195–196), in 1942, 77 percent of divorce cases in Beijing were initiated by women, and more than half of these cases were on grounds of either desertion or disappearance. These figures may suggest a wartime trend that contributed to the demographic shift.

13. Xu, *Gudu xinmao,* 270. For an examination of non-elite women and work in late Qing and early Republican Beijing, see Cheng, *City of Working Women.*

14. *Shehui tongji yuekan,* January 1938–December 1940.

15. Ma, *Runaway Wives,* 37–85.

16. *FNZZ* 2, no.1 (January 1941): 90–94; 3, no. 2 (February 1942): 24–33; *Shizheng tongji yuekan,* January 1941–March 1943.

17. The number of Japanese residents in Beijing was reported regularly in *Pekin Nihon Shōkō Kaigisho shohō* 北京日本商工会議所所報 (Beijing Japanese Chamber of Commerce gazette), 1938–1940, and *Keizai geppō/Pekin Nihon Shōkō Kaigisho* 経済月報/北京日本商工会議所 (Economics monthly/Beijing Japanese Chamber of Commerce), 1941–1943. Shanghai's wartime Japanese population increased about fourfold; Tianjin's, sixfold. Numerically, only wartime Shanghai housed more Japanese than Beijing. Ethnic Koreans and Taiwanese, as colonial subjects of the Japanese empire, also lived in occupied Beijing. It is possible that, in a few instances, the term "Japanese" used in sources cited in this chapter refers to Koreans and Taiwanese in addition to ethnic Japanese, but information relayed by these sources is insufficient to allow an exploration of the participation of Koreans and Taiwanese in the workplace and beyond.

18. Gaimushō, *Kaigai kakuchi zairyū honpō naichijin shokugyō betsu jinkō hyō.*

19. For a sampling of job advertisements placed by the North China Transportation Company in various Japanese newspapers, see Kishi, "Nit-Chū sensō to Kahoku Kōtsū no jidai," 58.

20. *HWBD* 1, no. 8 (August 1941): 8. Available sources do not allow an analysis of wage differences between Chinese male and female switchboard operators. But one article about a group of male operators, older than the young women profiled in this chapter, suggests that these men, with seniority in the company, earned at least double the salary of their junior, unmarried female colleagues. Nonetheless, by 1942, these men were not able to support their families with their meager income. *HWBD* 2, no. 7 (July 1942): 40–41.

21. *FNZZ* 3, no. 11 (November 1942): 13–15.

22. *FZNN* 3, no.1 (January 1942): 36–37; 4, no. 5 (May 1943): 24–27. Barnes, *Intimate Communities,* 3. Paralleling accounts provided by Barnes, in the spring of 1945, a group of sixteen-year-old Japanese schoolgirls in Beijing was pressed into nursing service for the Japanese military after a ten-day training course. Two days after graduating from their girls' higher school, sixty-six teenagers (nearly half of the graduating class), together with students from other Japanese girls' schools in the city, were dispatched to work at a military hospital that was set up on the campus of Qinghua University, which had been seized by the Japanese authorities in 1938. See *Pekin Nihon Daiichi Kōtō Jogakkō Shikisei no kiroku,* 225–329.

23. Xu, *Gudu xinmao,* 384–394.

24. Beijing Municipal Archives (hereafter BMA), J183-002-31189. One police department directive, marked secret and dated April 11, 1939, underscored the regime's insistence on conducting body searches on women, as well as on doing them in accordance with social and gender norms. During a wintertime high alert period that had just ended, male police occasionally searched women when female police were not able to reach a specific checkpoint on time. These incidents stirred up complaints among the people. The directive warned that policemen were absolutely forbidden to conduct body searches on women. When the need for a policewoman arose, the officer in charge should immediately request one by telephone. If a policewoman was not able to arrive in a timely fashion, a female family member of a police officer, or a female elementary school teacher in the jurisdiction, could be prevailed upon to conduct the search under the guidance of the police. The members of this "auxiliary branch" of the police force should be vetted by officers of rank ahead of time and compensated for their efforts with token remuneration. Available sources do not reveal how often this directive was consistently followed.

25. *FNZZ* 2, no. 3 (March 1941): 45–46. Xu, *Gudu xinmao,* 384–394. See also *Shizheng tongji yuekan.*

26. Ten women began working for the North China Transportation Company as security guards at Beijing Station in March 1939. As of September 1939, an additional eleven were being recruited; female guards were also working at the station in Jinan, and the same was planned for Tianjin. *Hokushi* 1, no. 9 (September 1939): 13–14. Kishi, "Nit-Chū sensō to Kahoku Kōtsū no jidai," 50. *Kōhō sasshi "Kahoku Kōtsū" Shōwa jūgonen kugatsu hakkō,* 279. Photographic evidence suggests that municipal policewomen inspected third-class passengers and North China Transportation Company female security guards checked first-class passengers, or perhaps these two groups worked at different stations in Beijing. See North China Railway Archive, Photo IDs 3601-002940-0, 3702-019282-0, 3702-019283-0, and 3702-019288-0.

27. This explains the proliferation of all manner of Japanese language classes in the city, as well as Chinese-language instruction for the Japanese (discussed in this chapter).

28. Mullaney: "Controlling the Kanjisphere" and *The Chinese Typewriter,* 172–178.

29. *FNZZ* 2, no. 2 (February 1941): 8.

30. Despite the efforts of the Japanese at learning Chinese, their facility with the language—and opportunities to use it—left much to be desired. In a 1988 group memoir published by the alumnae of a higher school for Japanese girls in wartime Beijing, the women were surveyed about various aspects of their lives in the occupied city. On the question of their facility with Chinese, no one rated herself as fluent; 26 percent were able to carry on daily conversation; the rest were able to communicate with family servants and shopkeepers. The majority of this group were born in Japan, not in Manchuria or China proper. On the question of how they met Chinese acquaintances and friends, about 70 percent said it was through their families and 11 percent through Chinese children of their age (possibly by playing outside their houses in the neighborhood). *Pekin Nihon Daiichi Kōtō Jogakkō Shikisei no kiroku,* 419. According to an edited exchange between Chinese and Japanese at a roundtable discussion about "how to get to know the other side," published in *FNZZ* 5, no. 8 (August 1944): 8–12, language barrier was identified as a significant obstacle.

31. *HWBD* 1, no. 8 (August 1941): 2–3.

32. *Chenbao,* June 4, 1937. In Shanghai, by contrast, women joined men to work as switchboard operators beginning in the early 1920s.

33. Gaimushō, *Kaigai kakuchi zairyū honpō naichijin shokugyō betsu jinkō hyō.*

34. Offering tips to the Japanese community on how to interact with Chinese domestic help, one Japanese woman relayed both practical advice and profound anxiety. See Andō, *Pekin annaiki,* 347–350; *FNZZ* 2, no. 3 (March 1941): 62.

35. *FNZZ* 2, no. 7 (February 1941): 8–13.

36. Ma, *Runaway Wives,* 272; *FZNN* 4, no. 5 (May 1943): 20–21; 5, no. 4 (April 1944): 46–47; 5, no. 11 (November 1944): 6.

37. Writers of the essays (length capped at five thousand characters) cited in this chapter usually received payments ranging from ¥30 to ¥80 for each selected submission, whereas the top winner in an essay competition underwritten by a regime-sponsored security-strengthening (i.e., anti-Communist) campaign in the summer of 1941 was promised ¥1,000 (for a submission also no longer than five thousand characters).

38. *FNZZ* 2, no. 8 (August 1941): 54; 79–81; BMA, J181-022-06761 and J181-022-10365.

39. *FNZZ* 2, no. 8 (August 1941): 79–81; 2, no. 11 (November 1941): 15–17; 3, no. 1 (January 1942): 37; 3, no. 3 (March 1942): 59–67. In a roundtable discussion hosted by the Beijing Telephone Company, two participants recounted their surprise when they realized, upon being hired, that they were assigned to work at the switchboard. One of them was quite unhappy because when she took the recruitment examination, she had thought she was applying for a conventional office job. *HWBD,* 1, no. 8 (August 1941): 6. See a sample of the written examination used to recruit female telephone operators in Jinan in *Hokuden* 2, no. 10 (April 1940): 10. The examination contained (1) a one-hour essay to explain the applicant's motivation for taking the examination; (2) a thirty-minute section containing five general-knowledge questions, such as the number of Chinese households and total population in the city, the date of Confucius's birthday, and the Fahrenheit and Celsius temperatures at which water boils and freezes; and (3) two quick assessments of the applicant's ability to hear, remember, and distinguish Arabic numerals. Those who passed the written examination had to pass both an oral and a physical examination before being hired. Note that Japanese was not a subject on the examination. Those who were hired were then given language instruction, along with technical training. For some positions at a higher job classification, applicants were examined on their command of Japanese, and such assessments, plus testing on technical subjects, continued for performance evaluations after hiring. For an example of the latter, see *HWBD* 3, no. 6 (June 1943): 6.

40. Complaining male customers were not identified by their nationality. *HWBD* 1, no. 8 (August 1941): 6–10.

41. *FNZZ* 3, no. 1 (January 1942): 38.

42. *FNZZ* 1, no. 1 (September 1940): 32–39.

43. *FZNN* 2, no. 9 (September 1941): 8–11; 2, no. 10 (October 1941): 32–34; 2, no. 11 (November 1941): 15–17.

44. *FNZZ* 6, no. 1 (January 1945): 33–34.

45. *FNZZ* 4, no. 10 (October 1943): 38; 5, no. 6 (June 1944): 2–3; 5, no. 7 (July 1944): 13. The episode about women sporting unusual hair ornaments happened in Zhangde, Shandong, and was first reported on July 2, 1944, in *Huabei xinbao,* the only daily still in operation in Beijing during the last year of the war. *FNZZ* reprinted the short article in its July 1944 issue.

46. "Introduction" in Higonnet et al., *Behind the Lines,* 7. Linda Grove ("Senjiki Chūgoku no shokugyō josei 'Shanhai fujo' sono ta no zasshi keisai kiji ni miru 'byōdō' no tsuikyū) discusses two gender discrimination disputes involving wartime Nationalist government

female civil servants against the state, which defended its position by claiming special wartime needs and customary gender assumptions but nonetheless made a few concessions.

47. *HWBD* 1, no. 8 (August 1941): 6–10. If possible, useful comparisons could be made between family expenditures during the occupation and family budgets of 1926–1927, recorded in Gamble et al., *How Chinese Families Live in Peiping.*

Bibliography

Manuscript Collections and Archives

Beijing Municipal Archives (BMA)

North China Railway Archive (North China Railway Archive Committee); http://codh.rois.ac.jp/north-china-railway/.

Newspapers and Periodicals Cited as Primary Sources

Chenbao 晨報
Funü zazhi 婦女雜誌 (*FNZZ*)
Hokuden 北電
Hokushi 北支
Huabei xinbao 華北新報
Huawen Beidian 華文北電 (*HWBD*)
Keizai geppō/Pekin Nihon Shōkō Kaigisho 経済月報/北京日本商工会議所
Peking Chronicle
Pekin Nihon Shōkō Kaigisho shohō 北京日本商工会議所所報
Shehui tongji yuekan 社會統計月刊
Shibao 實報
Shizheng tongji yuekan 市政統計月刊
Zhiye funü yuekan 職業婦女月刊

References

Andō Kōsei 安藤更生. *Pekin annaiki* 北京案内記 (A guide to Beijing). Beijing: Shinmin inshokan, 1942.

Barnes, Nicole Elizabeth. *Intimate Communities: Wartime Healthcare and the Birth of Modern China*. Berkeley: University of California Press, 2018.

Bernhardt, Kathryn. “Women and the Law: Divorce in the Republican Period.” In *Civil Law in Qing and Republican China*, edited by Kathryne Bernhardt and Philip C. C. Huang, 187–214. Stanford, Calif.: Stanford University Press, 1994.

Bock, Gisela. “Nazi Gender Policies and Women’s History.” In *History of Women*, edited by Françoise Thebaud, 5:149–176. Cambridge, Mass.: Harvard University Press, 1994.

Cheng, Weikun. *City of Working Women: Life, Space, and Social Control in Early Twentieth-Century Beijing*. Berkeley: Institute of East Asian Studies, 2011.

Gaimushō 外務省 (Ministry of Foreign Affairs). *Kaigai kakuchi zairyū honpō naichijin shokugyō betsu jinkō hyō* 海外各地在留本邦内地人職業別人口表 (Population of

Japanese living abroad in various regions, classified by occupation). Tokyo: Gaimushō chōsabu, 1940.

Gamble, Sidney D., et al. *How Chinese Families Live in Peiping*. New York: Funk and Wagnalls, 1933.

Glosser, Susan. *Chinese Visions of Family and State, 1915–1953*. Berkeley: University of California Press, 2003.

Grove, Linda. "Senjiki Chūgoku no shokugyō josei 'Shanhai fujo' sono ta no zasshi keisai kiji ni miru 'byōdō' no tsuikyū 戦時期中国の職業女性: "上海婦女"その他の雑誌掲載記事に見る「平等」の追求" (Professional women in wartime China: The pursuit of equality as reported in *Shanghai funü* and other journals). *Chūgoku joseishi kenkyū* 中国女性史研究 (Journal of Historical Studies on Chinese Women) 29 (February 2020): 1–16.

Hershatter, Gail. *Women and China's Revolutions*. Lanham, Md.: Rowman and Littlefield, 2019.

Higonnet, Margaret, et al., eds., *Behind the Lines: Gender and the Two World Wars*. New Haven, Conn.: Yale University Press, 1989.

Howard, Joshua H. "The Politicization of Women Workers at War: Labour in Chongqing's Cotton Mills during the Anti-Japanese War." *Modern Asian Studies* 47, no. 6 (November 2013): 1888–1940.

Jiang Weitang 姜緯堂, and Liu Ningyuan 劉寧元, eds. *Beijing funü baokan kao* 北京婦女報刊考 (A study of women's newspapers and periodicals published in Beijing). Beijing: Guangming ribao chubanshe, 1990.

Judge, Joan. *Republican Lens: Gender, Visuality, and Experience in the Early Chinese Periodical Press*. Berkeley: University of California Press, 2015.

Kishi Toshihiko 貴志 俊彦. "Nit-Chū sensō to Kahoku Kōtsū no jidai 日中戦争と華北交通の時代" (The Japan-China War and the Era of the North China Transportation Company). In *Kyōto Daigaku Jinbun Kagaku Kenkyūjo shozō: Kahoku Kōtsū shashin shiryō shūsei (ronkōhen)* 京都大学人文科学研究所所蔵：華北交通写真資料集成 (論考編) (Collection of photographs from the North China Transportation Company held by the Humanities Research Institute of Kyoto University [essay volume]), edited by Kishi Toshihiko and Shirayama Mari 白山眞理, 39–62. Tokyo: Kokusho kankōkai, 2016.

Kōain Kahoku Renrakubu 興亜院華北連絡部 (Asia Development Board, North China Liaison Division). *Hi Kahoku ni okeru shinbun zasshi, tsūshinsha chōsa* 秘 華北における新聞雑誌, 通信社調査 (A survey of newspapers, periodicals, and news agencies in North China [secret]). Chōsajo chōsa shiryō 調査所調査資料, no. 118; Bunka 文化, no. 7 (1941). Reprinted in *Chūgoku senryōchi no shakai chōsa I: Kyōiku, bunka* 中国占領地の社会調査. I. 教育 ・ 文化 (Social survey of occupied China, I. Education, culture), edited by Nagaoka Masami 永岡正己 and Shin Ketsu 沈潔, 15:13–151. Tokyo: Kin-gendai shiryō kankōkai, 2010.

Kōhō sasshi "Kahoku Kōtsū" Shōwa jūgonen kugatsu hakkō 弘報冊子 "華北交通" 昭和十五年九月発行 (Publicity booklet "North China Transportation Company," published in September, Shōwa 15 [1940]). Reprinted in *Kyōto Daigaku Jinbun Kagaku Kenkyūjo shozō: Kahoku Kōtsū shashin shiryō shūsei* (*ronkōhen*), edited by Kishi Toshihiko and Shirayama Mari, 257–298. Tokyo: Kokusho kankōkai, 2016.

Li, Danke. *Echoes of Chongqing: Women in Wartime China*. Urbana: University of Illinois Press, 2009.

Ma, Zhao. *Runaway Wives, Urban Crimes, and Survival Tactics in Wartime Beijing, 1937–1949*. Cambridge, Mass.: Harvard University Asian Center, 2015.

Mullaney, Thomas S. "Controlling the Kanjisphere: The Rise of the Sino-Japanese Typewriter and the Birth of CJK." *Journal of Asian Studies* 75, no. 3 (August 2016): 738–744.

———. *The Chinese Typewriter: A History*. Cambridge, Mass.: MIT Press, 2017.

Pan, Yihong. "Surviving under the Enemy: Oral Narratives of Middle-Class Women in Japanese-Occupied China (1931–1945)." *Frontiers of History in China* 14, no. 3 (2019): 323–352.

Pekin Nihon Daiichi Kōtō Jogakkō Shikisei no kiroku: Haruka kokoro no furusato Pekin ni kyōshū o komete 北京日本第一高等女学校四期生の記録: はるか心のふるさと北京に郷愁をこめて (A chronicle of the Fourth Class of the Beijing Japanese Number One Higher School for Girls: With nostalgia for Beijing, a distant place dear to our hearts). Tokyo: Pekin Nihon Daiichi Kōtō Jogakkō Shikisei Kiroku Hensan no Kai, 1988.

Taylor, Jeremy. "Gendered Archetypes of Wartime Occupation: 'New Women' in Occupied North China, 1937–40." *Gender and History* 28, no. 3 (November 2016): 660–686.

Wu Jen-shu (Wu Renshu) 巫仁恕. "Jiehou funü: Kangzhan shiqi Suzhou lunxianhou de funü shenghuo 劫後婦女: 抗戰時期蘇州淪陷後的婦女生活" (Surviving calamity: Women's lives in occupied Suzhou). *Jindai Zhongguo funüshi yanjiu* 近代中国妇女史研究 (Research on women in modern Chinese history) 35 (May 2020): 1–65.

Xu Huiqi 許慧琦. *Gudu xinmao: Qianduhou dao kangzhanqian de Beiping chengshi xiaofei*, 1928–1937 故都新貌: 遷都後到抗戰前的北平城市消費 (1928–1937) (New face of the old capital: Urban consumption in Beiping after the transfer of the capital and before the war [1928–1937]). Taibei: Xuesheng shuju, 2008.

PART II

Living and Working with Culture

Tea, Film, Calendars

CHAPTER 3

Drinking Tea and National Fate

Teahouses and Teahouse Politics in Wartime Chengdu

DI WANG

The War of Resistance brought Sichuan and Chengdu onto a central stage in national politics.[1] The Nationalist government's move to Chongqing had a profound impact on Chengdu and the relationship between Sichuan and the central government. Many offices of the central government and other provincial governments, social and cultural organizations, schools, and factories moved to Chengdu. A huge number of refugees flooded the city, bringing many new cultural elements with them.[2] Those outsiders were surprised at the large number of teahouses and teahouse goers.

This chapter will discuss how the war brought politics into teahouses to an unprecedented degree. Social groups and government officials used teahouses to spread propaganda; display slogans, posters, and public notices; and oversee performances and public meetings related to the resistance effort and patriotism. Teahouses actually became a stage for "saving the country." Discussions in teahouses focused on the war; there people could learn the latest news from the front lines, as well as stories about the resistance, the ruthlessness of the Japanese invaders, and wartime tragedies. Although people still went to teahouses—an activity still criticized by elites and the government—they could not escape the impact of the war there and were inevitably drawn onto a political stage.

I argue that during wartime, the national crisis gave the state more opportunities to engage with teahouses and use them as tools for political propaganda. Remarkably, the teahouse also created a kind of amateur politicians known as "teahouse politicians" (*chaguan zhengzhijia* 茶館政治家), whose opinions and behavior became an indicator of trends in local and national politics. This chapter discusses how public space, leisure activities, and entertainment were always connected with politics; how they were closely associated with changes in the economy, social inequality, and political movements; and how various political forces were always trying to control or enforce their influences in these domains. Government was intended to suppress the spread of any political ideology or activity that could jeopardize the GMD's rule. Teahouse owners did their best to stay away from politics but often failed because both the government and patrons enforced their politics there.

Rediscovery of Teahouses in Chengdu

In the Republican period, many visitors to Chengdu, whether Chinese or foreign, were impressed by the city's teahouse life and culture, and they included descriptions of teahouses in their travel notes.[3] Some described old Chengdu as a city of "three plenties:" plenty of idle people, plenty of teahouses, and plenty of lavatories.[4] The city was best known for having the most teahouses, the most patrons, and the most people who spent the most hours each day at a teahouse. Visitors often compared the teahouses in Chengdu to those in other regions. For example, Westerners found that in Chengdu "there are also restaurants and tea-drinking saloons open to the street. The latter take the place of the public-houses in England, and are a great deal less harmful. Friends meet there for social chat." He also noticed that "a large proportion of . . . business is also done there." The most detailed descriptions of teahouses came from Chinese travelers. When Shu Xincheng, a famous educator in the Republican period, visited Chengdu in the 1920s, the most remarkable characteristic he found was the feeling of "special leisure in people's lives."[5]

However, the teahouse life in Chengdu that became nationally known, or rediscovered, was during wartime. There were increasingly more reports, essays, and discussions on teahouses. For instance, from the *West China Nightly News* (*Huaxi wanbao* 華西晚報) of 1942 alone, I found at least five such articles, including the following: Ci Jun, "Teahouses in Chengdu"; Lu Yin, "A Chat about Waitresses in the Teahouse"; Zhou Zhiying, "A Random Talk about Waitresses in Chengdu Teahouses"; Ju Ge, "Ideal Teahouses"; and Lao Xiang, "A Chat on Tea Drinking by Chengdu People." The same newspaper published a similar article in January 1943, Yu Xi's "Teahouse Politicians."[6] In 1944, Wang Qingyuan's "Rural Teahouses on the Chengdu Plain" appeared in the journal *Folkways*.[7]

Many observers wrote their impressions of teahouses in Chengdu. Xiao Jun 蕭軍, a well-known leftist writer who came to Chengdu in 1938, was surprised by the large number of teahouses and exaggerated, "There is a willow tree every ten steps in Jiangnan, but there is a teahouse every ten steps in Chengdu." Wu Zhihui 吳稚輝, an important figure of the Nationalist Party who had once studied in Paris, said in 1939, "Teahouses in Chengdu are as popular as coffeehouses in Paris."[8] He Manzi 何滿子, one of China's most prolific contemporary writers and literary critics, recalled, "When I was a child, I thought that Jiangnan had the most prosperous teahouses. After I grew up and visited Yangzhou, I found that it had many more teahouses than Jiangnan. But upon my arrival in Chengdu during wartime, I found that the teahouses there were the best to be found anywhere on earth or in heaven!"[9] He likes to discuss teahouses in Chengdu although he was born and reared in Jiangnan and spent almost all of his life there except for a few years during the War of Resistance. Teahouse life is one of his favorite topics, and he has written extensively about his most memorable experiences in the teahouses of Chengdu.[10] In fact, He Manzi was just one of many visitors to Chengdu who were surprised to discover the richness of teahouse culture and found that the teahouse was a complex social institution that served various economic, social, and cultural functions.

In 1943 one person wrote a very interesting article, "On Teahouses" (Guanyu chaguan 關於茶館), which described his experiences in the teahouses of different cities. The author, not a Sichuan native, arrived there during the war. As a child, he wrote, his parents had not allowed him to go to the teahouse because it was a place for "lower society"—opium users and gamblers. His parents would beat him for merely standing at the door and watching the show inside. Therefore, although he was curious about teahouses, he never entered one until he was eighteen years old and moved to Wuhan. Teahouse goers in Wuhan were also "indecent" people, and from them he learned to gamble, feed birds, and speak the language of hooligans. He became known as an "evil young man" (*eshao* 惡少). Later, he traveled to many cities and towns but seldom visited teahouses, except in Shanghai and Nanjing, where the women singers who performed on the stage to an audience of well-dressed men made a deep impression on him. Then during the war, he went to Sichuan and lived in Chongqing for five years, spending "more than one hundred nights in the coffeehouses," which were nicknamed "foreign teahouses" (*waiguo chaguan* 外國茶館). Eventually, he arrived in Chengdu and was surprised to find that teahouses provided a comfortable setting for customers of all social classes. He wrote that "The teahouses in Chengdu are the greatest among all cities" and that a teahouse there was probably the "only place today where one could spend more than half a day at a price of five yuan."[11]

These writers had different backgrounds and their observations came from a variety of angles, but their impressions of teahouse life were remarkably similar. They all believed that the teahouse was an especially important part of Chengdu daily life and that teahouse culture in Chengdu was prominent and unique because teahouses there were more accessible and served all classes of customers, and for longer hours, than anywhere else in China.

"Chengdu under the Microscope"

As soon as people rediscovered teahouses in Chengdu, a debate was raised under the concerns of "healthy lifestyles," "city images," and "civilization."[12] During wartime reformist elites and the government all framed their constant attacks on teahouse culture in the larger context of the war. Their basic point was that when the very fate of the nation was at stake, people should devote their money and energy to saving the country rather than squandering resources in the teahouse. They often compared the plight of soldiers fighting on the bloody battlefields with people whiling away the hours at teahouses, turning leisure pursuits into shameful activities. According to the author of "The Social Situation in Wartime Chengdu" (Zhanshi Chengdu shehui dongtai 戰時成都社會動態), published in 1938 (the second year of the Japanese invasion), Chengdu residents seemed to care little about the war. The essay stated that there were two kinds of "special people": those who played mahjong and those who lingered in the teahouse. Sitting in the teahouse was "surely the Chengdu people's pastime." Although some might go to the teahouse for business purposes, the essay claimed that 50–60 percent of teahouse goers went "purely to drink tea" (*weichicha er chicha* 為吃茶而吃茶), ensuring that teahouses always did a good business. This essay urged those who were selfish and insensitive to wake up and care more about the fate of the nation.[13]

In a letter to a friend, Zhou Wen 周文 described what he saw when he arrived in Chengdu in the late 1930s, when the "movement for saving the country from crisis" was at its highest point. He describes a group of students carrying flags in a teahouse, with one student, intensely emotional, standing on a chair and giving a speech as all of the patrons listened. Yet Zhou also found that the war did not seem to change daily life much; just a few days later, he saw people passing through the streets beating drums to advertise theater performances and noted that the theaters were still crowded. Zhou was not the only one to comment on this phenomenon. For a period, the government tried to "regulate wartime life" and generated a discussion that linked the "national fate" to "tea drinking" (*chicha yu guoyun* 吃茶與國運).[14] A report titled "Chengdu under the Microscope" (Xianweijing xia zhi Chengdu 顯微鏡下之成都) criticized residents for living lives of leisure at teahouses and theaters when the whole nation was caught up in bloody battles with the Japanese. It condemned Chengdu as a "grotesque and gaudy society" (*guangguai luli de shehui* 光怪陸離的社會). Zhou and the author of the report might have seen only the surface of Chengdu society; in fact, the war inevitably affected many aspects of daily life. Although people still frequented teahouses and theaters, the kinds of performances they watched might have already changed. For example, the editor of the publication *New Chengdu* (*Xin Chengdu* 新成都) wrote that "in the past, storytellers' language was licentious and plots were bizarre, which unconsciously corrupted the thoughts and behaviors of the masses." After the Japanese aggression, storytellers still used well-known materials as the basis for their stories but inserted patriotic and anti-Japanese themes.[15]

In 1941 a critic condemned the so-called Chengdu phenomenon (*Chengdu xianxiang* 成都現象), in which central areas such as Warm Spring Road and Main Mansion Street had more than ten teahouses, all of which were crowded day and night. The author criticized some "boring and idle people" (*baixiang deren* 白相的人) for sitting in a teahouse all day "without rhyme or reason." He observed that "teahouses have recently become an unusual place, where waitresses publicly flirt with customers and even charge four to five times more for tea served in private rooms." Another article also condemned the prosperous entertainment trade during an era of rampant inflation; people wasted time and money on entertainment when they should be frugal.[16] In 1942, "Chatting about Chengdu" (Xianhua Rongcheng 閒話蓉城) described the city as not appearing to be in a country at war; people still flocked to the splendid shops, entertainment venues, and teahouses. The population increase meant that these places were emerging like "bamboo shoots after a spring rain," an occurrence that elites lamented during the national crisis. Another article quoted Chiang Kai-shek as saying that "the Chinese revolution would have been successful if people had used the time they spent in the teahouse for the goal of the revolution." Many elites thought that teahouses reflected the "inertia" of people "who have nothing to do and stay at the teahouse for a whole day." *New Chengdu* claimed that these patrons "kill time in the teahouse, telling stories from ancient and modern times, commenting on society, playing chess, gambling, criticizing public figures, and gossiping about private matters and secrets of the boudoir." The author wondered, "How could there be so many idlers in this land who spend their money while doing nothing?"[17] The teahouse was multifunctional, and these criticisms focused only on the pursuit of leisure in an effort to make the teahouse seem diametrically opposed to patriotic pursuits. (The sketches of teahouse life in figure 3.1 use humor to give an idea of the wide range of activities conducted there.)

"Mere Talk Hurts the Country"?

Some elites treasured and defended teahouse life in Chengdu. They pointed out that tea was the cheapest of all drinks and that teahouses were not the exclusive domain of gossip and rumors. They acknowledged that teahouses had many problems and that it was necessary to limit them, enforce registration and hygiene standards, and forbid gambling and "lecherous" shows, but they disagreed with the radical measure of permanently closing teahouses. One writer gave some concrete examples of teahouse culture's good qualities, one of which was that a

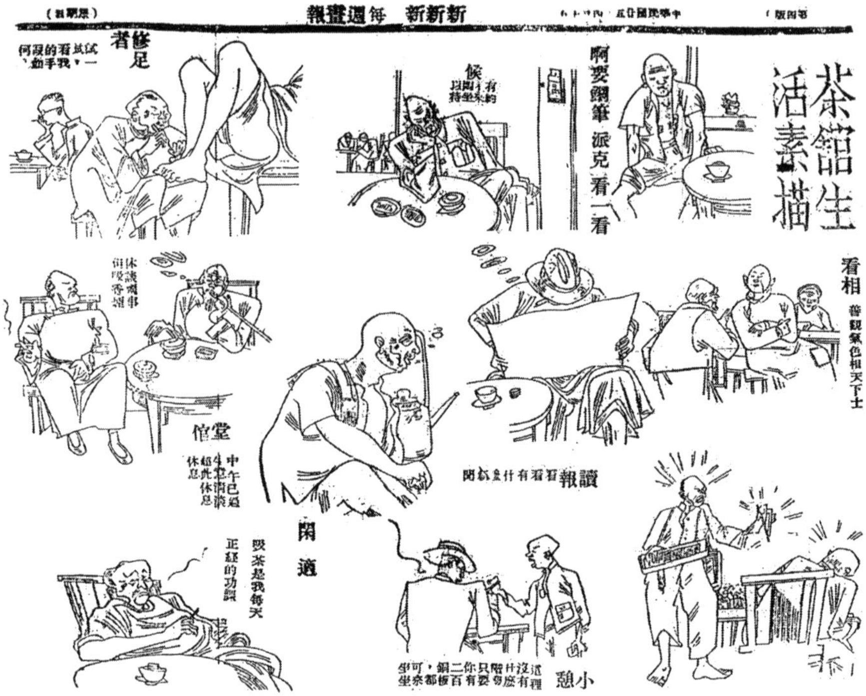

Figure 3.1. Sketches of teahouse life. Left to right, top to bottom: (1) A pedicurist: "Try and see my skill." (2) "Waiting quietly for an appointment." (3) I buy pens: "Show me if you have a Parker." (4) "Don't talk about national affairs, but smoke freely." (5) A waiter: "When business slows down in the afternoon, the waiter takes a moment to rest." (6) Reading the newspaper: "Take a look and see what's in the news." (7) A fortune-teller: "Inspecting people's faces and complexions." (8) Leisure: "Drinking tea is my daily routine." (9) Taking a break: "There is no class system here, and you can sit as long as you have 200 coppers." (10) A peddler. Source: *Xinxin xinwen* (Latest news), April 19, 1936.

man who quarreled with his wife was likely to forget his troubles after a few hours spent chatting with friends or reading a few newspapers at a teahouse. Another explained that the many young people who were unemployed found the teahouse to be the cheapest place to kill time, relieve frustration, and even find a job if they were lucky.[18]

The most passionate defense of teahouse culture came from a writer who used the pen name Lao Xiang (Old Fellow) in a long series, "A Chat on Tea Drinking by Chengdu People," published in the *West China Nightly News* in 1942. The author pointed out that drinking tea had always been a part of daily life in Chengdu, where it was "neither cherished nor despised," and that it had not become a "serious issue until some people began to talk about it." In response to the criticism that people wasted too much time there, the author wrote mockingly, "It seems these people treasure every minute but sometimes they let the cat out of the bag because they also like to play cards, chat, and watch local operas, spending more time in these activities than people in Chengdu do drinking tea." Those who had different hobbies and preferences joined the critical chorus of teahouse goers. Lao Xiang, responding to the description of the teahouse as the "devil's den" (*moku* 魔窟), where students ignored their studies, argued that "we cannot claim that all bad things originate in the teahouse." He suggested that educators find out why students liked to go to the teahouse and pointed out that "everything has both advantages and disadvantages" and that "we do not destroy an entire society just to get rid of a few bad people." Lao Xiang further stated that many teahouse goers were poor and liked to relieve their fatigue by meeting friends at the teahouse and conversing about things "as big as space to as small as a fly; from Aristotle to the shape of a woman's body; and from skyscrapers in New York to the Peace and Joy Temple (Anle si 安樂寺)." While some people discussed topics at random and some conducted business, others just sat alone, reading books. Lao Xiang even gave a foreign example to support his point: "The great French writer Balzac drank foreign tea and coffee while writing his book *The Human Comedy*." Even commoners might be inspired to do great things while drinking tea: "They do not gamble, drink much alcohol, watch local operas, or frequent prostitutes, so who are we to say they have enjoyed themselves too much?"

Lao Xiang also addressed the claim that "mere talk hurts the country" (*qingtan wuguo* 清談誤國) by responding that critics considered the national interest a top priority, but while they despised "mere talking," they never volunteered to go to the front lines to fight the Japanese but only engaged in empty talk themselves. He placed opposing ideas in extreme juxtaposition. If the claim that "mere talk hurts the country" were correct, then "teahouse goers would be traitors and should be put in jail and given the death penalty." He claimed that critics either did not know the cause of the country's calamities or "they know but pretend not to see." He added sarcastically, "They should follow Hitler and burn all books about tea." Lao Xiang further asked, "Is drinking tea [in the teahouse] really a crime?" There were reasons that Chengdu had so many teahouses, tea gardens, tea balconies, and tea halls. A teahouse functioned as a market, where people traded goods and settled disputes. Teahouses provided a resting place for travelers and traders from outside the city. Therefore, teahouses provided a convenience for travelers and others who regularly went there to drink "early tea" (*zaocha* 早茶), "noon tea" (*wucha* 午茶), and "evening tea" (*wancha* 晚茶). "They are addicted," Lao Xiang argued, "so spending 20 cents on tea is not a luxury." Lao Xiang asked why drinking coffee in a coffee shop was "fashionable" but drinking tea was considered "backward." The two activities were similar; those who praised coffee but ridiculed tea were "too snobbish" (*guoyu shili* 過於勢利). Lao Xiang even noted that he had written the article from a teahouse balcony; he added, "If more public spaces were built for appointments and gatherings of friends in the future, people would spend less time in the teahouse. We do not cry out, 'Long live teahouses!' but we also disagree that teahouses should be forbidden. When a better alternative emerges, teahouses may fade away. In the meantime, however, we have to go to teahouses to drink, rest, chat, do business, meet friends, and so on. We still repeat the old saying, 'Let's drink tea on the street corner.' "[19]

Lao Xiang's article is the most comprehensive defense of teahouses and teahouse life that I have found to date. Although it was a lone voice in a tidal wave of criticism, it at least reflected the opinion of most Chengdu residents, who resisted the efforts to change their lifestyle. Lao Xiang's article also suggested that a gap existed between Chengdu natives and outsiders. His article implied that most critics were outsiders. He believed that these critics were do-nothings who had come to Chengdu during the war and, because they could not criticize the rich and powerful, found a convenient target in Chengdu's teahouse culture, which they attacked as "senseless" (*wuliao* 無聊) and "harmful to the country" (*wuguo* 誤國). He mocked critics as having "the face of a Western dog" (*xizai xiang* 西崽像), suggesting that only those who embraced Western attitudes would attack Chinese tradition and reflecting his own hostility to the "other," underscoring ethnic and geographical conflict. Therefore, during the war, the debate over teahouses was actually a debate of issues far beyond the scope of teahouse life, a cultural conflict that reached a new level with the influx of down-river people (*Xiajiang ren* 下江人) to Chengdu. When the elites from downriver picked the teahouse as their target of criticism, the debate to some extent became a fight between Sichuanese and coastal people over the evaluation of culture and lifestyle. Lao Xiang's article, however, indicates that Chengdu people lacked the confidence to support their teahouse life and culture. Even though Lao Xiang enthusiastically defended teahouses, he believed that a new type of public facility would eventually replace them. Although he repeatedly emphasized their useful functions, he seems to have agreed that they were a token of "old society" that would be abandoned as society became more "progressive." He likely never anticipated that more than fifty years later, when society had indeed become much more "progressive," teahouses would be flourishing to an unprecedented degree.[20]

Wartime Propaganda

The government tightly controlled public entertainment and tried to shape public perceptions during the war by seeking to use teahouses as places of wartime education, bringing innovations to storytelling, providing new books and newspapers, putting new pictures and slogans on the walls, and facilitating "patriotic" forms of entertainment. It required plays to include some patriotic and anti-Japanese terms and content even though the old genres and materials could still be used.[21] A new organization called the Temporary Instructive Committee of the Chinese Nationalist Party for People's Organizations in Chengdu (Zhongguo Guomindang Chengdu Shi Renmin Tuanti Linshi Zhidao Weiyuanhui 中國國民黨成都市人民團體臨時指導委員會) was responsible for examining scripts, some of which are still available in the archives and reveal how politics entered this facet of public life. I have found twelve scripts, all of which focus on the war. Some recall the history of Japanese aggression against China; some praise the brave resistance movement; some commemorate the heroes who lost their lives on the battlefield; some express yearning for the lost motherland; some list Japanese crimes committed in China; some bemoan the nation's sad situation; and some recount bloody battles. The kinds of performances varied and included storytelling and the singing of folk songs. The powerful content and language were intended to wake up and mobilize audience members.[22]

For example, the story *Recovering the Motherland* (Huanwo heshan 還我河山), describes China's beauty, vast territory, rich natural resources, long history, and wonderful culture. The calligraphy of the four characters, *huan wo he shan,* written by the Chinese national hero Yue Fei during the Song era, was well known and could be found throughout the country. The use of these characters in the title had a powerful influence on people's hearts and minds. This story described crimes the Japanese invaders committed and called on fellow countrymen to organize means for self-protection as all Chinese fought for their lives. The script claimed, "We will fight to the victory to recover our motherland. We would rather die as heroes than live as slaves without a country." The story told how the Japanese empire wanted to take China's land because its own lacked natural resources and markets. Japan invaded Manchuria and set up Pu Yi as a puppet ruler. Then it occupied North China, where it forced Chinese to study Japanese and destroyed Chinese education. Under Japanese occupation, people suffered greatly, and young people were forced to serve in the Japanese military. The Japanese Army ruined and burned to the ground any property it occupied and shipped stolen property back to Japan. The Japanese killed countless people—many by burying them alive—tore apart families, and raped women.[23]

One play, *The Exposure of Traitors* (Hanjian timing 漢奸題名), denounced the crimes of the Japanese invaders and named eight traitors, exposing them to public shame and adding that there were too many traitors to name all of them individually. This program also tells how they became traitors. Another play with a similar topic, titled *The Fate of Traitors* (Hanjian de xiachang 漢奸的下場), warned that "the heads and bodies of traitors would fall apart if they were caught" and their families would be implicated in their crimes, not only losing their property, but also permanently tarnishing their reputations. It cautioned traitors to avoid such an unfortunate fate.[24] These scripts, which used rhymes and song lyrics, were full of political ideas, unlike the traditional style of popular entertainment. Such materials targeting the Japanese or traitors obviously met the government's need for a powerful tool of propaganda, and they became part of the wartime political culture. Without question, they played an active role in mobilizing people to join the movement to save the country.

Of course, one of the motivations behind these patriotic programs was to promote business, and the theaters and entertainers knew how to deal with the government for survival. In 1939, folk singer Wang Qingyun applied for a permit to perform folk songs in the Pleasant Wind Teahouse (Huifeng 惠風). He claimed that he wanted "to spread propaganda to support the government" in the War of Resistance. He promised not to perform any "lecherous songs" but to "wake people up to mobilize the nation." He said, "The final victory must be ours, and we must strongly support Chiang Kai-shek and struggle until the end." In 1941, three people from Jiangsu requested permission to perform operas, claiming that the Nanjing National Opera Stage (Nanjing Guoju Shuchang 南京國劇書場) promoted "noble entertainment" and helped "change social customs." They said that they had witnessed the Japanese invasion and the killing of Chinese and that it was imperative that anyone who had "blood and breath" should fight the invaders and recover the stolen land. Their performances could inspire patriotism and mobilize the masses behind the front lines.[25]

In 1941, the government ordered all teahouses to purchase portraits of Sun Yat-sen and other GMD leaders and to prepare space for a lectern, blackboard, GMD party flag, and national flag. The Teahouse Guild issued a deadline for satisfying this new rule "in order to avoid investigations by the municipal government and trouble for teahouses that do not have these items."[26] The military was also involved in wartime propaganda. The military's division headquarters inspected the eleven teahouses for the required items on the six streets that made up the Imperial City district. When it was found that none of the teahouses was in compliance, Mayor Yu issued an order to the president of the Teahouse Guild that these items were mandatory and that the guild should require all teahouses to comply with the regulation.[27] The executive committee of the GMD in Sichuan enacted the "Plan for Propaganda in Teahouses" (Chaguan Xuanchuan Shishi Jihua 茶館宣傳實施計畫), issued by the mayor of Chengdu, which stated that the authorities regarded teahouses as important arenas for propaganda. Under the plan, the 640 or so teahouses in Chengdu were divided into three classes (A, B, and C), each of which had different requirements for propaganda.[28]

The government even dictated the messages to be put on the blackboards in each teahouse. The Provincial Mobilization Committee (Sheng Dongyuan Weiyuanhui 省動員委員會) was established and issued a weekly "summary of current news" to display. An example of these summaries had three pieces of news: a two-line update on the war in Europe; a longer description of the Chinese victory in battles in south Hubei and north Hunan, which told how many Japanese were killed and injured; and an item about diplomacy, such as that China had signed an agreement for a loan of five million pounds from Britain. This example also included one sentence about diplomatic problems caused by the U.S. refusal to sign a treaty of nonaggression with Japan.[29] From these passages, we see that the government focused on positive news to promote patriotism and inspire optimism.

The government also asked each police district to set up a large, well-financed, and centrally located "model" teahouse as an example for all teahouses in the district. These model teahouses had a simple platform for propaganda, which included newspapers and posters, a radio or record player, and maps of Sichuan and the world. The dictum also gave nine categories of slogans to be put on the walls; these concerned the uprooting of traitors, military service, transportation, air defense, economizing and saving, raising money, "general mobilization of the spirit," the New Life Movement, and the "citizens' pledge." In the category of the uprooting of traitors, the government wanted people to follow its policies, carry out military orders, and destroy Wang Jingwei's puppet regime. By using propaganda, the government encouraged people to support military service and recognize that "avoiding military service is the most shameful of actions." It wanted people to believe that "the War of Resistance would be won if everyone joined the army" and that giving favorable treatment to servicemen's families and serving in the military were "citizens' obligations."[30]

In the slogans, the government gave specific guidelines about what people should know and do.[31] While the government mobilized people, it also tried diligently to control people's thoughts and ideas in the name of the national interest, and a so-called general mobilization of the spirit was conducted to promote ideas such as the supremacy of the state and nation and that "selfishness" and "different and wrong thoughts" should be overcome. Whereas the "general mobilization of the spirit" was aimed at mind control, the "New Life Movement" targeted behavior. It applied Confucian doctrines such as "The [Confucian] rite is a serious principle," "The righteous are brave to die," and "The sense of honor is a struggle on a grand and spectacular scale."[32] Thus, the government used traditional values to connect daily life with current national affairs. The government required all teahouses to post the "citizens' pledge" (guomin gongyue 國民公約) as part of the wartime propaganda. The pledge had twelve items and required citizens to never do any of the following: violate the Three Principles of the People; violate government regulations; violate the interests of the country and nation; surrender to the enemy; join the organizations of traitors; serve in the armies of enemies and traitors; help enemies and traitors; collect information for enemies and traitors; work for enemies and traitors; use the currencies of the banks of enemies and traitors; buy goods from enemies and traitors; or sell grain or other goods to enemies and traitors. In addition, government regulations required all teahouses to provide government-selected books and newspapers. These books covered many topics, such as praise for war heroes and members of the resistance, condemnation of traitors, mobilization, and ideologies of the GMD, as well as anti-CCP (Chinese Communist Party) sentiments.[33]

As the war became a major focus, the government adopted a policy of suppressing all criticism of state power and its representatives. In 1940, for example, the government asked the Teahouse Guild to "stay on high alert" for 120 students from the Resistance University in North Shaanxi (Shanbei Kangda 陝北抗大) who were coming to Chengdu and Chongqing.[34] The CCP had established the university to cultivate leaders in the movement. Therefore, the students' arrival concerned the local government, which tried to limit their activities. In the political atmosphere of that time, teahouse employees had to work with the police to enforce local "security." In the same year, the police claimed that some traitors and hooligans plotted their activities in teahouses and demanded that the Teahouse Guild provide "secret reports" about them. The guild had no choice but to cooperate. The government used the term "traitors" loosely during wartime, frequently using it to describe anyone who spoke out against the government. For example, the government defined "anyone who thwarts government regulations" as "a traitor" and demanded "the cleaning up of traitors and the strengthening of the rear area of defense."[35]

It is obvious that government control over the teahouses caused tremendous resentment. In 1942, the *West China Nightly News* published Ju Ge's satirical essay describing a so-called ideal teahouse as a "municipal teahouse" in the heart of the city. The teahouse should have a director and associate director, and all customers should follow their instructions. The teahouse was to serve only Chinese tea, and the quantity of tea leaves in each bowl should be standardized:

two millimeters per bowl of green tea, five millimeters for red tea, and three pieces for chrysanthemum tea. There was no limitation in the number of times a bowl could be refilled, but the quantity of water should not exceed 0.5 *sheng* (about 0.56 quart); customers who weighed more than sixty kilograms or had walked more than two kilometers under the hot sun could request 0.75 *sheng*. The teahouse should be open from 6 to 7 a.m., from 12 to 1 p.m., from 4 to 5 p.m., and from 9 to 10 p.m. Patrons who spent more than two hours in the teahouse per day would be punished for wasting time. A teahouse goer had to get a "card for drinking tea in the teahouse" (*yincha zheng* 飲茶證) that certified that he was at least twenty years old and employed and had received approval from the authorities to patronize the teahouse, including a reason why his home was too small to accommodate tea drinking. Patrons would be required to dress formally, to "straighten their clothes and sit properly," and to sip tea slowly. "Bizarre clothes," "exposing one's neck and shoulders," "whispering," "yelling," and especially "loud talking" would be prohibited. All patrons would be required to be at the teahouse at a certain time and would not be allowed to enter late or leave early. Before drinking, all patrons would be required to stand up and then be seated. Reading newspapers and playing chess would be forbidden. The teahouse should have a radio tuned only to certain programs of the central broadcast station, such as news and market information. All patrons would be required to exit the teahouse by marching out in single file.[36] Ju was deliberately mocking the teahouse regulations, such as basing the quantity of boiled water on a patron's weight and requiring patrons to enter and leave at the same time. The "ideal teahouse" he described was more like a military camp, an image that reflected people's dissatisfaction with increasing government controls.

Never before had there been such a large-scale distribution of government propaganda. This movement was well organized and highly controlled. Obviously, teahouses became a "battlefield" in the government's "war" for control. In teahouses, patrons could see and hear only what the government wanted them to see and to hear. We can only imagine the political environment and atmosphere created by the new dramatic performances and the portraits, slogans, and pledges that were posted on the walls. Thus, under its wartime propaganda, the GMD successfully extended its political control into public space and public life. On the surface, teahouse life did not appear much changed, but to a great extent, the core of teahouse life was altered by the domination of the national crisis and political orientation.[37]

In March 1945, on the eve of victory against the Japanese, the provincial government enacted the Regulations of Teahouses in Sichuan (Sichuan Sheng Guanli Chaguan Banfa 四川省管理茶館辦法), which covered eleven issues ranging from the location of teahouses to hygiene. Under these regulations, all teahouses had to be registered under the new law, and the number of teahouses would be gradually reduced in areas where supply exceeded demand. The new regulations further prohibited the hiring of waitresses, bringing an abrupt end to the short history of women employees. The regulations forbade some services that had been offered for decades, including haircuts and pedicures, for reasons of hygiene. The regulations also brought new force to bear on the ban on some activities, such as gambling and the singing of "licentious" songs, that had been long been ignored. Some trends, including the private "family tearooms" that had emerged in the late Qing era, were also outlawed.[38]

"Do Not Talk about National Affairs"

The opportunity to speak freely was one attraction of the teahouse, but this freedom was often challenged by the government, which used its power to suppress the comments of people who expressed political ideas and criticized authorities. Discussing politics in a teahouse was risky. The police and the government could use whatever was said in public against the speaker, and some people became political prisoners. The government commonly planted secret agents in teahouses to eavesdrop. Those who dared publicly criticize the government were punished harshly, and such punishments became a means of suppressing dissent. The teahouse also was implicated, even to the point of being forced to close.

According to Yu Xi, in his essay "Teahouse Politicians," "In the past, a public notice stating, 'Do not talk about national affairs' [*Xiutan guoshi* 休談國事] was posted in many teahouses."[39] The drawing of Chengdu teahouses has the caption, "Don't talk about national affairs but smoke freely," giving visual evidence supporting the existence of such a public notice (see figure 3.1). It is difficult to trace the origins of this public notice. In his novels about late-Qing Chengdu, Li Jieren 李劼人 did not mention such a notice in his detailed accounts of teahouses. Yu Xi's article was published in 1943, when he regarded the notice as being "in the past," which means that at least in 1943 the notice was no longer popular.

Another account from 1942, however, indicated that such a notice was still publicly displayed, although in the form of humorous couplets: "If someone asks your opinion, do not talk about national affairs, just drink your tea" (Pangren ruowen qizhong yi, guoshi xiutan qie hecha 旁人若問其中意, 國事休談且喝茶).[40] In March 1945, when the war was almost over, Bai Yuhua wrote "A Chat on 'Do Not Talk about National Affairs'" about this phenomenon. According to Bai, "At the teahouses away from the main roads in Chengdu and those in the market towns and settlements outside the city, a public notice 'Do Not Talk about

National Affairs' can often be seen." He in fact suggested that such notices could still be found at some out-of-the-way teahouses in wartime Chengdu, causing him to comment further:

> This is a backward, not a progressive, phenomenon. A strong democratic country should not have such a detrimental shortcoming, especially during a war that is crucial to the survival of the nation. The people's involvement in national politics, the military, and the economy can give the greatest and most effective aid in the War of Resistance. A country's success in political, military, and economic affairs cannot be based simply on reading the outlines and principles of a few books. What can we not discuss? It should be all right as long as there is a limitation. The folks who hold conservative ideas should open their minds. Here, I hope that local authorities can tolerate the following three topics: the war that decides the fate of the nation, current affairs, and the resistance movement. As long as we act under the government's leadership and instruction, what national affairs can we not talk about?[41]

Bai expressed his dissatisfaction with governmental control, although he was not overtly critical. Here, he did not risk requesting true freedom of speech but simply asked for permission to discuss the war and its progress.

Some writers felt that such a public notice to not talk about national affairs was indicative of Chengdu residents' apparent blind obedience and lack of courage to speak out against authority. Such blame seems unfair; notices could be found at teahouses in other regions as well. In Lao She's drama *The Teahouse,* a similar public notice—*motan guoshi* 莫談國事—was also posted at the teahouses in late-Qing and Republican-era Beijing. Although the wording differed slightly (*xiutan* or *motan* or *wutan* 勿談), these notices had the same meaning.[42] From a certain perspective, a sign that read "Do not talk about national affairs" was itself evidence of people's anger and desire to complain about the dictatorship under which they lived, and it might serve a similar function as the message sent by those who taped their mouths shut in demonstrations for free speech.

"Teahouse Politicians"

Ultimately, the government could not suppress the topic of politics in wartime conversations. Patrons who frequently discussed politics in teahouses and whose opinions drew attention were humorously known as "teahouse politicians" in Chengdu. In his 1943 article, Yu Xi stated that after the war broke out, people talked about politics more than ever before. It seems that he was uncomfortable hearing political talk. "National affairs," he wrote, "do not concern us." He claimed that his attitude was not one of indifference but that he considered those who claimed to be "concerned with the nation" and "having a political mind" in their loud arguments over politics in the teahouses every day as pitiful and stupid. For example, those who often proclaimed that "So-and-so is a great man" or "So-and-so is hiding a conspiracy" irritated him. People who "thought of themselves as having political insight" often deliberately and mysteriously revealed one or two pieces of "important news," which they immediately emphasized would never be reported in newspapers. This essay mocked ignorant "teahouse politicians" who liked to show off by telling "important news" and name dropping.[43]

"Teahouse politicians" were usually those who read newspapers and liked to discuss politics. They lingered for hours each day in the teahouse, and what they heard became fodder for future discussions. They usually believed they were superior to those who did not understand politics and always wanted to be the center of teahouse discussions. They spoke loudly and disliked opinions that differed from theirs. They wanted others to believe that they were always right. Of course, some teahouse politicians earned a positive social reputation while others became objects of ridicule. They behaved like actors on a stage and often gave speeches in public. To a certain extent, they could influence public opinion. Although most public talk was not taken seriously, the teahouse did provide an informal forum in which people could express political views. The government, however, used force to put an end to any remarks that it considered negative. In fact, talking about national affairs went on every day and in every teahouse; the notice that read "Do not talk about national affairs" was more a means for teahouse managers to deal with the government than with patrons because through it they could avoid responsibility for conversations the government did not like.

Yu Xi's article reveals some interesting things "between the lines." The author disliked "teahouse politicians" probably because he resented the government's treatment of patriotic people and because it punished those who expressed unpopular ideas. So from the author's point of view, "teahouse politicians" were very stupid to get involved in politics, a stance that the government never allowed. Or the author probably was unhappy with the teahouse politicians' irresponsible claims or resented their allegiance to a broader cause. Some elites thought that only they were qualified to talk about politics and became uncomfortable and even threatened when someone they considered inferior engaged in political talk. They did not want such people to be in the spotlight. In fact, despite the fact that some political views seemed "unprofessional" or "silly," these discussions were the only outlet available to most people. Some people who talked about politics might know little about the subject, resulting in derision from others. Still, the teahouse was an important venue for making their voices heard, and certain factions always shared their opinions.

Conclusion

The teahouse was a true witness of daily life in the rear area of wartime China. Although teahouses filled people's needs in terms of leisure, business, and public life, they often became an arena of political struggle or were forced into the political orbit. In fact, local and national political developments at wartime were always in evidence in the teahouse and teahouse life. From this point of view, the teahouse could be considered a political stage where all kinds of people and powers played roles in the ongoing drama of wartime politics.

The debate about frequenting a teahouse (or not) in wartime had significance far beyond teahouse life. On the surface, it was about patronizing a teahouse, but it reflected deep conflicts between the following pairs of relations. First was the conflict between coast and inland because there was a cultural gap between regions, and such a conflict became worse after a large number of war refugees arrived in Chengdu. Second was the conflict between coastal culture and inland culture. When the elites from the coastal areas attacked teahouses, the debate over the teahouse became a conflict of different cultures and lifestyles, between inland residents and "lower Yangzi people." Third was the conflict between elites and commoners. Elites, who had some authority and represented state ideology, placed their cultural hegemony onto ordinary people, but people resented and resisted the elites' effort. Fourth was the conflict between elite culture and popular culture. The debate over the teahouse was a continuance of the anti-popular cultural movement beginning in the late Qing period, which showed a conflict between elite culture and popular culture. Fifth was the conflict between local culture and national culture. The latter, supported by state power, forced the former, which was weak and on the defensive, to move toward a unified national form, and it met the "resistance of the weak." The final conflict was between local places and the nation. Sichuan, located in the Upper Yangzi region, had enjoyed relative independence for a long period after the 1911 revolution, and the nationalist government was able to extend its power into this region only right before the war, but localism still had its momentum.

During the war, the teahouse became part of the state's propaganda machine. The government wanted to accomplish several goals through the teahouse: mobilize people, inspire patriotic zeal, suppress activities that threatened authority, and enforce its absolute power in wartime. By using slogans and the "citizens' pledge," the government wanted people in the teahouses to mobilize and participate in official movements, such as opting for military service, raising money, and promoting patriotism and the New Life Movement. One of the government's most important targets was the so-called traitors, a term that was used for those serving Japanese interests but one that eventually was often used to persecute anyone who challenged government power and authority. During the civil war, any political gathering became taboo and any political talk became dangerous as the democratic movement gained momentum and the economy deteriorated.

This study confirms that the teahouse played an important role in politics, especially in an era when people received most of their information on current events there and used teahouses as sites for political activities. Politics infiltrated the teahouse through other means as well. In fact, it is clear that many people liked to discuss wartime politics in the teahouse. Regardless of their ability to articulate their views, their knowledge of current events, or their political orientation, people involved in political discussions had an impact on others. "Teahouse politicians" during wartime could at least make a voice heard that was different from the official one. Throughout the Republican period, the government demanded that teahouse managers report conversations critical of the government and its policies. The public notice "Do not talk about national affairs" might also have been a kind of protest by serving as a prominent indication that free speech was not allowed. To a great extent, the teahouse was a barometer of politics, where the topics of conversation and patrons' freedom to express themselves changed along with the political situation.

Notes

1. For a period after the 1911 revolution, Sichuan fell into chaos. In the period between 1928 and 1936, Sichuan was most autonomous but warlord power was strongest, although China was largely united under the Nationalist Party. During 1932 and 1933, the Red Army entered Sichuan and established its base in the northern part of the province. As a result, the warlords had to change their focus to fighting the Communists and were forced to seek support from Chiang Kai-shek; the central government took this opportunity to finally extend its power into Sichuan during 1935 and 1937. See Kapp, *Szechwan and the Chinese Republic,* chs. 3, 4, 5; Qiao, Li, and Bai, "Chengdu shizheng yange gaishu," 15; and He Yimin, *Biange yu fazhan: Zhongguo neilu chengshi Chengdu xiandaihua yanjiu,* 345–346.

2. Chengdu had one of the largest populations among the country's inland cities in the late nineteenth and early twentieth centuries. In the 1900s through the1920s, its population was 340,000–350,000, and in the 1930s and early 1940s, 440,000–450,000. In 1945, its population reached the highest point, 740,000, falling to 650,000 in 1949. See Shi, *Sichuan renkou shuzi yanjiu zhi xinziliao; Xinxin xinwen,* April 5, 1934, and November 25, 1935; *Chengdu kuaibao,* November 29, 1938; Archives of the Police Force in the Capital City of Chengdu,

93-1-900; He Yimin, *Biange yu fazhan,* 574, 578, 581–582; Zhang Xuejun and Zhang Lihong, *Chengdu chengshi shi,* 229–330; Qiao, Li, and Bai, "Chengdu shizheng yange gaishu," 12.

3. Ye, "Chengdu chazuo fengqing"; Wen, *Sichuan fengwu zhi,* 452.

4. Chen, *Sichuan chapu,* 32.

5. Davidson and Mason, *Life in West China,* 86; Shu, *Shuyou xinying,* 142. All data from Chinese sources are my translations.

6. Lai, "Chengdu shi chashe zhi jinxi"; Ci, "Chengdu de chaguan"; Lu, "Xianhua nü chafang"; Zhou Zhiying, "Mantan Chengdu nü chafang"; Ju, "Lixiang de chaguan"; Lao Xiang, "Tan Chengduren chicha"; Yu, "Chaguan zhengzhi jia."

7. Wang, "Chengdu pingyuan xiangcun chaguan."

8. Xiao and Wu are quoted in Li, "Jiu Chengdu de chaguan."

9. He Manzi, *He Manzi xueshu lunwenji,* 270–271.

10. Most of his writings on teahouses in Chengdu are collected in He Manzi, *Wuzakan* and *He Manzi xueshu lunwenji.*

11. *Xinminbao wankan,* October 27, 1943. Wang, "Chengdu pingyuan xiangcun chaguan," offered a comprehensive description of teahouses in the small market towns on the Chengdu Plain, but teahouse culture there was similar to that found in the city proper.

12. Throughout the first half of the twentieth century, debate raged over the popularity of teahouses. Elites' debates on the teahouse reflected their different attitudes toward popular culture. The criticism of teahouses was a continuance of this trend of anti-popular culture.

13. The essay appeared in *Xinxin xinwen,* April 29, 1938. For more such articles, see Jian, "Xianhua Rongcheng," and Qiu, "Chengdu de chaguan."

14. Zhou Wen, "Chengdu de yinxiang," 229. There is no study of wartime Chengdu, but there are a few of wartime Chongqing. See McIsaac, "The City as Nation," and Zhang Jin, "Faxian shenghuo."

15. *Xinxin xinwen,* April 9, 1938; Zhou Zhiying, *Xin Chengdu,* 224. Teahouses and teahouse theaters took part in patriotic activities, especially fund raising, from the early stages of the War of Resistance (*Chengdu kuaibao,* August 25, August 27, and September 1, 1938).

16. The articles appeared in *Huaxi wanbao,* June 16 and November 23, 1941.

17. Jian, "Xianhua Rongcheng"; Qiu, "Chengdu de chaguan"; Zhou, *Xin Chengdu,* 246.

18. *Sichuan sheng zhengfu shehuichu dang'an,* 186–1431; Ci, "Chengdu de chaguan"; Qiu, "Chengdu de chaguan."

19. Lao, "Tan Chengduren chicha."

20. Lao, "Tan Chengduren chicha." In 2000, Chengdu had at least three thousand teahouses. See *Shangwu zaobao,* May 19, 2000.

21. Wang, "Chengdu pingyuan xiangcun chaguan"; Zhou, *Xin Chengdu,* 224.

22. Archives of Industry and Commerce in Chengdu, 38-11-1103.

23. Ibid. Regarding Yue Fei's historical memory, see Huang, "Yue Fei Miao."

24. Archives of Industry and Commerce in Chengdu, 38-11-1103.

25. Ibid., 38-11-950, 38-11-951.

26. The guild especially organized a committee called the Committee of Stages for Lectures (Jiangtai Weiyuanhui 講台委員會), each district having three to five members, for a total of nineteen people; Archives of the Chengdu Chamber of Commerce, 104–1401.

27. Archives of Industry and Commerce in Chengdu, 38-11-952.

28. Class A teahouses were required to display the GMD and national flags and portraits of the founding father Sun Yat-sen, as well as the president and chairman of the national

government (the chairman's portrait on the left and the president's on the right). A blackboard, a lectern, magazines and newspapers, pictures, and slogans were also required. Class B and C teahouses had to have all of the above items except the lectern. Those that did not meet the requirements by a certain deadline would be fined, and those that refused to follow this order would be shut down. The mayor also required the Teahouse Guild to report the names, locations, and owners of all teahouses in Chengdu (Archives of the Chengdu Chamber of Commerce, 104–1384). The government enacted the Setting of Teahouses act, which gave concrete instructions about décor based on a teahouse's economic capacity, size, and class. Class A teahouses had to display cartoons and slogans, charts, pictures, books, and newspapers, and they had to provide a blackboard for the display of propaganda and news. Class B teahouses had most of the same requirements, but pictures and books were optional and the blackboard was smaller. Class C teahouses had to display the cartoons, slogans, and charts but not the pictures, newspapers, or blackboard (Archives of the Chengdu Chamber of Commerce, 104–1388).

29. Ibid., 104–1390.

30. Ibid., 104–1388.

31. Ibid. Here are some examples of the slogans. On transportation: "To develop transportation for taking military supplies to the frontlines"; "Transporting in the rear areas is just like fighting on the front lines"; "Transportation plays a key role in the War of Resistance"; and "Transportation depends on the power of humans and animals." On air defense: "No air defense, no national defense"; "Making an effort to construct air defense"; "To build air defense is to strengthen national defense"; and "Everyone contributes to buying aircraft for the killing of enemies." On economizing and saving: "Practicing strict economizing promotes saving"; "Economizing and saving establish a foundation for our offspring"; "Savings bonds benefit us and the nation"; and "To practice economizing is to strengthen the fight against the Japanese." The government also sought financial support and stressed the importance of raising money: "It is natural that the rich should donate more money"; "To donate money for the military is to improve the morale of soldiers"; and "Respond enthusiastically to the call to donate rice and money."

32. Ibid.

33. Some of the books and newspapers praised the heroes of the War of Resistance and ancient wars, such as *Stories of Bravery* (Yingyong shiji 英勇事蹟) and *Yue Fei*. Some books had anti-Communist themes, such as *Dismissing the New Fourth Army and Strengthening Military Discipline* (*Jieshan Xinsijun yu zhengchi junji* 解散新四軍與整飭軍紀). Some were about traitors, such as *Nets Above and Snares Below* (*Tianluo diwang* 天羅地網) and *This Is Wang Jingwei* (*Ruci de Wang Jingwei* 如此的汪精衛). Some promoted GMD ideology, such as *A Popular Reading of the Three Principles of the People* (*Sanmin zhuyi dazhong duben* 三民主義大眾讀本) and *A Brief Plan of National Construction* (*Jianguo fanglue* 建國方略). Some addressed the mobilization of the masses in the resistance movement, such as *The President's Call for Sichuan Folk-Followers* (*Zongcai gao Chuansheng tongbao shu* 總裁告川省同胞書) and *Outlines for Mobilizing the National Spirit and Its Implementation* (*Guomin jingshen zongdongyuan gangling ji shishi banfa* 國民精神總動員綱領及實施辦法). There were also some general-interest publications for social reform, such as *Sichuan Geography* (*Sichuan dili* 四川地理) and *A Story Collection of the New Life* (*Xin shenghuo gushi ji* 新生活故事集). Ibid.

34. Ibid., 104–1401.

35. Ibid., 104–1388, 104–1401.

36. Ju, "Lixiang de chaguan."

37. Propaganda in the teahouse became so important and popular that someone wrote an article entitled "Theory and Practice of Teahouse Propaganda," which discusses the importance and functions of teahouses, the value of teahouse propaganda and its relationship with the war, the preparation of teahouse propaganda, and how to do teahouse propaganda. Bo, "Chaguan xuanchuan de lilun yu shiji." The Nationalist government continued using this strategy even after the war ended. In 1948, the Sichuan Provincial Government enacted Regulations of Teahouses in Sichuan, which still required teahouses to hang slogans and pictures of the New Life Movement and enact measures of sanitation, air defense, and poison prevention. The government also asked teahouses to provide books and newspapers for customers. Archives of the Chengdu Chamber of Commerce, 38-11-298.

38. Ibid.

39. Yu, "Chaguan zhengzhi jia."

40. Ci, "Chengdu de chaguan."

41. Bai, "Tantan 'Xiutan guoshi.'"

42. Lao She, "Chaguan," 78, 92, 113.

43. Yu, "Chaguan zhengzhi jia."

Bibliography

Archives and Manuscript Collections

Archives of Industry and Commerce in Chengdu (Chengdu shi zhengfu gongshang dang'an 成都市政府工商檔案).

Archives of the Chengdu Chamber of Commerce (Chengdu shi shanghui dang'an 成都市商會檔案).

Archives of the Police Force in the Capital City Chengdu (Sichuan shenghui jingcha ju dang'an 四川省會警察局檔案)

Archives of the Social Bureau of the Sichuan Provincial Government (Sichuan sheng zhengfu shehuichu dang'an 四川省政府社會處檔案).

Newspapers and Periodicals Cited as Primary Sources

Chengdu kuaibao 成都快報 (Chengdu daily bulletin)

Chengdu wanbao 成都晚報 (Chengdu evening news)

Fuwu yuekan 服務月刊 (Service monthly)

Huaxi wanbao 華西晚報 (West China nightly news)

Shangwu zaobao 商務早報 (Commerce morning news)

Xinminbao wankan 新民報晚刊 (Nightly edition of *New Citizens' Daily*)

Xinxin xinwen 新新新聞 (Latest news)

References

Bai Yuhua 白渝華. "Tantan 'Xiutan guoshi' 談談 '休談國事'" (A chat on "Do not talk about national affairs"). *Xinxin xinwen,* March 18, 1945.

Bo Xing 博行, "Chaguan xuanchuan de lilun yu shiji 茶館宣傳的理論與實際" (Theory and practice of teahouse propaganda). *Fuwu yuekan*, no. 6 (May 1941): 5–10.

Chen Jin 陳錦. *Sichuan chapu* 四川茶舖 (Teahouses in Sichuan). Chengdu: Sichuan renmin chubanshe, 1992.

Ci Jun 此君. "Chengdu de chaguan 成都的茶館" (Teahouses in Chengdu), pts. 1–2. *Huaxi wanbao,* January 28–29, 1942.

Davidson, Robert J., and Isaac Mason. *Life in West China: Described by Two Residents in the Province of Sz-chwan.* London: Headley Brothers, 1905.

He Manzi 何滿子. *He Manzi xueshu lunwenji* 何滿子學術論文集 (An essay collection of He Manzi's academic writings), pts. 1–3. Fuzhou: Fujian renmin chubanshe, 2002.

———. *Wuzakan* 五雜侃 (Five series of random talks). Chengdu: Chengdu chubanshe, 1994.

He Yimin 何一民, ed. *Biange yu fazhan: Zhongguo neilu chengshi Chengdu xiandaihua yanjiu* 變革與發展中國內陸城市成都現代化研究 (Reform and development: A study of modernization in the interior city of Chengdu). Chengdu: Sichuan daxue chubanshe, 2002.

Huang Donglan 黃東蘭. "Yue Fei Miao: Chuangzao gonggong jiyi de 'chang' 岳飛廟: 創造公共記憶的 '場'" (Yue Fei temple: Creating the "field" of public memory). In *Shijian, jiyi, xushu* 事件, 記憶, 敘述 (Events, memory, and narrative), edited by Sun Jiang 孫江, 158–177. Hangzhou: Zhejiang renmin chubanshe, 2004.

Jian Fu 健夫. "Xianhua Rongcheng 閒話蓉城" (A random talk on Chengdu). *Huaxi wanbao,* June 17, 1942.

Ju Ge 居格. "Lixiang de chaguan 理想的茶館" (Ideal teahouses). *Huaxi wanbao,* October 17, 1942.

Kapp, Robert A. *Szechwan and the Chinese Republic: Provincial Militarism and Central Power, 1911–1938.* New Haven, Conn.: Yale University Press, 1973.

Lai Yeyi 來也乙. "Chengdu shi chashe zhi jinxi 成都市茶社之今昔" (Today and the past of teahouses in Chengdu). *Xinxin xinwen,* April 27, 1932.

Lao She 老舍. "Chaguan 茶館" (The teahouse). In *Lao She juzuo xuan* 老舍劇作選 (Selected plays of Lao She), 73–144. Beijing: Renmin wenxue chubanshe, 1978.

Lao Xiang 老鄉. "Tan Chengduren chicha 談成都人吃茶" (A chat on tea drinking by Chengdu people), pts. 1–3. *Huaxi wanbao,* December 26–28, 1942.

Li Ying 李英. "Jiu Chengdu de chaguan 舊成都的茶館" (Teahouses in old Chengdu). *Chengdu wanbao,* April 7, 2002.

Lu Yin 陸隐. "Xianhua nü chafang 閒話女茶房" (A chat about waitresses in the teahouse). *Huaxi wanbao,* February 25–28, 1942.

McIsaac, Lee. "The City as Nation: Creating a Wartime Capital in Chongqing." In *Remaking the Chinese City: Modernity and National Identity, 1900–1950,* edited by Joseph W. Esherick, 174–191. Honolulu: University of Hawai'i Press, 2000.

Qiao Zengxi 喬曾希, Li Canhua 李參化, and Bai Zhaoyu 白兆渝. "Chengdu shizheng yange gaishu 成都市政沿革概述" (General information about the course of change and development of the Chengdu municipal administration). *Chengdu wenshi ziliao xuanji* 5 (1985).

Qiu Chi 秋池. "Chengdu de chaguan 成都的茶館" (Teahouses of Chengdu). *Xinxin xinwen,* August 7–8, 1942.

Shi Jufu 施居父. *Sichuan renkou shuzi yanjiu zhi xinziliao* 四川人口數字研究之新資料 (New materials on the statistics of the Sichuan population). Chengdu: Minjian yishi she, 1936.

Shu Xincheng 舒新城. *Shuyou xinying* 蜀游心影 (My feeling in a Sichuan tour). Shanghai: Zhonghua shuju, 1934.

Wang Qingyuan 王慶源. "Chengdu pingyuan xiangcun chaguan 成都平原鄉村茶館" (Rural teahouses in the Chengdu Plain). *Fengtu shizhi* 風土什誌 (Folkways) 1, no. 4 (1944): 29–38.

Wen Wenzi 文聞子, ed. *Sichuan fengwu zhi* 四川風物志 (Customs in Sichuan). Chengdu: Sichuan renmin chubanshe, 1990.

Ye Wen 葉雯. "Chengdu chazuo fengqing 成都茶座風情" (Feelings about Chengdu teahouses). *Chengdu wanbao,* March 20, 1949.

Yu Xi 于戲. "Chaguan zhengzhi jia 茶館政治家" (Teahouse politicians). *Huaxi wanbao,* January 15, 1943.

Zhang Jin 張瑾. "Faxian shenghuo: Ershi shiji ersanshi niandai Chongqing chengshi shehui bianqian 發現生活:二十世紀二三十年代重慶城市社會變遷" (Discovering life: Changes of urban society in 1920–1930s Chongqing). In *Zhongguo de chengshi shenghuo* 中國的城市生活 (Urban life in China), edited by Li Xiaoti 李孝悌, 329–366. Taipei: Lianjing, 2005.

Zhang Xuejun 張學君 and Zhang Lihong 張莉紅. *Chengdu chengshi shi* 成都城市史 (A general history of Chengdu). Chengdu: Chengdu chubanshe, 1993.

Zhou Wen 周文. "Chengdu de yinxiang 成都的印象" (Impression of Chengdu). In *Wenhuaren shiyezhong de lao Chengdu* 文化人視野中的老成都 (Old Chengdu in the sight of intellectuals), edited by Zeng Zhizhong 曾智中 and You Deyan 尤德彥, 224–231. Chengdu: Sichuan wenyi chubanshe, 1999.

Zhou Zhiying 周止穎. "Mantan Chengdu nü chafang 漫談成都女茶房" (A random talk about waitresses in Chengdu teahouses). *Huaxi wanbao,* October 13, 1942.

———. *Xin Chengdu* 新成都 (New Chengdu). Chengdu: Fuxing shuju, 1943.

CHAPTER 4

Film Censorship during the Sino-Japanese War (1937–1945)

WANG CHAOGUANG

After its birth, film enjoyed enormous popularity for its intuitive and vivid features, and it soon became the most influential media for popular culture and consumption. For this reason film aroused wider public concern than any other art form, and a strong outcry for the elimination of its "negative" effects resounded in various countries. As a result, a variety of different manifestations of film censorship systems emerged around the world, and China was no exception. In 1931, four years after the Nationalist regime came to power in China, it began to implement a unified national system of film censorship, which to a considerable extent affected the development of the Chinese film industry. However, the outbreak of the full-scale Sino-Japanese War in 1937 split China's unified film censorship system into multiple regimes, including the rear areas controlled by the Nationalist government and the regions occupied by Japanese troops. The latter included the puppet state of Manchukuo in Manchuria (Northeast China) and the collaboration regimes in North and South China.

This chapter mainly deals with the origins, formations, content, effectiveness, and cultural and social influences of the film censorship systems in different places in China during the Sino-Japanese War.[1] By comparing film censorship among these regimes, we will be able to see considerable similarities in the approaches of even mutually hostile regimes. All of these regimes opposed "superstition," "immorality," "romance," "decadence," and content contrary to state interests, though, of course, the nature of state interests varied from regime to regime. At the same time, there was some variation, especially among the Japanese occupation regimes. Those occupation regimes that were established first (especially in Manchuria) were also those regimes geographically closest to Japan, and they had film censorship systems that resembled the system in the Japanese home islands. The farther away from Japan, the less the censorship system resembled Japan's, and the more likely the occupation regime had a measure of autonomy in establishing its own standards.

Film Censorship in the Nationalist Government-Controlled Areas

In the 1920s, the Beijing government, controlled by Beiyang (northern) Warlords, had instituted regulations on the censorship of films, but because the warlords had limited political control, the regulations were not actually implemented. Beginning in 1927, the Nationalist government gradually unified the country under single-party rule and "political tutelage," a concept that meant that the party had to make decisions for the good of the people. In relying on force to maintain power and unity, the Nationalists also placed great emphasis on the function of ideology. Chiang Kai-shek once remarked, "The unity of thinking matters more than anything else." The "unity of thinking" referred to the unity under Sun Yat-sen's "Three People's Principles," which the Nationalists regarded as "the foundation of the nation."[2] In June 1929, the Nationalist Central Propaganda Department convened a national meeting in which "Proposals on Establishing the Party's Literature and Art Policy" were approved; they required the creation of literature and art in line with the Three People's Principles and the clampdown on all the literary works in violation of those principles.[3] Film, which has a broad social impact, was naturally included in the cultural undertakings that needed priority control by the Nationalist regime. The Nationalists first set up a local film censorship system in Shanghai, China's most important film production base and market. In November 1930, the Legislative Yuan approved and promulgated the Film Censorship Act, and in March 1931 a Film Censorship Commission (FCC), formed jointly by the Ministry of Education and the Department of Interior, began to implement a nationally unified film censorship system under centralized authority.

The Film Censorship Act prohibited films in four categories: those that (1) undermined the dignity of the Chinese nation; (2) violated the Three People's Principles; (3) impaired good customs or public order; and (4) promoted superstition and heresy. The first two criteria were highly political and reflected the Nationalists' attempts to establish "party rule" based on a national identity oriented toward a unified ideology with the Three People's Principles as the core. The other two criteria were closely related to the regulation of the Chinese cultural tradition, and they might also have been moves made by the authorities after taking the actual situation of the film industry into consideration.[4] Overall, the film censorship system of the Nationalist era showed both distinctive party and Chinese characteristics.

After its establishment, the national unified film censorship system received strict and effective implementation. Compared with many laws and regulations with lax implementation during the Nationalist era, the film censorship system could be described as one of the rare legal systems that was strictly enforced from beginning to end. In March 1934, the FCC was restructured, and the Central Film Censorship Commission (CFCC) was established directly under the Nationalist Central Publicity Committee, but its applicable law, organizational structure, and functional authority basically remained unchanged, and these conditions continued until the outbreak of the Sino-Japanese War.

In July 1937, the Sino-Japanese War broke out in full scale. In less than six months, Shanghai, China's largest industrial and commercial city and its key film center, as well as Nanjing, the capital and the seat of the Nationalist government had fallen into the occupation of the Japanese Army. The CFCC had to move westward with the Nationalist government. In the chaos at the initial stage of the war, the committee's work came to a temporary standstill until November, when it again set up an office in Guangdong Province to continue its work in the region unaffected by the war. However, the film industry in the territories occupied by the Japanese Army, in particular in Shanghai was actually detached from the Nationalist government's censorship.

When the fighting ceased and film screenings were restored in November 1937, Shanghai cinemas were divided into two categories based on their geographical locations. Cinemas in the areas occupied by the Japanese Army were naturally beyond the jurisdiction of the Nationalist government. Cinemas in the "isolated island" foreign concessions were not under the direct control of the Japanese Army at that time. Thus the CFCC stationed Luo Gang, chairman of the committee, and others in isolated-island Shanghai to continue film censorship work. Due to a variety of restrictive conditions, however, "the environment became worse day by day, and the managers from foreign film companies deliberately made things difficult, leading to the failure of the censorship work, so we have determined to retreat."[5] In the middle of 1938, the film censorship system led by the Nationalist government in Shanghai was suspended.

The war caused the Nationalist government to lay greater emphasis on the advocacy and mobilization roles of film. At the initial stage of the war, the fiftieth meeting of the Nationalist Central Standing Committee adopted "Control of the Film Industry in Wartime" regulations that stated, "During the war, equal emphases shall be placed on both ideology and strength. Films with popular and in-depth contributions to ideological warfare actually override all written propaganda."[6] Since the CFCC actually could not fulfill its functions in the Japanese-occupied areas, in July 1938 the Nationalist government decided to restructure the CFCC into the Film Censorship Institute of the Period of Emergency (FCIPE). Directly under the authority of the Executive Yuan, its censorship provisions aimed "to meet the need of the Anti-Japanese War, clamping down on the films advocating romance or corruption or going against the War and unity." It provided direction for "the Anti-Japanese War and nation building to move forward together" as a guideline to promote the shooting of films to "fit reality, to grasp the pulse of the times so as to seize the public's mind, and then direct them upward [toward the duty at hand]."[7]

In August 1938, the FCIPE was set up in Guangzhou (in September, a Chongqing office was established), and it paid special attention "to the elimination of all non-war, pro-enemy, romantic, depraved, or reactionary films and those films threatening the Anti-Japanese War and undermining unity."[8] However, four months later, Guangzhou fell to the Japanese occupation, and the FCIPE was forced to move to Chongqing, the wartime capital of the Nationalist government.

Compared with prewar Shanghai and other cities in eastern China, the cities in the western region of China, where the Nationalists established their wartime government, were limited, both in number and size, and their film markets were not very developed. As explored in the chapters by Micah Muscolino and Matthew Johnson in this volume, however, the war changed the relationship between center and periphery in China. After the Nationalist government moved to Chongqing, the cities in the western region expanded greatly in size along with the move of the government and incoming industry and the consequent displacement of populations to the west. Cities that grew rapidly included Chongqing; Chengdu, the capital of Sichuan Province; Kunming, the southwest external transport hub; and Xi'an, a city of military importance in northwestern China, as well as other cities that all experienced a significant process of urban expansion. In this process, the film market expanded accordingly.

After the outbreak of the Pacific War in December 1941, the United States became China's main ally. With the arrival of U.S. military aid to China, the film market in the southwest region was further expanded, and Hollywood films came in great numbers. Although the subject of film in Nationalist government–controlled areas centered on the Anti-Japanese War, film production was very limited and subject to restrictions on materiel. From the outbreak of war in 1937 to the end of the war in 1945, a total of nineteen films were produced, only about one-third of the average annual output in prewar Shanghai. Domestic film production in Shanghai's concessions—the "isolated island"—resumed, but due to environmental, communications, and other restricting factors, the films could not publicize the Anti-Japanese War, and their circulation was also subject to certain obstacles. The existence of the above-mentioned factors, in varying degrees, affected the work of the Nationalist government's film censorship.

Although the film industry was greatly impacted by the war, the Nationalist government strengthened film's use in propaganda and mobilization.

In 1939, after the FCIPE moved to Chongqing, its work was influenced by the ongoing Anti-Japanese War, the features of Nationalist government–controlled areas, and the status of film imports. The FCIPE focused its work on three aspects. In terms of content, it mainly suppressed the films perceived as adverse to the Anti-Japanese War, supported those that promoted morale, and encouraged the production and screening of Anti-Japanese War films. In terms of geographic reach, its work was mainly carried out in the large cities controlled by the Nationalist government, particularly Chongqing, Chengdu, Kunming, and Xi'an. In terms of the countries of origin, it mainly focused on checking films from the United States and those made in Shanghai's "isolated island."

In the inspection of foreign films, the FCIPE stated, "Most foreign-import films have content concerning wartime propaganda and promote faith in the victory of the allied forces, but many involve romance, love, fantasy, and absurdity, contrary to film censorship standards." In particular, Hollywood films, because of cultural differences between China and the United States, had been the focus of the prewar film censorship, and in wartime they were still a matter of concern.[9] The FCIPE excised a lot of scenes from U.S. films. In American films with Chinese themes, portrayals of China's poverty and backwardness, Chinese men gambling and smoking opium, Chinese women with bound feet and acting as maids, and the like would be deleted. In the films about the United States, mysteries, robbery, theft, dancing, kissing, and nude bathing scenes were cut, and all the scenes with direct references to Japan and the Japanese occupation were as well. Even Charlie Chaplin's classic *The Great Dictator* was considered to be "a problem movie" that needed the cooperation of the authorities to get through censorship.[10] However, because the Chinese audiences in general could not speak English and they had never seen the original film, they were usually unaware of such excised scenes.

Most domestic films were not particularly affected by censorship. There was limited film production in the Nationalist government–controlled areas, and all the films were produced by state-owned film studios with themes about the Anti-Japanese War. Therefore, only individual films were considered to have problems and needed to be excised.[11] Among Chinese films, the FCIPE was primarily concerned about Shanghai concession "isolated island" films. These films were quite numerous and were filmed in the international concessions surrounded by the Japanese during wartime. Although their production was out of Japanese control, because of their location in the middle of occupied Shanghai, they could not advocate for resistance in the Anti-Japanese War publicly and on a grand scale.

Given these environmental factors, most films had themes about ancient history and swordsmen, combat in traditional Chinese style, and plots about conflicts. In addition, they tended to have rough performances and productions. They were regarded by the censoring authority as having "few revolutionary and nation-building themes. In terms of the ethical significance of social education, this kind of commercial companies' films may still exist, but those involving romantic love should be immediately sent back for rigorous review."[12] These films had a high degree of censorship, and the majority of the excised scenes were considered to involve absurdity, traditional Chinese fighting, pranks, and flirtation.

Censorship differed for films from Shanghai's "isolated island" compared with those from America. American films had Chinese subtitles and English dialogue, but the majority of Chinese audiences and even inspectors could not speak English, so film dialogue was seldom censored, while the Chinese dialogue in the "isolated island" films was an important priority for excision. For example, in the "isolated island" Xinhua Company's film based on the famous writer Ba Jin's masterpiece novel *Family,* the protagonist's lines of dialogue such as "to be born for death," "to resist," and "in society those thieves and robbers remain at large," were ordered to be deleted.

In addition to the censorship of U.S. and Shanghai "isolated island" films, the Nationalist government also censored Soviet films. Due to the restoration and improvement in the Sino-Soviet relationship in wartime, the Soviet Union became one of China's allies; therefore the Soviet films rarely screened in China for political reasons before the war had quite a number of screenings during the war. But the truth was that although the Nationalist government publicly maintained a friendly attitude toward the Soviet Union, in private it was still vigilant against Soviet influence. In particular, it was worried that the Soviet Union would back the Chinese Communist Party (CCP), which was not conducive to Nationalist rule. Therefore, the Nationalist officials in charge of propaganda, especially local officials who did not actually deal with the Soviet Union, were considerably vigilant in regard to Soviet wartime cultural propaganda activities in China, and film was no exception. As the Soviet films "kept flowing in constantly," the central authorities believed that the films "had their own advocacy role, [so] with no great hindrance to the nation-state and modern society, their screening cannot be denied."[13] However, although the FCIPE exercised strict censorship toward Soviet films, the screening of many Soviet films approved by the institute encountered additional obstacles in various places. "Many local governments are not sure about the central government's attitude and constantly make things difficult, thus arousing disputes time and again." For example, the Bureau of Social Affairs of the Chongqing municipal government stopped the screening of the Soviet film *Golden Key,* and Hanzhong, Shaanxi, banned Soviet films entitled *Flesh and Blood for Freedom* and *Hero Yaerxun,* "causing the Soviet Union to protest . . . and the Soviet Union's ambassador repeatedly expressed dissatisfaction with such occurrences."[14] In this case, the Nationalists had to take some measures to maintain friendly relations with the Soviet Union in wartime. The FCIPE issued special instructions by the Executive Yuan, objecting to the fact that "those films already censored in accordance with the law and that obtained a public screening license are in reality subject to unlawful interference. At the same time, those uncensored remain at large. [This situation] has affected the unity of the government laws, the dignity of the legal system, and even diplomatic relations, thus providing others with a pretext. This is wrong." It also requested that "various local governments shall not stop the screening" of films approved by the censorship institution in accordance with the law.[15] After the Soviet-German War broke out in 1941, the Soviet Union was drawn into a bitter struggle, and its film industry was greatly affected. Production declined, with a corresponding reduction in the number of films exported to China, thus easing the conflicts concerning the censorship of Soviet films.

After the FCIPE moved to Chongqing, its work was smooth on the whole. Of course, "Due to the vast territories, non-uniform local ordinances, and the limited reach of jurisdictions . . . film speculators screened films by stealth or screened expired films in remote areas, or scared by legal sanctions, [they] dished up the same old stuff in a new form and found all sorts of excuses to deceive the public."[16] However, these phenomena occurred only in some areas at certain times and did not fundamentally affect the overall work and efficiency of film censorship.

In August 1944 and through the end of the war, the FCIPE was reorganized into the Central Drama and Film Censorship Institute (CDFCI) under the leadership of the Central Books and Magazines Censorship Committee, but its organizational structure and censorship system underwent no major changes.

According to its records, from May 1942 to July 1944, the FCIPE reviewed a total of 1,312 films (including the initial review and reexamination of films and also including feature films and documentaries); of these 358 were Chinese, 954 were from the United States, 242 were from Britain (the vast majority documentaries), 266 were from the Soviet Union (nearly half documentaries), 1 was from Spain, and 1 was from the Netherlands. Of these films, a total of 138 were censored; of these 105 were Chinese, 26 were from the United States, 4 were from Britain, 2 were from the Soviet Union, and 1 was from the Netherlands. A total of 66 films were banned from screening, including 56 Chinese films (mostly Shanghai "isolated island" productions with themes of ancient history and swordsmen),

9 American films (mostly crime and ghost films), and 1 British film. Usually lack of suitability for wartime needs was the reason cited for banning films.

In sum, within the jurisdiction of the Nationalist government during wartime, the prewar regulation and inspection system of film censorship basically continued into wartime and was adjusted only according to the needs of the war, with emphasis on suppression of those films considered detrimental to the war, especially the Shanghai "isolated island" films. At the same time, the censorship of American films, which had been strictly inspected before the war, was somewhat relaxed.[17]

A New System?

Film Censorship in the Japanese-Occupied Areas

Film censorship in occupied China reflected the piecemeal fashion of the occupation itself. Occupation governments established film censorship regimes first in the puppet state of Manchukuo (occupied by Japan in 1931); then in the provisional government of North China in Beijing and the Reformed government of Central China in Nanjing (both following the Japanese invasion of 1937); then in the Wang Jingwei regime (1940) in Central and South China in Nanjing, with titular, but little real, authority over North China; then in those parts of the foreign concessions in Shanghai and other cities taken over after the outbreak of the Pacific War in December 1941.

In order to suppress and soften the resistance among the Chinese people in its occupied areas, Japan implemented a policy of ideological and cultural control, depending on different regions and different circumstances. Since film has a broad social impact, it naturally became an integral part of Japan's official policy for its invasion and occupation of China. Japanese film inspectors admitted, "We censor films from the administrative point of view. For the artistry of film, we take an indifferent attitude to this problem [to eliminate] the things our country does not need, even if the artistic will be ignored." These words plainly reflected the purposes of Japanese film censorship in the occupied areas. In August 1937, when the Sino-Japanese War broke out, the Japanese minister of the interior asked the film companies "to exert great efforts in encouraging people to carry forward the traditional spirit of sacrificing their lives for the country."[18] The Propaganda Department of the Japanese invading troops, led by Terauchi Masatake, put forward the idea that propaganda should pay attention to concrete and effective evidence and require a focus on exposing the inhuman tyranny of the CCP and the Nationalist Army, show the Japanese Imperial Army's humanitarian rules and goodwill, strengthen anti-Communist propaganda, and cite examples of military frustration of the Chinese people. After the outbreak of the Pacific War in 1941, the Japanese authorities also requested that films serve the "Greater East Asia War" and "Greater East Asia Co-Prosperity Sphere," creating "national policy films" advocating for the war.[19] Japan's film censorship system in its occupied areas, from creation to implementation, upheld all such concepts, though with some differences.

The puppet regime of Manchukuo in China's northeast had basically the same system as in Japan because it had directly inherited Japanese film censorship standards. Because Japan had invaded Northeast China in 1931 and established quasi-colonial rule there, its puppet Manchukuo regime had the least "independence" among the collaboration regimes in the Japanese-occupied areas.

After the establishment of the Manchukuo regime in March 1932, security bureaus in various regions started film censorship as early as July, but because of "a serious shortage of personnel and inadequate equipment . . . the work produced was not only small, but [also] rarely effective." In April 1934, Manchukuo film censorship was transferred to the Auditing and Inspection Section, Secret Service, of the Police Division of the Ministry of Civil Affairs. In June 1934, the Manchukuo Ministry of Civil Affairs announced "Rules on Banning Motion Pictures," which institutionalized film censorship more formally.[20] According to the rules, all the films that "offend [Japanese] imperial dignity," "violate the benevolence of the government," "disrupt national harmony," and "undermine the prestige of the officials and the state" (among others) were on the banned list. Punishment ranged from fines to imprisonment.[21]

Manchukuo film censorship was consistent with that of Japan—namely, that "all censorship must be observed from the ideological point of view"; as long as an inspector believed that a film had "ideological" problems, the punishments ranged from cutting inappropriate scenes to outright banning of the film. Artistic content and performance did not receive important consideration. The focus of the censorship was on U.S. films and prewar Chinese films produced in Shanghai because the Manchukuo authorities thought that "many of these films [were] not conducive to law and order in national and ideological education in Manchuria. [To attain these goals], it is necessary to swiftly contain them."[22] In particular, prewar Chinese films produced in Shanghai were considered to be "under Soviet influence, with a strong taint of communism. From the Manchurian Incident to the early events of the war in China, they have been extremely anti-Japanese and insulting to Japan." It was considered that the works produced after the outbreak of the war in 1937 "had subtly transformed their approach, changing from blatantly anti-Japanese content into comedies, cartoons, or modern films in order to stir up anti-Japanese consciousness. These changes in the nature of Shanghai films put forward a delicate and intricate task for our censorship work."[23] Therefore, Manchukuo film censorship institutions held to a high degree of vigilance, strictly prohibiting any film that might portray the Chinese people's anti-Japanese feeling or patriotic themes or plots, even those in the forms of ancient history and swordsmen.

In October 1937, the Manchukuo government announced the Motion Picture Act, an exact copy of the Japanese film management system. It listed film as one of the most highly controlled items by stipulating that those who wished to operate in the film industry "must hold a license issued by the prime minister of the State. . . . Films without the censorship of agencies designated by the Minister of Public Security shall not be exported or released." Under the act, those who exported or released films without censorship review could, in addition to penalties, also be sentenced to six months in prison. In addition to penalties imposed on the persons involved, the owners of the business would also be punished.[24] Under this harsh act, violators bore not only the economic loss, but also criminal liability. Persons involved were subject to penalties, and the owners also bore joint responsibility. After the law was passed, the Film Censorship Section of the Public Security Department took over the responsibility for Manchukuo film censorship. In January 1941, the responsibility of film censorship was shifted to the Motion Picture Unit of the Intelligence Bureau under the Office of General Services affiliated to the State Department.

According to available statistics, from July 1934 to June 1935 and in 1940, the Manchukuo government censored 4,812 films, of which 1,872 were Japanese, 1,413 were made in Manchukuo, 846 were American, 419 were Chinese, 239 were European, and 16 came from the Soviet Union and other countries.[25] These numbers were generally consistent with the actual ratio of countries' film screenings in the Manchukuo film market. Under the severe control of the authorities, the number of Japanese and Manchukuo films grew rapidly, while the number of Chinese films dropped greatly, and American films gradually withdrew from the Manchukuo market. Among the restricted films, 293 were excised in 1939; of these, 106 were Japanese, 89 were from Manchukuo, 49 were Chinese, 28 were German and Italian, and 7 were French. Twenty-three films were banned; of these, 10 were Chinese, 6 were German and Italian, 5 were French, and 2 were Japanese.[26] The proportion of excised films was roughly the same as the proportion of the countries with films released in the Manchukuo market; as for banned films, the proportion of banned Chinese films was higher than their actual screening ratio, while the proportion of the banned Japanese films was far lower than their actual screening ratio. Thus the focus of Manchukuo film censorship on Chinese films was clear at a glance.

In July 1937, the Japanese began the invasion of China south of Manchukuo. North China fell first into Japanese occupation, and it was also the place where Japan established its first collaboration regime. Prior to the establishment of a unified system of film censorship in North China, however, many localities occupied by the Japanese had their own censorship systems, and the censorship standards were not the same.

Of all the various local film censorship regulations in North China, none specifically mentioned the prohibition of a "breach of the Three People's Principles." Rather, they emphasized the prohibition of the doctrines of both the Nationalists and the CCP. Because at that time the Japanese were engaged in fierce fighting with the Chinese armed forces in the frontline battlefields and the Nationalist-Communist cooperation was at its height, Japan was hostile to both the Nationalist and Communist Parties, and this situation was also highlighted in the film censorship in North China, where censorship was basically in the charge of the police authorities, with strict implementation and stringent penalties. Those in severe violation of the regulations were penalized and sometimes also ordered to close down.

In August 1937, the Beijing Peace Preservation Association was set up, proposing in its prepared "Film Censorship Approaches" to "reward the films that promote Sino-Japanese goodwill" and to ban films with "misleading aims" and those "hindering diplomatic relations." It also proposed that Japanese consultants provide guidance in film censorship.[27] The severity of regulation is seen in the fact that in Beijing notice of all film censorship was supposed to be sent to the Japanese military police. Tianjin stipulated that if a released film impeded "Sino-Japanese-Manchu goodwill," the cinema manager would be seized and would be subject to "strict punishment."[28] In February 1938, the Beijing Capital Cinema showed the American film *The Good Earth*. Because there were scenes in which some farmers put up anti-Japanese slogans, the film was forcibly cut and confiscated by the Japanese Secret Service and the manager was beaten.[29]

In December 1937, the Japanese-supported Provisional Government of the Republic of China was established in Beijing, offering cultural policy guidelines to "sweep away the deformed culture under the guidance of the Nationalist Party" and "get rid of the international 'poison' culture of communism."[30] The Beijing Provisional Government was mainly composed of the former Beiyang warlord government officials, who had no historical ties to the Nationalist movement and who did not agree with the movement's ideology and organizational structure. They had been in long-term idleness during the reign of the Nationalists and were grateful to the Japanese, who helped them to reenter the political arena; thus they held an even more humble attitude toward Japan than did subsequent southern regimes. Therefore, the film censorship of the Beijing Provisional Government made a new start and had its own censorship system and standards.

In Central and South China, after Japanese troops occupied Nanjing, they first fostered the establishment of the Reformed Government of the Republic of China in March 1938. In May 1939 the Propaganda Bureau of the Reformed Government and representatives of Japan's Kōa Institute agreed on a "Chinese Film Policy Implementation Plan" and intended to set up a film control committee as a "film policy control and guidance agency" that would include a film censorship commission. However, as Shanghai's isolated island concession areas, with the most developed film industry, were beyond the complete control of the collaboration regime at that time, the plan failed to be put fully into practice.[31] Outside of the foreign concessions, film censorship within the jurisdiction of the Reformed Government was generally implemented by the local police or the Bureau of Social Affairs. For example, the inspection regulations developed by the Wuhan municipal government especially prohibited content going against the construction of a new order in East Asia and making false publicity for the Nationalist government.[32]

In January 1940, the Ministry of the Interior of the Reformed Government promulgated the "Film Censorship Provisional Orders" to implement unified film censorship within its jurisdiction. The censorship standards generally followed the four criteria of prewar Nationalist government film censorship, but the second stipulation (forbidding films "in violation of the Three People's Principles") was replaced by the prohibition of films "in breach of peace in East Asia," a stipulation that was clearly adapted to Japan's demands.[33] Also, ethnic Japanese accounted for half of the membership of the film censorship board of the Reformed Government. However, after the publication of the censorship order, one official noted that "restricted by the environment, [the order] has not been strictly implemented, and only a small number of Chinese-made films have been censored, while the foreign film managers refuse to give in, so the order has not reached its original legislative purpose."[34]

In March 1940, the Wang Jingwei regime, supported by Japan, was set up in Nanjing, and the Reformed Government Film Censorship Commission was taken over and reorganized. Wang Jingwei considered himself an orthodox Nationalist Party member, so his regime still raised the banner of the Nationalist Party and government, and (in a manner similar to the promulgation of holidays as seen in Maruta Takashi's chapter in this volume), its institutions, regulations, and structure basically inherited the former practices of the prewar Nationalist government. Film censorship was not an exception. In October 1940, the Nanjing Legislative Yuan passed amendments to the Film Censorship Act, whose provisions were substantially the same as the prewar Film Censorship Act. Similar to the case with the previous collaboration government, only the film censorship standard that prohibited "violating the Three People's Principles" was changed to prohibit "violating the Three People's Principles and existing national policy." Thus, on the one hand, the Wang Jingwei regime continued to highlight the observance of the Three People's Principles, and, on the other hand, used "existing national policy" instead of the "breach of peace in East Asia" as in the former Reformed Government censorship standards. In any case, the essence had not changed.[35] According to the provisions in the Sino-Japanese New Relationship Adjustment Outline agreed to by Wang Jingwei and Japanese representatives in December 1939 before the establishment of Wang's regime, "with regard to ideology, education, propaganda, cultural undertakings, and police, Japan and China shall work together closely."[36] Meanwhile, a large number of Japanese troops were still stationed in the areas of the Wang Jingwei regime; therefore, the Wang regime's policies and measures in fact were never completely rid of Japanese control.

In November 1940, the Wang regime's Film Censorship Commission (FCC) was formally established, subordinate to the Executive Yuan's Propaganda Department, and its mandate was to "actively promote the action of film censorship, completely ban all harmful films, correct domestic film culture, and use films as the tools to promote peace, anti-communism, nation building, and education."[37] However, because Shanghai was the center for film production and screening, the FCC thought that "Shanghai concessions have special circumstances, and Western studios may not be able to submit their films for censorship according to the law. Therefore, China and Japan shall cooperate with each other, using all kinds of power to pressure [the concessions and the Western studios] and bring them under control." The decision was made to locate the FCC in Nanjing, as well as to establish an office in Shanghai, where a specially appointed commissioner would carry out censorship.[38]

According to statistics, from January to April and September to December 1941, a total of 1,213 films were reviewed by the FCC; of these, 441 were Chinese, 391 were American, 357 were Japanese, 14 were German, 9 were French, and 1 was Australian. The proportion of American films among the films censored was significantly lower than their actual market share because American film companies relied on the foreign concessions for protection and were beyond the reach of the FCC.[39] However, over time American films accounted for a greater proportion of the total number of censored films, and by the time the Pacific War broke out in 1941, the proportion was close to the actual screening ratio. This reflected increasing tensions in Japan-U.S. relations, and the American film companies were under increasing pressure.

The films that had portions censored were mostly Chinese. In addition to the plots and descriptions concerning morality and customs (such as flirting, bathing, topless shots, and the showing of legs), the main reason for excision was "violation of the Three People's Principles and existing national policy." Parts removed from movies included dialogue such as the following: "Did not expect grandfather to die such a tragic death"; "Do not know how many thousand innocent people died from this injustice"; and "Yue Fei and Han Shizhong [two figures from Chinese history] were patriotic." Gone too were scenes of the Chinese national flag, panoramic maps, and lyrics such as "[I] cannot sing about Changbaishan Mountain and Heilongjiang River, which breaks my heart" scenes and lyrics that, although not directly related to the war, were excised for "anti-Japanese irony."

Compared with its practices in Manchuria and North China, Japan was more conciliatory with the Wang Jingwei regime. In order to show the "independence" of the regime, as well as Japan's support for it, the FCC also cut some lines in Japanese films that might provoke the Chinese people, such as "the violent Chinese army," "The enemy troops in Shanghai were routed all along the line and in full retreat," and "[The Japanese] Imperial Army was active in Nanjing."[40]

The entry of Japanese troops into Shanghai's International Concession in December 1941 ended the period of the isolated island. In January 1943, the Wang Jingwei regime declared war against the United States, Britain, and other countries and ordered film theaters "to completely stop the screening of American and British enemy films" and "to screen only domestic films and films made by friendly nations."[41] In June, the Wang Jingwei regime announced the "Basic Framework of Wartime Cultural Propaganda Policy," advocating that "China and Japan share a common destiny, striving for coexistence and common prosperity in East Asia," a goal that requires the adjustment, enrichment, and strengthening of the various censorship agencies for the purpose of unified authority, clear responsibilities, close contact, and strict censorship.[42] However, as the FCC could monitor films only from Japan, the Axis nations, and Japanese-occupied areas and these films were basically consistent with the wartime "national policy," the banning and excision of films was correspondingly reduced.

Although the Wang Jingwei regime claimed to be the Nationalist government "returning to the capital" in Nanjing, its jurisdiction was mainly in the eastern, central, and southern parts of China. The North China collaboration regime stood apart and Manchukuo in the northeast then regarded itself as an "independent state," so the Wang regime's film censorship was limited to the eastern, central, and southern parts of China.

After the establishment of the Wang Jingwei regime in March 1940, the Beijing Provisional Government was nominally merged with it and renamed the North China Government Affairs Committee, but it basically maintained its status quo independence, not actually under the jurisdiction of Wang's regime, and its officials at all levels had no sense of identity and affiliation to the regime. Therefore, film censorship in North China still showed different characteristics from the film censorship of the Wang regime.

In November 1940, the North China Government Affairs Committee published the "North China Film Censorship Provisional Rules" and in January 1941 set up the North China Film Censorship Institute (NCFCI) under the aegis of the Public Security Administration (and later successively the Internal Affairs Administration and the Intelligence Bureau of the Public Management Ministry) to be responsible for North China's film censorship. After that, even if a film was reviewed under the Nanjing film censorship system, if it was to be shown in North China, it was still subject to check by the NCFCI. Although "the film operators may have a sense of inconvenience and the censorship administration is considered repetitive," the Wang Jingwei regime could do nothing but accommodate itself to this reality.[43]

According to the "North China Film Censorship Provisional Rules," there were seven censorship standards, with particular reference to the prohibition of films in "breach of government policy" and "having a negative impact on national education or thinking," and the rules also provided that the screening of films approved by the Censorship Institute, if necessary, still had to be limited. Rules for the implementation of the provision were divided into two major categories: public security and customs. In the public security category, the first order banned films that touched on the state system. (For example, the Japanese emperor's status rises above all else, and slandering the Japanese emperor would be regarded as slandering Japan.) At the same time, it strictly prohibited films violating state law, inciting revolutionary consciousness or anti-war ideology, advocating communism, hindering foreign policy, provoking class struggle, and describing soldiers' dissatisfaction or uncomfortable family life (among other things).[44] These prohibition articles were in fact similar to Japanese film censorship standards on the home islands and very different from the film censorship standards of the Wang Jingwei regime.[45] In addition to the fact that North China was actually not subject to the jurisdiction of the Wang Jingwei regime, the regulations also derived from the influence of Japanese attitudes and policies. The Japanese Army deeply felt the threat from its enemy's rear area and launched several campaigns "to strengthen law and order." In North China, it put more emphasis on high pressure and control, in sharp contrast with its appeasement policy toward the Wang Jingwei regime; therefore, it was natural that the North China film censorship standards were much closer to the Japanese standards than to the Nanjing standards.

According to incomplete statistics, 2,035 films were reviewed in North China in 1943; of these, 344 were Japanese films; 169 were domestic; 42 were Manchukuo films; and 42 were from Germany, France, and other countries.[46] Clearly, Japanese films occupied the dominant position in North China, unlike South China, where Chinese-made films were still central. This dominance also demonstrated that Japan's control of North China was more stringent than its control of the Wang Jingwei regime. Twenty-seven films were banned in 1943, with "inappropriate" listed as the reason for the largest number (9), followed by "indecent" (6). A total of 5,103 meters of film were excised, of which 4,469 meters were cut from Chinese-made films, 352 meters from Japanese films, and 282 meters from European films. The most common reason to cut scenes was for "public security" (accounting for 67 percent of the total, and all were Chinese-made films), followed by "customs" (accounting for 33 percent, also mostly Chinese-made films).[47] From this, it can also be seen that the North China film censorship focused on "public security" in excising the films, among which the Chinese-made films were the most affected. During the prewar Nationalist government period, film censorship focused on the excision of films from the United States and films about martial arts and customs. In contrast, the wartime situation in North China showed that film censorship was to control thought, in essence reflecting the harsh nature of politics in war.

Film Censorship and Political Correctness

During the Sino-Japanese War, different film censorship systems were implemented in the Nationalist government–controlled area and the various Japanese-occupied areas. Although they had different regimes and geographic locations, their purpose was to carry out the ideological mobilization of the public and advocacy to support the war, but for China, it was the war of independence to defend the homeland, and for Japan, it was the war of aggression for external expansion. Although the nature of the war varied, the means of supporting the war were the same, and thus similarities existed within differences. Just as observers said at that time, "Film censorship . . . is inevitable and necessary for any country, especially in time of war to govern any work or undertaking on a reasonable basis."[48] Thus, whether this was the Nationalist government in Chongqing or the regimes supported by Japan (such as the Manchukuo, North China, and Wang Jingwei regimes), all regarded film as an important "spiritual power," and all proposed that "equal emphasis should be put on spirit and the material, to unleash the spiritual power as well as enhance physical strength."[49] Their established systems of film censorship took it as a guideline to ban political and ideological content perceived as impeding the war and also gave a considerable degree of attention to plots that reflected "decadent" morality and traditional customs, films that might affect the morale of the people. With the exception of the early chaotic months of the North China regime, in all other cases, censorship featured a central control, with top-down and unified management designed to resist what the authorities thought of as politically "incorrect" films.

The film censorship of the Chongqing Nationalist government, however, emphasized its legitimacy and therefore demonstrated greater continuity with the prewar censorship system, mainly following the old system and only making some adjustments. The three different regimes in the occupied areas supported by Japan, in contrast, established new systems of film censorship that varied along with Japanese policies. Japan's policies were more conciliatory to the regime of Wang Jingwei in Nanjing and thus allowed it to have a measure of independence, but they placed greater emphasis on control in North China and Manchukuo. Also in view of the ties between the Wang Jingwei regime and the Nationalist Party, as well as its purported "independence," film censorship of the Wang Jingwei regime was more similar to that of the Nationalist government in Chongqing, while the North China and Manchukuo regimes were much closer to that of Japan.

In terms of censorship results, the work of the Nationalist government in Chongqing was more effective, completely blocking the influx of films produced in Japan and its occupied territories. Domestic anti-Japanese films were warmly welcomed because the Chinese people's enthusiasm to defend the homeland and support the Anti-Japanese War was not diminished. In contrast, in Japanese-occupied territories, the effectiveness of film censorship was still more or less influenced by the passive resistance of the people because Japan and the regimes supported by it found it very difficult to explain the war of aggression in terms of moral justice. For example, the Roxy Theater in Shanghai, which showed only Japanese films, had very small audiences. The opening film, entitled *The Day Britain Collapses,* which promoted Japan's "feats" in the Pacific War, attracted only 2,900 people in six days. The film that attracted the smallest audience in 1943 was *East Asia's Song of Victory,* which publicized "the Japanese Imperial Army's feats" and whose three-day showing attracted only 1,300 spectators, with attendance of only about 10 percent of capacity.[50] This could be seen as a silent resistance to Japanese aggression by the Chinese audience living in Japanese-occupied areas, and this resistance was unaffected by film censorship. Rather, this resistance reflected the trend of popular sentiment, and it was a natural expression by the people voting with their feet. Though often subject to the strong influence of politics, such as the film censorship system, film still had long-term associations with nationalism above politics.

Notes

1. Research on this topic is very limited. Chinese readers can refer to Wang Chaoguang's studies such as *Yingyi de zhengzhi*. English readers can refer to Po-shek Fu's studies such as *Passivity, Resistance, and Collaboration.*
2. Chiang, "Zhongguo jianshe zhi tujing," 323. Unless otherwise noted, all translations are mine.
3. Zhonggong Shanghai Shiwei Dangshi Ziliao Zhengji Weiyuanhui, *Shanghai geming wenhua dashiji, 1927–1937,* 229.
4. *Guominzhengfu gongbao,* no. 614.
5. "Woguo dianying jiancha xingzheng zhi yange."
6. "Zhanshi dianying shiye tongzhi banfa."
7. "Dianjiansuo zhuren Xu Hao di Gang shangqia qudi dusu yingpian."
8. "Feichang shiqi dianying jianchasuo zanxing guicheng."
9. "Feichang shiqi dianying jianchasuo dianying jiancha gongzuo baogao."
10. "Zeng Xubai gongzuo riji," 27.
11. The film *Riben jiandie* 日本間諜 (A Japanese spy), produced by the China Film Studio affiliated to the Nationalist Government Military Council, was considered to have "inappropriate content [that] could easily cause a negative impact on the audience," so the studio was asked to make adjustments. "Feichang shiqi dianying jianchasuo dianying jiancha gongzuo baogao."
12. Ibid.
13. "Feichang shiqi dianying jianchasuo minguo sanshi nian niandu gongzuo jihua."
14. "Feichang shiqi dianying jianchasuo zhuren Xu Hao cheng xingzhengyuan," 259.
15. *Xingzhengyuan xunling,* February 27, 1941.
16. Luo, "Kangzhan simian lai de dianying," 444.
17. "Dianying Jiancha Weiyuanhui gongbao," Chongqing Municipal Archives, file nos. 0002-1-12, 0061-15-3518, 0065-1-586, Chengdu Municipal Archives, file no. 38-4-5504, Hunan Provincial Archives, file no. 59-11-1544.
18. Zhong, *Riben dianying shi,* 156–157.
19. Hokushi Manshū Eiga Kansatsudan, "Nihon eiga no hokushi shinshutsusaku," 23–27.
20. Jilin Sheng Gong'an Ting Gong'anshi Yanjiushi, *Manchukuo,* 369; Tanaka, *Manshū nenkan,* 422.
21. Jilin Sheng Difangzhi Bianji Weiyuanhui, *Jilin shengzhi,* 252.
22. Hu and Gu, *Manying,* 33.
23. Jilin Sheng Gong'an Ting Gong'anshi Yanjiushi, *Manchukuo,* 370.
24. Hu and Gu, *Manying,* 226–228.
25. Jilin Sheng Gong'an Ting Gong'anshi Yanjiushi, *Manchukuo,* 370–371. In the original, the total sum of all the separate statistics is not consistent with the given total number, and

here the total number and the proportions are calculated by the author; Hu and Gu, *Manying,* 13–14, 160–161.

26. Tanaka, *Manshū nenkan,* 422; *Manshū nenkan,* 365.
27. "Beijing difang weichihui baogaoshu," 2:274–277.
28. Beijing Tebie Shi Gongshu Jingchaju, *Beijingshi jingcha fagui huibian,* administrative category, 8–9, 44–48; "Tianjin tebieshi gongshu xingzheng jiyao," 45–47, 173–176.
29. Tian, *Beijing dianyingye shiji,* 1:84–85, 134.
30. Zhang and Zhuang, *Kangri zhanzheng,* 6:246.
31. Zhongguo Di er Lishi Dang'an Guan, *Zhonghua minguoshi dang'an ziliao huibian,* series no. 5, edition 2, appendix, 1:548–551.
32. "Wuhan Tebieshi Zhengfu guanli yule changsuo guize."
33. China's Second Historical Archives, file no. 2010-3767.
34. "Woguo dianying jiancha xingzheng zhi yange."
35. "Dianying jianchafa jiqi xiuzheng caoan."
36. Zhang and Zhuang, *Kangri zhanzheng,* 6:826, 832, 840.
37. "Woguo dianying jiancha xingzheng zhi yange."
38. "Xuanchuanbu cheng xingzhengyuan yuanzhang Wang Jingwei."
39. "Xuanchuanbu di yi jie quanguo xuanchuan huiyi baogao huibian," Series No. 6, Vol. 3, 766–769, 862.
40. "Dianying jiancha baogaoshu."
41. Zhonggong Shanghai Shiwei Dangshi Ziliao Zhengji Weiyuanhui, *Shanghai geming wenhua dashiji* 1937.7–1949.5, 134, 141.
42. China's Second Historical Archives, file no. 2010-3764.
43. Huabei Zhengwu Weiyuanhui Zongwuting Qingbaoju, *Dianying jianyue lun,* 40–41.
44. Ibid., 125–127, 52–59.
45. Huabei Zhengwu Weiyuanhui Zongwuting Qingbaoju, *Geguo dianying jianyue zhidu,* 8–10.
46. Huabei Zhengwu Weiyuanhui Zongwuting Qingbaoju, *Dianying jianyue lun,* 91–96. Domestic films include those produced prewar and in the wartime Shanghai "isolated island" and those produced in Japanese-occupied areas in North and Central China. The total number includes those films re-censored.
47. Huabei Zhengwu Weiyuanhui Zongwuting Qingbaoju, *Dianying jianyue lun,* 107–120.
48. Luo, "Kangzhan simian lai de dianying," 443.
49. "Lin xuanbuzhang chanming mubiao," 2.
50. *Dahua daxiyuan baogaoshu,* 20–25.

Bibliography

Archives and Manuscript Collections

Chengdu Municipal Archives
China's Second Historical Archives, Nanjing
Chongqing Municipal Archives
Guangzhou Municipal Archives
Hunan Provincial Archives
Kuomintang [Nationalist] Central Committee Party History Museum

Sichuan Provincial Archives
Wuhan Municipal Archives

Newspapers and Periodicals Cited as Primary Sources

Guominzhengfu gongbao 國民政府公報
Shenbao 申報

References

"Beijing difang weichihui baogaoshu" 北京地方維持會報告書 (Report of the Beijing local peace preservation association), vol. 2. 1938.

Beijing Tebie Shi Gongshu Jingchaju 北京特別市公署警察局 (Beijing Special Municipal Commission Police Station). *Beijingshi jingcha fagui huibian* 北京市警察法規彙編 (Compilation of Beijing police laws and regulations). Beijing: Beijing tebieshi gongshu jingchaju, 1938.

Chiang Kai-shek (Jiang Jieshi) 蔣介石. "Zhongguo jianshe zhi tujing 中國建設之途徑" (The path of China's construction). July 18, 1928. In *Xianzongtong Jiang gong sixiang yanlun zongji* 先總統蔣公思想言論總集 (The complete thoughts and speeches of former president Chiang Kai-shek), edited by Qin Xiaoyi 秦孝儀, vol. 10. Taipei: Zhongguo Guomindang Zhongyang Weiyuanhui Dangshi Weiyuanhui, 1984.

Dahua daxiyuan baogaoshu 大華大戲院報告書 (Roxy Theater report). Shanghai: China Film Research Institute, 1944.

"Dianjiansuo zhuren Xu Hao di Gang shangqia qudi dusu yingpian" 電檢所主任徐浩抵港商洽取締毒素影片 (Xu Hao, director of the Film Censorship Institution, arrived in Hong Kong to negotiate the banning of toxic films). *Shenbao*, September 19, 1938, section 4.

"Dianying jiancha baogaoshu" 電影檢查報告書 (Film censorship report). Nanjing: China's Second Historical Archives, file no. 2040-9.

Dianying Jiancha Weiyuanhui 電影檢查委員會 (Film Censorship Commission). "Dianying Jiancha Weiyuanhui gongbao" 電影檢查委員會公報 (Film Censorship Commission communiques). Chongqing: Chongqing Municipal Archives, file nos. 0002-1-12, 0061-15-3518, 0065-1-586.

———. "Dianying Jiancha Weiyuanhui gongbao" 電影檢查委員會公報 (Film Censorship Commission communiques). Chengdu: Chengdu Municipal Archives, file no. 38-4-5504.

———. "Dianying Jiancha Weiyuanhui gongbao" 電影檢查委員會公報 (Film Censorship Commission communiques). Changsha: Hunan Provincial Archives, file no. 59-11-1544.

"Dianying jianchafa jiqi xiuzheng caoan" 電影檢查法及其修正草案 (The film censorship act and its draft amendments). Nanjing: China's Second Historical Archives, file no. 2008-368.

"Feichang shiqi Dianying Jianchasuo dianying jiancha gongzuo baogao" 非常時期電影檢查所電影檢查工作報告 (Film censorship work report of the Film Censorship Institution in the time of emergency). Nanjing: China's Second Historical Archives, file no. 2-6091.

"Feichang shiqi Dianying Jianchasuo minguo sanshi nian niandu gongzuo jihua" 非常時期電影檢查所民國三十年年度工作計畫 (Annual working program of the Film Censorship Institution in unusual period for 1941). Nanjing: China's Second Historical Archives, file no. 2-6090.

"Feichang shiqi Dianying Jianchasuo zanxing guicheng" 非常時期電影檢查所暫行規程 (Provisional Regulations of the Film Censorship Institution in the time of emergency), June 17, 1938. Guangzhou: Guangzhou Municipal Archives, file no. 10-4-6.

"Feichang shiqi Dianying Jianchasuo zhuren Xu Hao cheng xingzhengyuan" 非常時期電影檢查所主任徐浩呈行政院 (Report submitted to the Executive Yuan by Xu Hao, director of the Film Censorship Institution, during the time of emergency). February 18, 1941. In *Zhongguo xiandai zhengzhi shiziliao huibian* 中國現代政治史資料彙編 (Compilation of China's modern political historical materials). Nanjing: China's Second Historical Archives, 1964, series no. 3, vol. 92.

Fu, Po-shek. *Passivity, Ressistance, and Collaboration: Intellectual Choices in Occupied Shanghai 1937–1945*. Stanford, Calif.: Stanford University Press, 1993.

Hokushi Manshū Eiga Kansatsudan 北支滿洲映画観察団 (North China–Manchukuo Film Censorship Commission). "Nihon eiga no hokushi shinshutsusaku" 日本映画の北支進出策 (Japanese film policy in North China). No publisher given. 1939.

Hu Chang 胡昶 and Gu Quan 古泉. *Manying—guoce dianying mianmianguan* 満映-國策電影面面觀 (Manchukuo films—A panorama of national film policy). Beijing: Zhonghua shuju, 1990.

Huabei Zhengwu Weiyuanhui Zongwuting Qingbaoju 華北政務委員會總務廳情報局 (Information Department of the General Affairs Bureau of the North China Political Affairs commission). *Dianying jianyue lun* 電影檢閱論 (On film censorship). Beijing: Huabei Zhengwu Weiyuanhui Zongwuting Qingbaoju, 1944.

———. *Geguo dianying jianyue zhidu* 各國電影檢閱制度 (Various nations' film censorship systems). Beijing: Huabei zhengwu weiyuanhui zongwutingqingbaoju, 1945.

Jilin Sheng Difangzhi Bianji Weiyuanhui 吉林省地方志編輯委員會 (Jilin Province Local Gazetteer Compilation Committee), ed. *Jilin shengzhi* 吉林省志 (Jilin Province Gazetteer), vol. 39. Changchun: Jilin renmin chubanshe, 1996.

Jilin Sheng Gong'an Ting Gong'anshi Yanjiushi 吉林省公安廳公安史研究室 (Public Security Research Office of the Security Department of the Jilin Provincial Public Security Bureau), trans. *Manchukuo* [Manzhouguo] *jingchashi* 滿州國警察史 (from the Japanese *Manshū koku keisatsu shi* 滿州國警察史, 1942). Changchun: Jilin sheng gong'an ting gong'anshi yanjiushi, 1990.

"Lin xuanbuzhang chanming mubiao 林宣部長闡明目標" (Propaganda Minister Lin clarified the goal). *Shenbao*, June 12, 1943, 2.

Luo Xuelian 羅學濂. "Kangzhan simian lai de dianying 抗戰四年來的電影" (Films in the last four years of the Anti-Japanese War). In *Kangri zhanzheng shiqi de Chongqing dianying* 抗日戰爭時期的重慶電影 (Chongqing films during the Anti-Japanese War), edited by Chongqingshi Wenhuaju dianyingchu 重慶市文化局電影處 (Film Department of the Chongqing Municipal Bureau of Culture). Chongqing: Chongqing chubanshe, 1991.

Manshū nenkan 満州年鑑 (Manshū yearbook). Dalian: Manshū nichinichi shinbunsha, Kangde 9 (1942).

Tanaka Soichiro 田中総一郎. *Manshū nenkan* (Manshū yearbook). Dalian: Manshū nichinichi shinbusha, Kangde 7 (1940).

Tian Jingqing 田靜清. *Beijing dianyingye shiji* 北京電影業史跡 (History of the Beijing film industry). Beijing: Beijing chubanshe, 1990.

"Tianjin tebieshi gongshu xingzheng jiyao" 天津特別市公署行政紀要 (Administrative summary of the Tianjin special municipal commission). Tianjin: No publisher given. 1939.

Wang Chaoguang 汪朝光. *Yingyi de zhengzhi: Minguo dianying jiancha zhidu yanjiu* 影藝的政治: 民國電影檢查制度研究 (The politics of film art: Research on film censorship system during the Republic of China). Beijing: Renmin daxue chubanshe, 2016.

"Woguo dianying jiancha xingzheng zhi yange 我國電影檢查行政之沿革" (The history of film censorship in China). Report submitted to Wang Jingwei, director of the Executive Yuan by the Propaganda Department. Nanjing: China's Second Historical Archives, file no. 718–967.

"Wuhan Tebieshi Zhengfu guanli yule changsuo guize 武漢特別市政府管理娛樂場所規則" (Management regulations for places of entertainment for the Wuhan Special Municipal Government), September 19, 1939. Wuhan: Wuhan Municipal Archives, file no. 9-31-323-J22.

"Xingzhengyuan xunling" 行政院訓令 (Order of the Executive Yuan), February 27, 1941. Chengdu: Sichuan Provincial Archives, file no. 41-6306.

"Xuanchuanbu cheng xingzhengyuan yuanzhang Wang Jingwei" 宣傳部呈行政院院長汪精衛 (Report submitted to Wang Jingwei, director of the Executive Yuan, by the Propaganda Department). Nanjing: China's Second Historical Archives, file no. 2002-500.

"Xuanchuanbu Di Yi Jie Quanguo Xuanchuan Huiyi baogao huibian 宣傳部第一屆全國宣傳會議 報告彙編" (Compiled reports of the First National Publicity Conference of the Propaganda Department). In *Zhonghua minguo zhongyao shiliao chubian* 中華民國重要史料初編 (Initial compilation of the important historical materials of the Republic of China), edited by Qin Xiaoyi 秦孝儀. Taipei: Chinese Kuomintang Central Committee Party History Commission, 1981.

"Zeng Xubai gongzuo riji 曾虛白工作日記" (Zeng Xubai work diary). *Mingguo Dangan* 民國檔案, no. 2 (2000): 20–32.

Zhang Bofeng 章伯鋒 and Zhuang Jianping 庄建平, eds. *Kangri zhanzheng* 抗日戰爭 (The Sino-Japanese War). Chengdu: Sichuan daxue chubanshe, 1997.

"Zhanshi dianying shiye tongzhi banfa 戰時電影事業統制辦法" (Methods of control of the wartime film industry), August 12, 1937. Taipei: Kuomintang [Nationalist] Central Committee Party History Museum, file no. 5.3/297.

Zhong Li 鍾理, trans. *Riben dianying shi* 日本電影史 (Japanese film history from the original book by Iwasaki Akira 岩崎昶. Beijing: Zhongguo dianying chubanshe, 1981.

Zhonggong Shanghai Shiwei Dangshi Ziliao Zhengji Weiyuanhui 中共上海市委黨史資料徵集委員會 (Historical Materials Compilation Commission of the Shanghai Party Committee), ed. *Shanghai geming wenhua dashiji, 1927–1937* 上海革命文化大事記 1927–1937 (Cultural chronicle of the Shanghai Revolution, 1927–1937). Shanghai: Shanghai shudian chubanshe, 1995.

Zhonggong Shanghai Shiwei Dangshi Ziliao Zhengji Weiyuanhui 中共上海市委黨史資料徵集委員會 (Historical Materials Compilation Commission of the Shanghai Party Committee) et al., eds. *Shanghai geming wenhua dashiji 1937.7–1949.5* 上海革命文化大事記 1937–1949 (Shanghai revolutionary and cultural chronicles, July 1937–May 1949). Shanghai: Shanghai fanyi chuban gongsi, 1991.

Zhongguo Di er Lishi Dang'an Guan 中國第二歷史檔案館 (China's Second Historical Archives), ed. *Zhonghua minguoshi dang'an ziliao huibian* 中華民國史檔案資料彙編 (Compilation of Republic of China history archives), series no. 5. Nanjing: Jiangsu Guji Chubanshe, 1997.

CHAPTER 5

Regulation of Time and Folk Customs in North China during the Sino-Japanese War

MARUTA TAKASHI (TRANSLATED by BRETT SHEEHAN)

The control of calendars and time is critical in the formation of the modern nation-state. On the one hand, the state establishes holidays, memorial days, and methods of memorial. Power holders ask the people to acknowledge these memories to support legitimacy and demand that the people act together accordingly. On the other hand, with the development of industrialization, time becomes strictly measured, and in order to unify the management of the lives of the nation's people, states take steps to strictly manage calendars and time.

During the Sino-Japanese War, the Nationalist government, the Japanese-controlled puppet governments, and the Communists each had power in different parts of China. This chapter explores the political policies and social reactions to those policies adopted by these various regimes in North China in regard to time and symbolism.

The study of the holidays of the various regimes is consistent with Wang Chaoguang's conclusions in this volume about film censorship. There was great diversity across China even as the various regimes shared a larger commitment to certain ideals. In terms of diversity, the picture is complicated by the on-again, off-again alliance between the Chinese Nationalists and Communists, as well as the fact that the Wang Jingwei puppet regime claimed to be the legitimate Nationalist government. As a result, there was a certain amount of overlap in memorial days and holidays among the regimes. At the same time, variation was more salient. Japanese-controlled puppet regimes initially suppressed Nationalist holidays associated with revolution and nationalism, and Communists introduced holidays from the international socialist movement. At the same time, puppet regimes often tried to use or repurpose Buddhist holidays, but the Communist governments rarely did. Within regimes, we see variations among the different puppet governments, as well as between the front lines and the rear base areas of the Communists. In spite of this great variability, Nationalists, puppet governments, and Communists alike shared a commitment to modernity; anti-superstition; the precise regulation of time; and a predilection to emphasize community, group, and nation over the individual.

Cohesion, however was often not the result. For example, the competing regimes utilized the rhetoric of a new international order, nationalism, and folk beliefs for the general mobilization for war and as an important basis of state legitimacy. In regard to the reorganization of the international order, however, there were differing concepts, such as the allied front against fascism, "the New Order in East Asia," and "the Greater East Asian Co-Prosperity Sphere." In regard to nationalism, there existed various levels and various ethnic or national identities, such as the Republic of China, the Nationalist Party, the united front to resist Japan, and the peaceful movement to overturn communism and build the nation. In addition, for policies about symbolism and time, the use of folk customs was common in political mobilization and propaganda.

Research on time, calendars, and memorial days in modern China has included work on folk customs, the establishment of particular memorial days, and changes over time. There has also been research describing changes in concepts of time during the process of building the state and national mentality since the late Qing period.[1] In addition, there has been research on the warlord period, the Nationalist government, and the Chinese Communist Party (CCP) base areas, analyzing policies shaping political legitimacy and national mentality, as well as deeply exploring social processes and the use of clock time as a concept to control the body.[2] To extend this conversation, this chapter will focus on a direct comparison of the policies of the various wartime regimes in North China in regard to memorial days and calendar time.

The regulation of memorial days and time was complicated by the coexistence of the new solar calendar and the traditional lunar calendar. This chapter will first look at the memorial days established on the new calendar while the remainder of the chapter will be devoted to the legacy of the lunar calendar and its uses by various regimes.[3]

Solar Calendar Memorial Days

As early as 1930, before the war, the Nationalist government copied the Japanese example and issued an order to replace the lunar calendar with the solar calendar.[4] The Nationalist government believed that the new calendar represented not only advanced civilization and rational time, but also the legitimacy of the republic and Sun Yat-sen's will. Thus, the choice of calendar and politics was in strict accordance.[5]

The Japanese puppet regimes used a mix of the solar and lunar calendars, but the long-term trend was in favor of the former. Between 1942 and 1943 the Japanese Bureau for East Asian Rejuvenation of the Imperial Rule Assistance Association

(Taiseiyokusankai Kōakyoku 大政翼賛会興亜局) discussed creating and propagating in "Greater East Asia" a solar calendar more rational than the Gregorian version.[6]

For the puppet regimes, emphasizing the new calendar also had the significance of emphasizing the control of time as reflected in numerous activities of daily life. In 1938, after the railroads and radio stations began using Japanese time, the broadcast of calisthenics (*xinmin* [or "New People's" calisthenics] in the formulation of the North China puppet government) brought home the regulation of time.[7] During activities on memorial days, each locality would use broadcasts and sirens to have moments of silence or flag raisings in strict unison.[8] In training classes for the New People's Association there would be ceremonies for flag raising and lowering at exactly the same time.[9]

In spite of their both adopting the solar calendar, the Nationalist and North China puppet regimes took a very different approach to memorial days. Before the war, the Nationalist government had based its memorial calendar on the history of the revolution and completion of Sun Yat-sen's legacy; on the death and martyrdom days of Chinese leaders (the primary part of Nationalist Party memorial days); on days for mass movements or mass corporate bodies (such as the February Seventh massacre, International Women's Day, the May Fourth movement, etc.); and on traditional memorial days such as the folk Qing Ming (tomb sweeping) festival, marking the twenty-four solar positions, and Confucius's birthday.[10] In contrast, the puppet "Chinese Provisional Government" founded in Beiping (Beijing) in December 1937 repealed the Nationalist government's memorial days and instituted a unique system of memorial days. The North China puppet regime kept only two memorial days that marked republican rule (Establishment Day of the Republic of China and National Day). It repealed other memorial days of the Nationalist government, and it did not restore the memorial days of the earlier warlord government. In this way, it eliminated the revolutionary and Republican significance of "the Republic of China." In Beijing and other large cities, there were no overly large celebrations of National Day but only ceremonies at municipal offices. In the face of the rise of patriotic feeling in cities, the government had to be careful. Of the mass memorial days and corporatist memorial days, the regime's aversion to revolution and republicanism led it to repeal every holiday except for Children's Day. The Japanese-sponsored puppet government kept Children's Day because it recognized the importance of the influence of education on the young. In addition, memorial days of concern to the political situation were established such as "Rejuvenation of Asia Holiday" (the September 7 invasion of China), the days of the entrance of the Japanese Army into various localities, the days of the establishment of the Japanese-sponsored puppet government, and the like. Finally, the regime instituted memorial days celebrating Japan, such as Kigen-Setsu (紀元節) (February 11, the founding of Japan); Japanese Army Day (March 10); and Tenchō-Setsu (天長節) (April 29, the emperor's birthday). These all reflected Japanese control of the puppet government and were meant to reinforce "friendship and cooperation" between Japan and China and the establishment of the "new order in East Asia." Japanese officials held a certain number of positions in the Japanese-sponsored puppet regime. Acting as leaders, these officials and their sections celebrated Japanese memorial days along with the Japanese.

In March 1940, with the founding of the Wang Jingwei "Nanjing Nationalist Government" in Nanjing, the "provisional government" in Beijing was renamed the North China Political Affairs Commission (Huabei Zhengwu Weiyuanhui 華北政務委員會) and theoretically became a subsidiary of the former. Since the Wang regime claimed to be the legitimate Nationalist state, its memorial days reverted to the basic structure of the prewar Nationalist regime. In contrast, the North China Political Affairs Commission kept its independence and adopted only four of the Wang regime's memorial days (Sun Yat-sen's birthday and death day, the anniversary of the return of the capital to Nanjing, and the memorial day for the martyrs of the peaceful opposition to communism and construction of the country). The events celebrating these days, however, were rather small. As a result, the Wang regime could not demonstrate its control of the entirety of occupied China through its system of memorial days.

After January 1943, in order to advance cooperation with the Wang regime, Japan more actively started using the "new policies toward China," which to a certain extent respected and completed the legitimacy of Wang's regime. As a result, memorial days in Nanjing and North China began to gradually become unified. For example, North China actively organized the anniversaries of Sun Yat-sen's birthday and death day. In addition, the north also adopted the Wang regime's Youth Day, Teachers' Day, and other corporatist memorial days. In this way North China copied the Nationalist government's system of mobilization through corporatism. Besides Army Memorial Day, the puppet government did not observe any other Japanese memorial days, in place of which it celebrated "the Rebirth of China's 'Return of the [Foreign] Concessions,'" and thus emphasized Chinese "independent governance." Activities related to the political situation were still held on a large scale. The Dedication to the Rebirth of Asia Day, on the first day of every month, changed to the Memorial Day for the Greater East Asian War (East Asian Defense Day) on the eighth of every month. These were calendar days used by Japan and other Japanese colonies and possessions. After 1943, War Day (the ninth of every month, the anniversary of the Wang regime's declaration of war) was added. These memorial days each month were times when work continued, but drinking and smoking were prohibited; banquets, entertainment, games, and gambling were all stopped to emphasize discipline and mobilize the strength of the people and goods.

The systemization of memorial days in the Communist base areas was slower than in either the Nationalist or Japanese-occupied areas. Besides those memorials days that the government and party organs would occasionally order celebrated, only a few laws about days of rest from labor can be found. The lack of systemization stemmed from the fact that the soviets came from the viewpoint of class struggle and internationalism and did not worry about national or ethnic cultural symbols. For example, labor laws legislated as holidays the anniversary of Lenin's death, the anniversary of the February 7 crackdown on mine workers, the anniversary of the Paris Commune, Labor Day, the anniversary of the October Revolution in Russia, and the anniversary of the Canton Massacre, all of which emphasized the international Communist movement.[11]

After the beginning of the war with Japan, because the base area government became a titular part of the Nationalist government, the Communist regime lost the freedom to determine its own system of memorial days. Because of this, up through 1939 the Communist Party, especially in the base areas on the front lines, essentially observed the form and activities of the Nationalist government's memorial days. Later, as the war between China and Japan continued, the Communist Party's system of memorial days included national holidays determined by the Nationalist government and a portion of revolutionary memorial days (originally Nationalist Party memorial days); mass movement corporatist memorial days; memorial days for the international Communist and Chinese Communist movements (such as the October Revolution in Russia, International Labor Day, the founding of the CCP, and the founding of the Red Army); and holidays for the people's united front against Japan and the international united front against fascism (memorializing the Manchurian Incident when Japan took over Manchuria, the Marco Polo Bridge Incident, the international war of opposition day, and United Nations Day, among others).

As the relationship between the Nationalists and the Communists worsened, after 1940, the Communist Party abandoned the use of Nationalist government authority as a means to legitimize itself and began emphasizing memorial days that represented its own authority. Among the memorial days of the Nationalist government, the Communists emphasized only National Day and in this way demonstrated their respect for the legal system of the Republic of China and advocated the position that only they could truly represent the interests of the people. In an unusual twist, when the Communists no longer emphasized the memorial days of the Nationalist government, the puppet authorities in occupied North China began respecting those days and in this way demonstrated their own legitimacy. In other words, the Communists were not going to use the Nationalist government and its symbols as a basis for struggle with the puppet government in North China, but the puppet government was.

Conflict among Political Authorities over Memorial Days

There was a clear conflict over memorial days among the Nationalist government, the puppet governments, and the Chinese Communists. The anniversary of the July 7 Marco Polo Bridge Incident, which marked the Japanese invasion of China south of the Great Wall, for example, was for the Nationalist government a remembrance of the war of resistance and national reconstruction led by the Nationalist Party. For the puppet government it was a "resurgence of Asia" holiday, marking the construction of "New Asia" through "friendship and cooperation between Japan and China." Elsewhere, after the beginning of the War of Resistance, the Chinese Communists took July 1 as the anniversary of the founding of the party and after 1938 organized a memorial week between July 1 and July 7 to stress the contribution, or perhaps leadership, of the Chinese Communists in resistance to Japan.[12] In another example, the 1942 regulations for primary school holidays issued by the Communist Shanxi-Hebei-Shandong-Henan base area did not record regulations on memorial days—that is to say, this base area did not accept the Nationalist government holidays.[13] Even when memorial days coincided, there were differences. The puppet government emphasized the anniversary of the prohibition of opium (June 3) to promote anti-European and anti-American feeling. The Nationalists and Communists also celebrated Opium Prohibition Day, but their spearhead was directed against Japan.

The three competing regimes often changed holidays in response to the actions of one of the others, such as memorial days regarding Sun Yat-sen and Confucius, two figures that had significant implications for the political legitimacy of various regimes. The Chinese Communists paid attention to the anniversary of Sun Yat-sen's death because of his political policy of contact and cooperation with the Soviet Union and CCP during his later years. At the end of the Anti-Japanese War in regard to the question of postwar political leadership and after severe conflict broke out between the Communists and the Nationalists, the Communists used Sun Yat-sen's political authority and claimed that the CCP and Mao Zedong were the true heirs of Sun Yat-sen's revolutionary thinking while at the same time rejecting Chiang Kai-shek's political authority. In the

Hebei-Shandong-Henan base area, there was an educational movement to teach this kind of thinking on the anniversary of Sun Yat-sen's death in 1944. On this day in 1945, *Liberation Daily* published an editorial titled "In Memory of Sun Yat-sen, Criticism of Chiang Kai-shek." Thus, the party took the opportunity to promote an ideological mobilization campaign inside the base area.[14] Wang Jingwei was one of the primary authors of Sun Yat-sen's last will.[15] As a result, the Wang puppet regime also emphasized this anniversary and used it to explain that its own power derived from the sincere inheritance of Sun Yat-sen's ideas. In 1930 the Nationalist government issued a regulation that the anniversary of Sun Yat-sen's death be a school holiday. In 1941, the Wang regime too ordered that it be a day off school. After 1943 the North China puppet regime started celebrating the anniversary of Sun's death. When the Nationalist government undertook a major reorganization of its memorial days in 1942, the anniversary of Sun's death was removed from the list of national holidays, and it was no longer a school holiday.[16] In a similar vein, in 1939 the Nationalist government issued instructions to make the anniversary of Confucius's birthday a new Teachers' Day, but this was not adopted by the Communists or the Wang regime.[17] In 1941 the Wang regime revised its regulations on school holidays, changing the order of holidays beginning with Confucius's birthday, set by the Nationalist government, to January (because the school year began in August, the order of holidays began in August). In this way the first holiday of the year was the anniversary of the founding of the Republic of China, and the second was the anniversary of Sun Yat-sen's death.[18] Although the Nationalist government in Chongqing had removed the anniversary of Sun Yat-sen's death from its national holidays in 1942, it still kept Confucius's birthday. From this it is possible to see that in comparison with the Nationalist government, the Wang regime placed greater emphasis on the image of Sun Yat-sen's later years, and it always put Sun Yat-sen's political power at the center of its own political legitimacy while the Nationalist government not only relied on Sun Yat-sen, but also emphasized the power of traditional culture as a means of strengthening its own legitimacy. The Chinese Communists did not normally place Confucius's birthday among the list of officially designated holidays, though in 1946, after the conquest of Tai'an, the ceremonies surrounding Confucius's birth were made according to the lunar calendar; perhaps the Communists thought of it as a popular custom.[19]

Teachers, youth, children, and peasants, in particular, were all important targets of recruitment by these regimes, so in the handling of holidays there was a natural overlap and conflict. In 1938 the Nationalist government accepted the suggestion from the Northwest Youth National Salvation Society to make a memorial day for the May 4 Movement National Youth Day, but in 1943, the

Three People's Principles Youth Corps decided to establish the Revolutionary Martyrs' Day youth day to show its leadership position among youth movements.[20] For the Communists, the Shaan-Gan-Ning base area (Shaanxi base area) held activities to celebrate that day but kept May 4 as Youth Day.[21] At that time, the Wang puppet regime took Revolutionary Government Day as its Youth Day.[22] After 1941 the Communist Party did not celebrate Revolutionary Government Day but changed that day to celebrate Marx's Birthday (Study Day). The meaning of May 4 originally had anti-Japanese overtones, and it was also an important beginning for the appearance of communism on the political stage, so the Japanese took the opportunity to dilute the significance of this day. There appeared a system of holidays including Children's Day, Youth Day, Teachers' Day, Asia Rejuvenation Day, and National Day. For the North China puppet regime, the Information Bureau of the Operating Office of the North China Political Affairs Commission issued "The Nation's Important Holidays" in 1945 and divided them into "memorial days" and "holidays." There were lunar holidays and solar holidays made up of Children's Day, Youth Day, and Teachers' Day.[23]

Within the Communist-controlled areas, in particular, there was variation between holidays celebrated on the front lines near puppet regime territory and holidays in the interior, away from the war front. For example, in the interior, the Shaan-Gan base area did not organize special activities for Opium Prohibition Day or Teachers' Day, but those days were actively celebrated in the front-line base areas. This shows that the CCP wanted to oppose the Japanese puppet government and mobilize the masses in front-line areas, so it adjusted its emphasis on different memorial days in different places.

The Lunar Calendar and Popular Customs

After the Nationalist government established its solar calendar, fragmentary sources show the occasional reference to customary holidays from the lunar calendar such as Spring Festival, Qing Ming (tomb sweeping), and the Mid-Autumn Festival. During the latter half of the 1930s, the Nationalist government used solar terms and the solar calendar to create several memorial days drawn from the lunar calendar, such as Li Chun (the first day of spring) and Qing Ming. In this way it emphasized nationalism while carrying out the principle of the new calendar.[24]

However, the influence of the lunar calendar had deep and firm roots among the people. Especially in the countryside, the lunar calendar was still an important standard for living for the common people in their work and beliefs. The people adopted special activities according to their own habits and customs, including common expectations and hopes. The ability to control these kinds of feelings, choose special times and places, and conduct propaganda at appropriate times to mobilize could bring great rewards. The North China puppet government and the Communists were both able to depart from the principles of the Nationalist government to use the lunar calendar and customs to mobilize the masses.

The North China puppet regime used "Carry Forward East Asian Cultural Morality" and "Construct a New Order in East Asia" as slogans, and the work of using popular customs in propaganda and mobilization became an important opportunity to put into practice these concepts. Japan and the puppet regime presented themselves as protectors of traditional culture and emphasized the commonality of Japanese and Chinese culture. After initial Japanese occupation, the "provisional government" in Beijing restored many old rituals, traditional memorial days, and traditional holidays of the former warlord government, all according to lunar calendar time. In addition, it restored representative temple festivals and used them as general occasions for ceremonies. During the festivals it conducted propaganda; held mass meetings; and held various meetings, memorials, exhibitions, sports events, and entertainment. On traditional holidays and festival days the regime conducted such traditional activities as meetings to respect the elderly, events to praise filial piety and virtuous women, and soup kitchens. The government also used folk beliefs about the lunar calendar to conduct propaganda and health clinics. On traditional Buddhist holidays, days to worship the god of war and temple festival days, the regime often held Sino-Japanese memorial services for the dead. Temples, monasteries, and temples to the god of war became important ceremonial spaces.

However, the "tradition" restored by the puppet regime was chosen to reflect the political interests of Japan, and neither folk nor imperial rituals always fit comfortably. For one thing, some of the so-called "common customs" of the Chinese and Japanese seemed real but were really fake. The puppet government emphasized Buddhist customs and holidays but in ways not in tune with Chinese popular custom. For example, the puppet government held an activity to pay homage to fallen soldiers during the Zhongyuan Festival (the festival to feed hungry ghosts), but according to folk customs this was the day ghosts wandered the earth and some people did not go outside.[25] In addition, in Japanese Buddhism there is the hierarchical organization of head temples and branch temples, which is rich in mobilizing possibility, but Chinese Buddhism does not have this organizational structure and is thus without the strength to mobilize the masses. The puppet government could step forward only with an organizational support structure of its own.[26]

On the other hand, imperial rituals did not always suit an occupation puppet government. For example, since the failure of Yuan Shikai's restoration of the emperorship in 1915, the Republic of China had not again had a holiday to worship heaven at the winter solstice. The mandate of heaven no longer gave effective legitimacy to the Republican government, and that ideology was like oil and water with the universal imperial system of Japan. Instead, the puppet regime conducted rituals at the temple of the god of war that included worship of Japanese "Martyrs of the Rejuvenation of Asia and Construction of the Country." The regime did not restore the rituals to the god of war of the Beijing warlord government period, however, because the Japanese wanted to suppress the association of the god of war temple with Yue Fei, a Chinese general during the Song dynasty who had opposed invaders.

In examples of other conflicts, the Japanese did not have the Qing Ming tomb-sweeping custom, so Qing Ming became a memorial to plant trees. For Qing Ming in 1944, the puppet government in Beijing held a ceremony in honor of the three hundredth anniversary of the end of the Ming dynasty and finally separated itself from Japanese customs by emphasizing nationalism in the form of remembrance of a long-gone dynasty. In the end, though, the puppet regime conducted the war and its administration according to the new solar calendar, so restoring the rhythms of the lunar calendar to a large scale was not reasonable.

In addition, the biggest problem was that the Japanese did not understand the nature of Chinese customs and sometimes subjected them to unfeeling attack and suppression. As the Japanese Army waged war, sometimes it chose holidays to act, and sometimes it used temples as execution grounds or destroyed the temples. Also, the government ordered the people to wear coarse clothes and eat coarse grain, destroying the festival atmosphere.

The long-term trend, however, favored use of the solar calendar. After the formation of the Wang Jingwei regime, the puppet governments undertook the process of unification of the calendar. The regime changed the memorial day for Confucius's birthday from the lunar to the solar calendar in 1942 and in 1944 canceled the rituals to Confucius at Mid-Autumn Festival and placed the rituals of the Wang regime (Qing Ming and Confucius's birthday on the new calendar) on the same day.[27]

In the war of calendars, the Japanese Fourth Law and Order Campaign targeted some folk practices of the lunar calendar, criticizing them as "empty rituals," "a waste," and "superstition." In 1944 an editorial in the Shanxi edition of the *New People's Gazette* (*Xinmin bao*) advised the government, schools, banks, and shops to eliminate the customs under the system of the lunar calendar.[28] Although the holidays of the lunar calendar had not been eliminated, by the end of the war, the lunar calendar had lost its previous status.

The view of the Communist Party in regard to the new calendar in principle was the same as that of the Nationalist government, but when official newspapers (among others) undertook enlightenment propaganda, the emphasis was on the new calendar's rationality and not on the system of thought. Of course village-level cadres originally had lived under the rhythms of the lunar calendar, and its customs were in the blood. Early in the Soviet revolutionary period the Communist Party already had experience using folk customs in propaganda activities. In the latter half of 1938, after the introduction of the "[Chinese] nationalization of Marxism," there was a theoretical basis for using folk customs in party activities. In addition, there is some evidence that the Japanese use of folk customs and holidays spurred the Chinese Communists to do the same. Actual use of the lunar calendar, however, varied widely in different base areas, especially between the front lines and the interior areas. On the front lines of the Eastern Shanxi base area (the fronts of the Taihang and Taiyue areas) Communists were ahead of party headquarters in Shaanbei (North Shaanxi) in using traditional holidays to conduct mobilization propaganda. The reason lay in the fact that the united front government of the front line (the Shanxi provincial government) already had laid a foundation of using folk customs, and in the atmosphere of the front lines it was truly necessary to use folk customs because the Chinese Communists felt threatened by the puppet government's use of folk customs. The puppet government's medical clinics, distribution of medicine, and holding of meetings for production and respect for the elderly on holidays and temple festival days were similar to the Communist holding of production hero meetings at temple festivals and celebration of long life, for example. Also, during the Sino-Japanese War the Japanese side first began to use such methods. Some research indicates that the Japanese use of traditional New Year paintings in propaganda instigated the Communists to use New Year paintings as well.[29] It is impossible to deny that the large-scale use of folk customs by the Japanese in anti-Communist propaganda promoted the use of folk customs by the Communists.

To mobilize the masses, the Communists fully used traditional household concepts from the common people, such as the avoidance of evil and the pursuit of wealth, becoming an official and getting rich, and making one's family wealthy.[30] Rural mobilization also included the establishment of new holidays. Originally there were no peasant memorial days in the system of Japanese corporatist memorial days of the new calendar, but the Communists had been working to establish one. In 1938 in the system of corporatist memorial days, the Southeast Shanxi base area set up national salvation associations for people from different circles. The Southeast Shanxi base area peasants' national salvation association meeting day was the anniversary of Sun Yat-sen's death (also Arbor

Day), so it is clear that the day had significance for the united front with peasants.[31] On the "Hundred Groups Great War Memorial Day" in 1941 (August 20 on the new calendar) the second meeting of representatives of the Southeast Shanxi Peasants' National Salvation Association was held, and a resolution was passed to make that Peasants' Day.[32] The Communists' decision to establish a "peasants' day" shows that they no longer relied on the authority of the Nationalist government. The suggestion was made by a "gentry representative," however, indicating that the direction of the base area was set in cooperation with landlords. The Shanxi-Hebei-Shandong-Henan Base Area Labor Protection Regulations stipulated that "Peasants' Day" was a holiday for workers, but it is impossible to confirm activities after 1942, so it is possible that the regulations became empty verbiage.[33] At that time the Nationalist government was also paying attention to the problem of a peasants' holiday. In December 1941 it used popular customs to make Li Chun (the first day of spring) "Peasants' Day."[34]

Art and literature workers took their experience using folk customs to the Shaanxi base area in the interior. As these practices became common after the 1942 rectification movement, the use of lunar calendar folk customs also grew. In the process of emphasizing the lunar calendar, peasant time, including the significance of peasant holidays, started to come to the fore. Activities of support for the government and "cherish the people" campaigns at Spring and Mid-Autumn Festivals, as well as labor hero meetings at market fairs, got the status of peasant holidays.[35]

Many peasant holidays were originally times to pray for the good fortunes of families, but the Communists planned to change holidays into ceremonies for villages as a whole, with low-level cadres to facilitate propaganda and mobilization. In 1944 Taihang used the mid-autumn festival to spread cooperative work. Huangyingjun village in Piancheng County held an "all-village mutual aid organization for unity" celebration at the Mid-Autumn Festival. The village head said, "In the past on August 15, each family separately took care of its own affairs. This year with mutual aid organizations, the mutual aid organization is the unit [of celebration], and we are all unified as a village. We have 'organized,' and the whole village has become a family."[36] Someone in the Dongbao production committee of the second area of Wu Township suggested organizing mobilization for the harvest and war preparations on the evening of the Mid-Autumn Festival entertainment. The next day labor cooperation for the whole village began.[37] The agricultural labor cooperative in Wenjia village in Taigu County unified the distribution of flour at the Mid-Autumn Festival.[38]

With the promotion of cooperative work during the production campaign, villages in the central area tried a unified management of time. In the Taiyue area, Yanshan village in Yangnan County, a village in Wuxiang County, and Caozhuang village in Libei County all used drums, speakers, and whistles to unify management of the villagers' time to get them out of bed, go to the fields, and the like.[39] Taoyang village in Yushe County used the positions of the sun as a standard to establish production plans for the entire village, and it is possible to verify the existence of an all-village production plan during the production campaign.[40] The increasing strictness of time management accompanied the measurement of labor time during the mutual aid campaign. Making time measureable set the stage for rural assistance plans such as the army production, support the government, and cherish the people campaigns.

To create village collectivism the Communists also used life habits. At Spring Festival in 1945 the Wuxiang County government in the Taihang area organized a celebration of old age in the villages, and the sweeping of tombs at Qing Ming became a memorial day for martyrs.[41] But there were many difficulties in creating village cohesion. Along with the constant struggles over accounts and the development of land reform, plans for cooperatives centered on labor heroes became frustrated, and the symbolic expressions of village cohesion did not continue.[42]

The Communists intended to use lunar calendar folk customs to make the people accept the memorial days on the new calendar. When the memorial days and folk holidays were close or duplicated each other, they audaciously used folk thinking to promote the significance of the memorial days. In New Year's activities they used various customs and habits to make the masses feel the memorial day was their own holiday. In 1940 in activities to memorialize the anniversary of the Manchurian Incident, the Shanxi-Hebei-Henan base area held a propaganda week for the one hundred regiments offensive in order to communicate the war results. The area also held a large memorial meeting and exhibitions of industrial and agricultural production. The Mid-Autumn Festival during the propaganda week was made a memorial day for the one hundred regiments offensive.[43] Since the interior Shaanxi base area did not designate traditional holidays as memorials for political incidents, it is possible to see the active approach of the front line base areas in using the lunar calendar. In the next year, however, the Shanxi-Hebei-Henan base area did not use the Mid-Autumn Festival as the memorial day for the war. As noted above, the memorial day for the one hundred regiments offensive was August 20, showing the ongoing variability and lack of systemization.

There were many examples of combining political and folk holidays. In 1942 the memorial days for the Paris Commune and the Beijing Massacre were also on the day the dragon raises his head on the lunar calendar. The Shanxi-Hebei-Shandong base area government issued instructions to hold a troop review and held memorial services for generals Fan Zixia and Guo Guoyan together with the 129th Division's headquarters.[44] Elsewhere, in Liao County, because of the Japanese Army's attack, there was no celebration of Spring Festival. The people of the county and government organs decided to create a "makeup New Year" and organized entertainment and decided to declare that day a "new calamity festival." In folk custom the "calamity festival" was January 16 on the lunar calendar, and it was said that after worshiping on that day, one would have fewer illnesses during the year. Using this kind of folk feeling, "places in the entire county undertook a cleanup to reduce the chance of the spread of disease."[45] In addition, at the Zhenwudong market in Anji County, Shaanxi, International Women's Day was held on market day on February 14 on the lunar calendar. That was also the day to reward labor heroes and mobilize for agricultural production. Two days previously had been two lunar calendar holidays: the waking of the insects and the day the dragon raises his head. On February 14 the area held the waking of the insects ceremony of wrapping a cow's horns with red cloth as a prize to give to a labor hero. That night, the game "*zhuan jiu qu*" (turn nine bends) was played in accordance with the custom of the dragon raising its head.[46] In Taihang, in consideration of the rhythms of agriculture, the memorial days and troop reviews for the Paris Commune and Beijing Massacre (March 18) and the memorial day for the Manchurian Incident (September 12) were divided over the year between periods when agriculture was more or less busy. The two memorial days used spring planting and autumn harvest as standards. In the atmosphere of the guerilla war an important memorial day was organized to celebrate the people's protection of production.[47]

In addition, the Communists actively used folk customs about the position of the sun to hold large production meetings. The positions of the sun and rhythms of the sun in the solar calendar are in truth the same. Rhythms of agriculture and the mobilization of programs of the new solar calendar together make up the rhythms of time of the base area. The Communists propagated these rhythms through the leadership of labor heroes in mobilizing production and in the issuance of rural household calendars.

When the Communist Party was concentrating on its own power, it virtually never used Buddhism and its related organizations. This is very different from the Japanese puppet government, which actively used these holidays and organizations. Buddhist organizations had their own internal logic of activities and an independent worldview that were in conflict with the principles and worldview of the Communists. Not only did the Communists not rely on Buddhist organizations when they ran campaigns, but when possible they also did their best to eliminate these organizations and bring the masses into the revolutionary corps.

This is fundamentally opposed to the puppet government's active use of these organizations and its political cooperation with them. The Chinese Communists inherited the Chinese political mentality and wanted to put forth the new age's son of heaven, Mao Zedong, and carry out the concept of equality in the process of land reform, but the Communists maintained their attitude toward Buddhists and from beginning to end tried to eliminate them.

For the most part, however, like both the Nationalist and puppet regimes, Chinese Communist power lay in new calendar time. Except for the Spring Festival, Mid-Autumn Festival, and Qing Ming, the Communists did not engage in any area-wide holiday activities and did not provide any organizational basis for them. Miscellaneous holidays were used only on an individual basis and were sometimes criticized as wasteful and superstitious and thus suppressed.

For example, the base areas gave special privileges to military dependents not only at Spring Festival and Mid-Autumn Festival, but also on holidays in the system of the solar calendar such as International Labor Day, Memorial Day for the War of Resistance, the anniversary of the founding of the Red Army, and the October Revolution.[48] Work holidays in the Shanxi-Hebei-Shandong-Henan base area were essentially set according to the solar calendar. Lunar calendar holidays were "handled based on custom" and did not have clear regulations, but wages were paid as conditions permitted according to folk customs on the lunar calendar.[49] Government employees and teachers received subsidies and distributions of grain not only on traditional holidays such as Spring Festival and Mid-Autumn Festival, but also on New Year's Day of the new calendar.[50] The Shanxi-Hebei-Shandong-Henan base area used the two-semester academic year of the new solar calendar in accordance with Nationalist government regulations.[51] It can be said that these practices gave people an opportunity to acknowledge the new calendar. In 1945 in the instructions of the Hebei-Shandong-Henan Area Number Eleven Bureau, those who entered before the end of the school year and those who entered after were to have different treatment of their dependents. Also in 1945 the regulations on grain supply of the Hebei-Shandong-Henan Number Four Bureau divided the times for distribution of wheat and millet according to the solar calendar. If this practice had continued, it could have brought the new calendar closer to the people, but the next year was again scheduled according to the lunar calendar.[52] In addition, when policies changed quickly, the Communists sometimes mobilized the masses based on the new calendar, such as in 1940, when the Hebei-Shandong-Henan area vigorously promoted class struggle and the Red May struggles of "anti-superstition" and "anti-feudalism."[53] In 1945, May 1 (International Labor Day) marked the beginning of the struggle to reduce rents and interest.[54]

In November 1946, *People's Daily* published an article titled "Miscellaneous Records of Township Residents in Wu Township (1)," which showed the actual holiday practices of villages, and it provides evidence about how the Communists mixed the solar and lunar calendars.[55] Wu Township had been a central part of the Taihang base area for a long time. According to the newspaper article, the villagers in Wu Township celebrated holidays on the new calendar, including Support the Cadres, Cherish the People Day (New Year's Day on the new calendar); March 8, Women's Day; April 4, Children's Day; May 1, Labor Day; May 4, Youth Day; June 6, Teachers' Day; July 7, All People's War of Resistance Unity Day; and October 10, Heroes of the Masses Day. The holidays on the lunar calendar included Respect the Elderly Day (Spring Festival), Support the Army, Excel at Resistance Day (Lantern Festival), Remember Martyrs Day (Qing Ming), and Kill the Enemy Heroes Day (Mid-Autumn Festival). From this list it is possible to see that the new calendar was used primarily for corporatist holidays, including days for youth and teachers, not according to the Nationalist government's regulations, but still maintaining May 4 and June 6 as originally celebrated by the Communists. New Year's Day on the new calendar was Support the Cadres, Cherish the People Day, where the masses and cadres could reflect about the year but without mentioning the founding of the Republic of China. October 10 was Heroes of the Masses Day, a holiday for summarizing production and choosing different kinds of heroes, but National Day was not mentioned. Corporatist holidays were adopted by various groups without need of reference to their political significance. The only holiday on the new solar calendar with direct political significance was the July 7, All People's War of Resistance Unity Day. It is clear that in accepting the new calendar, the rural masses did not pay too much attention to politics but focused on holidays that were corporatist or that marked the rhythms of agricultural life.

Of these holidays, the Shanxi-Hebei-Shandong-Henan Base Area Labor Protection Regulations, issued in 1941, established days off for May 1 and July 7 (with days off for holidays on the lunar calendar according to local custom). In addition, factories, workshops, mines, and shipping concerns took a holiday on February 7. Women had a holiday on March 8; children workers, on April 4, Children's Day; youth workers, on May 4, Youth Day; and hired laborers, on August 20, Peasants' Day. From these holidays, it is possible to see that the use of people's lives was a basis to penetrate all the strata of society. Also, the most recent research on the revolutionary history of the soviets shows that the main mobilizing factor for the masses in support of the revolution was not class struggle but the conflicts between old and young, men and women. Youth and women thus played an important role. In using these kinds of social conflicts, the campaign to divide the masses into corporatist groups was in accordance with the emphasis on this system of holidays.[56]

Among the memorial days and holidays mentioned here, the ratio between new solar calendar holidays and lunar calendar holidays is 8:4. Not counting some large festivals such as Dragon Festival (Duan Wu) and Winter Solstice (Dong Zhi) (not included here), the superior position of the solar calendar is clear. In addition, Qing Ming is based on the position of the sun and can be used to bring in the solar calendar, making the superior position of the solar calendar all the more salient. But from another standpoint, lunar calendar holidays and corresponding military mobilization, such as martyr memorials, concern for soldiers and dependents in the resistance, and rewards for militia, were closely related to everyday life and penetrated among the people. Holidays based originally on household activities (celebrations of long life, funerals) became activities for entire villages. It is clear that the Communists, on the one hand, worked toward the penetration of the solar calendar and, on the other hand, effectively used lunar calendar time to mobilize the masses. This kind of structure was very similar to that of the North China puppet authorities, who emphasized Japanese memorial days in conjunction with lunar calendar holidays to create new "holidays."

Also among the memorial days established by the Communists and Red Army, many villages actually held important mobilization or memorial activities, but they were not in the *People's Daily* report on Wu Township cited above. This is possibly because the report introduced "people's positions of the sun" and did not mention "cadre holidays" or "government holidays," which were more distant from the masses. For example, in Taihang, before the 1947 celebration of the founding of the CCP party organization was not made public.

Of course there was also a contradiction between the Communists and popular customs and ideas. Sometimes the Communists used methods to oppose popular culture as a way of reforming lunar calendar customs. The Communists also conducted various military mobilization activities at Spring Festival and Mid-Autumn Festival. At Spring Festival, at base areas on the front lines, they conducted a strict self-appraisal regarding support of the army to make village cadres thoroughly consider whether they behaved in ways that were not in cooperation with or were even opposed to the Eighth Route Army.[57] Also during the Support the Government Cherish the People movement soldiers had to consider whether or not they had opposed the people or if there was deceit or oppression of the masses.[58] Rectification of high-level cadres and the party in Taihang was also conducted at Spring Festival. Labor heroes who broke through traditional customs did not even rest on holidays, but ordinary people would have a hard time accepting such an approach.

When the new calendar gradually penetrated society, the common people also celebrated their new holidays according to their own customs. As a result, the Communists also wanted to prohibit so-called obscenity, superstition, waste, and the like, and their intent was naturally reflected in the new calendar. The military in Taihang killed draft animals at will during the new calendar New Year.[59] Various organs in Yangcheng attacked the wasteful popular practice of setting off "New Year's thunder" fireworks at New Year's on the new calendar and Spring Festival.[60] There was an "emancipated hero," who wanted to use Mao Zedong's picture as an object of worship on New Year's Eve of the new calendar. In some villages there was "obscene" entertainment at New Year's on the new calendar, and some businesspeople and cadres watched and cheered.[61] At New Year's on the new calendar during land reform, there were some middle peasants who, afraid of having their their property divided, killed sheep to make dumplings for a big banquet.[62] These examples show the resilience of popular culture.

Conclusion

According to the idea to "Carry Forward East Asian Morality," the Japanese criticized the Chinese Communists; the Nationalists; and powers such as the Soviet Union, England, and the United States for weakening the power of traditional morality. The Japanese also used popular customs to mobilize propaganda activities. As a result, the North China puppet government restored and promoted traditional ceremonies, holidays, and temple festivals of the lunar calendar on a large scale. In these ceremonies, Confucian morality and Buddhism were shown to the people as common moral values of the Chinese and Japanese. The North China puppet regime eliminated memorial days on the new calendar relating to the revolution and the republican system. As a result, this led to a significant lack of unity between the system of holidays of the Wang Jingwei regime and that in North China. But after Japan instituted new policies toward China in 1943, holidays in the north and south gradually became unified and took the form of ceremonies to support state legitimacy.

The customs of "East Asian Cultural Morality" used by the Japanese puppet regimes were in truth customs based on the logic of Japanese rule. Moral rules about holidays and timekeeping promoted by the puppet regimes suppressed customs based on the household. Because of the destruction of war and economic embargo, there were very few temple festivals and markets that could be restored and used by the puppet authorities. Turning away from original intentions, they sometimes vigorously attacked and suppressed popular customs.

These ceremonies could not connect with people's hearts; some lunar calendar customs were criticized as empty, wasteful, and superstitious. The Japanese planned to use the elements of the traditional calendar to create a calendar more rational than the Gregorian one, but this plan could only bring them closer to the Nationalists' use of solar positions for a complete calendrical system.

To mobilize the masses the Nationalist Party, the Nationalist government, the Wang Jingwei government, the puppet regime, and the Communists all emphasized corporatist holidays. In the promotion of these holidays, there was no need for the people to understand the political background. The Wang Jingwei government, the North China puppet regime, and the Communists all used these holidays to create a system with special characteristics.

The North China puppet regime used holidays to get the masses to cooperate with Japan in prosecuting the war and also, through obligatory activities and donations during holidays, to extract labor and goods. Although the development of such activities under Japanese rule was limited only to the points and lines (cities and railways) successfully controlled by the Japanese occupation, the North China puppet regime, in the guise of a sovereign nation, used new media to continuously educate and train the people in occupied areas. These ceremonies gave the appearance of a nation to the people of the occupied areas and in this way spread the idea that China should be a sovereign nation.

The Communist base areas basically respected the Nationalists' system of holidays until 1939 and advocated political legitimacy based on the authority of the Nationalist government. But from the end of 1939, after relations between the Communists and Nationalists worsened, the Communists intentionally opposed the Nationalist government in their holiday activities. Many Nationalist government holidays were discontinued while the Communists used their own system of holidays to enhance their power.

The use of popular customs of the lunar calendar in propaganda mobilization and in the process of opposing the Japanese puppet regime's use of popular customs first started in the Southeast Shanxi base area. The Communists used various methods to introduce the new calendar into the villages, such as scheduling holidays in consideration of the rhythms of agricultural production, importing lunar calendar customs into the activities on the new calendar, and placing new holidays on or near lunar calendar holidays. Lunar calendar holidays were originally heavily based on household activities, and the Communists wanted to cultivate communality by using holidays as memorial days for peasants and villages. But with political campaigns like the struggle over accounts and the development of land reform, the policy to raise village cohesion through cooperative campaigns centered on labor heroes gave rise to conflict. As a result, many ceremonies could not be continued. The Communists also planned to reform the nature of folk customs, but folk customs are hard to manage, and the peasants just took customs prohibited by the Communists and celebrated them based on the new calendar.

The Chinese countryside lacked village community structures. In order to make the Communist base area societies more communal, it was necessary to control the individual nature of households and in this way create cultural cohesion. Because of the Communist policy to increase reliance on hired labor, they could not effectively create cultural cohesion. The fragmented small-peasant economy took on an extreme form during the process of land reform, and a new phenomenon of individualist households appeared anew. As a result, we can see the durability of folk customs.

Notes

1. Qiao Zhiqiang, *Jindai Huabei*; Jian, "Luelun jindai li chunjie jieri wenhua de yanbian"; Xie, Wu, and Hua, "Minguo shiqi de tiyu jie, yinyue jie, xiju jie yu meishu jie"; Wu and Ruan, "Minguo shiqi yifeng yisu"; Chen, "Guomindang dui shehui shijian de liyong yu zhizuo"; Usa, "'Jikanteikoku' no tasogare"; Yoshizawa, *Aikokushugi no sousei nashonarizumu.*

2. Maruta Takashi: "SenKannei-Henku," "KaHoku Kairai," and "Tiki to Kenryoku (I) (II)"; Harrison, *The Making of the Republican Citizen;* Onodera: "Minkoku" and "Nanjing"; Li, "Zongli jinianzhou yu minguo zhengzhi wenhua"; Ishikawa, "Omoidasenai hizuke"; Tanaka, "'Shūsen' 'kōsen shōri' kinenbi to Higashi Ajia"; Satō and Sun, *Higashi Ajia no shūsen kinenbi;* Huang, *Lishi, shenti, guojia.*

3. When different political regimes use different terms for memorial days, the nomenclature of the original sources is still respected.

4. "Feizhi jiuli jieri gaiding ti jieri an."

5. Zhongguo Guomindang Zhongyang Zhixing Weiyuanhui Xuanchuan Bu. On the penetration of the new calendar into society during the Republican period and the republic's policies about calendars, see Zuo, "Cong 'gaizheng shuo' dao 'fei jiuli.'"

6. Kanda, *Manshū-Koku jikesho no seitei to sono hukyū;* Nōuda: "Tōyō niokeru" and "Meixin to rekichuu"; Mori, "Shinareki to nenchū gyōji."

7. *BX*, April 26 and 27, May 15, 1938.

8. *SX*, November 2, 1942; December 24, 1943; February 8 and 10, 1944; Zhao, *Linfen xian diwuci zhian qianghua yundong huibian*, 26.

9. Xinminhui Zhongyan Zhidao Bu.

10. Memorial days here and for other regimes compiled from the following: Guoli Zhongyang Yanjiuyuan Tianwen Yanjiusuo, *Guomin li; Guomin zhengfu gong bao*, Order Yuzi No. 77 of the Nationalist Government, March 7, 1938, and Order Yuzi No. 30, March 12, 1938; *BX*, December 11, 1938, 3, and evening edition, November 4, 1939; *Huabei zhengwu weiyuanhui gongbao*, no. 171/172 (October 29, 1942), *benhuidu* (commission documents), 7–8; Guomin Zhongyang Guanxiangtai, *Zhonghua minguo shisan nian lishu; BX, SX, TH, RR.*

11. Han and Chang, *Xinminzhuyi gemming shiqi genjudi fazhi wenxian xuanbian,* 547, 572, 589–590.

12. Ishikawa, "Omoidasenai hizuke."

13. "Jin-Ji-Lu-Yu bianqu xiaoxue canxing guicheng," 369–370.

14. *JL,* February 27, 1944; *JR,* December 3, 1945; and *JL,* May 5, 1945.

15. Ishikawa, "Shigo no Sonbun."

16. "Jiaoyubu xiuzheng xuexiao xuenian xueqi ji xiujia riqi guiding"; "Jiaoyubu xiuzheng xuexiao xuenian xueqi ji xiujia riqi guiding (1941 Yiyue di'er ci xiuzheng)"; "Zhanshi geji xuexiao xuenian xueqi jiaqi fuwu jinjin zanxing banfa."

17. Jiaoyubu cheng, Li 裡12 zi 字 no. 11266 (1939-05-02) and ren 人 10 zi 字 no. 18577 (1939-08-06).

18. "Jiaoyubu xiuzheng xuexiao xuenian xueqi ji xiujia riqi guiding."

19. *JL,* October 6, 1946.

20. *XZ,* April 13, 1939; Xu, *Jieri jinianri jiaoxuefa,* 2.

21. *JR,* March 31, 1943.

22. *SX,* May 6 and 19, 1943.

23. Huabei Zhengwu Weiyuanhui Zongwu Ting Qingbao Ju, 4.

24. "Jinian jieri an (11)."

25. Taiyuanshi Nanjiaoqu Difangzhi Bianji Weiyuanhui, 847.

26. *Huabei jianshe nianshi,* 7; *Shanxi minbao,* February 16, 1941.

27. "Jiaoshu gongdu."

28. *SX,* January 22, 1944.

29. Kawase, *Sensō to nenga.*

30. Maruta, "Senkannei-Henku."

31. *XRH,* November 3, 1939.

32. Ibid., August 29, 1941.

33. "Jin-Ji-Lu-Yu bianqu laogong baohu zanxing tiaoli," 27; "Ji nan qu gugong zanxing tiaoli."

34. Jian, "Luelun jindai li chunjie jieri wenhua de yanbian"; Chen, "Guomindang dui shehui shijian de liyong yu zhizuo."

35. Maruta, "SenKannei-Henku."

36. Quoted in *TH,* October 9, 1944.

37. Ibid., October 15, 1944.

38. Ibid., December 19, 1944.

39. XTY, April 7, 1944; TH, August 29 and September 19, 1944.

40. *TH,* September 29 and October 3, 1944, and March 17, 1945; *XTY,* April 10 and June 22, 1944.

41. *TH,* February 17, 1945.

42. *XTY,* June 1, 1948.

43. XRH, September 9, 17, and 23, 1940; *TY,* September 17 and 23, 1940; "Guanyu Jin-Ji-Yu qu yinian xuanchuan gongzuo baogao."

44. *XRH,* March 13 and 25, 1942.

45. Ibid., March 18, 1942.

46. *JR,* March 17 and 24, 1943.

47. "Zhonggong Jin-Ji-Yu qu dangwei xuanchuan bu guanyu Jin-Ji-Yu qu yi nianlai xuanchuan gongzuo baogao; "Zhonggong Jin-ji-Yu qu dangwei guanyu fandui diren 'qingchao' 'dadang' de zhishi"; "1944 nian zhandou he shengchang jiehe de jinghan."

48. *TY,* August 24, 1942; *XRH,* November 19, 1942.

49. "Jin-Ji-Lu-Yu bianqu laogong baohu zanxing tiaoli"; "Ji nan qu gugong zanxing tiaoli."

50. "Guanyu zhixing xin gongji zhidu yu xiaoxue jiaoyuan daiyu wenti de mingling"; "Taiyuequ yige zhengmin ganbu zhi shenghuo Chengdu"; "Di si zhuanqu zhengminxue san shi si niandu gongji zhidu"; Jin-lu-yu xingshu.

51. "Jin-Ji-Lu-Yu bianxu xiaoxue zanxing guicheng"; "Xuexiao xuenian xueqi ji xiujia riqi guicheng."

52. "Di si zhuan qu zhengminxue san shi si niandu gongji zhidu"; *Ji-Lu-Yu qu san shi wu niandu gongji zhidu.*

53. "Taixi hong wu yue yundong"; "Luxi fujiu zonghui guanyu jinhou funv gongzuo de jueyi."

54. *JL,* May 15 and 27, 1945.

55. *RR,* November 10, 1946.

56. Tatahashi, *Tō to nōmin:Chūgoku nōmin kakumei no saikentō.*

57. *TH,* January 19 and February 15, 1946; *XTY,* March 3, 1945.

58. *TH,* February 6, 1944, and January 25, 1945.

59. *XRH,* December 18, 1942.

60. *XTY,* January 29, 1947.

61. *TH,* January 17, 1945.

62. Ibid., January 21, 1948.

Bibliography

Archives and Manuscript Sources

Archives of the Interior Ministry (Neizheng Bu 內政部), Academia Historica.
Archives of the Nationalist government, Academia Historica.
Shanxi Provincial Archives (Shanxisheng Dang'anguan 山西省檔案館).

Newspapers and Periodicals Cited as Primary Sources

Guomin zhengfu gong bao 國民政府公報
Huabei zhengwu weiyuanhui gongbao 華北政務委員會公報 (Official gazette of the North China Political Affairs Commission)
Jiefang ribao 解放日報 (*JR*)
Jiluyu ribao 冀魯豫日報 (*JL*)
Renmin ribao 人民日報 (*RR*)
Shanxi xinminbao 山西新民報
Taiyue ribao 太岳日報 (*TY*)
Xinhua ribao (North China edition) 新華日報 (華北版) (*XRH*)
Xinhua ribao (Taihang edition) 新華日報 (太行版) (*TH*)
Xinhua ribao (Taiyue edition) 新華日報 (太岳版) (*XTY*)
Xinmin bao (Beijing edition) 新民報(北京版) (*BX*)
Xinmin bao (Shanxi edition) 新民報 (山西版) (*SX*)

References

"1944 nian zhandou he shengchang jiehe de jinghan 1944 年戰鬥和生產結合的經驗" (Experience with combining production and war in 1944). In *Taihang dangshi ziliao huibian*, vol. 7 (2000), 390–391.

Chen Huihui 陳惠惠. "Guomindang dui shehui shijian de liyong yu zhizuo: Minguo nongmin jie yanjiu 國民黨對社會時間的利用與製作 – 民國農民節研究" (The use and establishment of social time by the Guomindang: Research on Republican rural holidays). *Jiangxi daxue xuebao* 江西大學學報 42, no. 6 (2009): 107–112.

"Di si zhuanqu zhengminxue san shi si niandu gongji zhidu 第四專區政民學三十四年度供給制度" (Supply system for 1945 for government, civil, and educational [employees] for the No. Four Special Area). August 1, 1945. In Jin-Ji-Lu-Yu bianqu genjudi lishi ziliao di 16 juan 晉冀魯豫邊區抗日根據地歷史資料, 第十六卷 (Historical materials of the Shanxi-Hebei-Shandong-Henan anti-Japanese base area, vol. 16), 889–890. No publisher given.

"Feizhi jiuli jieri gaiding ti jieri an 廢止舊曆節日改訂替節日案" (Abolishing old calendar holidays and changing to new holidays). March 4, 1930. Archives of the Interior Ministry, 026000012327A.

"Guanyu Jin-Ji-Yu qu yinian xuanchuan gongzuo baogao 關於晉冀豫區一年來宣傳工作報告" (Work report on propaganda work in the last year of the Shanxi-Hebei-Henan base area). August 1941. In *Taihang dangshi ziliao huibian Di si juan* 太行黨史資料彙編 第4卷 (Collected materials on Taihang party history, vol. 4), edited by Shanxisheng Dang'anguan 山西省檔案館 (Shanxi Provincial Archives), 599. Shanxi: Shanxi renmin chubanshe, 1994.

"Guanyu zhixing xin gongji zhidu yu xiaoxue jiaoyuan daiyu wenti de mingling 關於執行新供給制度與小學教員待遇問題的命令" (Order on implementation of the new system of compensation and supplies for primary school instructors). January 30, 1946. In *1946 nian zhongyao wenjian huiji* 1946 年重要文件彙編 (Collection of important documents for 1946), edited by Taihang xingshu 太行行署 (Taihang Bureau), 110. No publisher given.

Guoli Zhongyang Yanjiuyuan Tianwen Yanjiusuo 國立中央研究院天文研究所 (Academia Sinica, Institute of Astronomy and Astrophysics), ed. *Guomin li* 國民曆 (Calendar of the people [of China]). Nanjing: Department of Education 1938, 1941–1945.

Guomin Zhongyang Guanxiangtai 民國中央觀象臺 (Observatory of the Republic of China), ed. *Zhonghua minguo shisan nian lishu* 中華民國13年曆書 (Calendar of the Republic of China). 1924.

Han Yanlong 韓延龍 and Chang Zhaoru 常兆儒, eds. *Xinminzhuyi gemming shiqi genjudi fazhi wenxian xuanbian* 新民主主義革命時期根據地法制文獻選編 (Selection of base area legal documents of the new democracy revolutionary period), vol. 4. Beijing: Zhongguo shehuikexue chubanshe, 1984.

Harrison, Henrietta. *The Making of the Republican Citizen: Political Ceremonies and Symbols in China, 1911–1929.* Oxford: Oxford University Press, 2000.

Huabei jianshe nianshi 華北建設年史 (Yearly history of North China construction). *Shehui, wenhua bian* 社會・文化編 (Society and culture volume). Tianjin: Dongya xinbao, 1944.

Huabei Zhengwu Weiyuanhui Zongwu Ting Qingbao Ju 華北政務委員會總務廳情報局 (Intelligence Office of the Operating Bureau of the North China Political Affairs Commission). *Woguo zhongyao jinianri* 我國重要紀念日 (The nation's important holidays). Beijing, 1945.

Huang Jinlin 黃金麟. *Lishi, shenti, guojia: Jindai Zhongguo de shenti xingcheng 1885–1937* 歷史, 身體, 國家 近代中國的身體形成 18851937 (History, body, state: The formation of the body in modern China 18851937). Taipei: Lianjing chuban shiye gongsi, 2000).

Ishikawa Yoshihiro 石川禎浩. "Omoidasenai hizuke: Chūgoku Kyōsan-Tō no Kinenbi 思い出せない日付–中国共産党の記念日" (Remember the date: Memorial days of the Chinese Communist Party). In *Kinenbi no sōzō* 記念日の創造 (Creation of memorial days), edited by Koseki Takashi 小関隆, 126–166. Kyoto: Jinbun Shoin 2007.

———. "Shigo no Sonbun: Isho to kenenshū 死後の孫文--遺書と紀念週" (Sun Yat-sen after death: His last will and anniversaries). *Tōhō Gakuhō* 東方学報, no. 79 (2006): 162.

Jian Tao 簡濤. "Luelun jindai li chunjie jieri wenhua de yanbian 略論斤代立春節日文化的演變" (A brief essay on the evolution of the culture of spring festival). *Minsu yanjiu* 民俗研究 (Folk customs research), no. 2 (1998): 5872.

"Jiaoshu gongdu 教署公牘" (Education notices). *Huabei zhengwu weiyuanhui bao* nos. 313314 (November 9, 1944): 11–12, and nos. 317–318 (November 29, 1944): 12.

Jiaoyubu cheng 教育部呈 (Education Ministry memorials). Li 裡12 zi 字 no. 11266 (1939-05-02) and ren 人 10 zi 字 no. 18577 (1939-08-06). In *Zhonghua minguoshi dang'an ziliao huibian* 中華民國史檔案資料彙編 (Selection of archival materials on the history of the Republic of China). Di wu ji di'yi bian wenhua er 第五輯第一編文化 (二) (Series 5, vol. 1, culture [2]), edited by Guomin Zhengfu Xingzhengyuan Jiaoyubu Bianli Weiyuanhui (Nanjing) 國民政府行政院教育部編曆委員會 (南京) (Editorial Committee of the Education Department of the Administrative Ministry [Nanjing]), 530–531 and 581–583. Jiangsu: Jiangsu buji chubanshe, 1994.

"Jiaoyubu xiuzheng xuexiao xuenian xueqi ji xiujia riqi guiding 教育部修正學校學年學期及休日期規定 (Regulations on the revision of school years, terms, and holidays). In *Guomin li* 國民曆 (National calendar), edited by Guomin Zhengfu Xingzhengyuan Jiaoyubu Bianli Weiyuanhui (Nanjing) 國民政府行政院教育部編曆委員會 (南京) (Editorial Committee of the Education Department of the Administrative Ministry [Nanjing]), 101–103. Nanjing: 1941.

"Jiaoyubu xiuzheng xuexiao xuenian xueqi ji xiujia riqi guiding (1941 Yiyue di'er ci xiuzheng) 教育部修正學校學年學期及休假日期規定, (一月第二次修正1941)" (Regulations on the revision of school years, terms, and holidays (January, second revision, 1941). In *Guomin li* 國民曆 (National calendar), edited by Guoli Zhongyang Yanjiuyuan Tianwen Yanjiusuo 國立中央研究院天文研究所 (Academia Sinica, Institute of Astronomy and Astrophysics), 85–86. Nanjing: Department of Education, 1942.

Ji-Lu-Yu qu san shi wu niandu gongji zhidu 冀魯豫區三十五年度供給制度 (Supply system for 1946 for the Hebei-Shandong-Henan area). No publisher given. P. 2.

"Ji nan qu gugong zanxing tiaoli (1943) 冀南區雇工暫行條例 (1943)" (Southern Hebei base area provisional regulations on hiring [1943]). In *Jin-Ji-Lu-Yu qu kangri genjudi lishi ziliao, die r juan* 晉冀魯豫區抗日根據地歷史資料, 第二卷 (Historical materials on the Shanxi-Hebei-Shandong-Henan anti-Japanese base area, vol. 2). No publisher given. Holdings of the Nankai Daxue Lishi Xueyuan Zhongguo Xiandaishi Jiaoshi Cang 南開大學歷史學院中國現代史教研室藏 (Chinese Modern History Room of the Nankai University History Institute), 102.

"Jinian jieri an (11) 紀念日案 (11)" (Memorial days and holidays [11]). July 11, 1940, and December 30, 1947. Archives of the Nationalist government, 0010516160005.

"Jin-Ji-Lu-Yu bianqu laogong baohu zanxing tiaoli 晉冀魯豫邊區勞工保護暫行條例" (Provisional regulations on labor protection for the Shanxi-Hebei-Shandong-Henan base area). In *Jin-Ji-Lu-Yu bianqu faling bian* 晉冀魯豫邊區法令彙編 (Collected laws of the Shanxi-Hebei-Shandong-Henan base area), edited by Jin-Ji-Lu-Yu bianqu zhengfu 晉冀魯豫邊區政府. Taofen shudian, 1945.

"Jin-Ji-Lu-Yu bianqu xiaoxue canxing guicheng 晉冀魯豫邊區小學暫行規程" (Provisional regulations on primary schools in the Shanxi-Hebei-Shandong-Henan base area, January 10, 1942). In *Taihang geming genjudi congshu zhi ba Wenhua shiye* 太行革命根據地叢書之八, 文化事業 (Taihang revolutionary base area collection, vol. 8, culture), edited by Taihang Geming Genjudi Shi Zongbian Weiyuanhui 太行革命根據地史總編委會 (Taihang Revolutionary Base Area History Editorial Committee). Shanxi: Shanxi renmin chubanshi, 1989.

"Jin-Ji-Lu-Yu bianqu xiaoxue zanxing guicheng 冀魯豫邊區小學暫行規程" (Preliminary regulations for primary schools in the Shanxi-Hebei-Shandong-Henan base area, October 1, 1942). In *Taihang geming genjudi congshu zhi ba—wenhua shiye* 太行革命跟基地叢書之八—文化事業, (Taihang revolutionary base area collection, vol. 8, culture), edited by Taihang Geming Genjudi Shi Zongbian Weiyuanhui 太行革命根據地史總編委會 (Taihang Revolutionary Base Area History Editorial Committee), 369–370. Shanxi: Shanxi renmin chuban she, 1989.

Jin-Lu-Yu Xingshu 冀魯豫行署 (Hebei-Shandong-Henan Bureau). *Jin-Lu-Yu qu san shi wu niandu gongji zhidu* 冀魯豫區三十五年度供給制度 (Supply system for 1946 in the Hebei-Shandong-Henan area). No publisher given. P. 2.

Kanda Kiyoshi 神田清. *Manshū-Koku jikesho no seitei to sono hukyū* 滿洲國時憲書の制定と其普及 (The writing and propagation of the Manchukuo-period constitution). In Taisei Yokusankai Kōgyoku 大政翼贊會興亜局 (Japanese Bureau for East Asian Rejuvenation of the Imperial Rule Assistance Association), *Rekihou chōsa siryō* 暦法調査資料, 第 8 輯 (Imperial Rule Assistance Association, calendrical research materials), no. 8 (December 1942): 8–11.

Kawase Chiharu 川瀬千春. *Sensō to nenga: 'Jūgonen Sensō'ki no Nichū Rōkoku no shikakuteki puropaganda (Propaganda)* 戦争と年画:「十五年戦争」期の日中両国の視覚的プロパガンダ (War and new year paintings: Visual propaganda of Japan and China during the "Fifteen Years' War"). Matsudo Shi: Azusa shuppansha, 2000.

Li Gongzhong 李恭忠. "Zongli jinianzhou yu minguo zhengzhi wenhua 總理紀念週與民國政治文化" (Sun Yat-sen memorial week and Republican political culture). *Fujian luntan* 福建論壇, Renwen shehui kexue ban 人文社会科學版 (Humanities and social sciences edition), no. 1 (2006): 56–60.

"Luxi Fujiu Zonghui guanyu jinhou funü gongzuo de jueyi 魯西婦救總會關於今後婦女工作的決議" (Decision on future women's work of the Western Shandong Women's Salvation Association). June 16, 1941. In *Zhonggong Ji-Lu-Yu bianqu dangshi ziliao xuanbian, Di er ji, wenxian bufen (shang)* 中共冀魯豫邊區黨史資料選編 第二輯,

文獻部分(上) (Selected materials on party history of the Chinese Communist Hebei-Shandong-Henan base area, vol. 2, Documents section [Vol. 1]), edited by Zhonggong Ji-Lu-Yu Bianqu Dangshi Gongzuozu Ban Gongshi, Zhonggong Henan Shengwei Gongzuo Weiyuanhui 中共冀魯豫邊區黨史工作組辦公室・中共河南省委工作委員會 (Party History Group Office of the Chinese Communist Hebei-Shandong-Henan Base Area and the Chinese Communist Henan Provincial Work Committee, 637. Henan: Henan renmin chubanshe, 1988.

Maruta Takashi 丸田孝志. "Kahoku kairai seiken ni okeru kinenbi katsudō to minzoku riyō: Sansei-Shou o chūshin ni 華北傀儡政権における記念日活動と民俗利用–山西省を中心に" (Memorial days and folk usage in regard to the North China puppet government power in Shanxi Province). In *Kindai Chūgoku to Nihon: Teikei to tekitai no hanseiki* 近代中国と日本：提携と敵対の半世紀 (Modern Japan and China: A half century of ties and animosity), edited by Soda Saburō 曽田三郎, 291–326, Tokyo: Ochanomizu Shobou, 2001.

———. 丸田孝志. "SenKanNei-Henku no kinenbi katsudō to sinreki-noureki no jikan" 陝甘寧辺区の記念日活動と新暦・農暦の時間 (Memorial days and time in the new and old calendars in the Shan-Gan-Ning base area). *Shigaku kenkyū* 史学研究, no. 221 (1998): 16–39.

———. 丸田孝志. "Tiki to Kenryoku (I) (II): Chūgoku Kyōsan-Tō konkyochi no kinenbi katsudō to sinreki-nōreki no jikan 時と権力 (I, II) -- 中国共産党根拠地の記念日活動と新暦・農暦の時間" (Time and power (I, II): Memorial days and time in the new and old calendars in Chinese Communist Party base areas). *Shakai shisutemu (System) kenkyuu* 社会システム研究, nos. 9, 10 (2005): 27–46, 57–53.

Mori Shikazō 森鹿三. "Shinareki to nenchū gyōji 支那暦と年中行事" (The Chinese Calendar and yearly activities). *Rekihou chōsa siryō* 暦法調査資料 (Calendrical research materials), no. 5 (November 1942): 28–29.

Nōuda Chūryō 能田忠亮. "Meixin to rekichū 迷信と暦注" (Superstition and calendar notes). *Rekihou chōsa siryō* 暦法調査資料 (Calendrical research materials), no. 7 (November 1942): 5–7.

———. "Tōyō niokeru reki no seijiteki bunkashiteki yigi 東洋に於ける暦の政治的文化史的意義" (The significance of the political cultural history of calendar methods in Asia). *Rekihou chōsa siryō* 暦法調査資料 (Calendrical research materials), no. 4 (November 1942): 15–17.

Onodera Shirō 小野寺史郎. "Minkoku shonen no kakumei kinenbi: Kokkeibi no seiritsu wo megutte 民国初年の革命記念日—国慶日の成立をめぐって" (Revolutionary memorial days in the early republic: Establishment of the national holiday). *Chūgoku: Shakai to bunka* 中国–社会と文化, no. 20 (2005): 208–224.

———. 小野寺史郎. "Nanjing Guomin zhengfu de gemin jinianri zhengce yu guozuzhuyi 南京國民政府的革命紀念日與國族主義" (Revolutionary memorial day policy of the Nanjing Nationalist government and nationalism). In *Dongya shijiaoxia de jindai Zhongguo* 東亞視角下的近代中國 (Modern China looking from East Asia), edited by Peng Minghui and Tang Qihua 彭明輝 唐啟華, 83–115, Taipei: Guoli zhengzhi daxue lishi xi 國立政治大學歷史系, 2006.

Qiao Zhiqiang 喬志強, ed. *Jindai Huabei nongcun shehui bianqian* 近代華北農村社會變遷 (Changes in rural society in modern North China). Beijing: Renmin, 1998.

———. *Jindai Zhongguo shehui wenhua qianbian* 近代中國社會文化變遷錄 (Changes in social culture in modern China), vol. 3. Hangzhou: Zhejiang renmin chubanshe, 1998.

Satō Takumi 佐藤卓己 and Sun Anshi 孫安石, eds. *Higashi Ajia no shūsen kinenbi* 東アジアの終戦記念日: 敗北と勝利のあいだ (Memorial day for the end of the war in East Asia). Tokyo: Chikuma Shinsho, 2007.

"Taixi hong wu yue yundong 泰西紅五月運動" (The Red May movement in Taixi). In *Zhonggong Ji-Lu-Yu bianqu dangshi ziliao xuanbian, di er ji zhuanti bufen (zhong)* 中共冀魯豫邊區黨史資料選編 第二輯，專題部分(中) (Collection of party history documents of the Communist Party of the Hebei-Shandong-Henan area, vol. 2, Special topic section, vol. 2, edited by Zhonggong Ji-Lu-Yu qu Bianqu Dangshi Gongzuo Bangongshi 中共冀魯豫邊區黨史工作組辦公室 (Chinese Communist Party History Work Office of the Hebei-Shandong-Henan Area), 457–469. Shandong: Shandong daxue chubanshe, 1990.

Taiyuanshi Nanjiaoqu Difangzhi Bianji Weiyuanhui 太原市南郊區地方志編輯委員會 (Editorial Committee of the Gazetteer of the Nanjiao Area of Taiyuan City), ed. *Taiyuanshi Nanjiaoqu Zhi* 太原市南郊區志 (Nanjiao Area of Taiyuan City Gazetteer). Beijing: Sanlian shudian, 1994.

"Taiyuequ yige zhengmin ganbu zhi shenghuo Chengdu 太岳區一個政民幹部之生活程度" (Living standards of government and civil cadres in Taiyue). June 19, 1946. In *Jin-Ji-Lu-Yu bianqu kangri genjudi lishi ziliao di san juan* 晉冀魯豫邊區抗日根據地歷史資料, 第三卷 (Historical materials of the Shanxi-Hebei-Shandong-Henan anti-Japanese base area, vol. 3), 103. No publisher given.

Tanaka Hitoshi 田中仁. "'Shūsen' 'kōsen shōri' kinenbi to Higashi Ajia '終戦' '抗戦勝利' 記念日と東アジア" ("War" "resistance victory," memorial days, and East Asia). In *Gendai chuugoku chiiki kenkyuu no aratana Shiken* 現代中国地域研究の新たな視圏 (New views on regional research on modern China), edited by Nishimura Shigeo 西村成雄 and Tanaka Hitoshi 田中仁, 194–232. Kyoto: Sekai shisōsha, 2007.

Tatahashi Nobuo 高橋伸夫. *Tō to nōmin:Chūgoku nōmin kakumei no saikentō* 党と農民: 中国農民革命の再検討 (Peasants and the party: A new examination of China's rural revolution). Tokyo: Kenbun shuppansha, 2006.

Usa Tōro 遊佐 徹. "'Jikanteikoku' no tasogare: kindai Chūgoku ni okeru 'jikan' shisustemu [system]' no henkō '時間帝国'の黄昏—中国近代における '時間システム'の変更" (The last years of "imperial time": The "system of time" in modern China). *Okayama daigaku bungakubu kyou* 岡山大学文学部紀要, no. 43 (2005): 23–39.

Wu Yechun 伍野春 and Ruan Rong 阮榮. "Minguo shiqi yifeng yisu 民國時期移風易俗" (Changes in customs during the Republican period). *Minsu yanjiu* 民俗研究, no. 2 (2000): 59–70.

Xie Shicheng 謝世誠, Wu Yechun 伍野春, and Hua Guoliang 華國梁. "Minguo shiqi de tiyu jie, yinyue jie, xiju jie yu meishu jie 民國時期的體育節, 音樂節,戲劇節與美術節" (Sports, music, drama, and art holidays in the Republican period). *Minguo dang'an* 民國檔案, no. 1 (1999): 105–109.

Xinminhui Zhongyang Zhidao Bu 新民會中央指導部 (Central Guidance Bureau of the New People's Association). "Xinminhui Dingxian zhidao bu gongzuo gaikuang minguo 27 niandu 新民會定縣指導部工作經過概況, 民國 27 年度" (The general work situation of the Ding County New People's Association Guidance Office in 1938). *Gongzuo ziliao* 工作資料 (Work materials), no. 10 (1939): 48–49.

Xu Yupan 許育藩, ed. *Jieri jinianri jiaoxuefa* 節日紀念日教學法 (Teaching methods for holidays and memorial days). Shanghai: Shangwuyuan shuguan, 1948.

"Xuexiao xuenian xueqi ji xiujia riqi guicheng 學校學年學期及休假日期規程" (Regulations on holidays, school terms, and academic holidays). In *Guomin zhengfu xianxing fagui di er ji* 國民政府現行法規 第二集 (Laws in force of the Nationalist government, vol. 2, 16. Shanghai: Shangwu yuanshuguan, 1930.

Yoshizawa Seiichirou 吉澤誠一郎. *Aikokushugi no sousei nashonarizumu* [nationalism] *kara kindai Chūgoku o miru* 愛國主義の創成 ナショナリズムから近代中國をみる (The creation of patriotism: Seeing modern China through nationalism). Tokyo: Iwanami shoten, 2001.

"Zhanshi geji xuexiao xuenian xueqi jiaqi fuwu jinjin zanxing banfa" 戰時各級學校學年學期假期服務進進暫行辦法, (Provisional wartime regulations for all levels of schools for service years, terms, and holidays). In *Guomin li* 國民曆 (National calendar), edited by Guomin Zhengfu Xingzhengyuan Jiaoyubu Bianli Weiyuanhui (Nanjing) 國民政府行政院教育部編曆委員會 (南京) (Editorial Committee of the Education Department of the Administrative Ministry [Nanjing]), 35. Nanjing, 1945.

Zhao Jingtong 趙景桐. *Linfen xian diwuci zhian qianghua yundong huibian* 臨汾縣第五次治安強化運動彙編 (Collected materials on the fifth law and order campaign in Linfen County). 1942.

"Zhonggong Jin-Ji-Yu qu Dangwei Xuanchuan Bu guanyu Jin-Ji-Yu qu yi nianlai xuanchuan gongzuo baogao 中共晉冀豫區黨委宣傳部關於晉冀豫區一年來宣傳工作報告" (Propaganda work report for the past year of the propaganda in the Shanxi-Hebei-Henan base area by the Communist Party Committee Propaganda Department of the Shanxi-Hebei-Henan Base Area). August 1941. In *Taihang dangshi ziliao huibian* 太行黨史資料會編, vol. 4, 599.

"Zhonggong Jin-Ji-Yu qu Dangwei guanyu fandui diren 'qingchao' 'dadang' de zhishi 中共晉冀豫區黨委關於反對敵人'清剿' '掃蕩'的指示" (Instructions of the Chinese Communist Shanxi-Hebei-Henan Party Committee in regard to opposing the enemy's "sweep up" and "attack"). March 2, 1942. In *Taihang dangshi ziliao huibian*, vol. 5 (2000): 139.

Zhongguo Guomindang Zhongyang Zhixing Weiyuanhui Xuanchuan Bu 中國國民黨中央執行委員會宣傳部 (Propaganda Department of the Nationalist Central Executive Committee, ed. *Guoli zhi renshi* 國曆之認識 (Understanding the national calendar). 1929.

Zuo Yuhe 左玉河. "Cong 'gaizheng shuo' dao 'fei jiuli': Yangli jiqi jieri zai minguo shiqi de yanbian 從 '改正朔' 到 '廢舊曆' – 陽曆及其節日在民國時期的演變" (From "Correcting the new moon [first day of the month]" to "Abandoning the old calendar": The evolution of the solar calendar and its holidays during the Republican period). *Minjian wenhua luntan* 民間文化論壇, no. 2 (2005): 62–68.

PART III

Living and Working with Provisioning

Currency, Salt, and Jute

CHAPTER 6

Preserving the Value of Fabi *during Nationalist China's Currency War with Japan*

PARKS M. COBLE

A well-functioning financial system requires a reasonably stable currency. By that measure the currency of wartime Nationalist China, the *fabi* 法幣, failed miserably. Faced with the loss of its tax revenue in the eastern provinces, unable to develop new financial resources in the interior, and attempting to fund a major war, the Nationalist government resorted to covering deficits by simply printing *fabi*, a formula that led to a weakening of the currency and hyperinflation. In 1941, for instance, government expenditures were over ¥10 billion but revenue just ¥1.3 billion, leaving a deficit of ¥8.7 billion, covered primarily by the printing press. As the value of these notes diminished, the government increased the issue, and the deficit soared to over ¥20 billion in 1943 and ¥1.1 trillion in 1945.[1] In total during the war, the official banks extended advances of ¥1,261,921 million to the government.[2]

As the currency weakened, commodity prices rose. The American economist Arthur Young served as a financial adviser to the Chiang Kai-shek government, working primarily with the Ministry of Finance and Central Bank of China. Young calculated the change in retail market prices in Free China (that part of China controlled by the Nationalist government) using January–June 1937 as the base of 1.0. By December 1941, when the Pacific War began with the Japanese attack on Pearl Harbor, it stood at 19.8. A twentyfold increase since the start of the war in 1937 was a serious issue but still one that could be managed. Yet after the Japanese overran Burma and further isolated Free China's economy, the rate of inflation increased more rapidly. By the end of 1943 the price index stood at 228 from the base of 1 in 1937. In the last two years of the war this deterioration accelerated geometrically, reaching 755 in December 1944, then 2,167 in June 1945, and a staggering 2,647 in August 1945. The loss of value of the Chinese currency during these eight years of conflict gravely weakened Free China. The foundation of a sound financial system was destroyed.[3]

The steady erosion of the value of the Chinese currency was particularly hard on those individuals receiving a salaried income, including military and civilian government employees. As was widely recognized, few could survive on their official salaries, leading to a massive increase in corruption and black market activities, as well as a sharp decline in morale.[4] Yet victory over Japan brought no peace dividend as China headed to civil war. The Nationalist government continued to prioritize military spending, while foreign trade and the domestic economy were slow to revive. The printing presses poured out more banknotes. After only a brief respite the inflationary situation worsened. In January 1946 in Shanghai the price index stood at over 1,600 (with January–June 1937 as a base of 1). A year later the price index in Shanghai stood at 8,177, and in January 1948, at 140,743. In July 1948 it reached 2,877,000 before the government abandoned *fabi*.[5]

Was the collapse in value of the *fabi* inevitable? Perhaps so, given the circumstances of wartime China. But it was a relatively new currency when the war erupted, having been created only a few months earlier in November 1935, when China replaced the silver standard with fiat currency. Many nations use semiautonomous institutions to regulate the money supply, such as the Federal Reserve System in the United States. From the start the Chinese yuan was not insulated from political control in any way. Decisions about the money supply were decided by political authorities without outside review. Many of the Shanghai bankers were concerned about the new political control. They remembered earlier attempts by Yuan Shikai and the warlord governments to use banknotes as a source of revenue. Zhang Jia'ao (Chang Kia-ngau 張嘉璈), who had been removed as general manager of the Bank of China in 1935, expressed these concerns and later noted that this had set the stage for China's wartime inflation. Financial officials, Zhang commented, had recommended that the Central Bank of China become a central reserve bank with capital subscribed by private banks and citizens as well as the government. It should be separated from the Ministry of Finance and made independent so that the supply of money would be supervised by representatives of private business. In this way the government would not be dependent on deficit financing through note issue.[6]

That was precisely what happened during the war. Whether China had an alternative in the midst of the massive Japanese invasion is perhaps another question. Yet even before July 7, 1937, the inflationary aspects of the *fabi* system became apparent. As Zhang Jia'ao noted, "The Central Bank never gained independent status, and no serious attempt was made to reorganize government finances. From the time when the new currency system came into operation in 1935 to the middle of 1937 the note issues of the four government banks increased from CNC (Chinese National Currency) $453 million to CNC $1,477 million. Only about half of this increase represented notes issued against silver surrendered."[7] Initially this inflation benefited China's economy by reversing the deflationary impact of the rise in silver prices. But in the process the foundation for wartime inflation had been laid.

War and the "Isolated Island" in Shanghai

China was still a semi-colonial country when Japan invaded in July 1937. The International Settlement in Shanghai, dominated by foreign imperialism, was the major center for Chinese banking, with the foreign concessions in Tianjin a secondary center. Foreign banks, such as the powerful Hong Kong and Shanghai Banking Corporation (HSBC), were protected not only by their location in the treaty ports, but also by extraterritoriality granted to most foreigners under the unequal treaties. All Chinese modern banks in Shanghai had their headquarters in the International Settlement, which afforded them a measure of autonomy from Chinese authorities.

The consequences of this situation became immediately apparent after the Marco Polo Bridge Incident on July 7, 1937. Although this is now recognized as the official start of the War of Resistance against Japan, all-out war really began with the Battle of Shanghai-Wusong on August 13, 1937. In the nearly five weeks that elapsed between these two events, many Chinese and foreigners alike chose to move their assets out of harm's way. Nanjing had made *fabi* convertible to hard currency, such as the British pound sterling and the American dollar and was determined to maintain this policy. During the period between July 7 and August 13, 1937, according to Japanese sources, an equivalent of ¥423 million in foreign exchange fled China. The holdings of British pounds by the government banks in Shanghai fell by 7 million in that period, close to one-third of their total holdings of sterling. Nanjing remained committed to keeping the *fabi* convertible even as the flight of capital accelerated.[8]

Once the fighting erupted in Shanghai, the government had to take action. On August 15 it imposed a moratorium of sorts on Chinese banks. Deposits were frozen and weekly withdrawals were capped at 5 percent of the credit balance to a maximum of ¥150. This had the impact of freezing up much of the banking system in Shanghai. The daily volume of checks cleared in the city's banking network dropped from 169 million items to only 33 million items. The activities of the Chinese private banks in Shanghai were significantly reduced.[9] The government had to introduce a process of intra-bank warrants to prevent the system from completely shutting down. Foreign banks continued to be shielded by extraterritoriality and could skirt most regulations.

After weeks of determined resistance by the Chinese forces, the Nationalist military was forced to retreat, eventually abandoning the capital in Nanjing and relocating military headquarters to Wuhan. When the latter fell in October 1938, along with Guangzhou, the government then moved to Chongqing, which served as the capital of Free China until after the war ended. Although the Chinese city of Shanghai and the Japanese sector of the foreign city were occupied by the Japanese military, much of the International Settlement and the French Concession remained unoccupied. This became the famed "isolated island" (*gudao* 孤島), a neutral area surrounded by Japanese-occupied territory. After the Chinese armies retreated, an odd calm developed in Shanghai as foreign residents tried to carry on as if the war were not happening. As one foreign employee of Standard Oil remembered, "Watching the war spread across China, while working in Shanghai's International Settlement in 1938, was an odd experience. The Settlement was 'neutral' territory; the war was 'out there.' We were close enough to the assorted chaos to know what was going on, but distant enough to be little affected in our day-to-day living."[10]

The Currency War

From 1938 until after the outbreak of the Pacific War in December 1941, the "isolated island" probably held the most unusual environment in which any financial system has ever functioned. China's modern banks remained open in the "isolated island," and the Chiang Kai-shek government decided to continue to make *fabi* convertible to foreign exchange in what is still a contested decision. In effect, China's financial center, the "isolated island," tried to operate as before, despite now being surrounded by an enemy-occupied zone. Chinese bankers were at the center of what was widely termed the "currency war" as competing regimes tried to force exclusive use of their currency.[11] As Japanese forces attempted to penetrate the foreign settlements, they and their Nationalist opponents would often resort to a "war of terror," in which the personal safety of bankers and their employees was at risk. This created an extremely dangerous and difficult environment for the Chinese bankers.

The Japanese proclaimed a "New Order in East Asia" and made control of the currency a key element of their program. But Japanese victory in the "currency war" was elusive for two major reasons. First, the Japanese-backed currencies were chronically underfunded; Japan simply had not provided sufficient capital for its entire enterprise in China. Although the *fabi* was plagued with similar problems, it would be many months into the war before it fell in value below the Japanese-backed currencies. Second, the Japanese effort on the Asian mainland was marred by disunity on the Japanese side. In North China the Imperial Army dominated. Its policies were an outgrowth of existing structures in Northeast

China (Manchukuo) and Hebei Province. By contrast, in Central and South China, the Imperial Navy tended to prevail, and Japanese institutions were slower to emerge. In North China the Japanese chose to establish a currency tied to the yen bloc. In Central China the Japanese delayed an attempt to do so until 1941. As one Japanese scholar observed, "The Central China Area Army did not attempt to set up its own bank or currency. … Japan had decided to regard north China as an extension of the Japanese homeland but to treat central and southern China as a foreign territory like Hongkong."[12]

In North China, Japan had a tradition of linking the area with the yen bloc. The Manchukuo Central Bank, established in 1932, issued yuan-denominated banknotes that linked to the yen at parity in 1935. Japanese also widely circulated the banknotes of the Tianjin branch of the Bank of Chosen (Korea) that were tied to the yen. After July 7, 1937, the Japanese first used banknotes of the Bank of Chosen to pay their bills but without providing adequate reserves, so the currency began to depreciate. Soon the Japanese North China Army sponsored a pro-Japanese regime in Beijing under Wang Kemin. In March 1938, this government established the Federal Reserve Bank (Zhongguo Lianhe Zhunbei Yinhang 中國聯合準備銀行; FRB), which is sometimes (more correctly) translated into English as the China Reserve Bank. The Beijing regime enlisted a number of prominent bankers to serve on the board of directors, including those from the Tianjin branches of the Bank of China and Bank of Communications, the Jincheng Bank, the Dalu Bank's Tianjin branch, and the East Hebei Bank. The Japanese began replacing the notes of the Bank of Chosen, which they had been issuing with those of the FRB. Tight restrictions made it difficult to exchange the notes for foreign currency, even yen.[13]

In June 1938 the Wang Kemin regime mandated that everyone in its jurisdiction exchange the old *fabi* notes of the Chiang regime for the new FRB notes. They were permitted one year to do so. In fact, because the bank issued excessive amounts of currency, few wanted these notes. Often they required a 30 percent discount when exchanged in Tianjin.[14] John Hunter Boyle observed, "The currency, which had only nominal backing, fell in value as huge inflationary printings swelled the volume in circulation to higher and higher levels each month." Even Japanese businessmen disliked the currency since it was difficult to exchange it for yen to remit to Japan. Vast amounts of *fabi* were hoarded in the foreign concessions in Tianjin and widely used in areas outside of direct Japanese control.[15] As late as the spring of 1939 the FRB notes were still worth only 74 percent of the value of *fabi*.[16] Meanwhile, Nationalist Party authorities forbade any use of the FRB currency, placing Chinese banks squarely in the "crossfire" in the north.[17]

The Japanese military in Central and South China was much slower to set up a China-based bank. Initially it simply used military yen issued by Japanese banks, a currency that was not convertible even to Japanese domestic yen. This military yen was accepted in China only when backed by Japanese military force. As much as 600 million yen of this currency was in circulation in China by the summer of 1940.[18] In May 1939 a Japanese-backed client state in Nanjing established the Huaxing Commercial Bank (Huaxing Shangye Yinhang 華興商業銀行), but it lacked adequate reserves and its currency was not widely accepted. It was not made convertible with the yen but instead with the *fabi*. Only with the establishment of the Wang Jingwei regime would an effort be made to establish a viable currency for Central and South China.[19] For a variety of reasons, however, the Japanese establishment was slow to give full support to the new Wang government and its institutions. Not until January 1941 did the Nanjing puppet regime set up the Central Reserve Bank (Zhongyang Chubei Yinhang 中央儲備銀行; CRB), established in Nanjing with Zhou Fohai (周佛海) as director. The former Central Bank of China building on the Bund in Shanghai had been earlier seized by the Japanese, and this became the Shanghai branch of the CRB. Eventually the bank would have forty branches with a total of 1,600 employees. Although it was set up as a "Chinese institution," it had forty Japanese advisers to provide "assistance," a feature common to virtually all of the agencies of the client regimes set up by the Japanese.[20]

Each regime—Wang Kemin's in Beijing, Wang Jingwei's in Nanjing, and Chiang Kai-shek's in Chongqing—tried to get its currency accepted as widely as possible. Together with a number of minor currencies, the result was a "currency war," with Chinese bankers in the crossfire. As all sides attempted to ensure that their currency become dominant, one major initial advantage of the *fabi* was that it could be exchanged for foreign currencies, including the British pound and the American dollar.

Keeping *Fabi* Convertible

At the start of the conflict the Nationalist government decided that to preserve the prestige of the *fabi* it must continue to make it convertible into foreign exchange. At great cost in the first eight months of the war it tried to keep the value steady at the prewar rate of one yuan to U.S.$0.30. The Chiang government expended large amounts of foreign exchange to hold this rate until March 1938.[21] This policy was controversial at the time and even today provokes arguments among economic historians. Both the International Settlement in Shanghai and the foreign concessions in Tianjin were completely surrounded by Japanese-held territory, yet in effect they continued to operate as open financial markets. The Japanese apparently took advantage of this situation. A 2003 study by Qi Chunfeng (齊春風) argued that the Japanese collected *fabi* through trade with Free China and then used this to purchase foreign exchange in Shanghai.[22] Even at the time it was widely believed that the Wang Kemin bank in North China supposedly collected a large quantity of *fabi* that the Japanese converted to foreign exchange in Shanghai. The *Bankers' Weekly* (*Yinhang zhoubao* 銀行週報) warned that this was creating a dangerous situation in which China's foreign reserves could end up in enemy hands.[23]

In fact, the policy proved so costly that the Chiang government on March 13, 1938, announced very strict restrictions on foreign exchange. The Chinese government could not prevent the foreign banks from trading in *fabi*, so a disparity developed between the legal exchange rate and actual trading rate of *fabi*. China thus had to provide additional funds for foreign exchange, even though much of this might have ended up in Japanese hands. Meanwhile, the Japanese and their client regimes found the holding of *fabi* useful since it was a convertible currency while the puppet notes were not.[24]

Was this a sound policy? Chou Shun-hsin, in his study of wartime inflation, has argued that it was not: "Much of the trouble in the international sector resulted from the attempt on the part of the government to maintain the external value of the Chinese currency at a high level. The absurdity of this foreign-exchange policy was particularly obvious during the early stages of the inflation, when the Chinese government tried to maintain the external value of its currency by draining on its meager exchange reserves without the help of effective trade and exchange controls."[25] Others have argued that the open market in Shanghai undoubtedly served the interests of the Japanese in the short run. They used the foreign exchange acquired through *fabi* to serve as reserves for their own currencies and to finance the entire Japanese enterprise in China.[26] Some Chinese economists also felt that maintaining foreign exchange convertibility at Shanghai and Tianjin under wartime conditions primarily served the interests of the imperialist powers who controlled these areas, not the Chinese nation. Concerned that the Japanese might be gaining foreign exchange by acquiring *fabi*, the Nationalist government attempted to reduce this problem. In early 1938 it ordered local governments in the occupied areas and nearby to issue their own currency to replace *fabi*, thinking that this would prevent the Japanese from acquiring the convertible currency. But such an approach undermined the unity of the currency system and the strength of the *fabi* itself.[27]

Despite these concerns, most in the wartime government believed that defending the currency was crucial to China's success in the war. As the noted economist Ma Yinchu (馬寅初) wrote in March 1939, "The enemy knows that if it wants to destroy our country, it must first destroy our *fabi*." As long as *fabi* were widely used in the occupied areas, Chongqing felt, the Japanese could not establish complete economic control.[28] One fear was that a loss of faith in the currency in the occupied areas would cause the local population to abandon it and accept the puppet notes. This might result in a flood of *fabi* notes back into Free China, drastically increasing the money supply and inflation.[29] H. H. Kung (Kong Xiangxi 孔祥熙), then president of the Executive Yuan, telegrammed the American State Department in December 1938, urging support for the *fabi*, arguing that if one of the Japanese puppet currencies displaced it, "the Japanese could both finance thereby their political, financial and economic enterprises and could exert a strangle hold upon the foreign and Chinese activities to the extent that their control could be maintained."[30]

Arthur Young, who served as a financial adviser to the Chinese government, was a strong advocate of convertibility, and he defended this approach in his many writings. In the competition between the Wang Kemin currency and the *fabi*, he noted, the convertibility of the latter "was an outstanding advantage."[31] Young maintained that keeping the *fabi* convertible strengthened China's military position in the war. "The vast inland areas away from [Japanese-held] cities and ports were mostly held by guerrillas," he noted. They used the Chongqing currency, so "exports from this hinterland, even though sold through occupied ports, had to be ultimately paid in Chinese currency." The viability of the *fabi* weakened Japan's ability to exploit and control the "occupied" areas.[32]

But in a study written twenty-five years later, Young acknowledged the high cost of this policy. Operations were expensive, he admitted. "[It was] hardly surprising any sizable sales for market support should pain the Finance Minister and lead him to worry whether the foreign currency assets were going down a rat hole." Still Young did not change his fundamental view that this policy was correct and that exchange had not been accumulated by the Japanese. In April 1939 he had become aware that an official in the Japanese Embassy had apparently told American consul Horace H. Smith that the Japanese Yokohama Specie Bank had been converting *fabi* funds it acquired through control of customs revenue into foreign exchange as rapidly as it could do so without disturbing the market. But Young insisted he had counterevidence to dispute the significance of this claim.[33]

In 1958 Young talked in Tokyo with Japanese bankers who had been in China during this period. They believed that the chief buyers of foreign exchange using *fabi* in China during the 1938–1941 period had been Chinese, not Japanese, including many insiders. Young remained supportive of the Chiang government and named no names, but he acknowledged that "this aspect of the war period was least credible to China."[34] Chinese bankers may have been among the insiders. Private bankers, such Zhou Zuomin (周作民) of the Jincheng Bank, sent representatives to Hong Kong to buy foreign exchange after restrictions were put into place in Shanghai.[35]

Young acknowledged that he perhaps pressed too hard to get H. H. Kung to supply funds to cover foreign exchange. Little money was available. But he still concluded that "without the stabilization operations of 1938–1941, there is grave doubt whether China could have avoided financial collapse during the war, perhaps before Pearl Harbor."[36] But if Japan benefited from having *fabi* be convertible, many Japanese in China, especially military and intelligence commanders, were not convinced. They felt that attacking *fabi* was essential to destroying the Chinese government itself. They committed their government to a policy of overthrowing the currency on July 13, 1938.[37]

Both before and after Pearl Harbor, a number of American advisers went to China. Some, like Arthur Young, spent many years in China, but most simply made short visits there to dish out "advice." As China was in desperate need of foreign support, it had to give these foreign visitors a hearing. In retrospect, recommendations by American advisers, both those based in Washington or even (like Arthur Young) stationed in Chongqing, were not very imaginative. Perhaps this is not surprising. Although World War II had a significant impact on the United States, the American economy tended to operate along traditional lines, with the United States benefitting from increased war spending, which finally brought America out of the Great Depression. Perhaps American advisers would have had a deeper appreciation for the reality of China's circumstances had America found itself in a situation like China's. If the Nazis had invaded the United States and overrun the Eastern seaboard but somehow Manhattan and Wall Street had remained unoccupied, the situation would have paralleled that of China. Under those conditions would American financial officials have found that maintaining the global position of the dollar by keeping it convertible in New York was the highest priority? A radical rethinking of the American financial system would have been the first order of business. Even advisers like Young, who were in China, never quite seem to appreciate how completely the old imperialist order had been destroyed in East Asia.

Ultimately the Chinese government could not hold the line. The costs of converting *fabi* to foreign currencies was simply too much of a drain. Moreover, the Chongqing government (as well as the Beijing and Nanjing client regimes) printed banknotes to cover government deficits, leading to inflation in all zones. Wang Kemin's FRB expanded note issue by 450 percent from 1938 to 1941. But the *fabi* also lost value as China bled foreign exchange through Shanghai while continuing to print more currency. Despite the foreign exchange restrictions, some support from Britain, and to a lesser extent the United States, the exchange value of the *fabi* yuan fell from just over U.S.$0.29 in July 1937 to only $0.06 in December 1940. The flood of printed currencies created inflation in both occupied and Free China, but by late 1940 the value of the FRB notes surpassed that of *fabi* notes. During 1941 the notes of the Beijing regime "became the chief currency of occupied north China," noted Arthur N. Young.[38]

After Pearl Harbor

The situation changed drastically after the Japanese attack on Pearl Harbor. The neutrality of Shanghai ended, and Japanese forces quickly overran the "isolated island." Victory was theirs in the currency war, at least for the time being. When the "isolated island Shanghai" era came to an end with Pearl Harbor, the Wang Jingwei notes were still not popular. Arthur Young suggested that *fabi* notes far outnumbered CRB notes in late 1941. But the Wang regime acted quickly to end the role of *fabi*. The Wang government decreed that after June 1, 1942, *fabi* would no longer be considered legal tender and must be exchanged for CRB notes by that date.[39]

The CRB banknotes had been set at par with the *fabi* notes prior to December 1941, but the Wang government now mandated a 2:1 ratio in favor of its currency. All *fabi* being held in Shanghai and the occupied areas suddenly lost half of their value, a move that further alienated the local population and resulted in increasing inflation. The population of the old "isolated island" now found its living circumstances much worse under the occupation regime. Zhou Fohai later admitted that this had caused tremendous losses for the local population.[40]

The Wang regime had wanted its currency to be the sole Japanese-backed issue in China, but disunity among the Japanese prevented this from happening. The FRB in Beijing, which had been set up by the Wang Kemin government, was backed by the Japanese Army in the north. The Wang Jingwei regime fought a long and unsuccessful battle to assert its authority over the north. The Beijing currency, which was tied to the yen, was already well established, and Japanese authorities in the north refused to replace the currency with that of the CRB. The two regions became two separate currency zones—North China in the yen bloc, Central China using the yuan. For those traveling between zones, the exchange rate in 1943 was 100 yuan (Nanjing) to 18 yen (Beijing). Nanjing had difficulty holding this rate and eventually in March 1944 restricted conditions for exchange between the two currencies. This situation inhibited trade between North and

Central China in the occupied areas. Japan's "New Order in East Asia" was a dismal economic failure.[41]

The military yen, which the Japanese military had used to pay its bills in China, remained a common currency. Essentially unsecured, it could not even be converted to regular yen to be remitted to Japan. People in the occupied area had little choice but to accept these notes when the Japanese military asked. The CRB tried without success to eliminate the currency, indicative of the broad failure of the Wang Jingwei government to establish any real authority independent of the Japanese military. Finally, when Japan permitted the Wang government to declare war on the Allied Powers in January 1943, Nanjing requested that as a co-belligerent it should be allowed to replace the military yen. The Japanese finally agreed in April 1943 to phase the currency out over a gradual period, but in reality, large quantities remained in circulation until the end of the war.[42]

Resentment of Shanghai by Those in Free China

Conditions in Shanghai deteriorated over the last years of the war after it became part of the occupied zone. Yet few in Free China felt any sympathy for the now occupied Shanghai and its people. In the four-and-one-half years from the Marco Polo Bridge Incident to Pearl Harbor conditions in Shanghai had generally been much better than in the interior, at least for the wealthy elite. Particularly in 1938–1940 the economy of the "isolated island" had actually been rather vigorous. Many businessmen relocated their factories and workshops to the neutral foreign zone from the Chinese areas. By the fall of 1938, the "isolated island" had become a bustling center of economic activity. It was surrounded by a war-scarred and devastated hinterland, but the "isolated island" experienced an economic "flourishing" fueled by the influx of businesses from surrounding areas. While total economic activity in the greater Shanghai area might have declined, within "island Shanghai" a boom of sorts occurred. Production levels in such diverse areas as cotton and silk weaving and flour milling in Shanghai in 1939 were equal to or greater than levels in 1936. And some areas, such as wool weaving, paper manufacture, and machinery production, increased significantly. By the end of 1938 over 4,700 factories in the "island" employed 237,000 workers.[43]

Prices for industrial commodities soared because overall production declined in China. Those businessmen who were able to establish factories in the "isolated island" generally made significant profits. And the influx of refugees seeking shelter from the fighting provided a ready source of cheap labor. By 1940 an estimated 780,000 refugees helped swell the population of the "isolated island" to over 4 million. The number of commercial businesses increased to meet the demands of the influx of people and because many merchants had relocated.[44]

Meanwhile in Free China, the economy became more and more isolated. Moreover, in 1939 Japan began a massive campaign of bombing of the wartime capital, Chongqing, as well as other cities in the interior. Patriotic industrialists who had relocated had to move facilities into caves to prevent being bombed. Thus, a sharp contrast developed between their hardships and the "flourishing" conditions in Shanghai. Those in the interior imagined, and not without reason, a life of leisure by the elite in Shanghai. The city already had a reputation for prostitution, drugs, and wild night life, activities that no doubt increased in wartime. This resentment of Shanghai became increasingly vocal. Even Chiang Kai-shek, in a radio address in May 1939, lashed out at those who lived in Shanghai while patriotic Chinese were sacrificing to save China.[45] Leftist intellectuals who were associated with the National Salvation Movement were even less kind. An article in *Zhiye shenghuo* (職業生活) in April 1939, for example, accused the capitalists in Shanghai of hoarding funds in the imagined security of the "isolated island," while the interior desperately needed capital. As Japanese bombs fell on Chongqing, those in Free China certainly felt they were the patriotic citizens, while the Shanghai elite hid in the foreign zone.[46]

For many in Free China the flagging attempt before Pearl Harbor to shore up the foreign exchange value of the *fabi* primarily benefited the financial structure of Shanghai. Chinese and Western merchants in the "isolated island" wanted a convertible currency to send money out of China rather than to invest in Free China. It seemed that the Chiang government sought to prop up the old imperialist structure of the treaty ports rather than adapt to the new reality of the war. The hostility of those in the interior to the people living in occupied areas would also play a significant role in the aftermath of Japanese surrender. One of the great failures of the Nationalist government was its botched takeover of areas such as Shanghai, particularly in economic terms. Peace should have given the government an opportunity to stabilize the currency and reinvigorate the economy. But resentment of the elites who stayed in occupied China helped fuel a "botched liberation" that led to worsening hyperinflation and economic decline. Chiang Kai-shek may have won the war against Japan, but he lost the peace.

End Game: The Erosion of the *Fabi* in the Last Years of the War

In what turned out to be the final years of the war, the value of the *fabi* eroded at an accelerated rate. Despite becoming one of the "Big Four" Allied powers, Free

China was increasingly isolated from foreign connections. Some essential military supplies were flown in over "the Hump," but actual trade was virtually impossible even when the Burma Road reopened late in the game. But the heaviest blow to the stability of the *fabi* was dealt by the Japanese when they launched their massive Ichigo campaign in April 1944. Although the Allies were winning elsewhere, in mainland China the Japanese had the upper hand.

The Ichigo offensive was actually the largest military campaign of the war on the Asian mainland. The Japanese mobilized five hundred thousand troops, approximately 80 percent of the China Expeditionary Army. Operation Ichigo had two goals. The first was to capture the American air bases in China and the second, to secure an interior corridor to link North China, Manchukuo, and Korea with Japanese possessions in Southeast Asia. The Japanese wished to establish a direct rail link among Southeast Asia, Beijing, and Korea. Operation Ichigo was an astounding Japanese success. In phase one of Ichigo 140,000 Japanese forces crossed the Yellow River and swiftly captured Luoyang. In phase two, they attacked Hunan, capturing Changsha on June 18, 1944. Chinese forces put up a spirited defense at Hengyang but were finally defeated by the Japanese on August 8. These losses were an enormous blow to Chiang's standing as the leader of Nationalist China.[47] In early September 1944 Japanese forces entered Guangxi Province. In all the Japanese would capture the American airbases in Guilin, Liuzhou, and Nanning.[48] Japan moved forces north out of Vietnam to link up. Fuzhou fell without resistance on October 5, 1944.[49]

The Ichigo campaign is usually studied in terms of its impact on the decline in prestige of the Chiang Kai-shek government, Chiang's relations with the United States, and the balance of power between the Communists and the Nationalists. Often overlooked is the reality that Ichigo had a significant economic impact on Free China and the Chongqing government. The Japanese victory was a serious blow to the finances of the Chiang regime. As Wang Qisheng noted, "The Japanese north-south corridor cut in half the area under Nationalist rule. One-fourth of China's manufacturing base was destroyed. Revenue dropped sharply because of the loss of manufacturing and because of the Japanese occupation of grain resource areas, aggravating an already desperate financial situation."[50] Chongqing's revenues decreased at a time when military expenses increased with the intensity of Japanese attacks. Hyperinflation gained momentum.

Arthur N. Young wrote that "beginning late in 1944 the price rise became definitely faster. A shock to confidence resulted from the strong Japanese drive in the second half of that year." By the spring of 1945 the rate of inflation was almost 25 percent a month, which meant, Young argued, that China had passed "the almost irreversible stage of hyperinflation, and to financial collapse before war's end."[51] As noted above, Young had calculated the commodity price index in Free China using January–June 1937 as a base of 1. In December 1943 it had reached 228. The first six years of war had seen a serious decline in the value of the *fabi*. But with Ichigo the rate of decline increased geometrically. In December 1944 it reached 755, in June 1945 it reached 2,167, and in August 1945, 2,647.[52]

Even at a practical, everyday level, inflation made life difficult. The government strongly resisted creating larger-denomination banknotes, feeling that this would be psychologically damaging. For a long time, the largest bill was the ¥100 note. As hyperinflation increased, people had to carry large bundles of cash for even simple purchases at the market. And printing banknotes was costly. Most were produced in the United States and flown over "the Hump." The expense in producing large quantities of small-denomination notes was extraordinary. The United States granted China a $500 million loan in 1942, but fully $55 million went for banknotes, paper, and ink.[53]

Holding the Foreign Exchange Value of *Fabi*

Despite the rapid drop in the purchasing power of the *fabi* within China, the Chongqing government attempted to maintain its foreign exchange rate. In August 1941 Minister of Finance H. H. Kung decreed that the official exchange rate between the yuan and the U.S. dollar would be ¥18.8 to one dollar, later changed to 20:1. T. V. Soong (Song Ziwen 宋子文), a key financial official and brother of Madam Chiang Kai-shek, had advised against attempting to keep a fixed rate, but Kung persisted, supported by Chiang or perhaps dictated by Chiang.[54] This rate was unrealistic even when it was set and became even less so as inflation worsened. The black-market rate reached 600:1 in 1944. When the American military was building air bases and facilities in China, it had to pay at the official rate so that the costs of even moderate facilities seemed exorbitant. In early 1944 the U.S. Army calculated that at the official exchange rate, the cost of materials for building the air bases in China, including the base for long-range bombers near Chengdu, was 8–10 times what the cost would have been in the United States itself.[55]

Chiang Kai-shek could be notoriously stubborn.[56] When he decided on a policy, it could be difficult to get him to change his mind. Early on during the "currency war," he seems to have become convinced that the value of the *fabi* in the exchange market was a symbol of the strength of Free China, a sign that it was stronger than the puppet governments. Even when the reality of the huge gap between the official rate and the black-market rate of the *fabi* created major complications, he was loath to budge on the issue.

Unfortunately, this policy led to serious tensions between the United States and Chongqing and made American leaders wary of providing additional financial support to shore up the *fabi*. American journalist Theodore White wrote that "the extortionate exchange rate was known to every American GI in China, who felt that America was being swindled in the most scandalous and blatant fashion." White concluded that the Chongqing government had really shot itself in the foot with this approach, undercutting American support for Chiang by the end of the war.[57] Arthur Young agreed with this assessment, noting that the artificial exchange rate created a situation in which "it appeared that Uncle Sam was being taken for a ride."[58]

In early 1944 Washington sent Ted Acheson to negotiate the issue of the exchange rates in relation to the costs of building the American air bases. Acheson offered a rate of 100:1, much better than the official 20:1 but still well above the black-market rate. Kung adamantly refused to consider this on the grounds that it would undercut the value of the Chinese yuan. The U.S. Army retaliated by paying the American military in China in U.S. dollars, which theoretically would be sent home but which many exchanged on the black market. In early 1944 the army estimated its monthly expenses in China to be $17 million, but only $6 million was spent at the official rate.[59]

After it became clear that the United States and Britain were virtually granting their citizens the right to go to the black market, Kung relented a bit and gave diplomats a 50 percent supplementary raise, still far from the black-market price. The "fleecing of foreigners" alienated those who had been most supportive of helping China. Missionaries found that the dollars donated by American church groups for China relief, for instance, purchased little when converted at the official rate. Eventually Kung allowed missionary groups to get the supplement as well, but everyone had to go through the official Central Bank of China to get the rates. This strengthened the foreign reserve holdings of China at the expense of its trading partners and generated much ill will.[60]

Among those alienated was U.S. secretary of the treasury Henry Morgenthau, who had been one of the early supporters of China before Pearl Harbor. Morgenthau blamed Chiang for the problem. In a memorandum of June 8, 1944, to President Roosevelt, Morgenthau suggested that "the difficulties of financing our military program in China began, you recall, at the Cairo Conference, where the Chinese leaders request a $1 billion loan." He had advised FDR to deny the loan and noted that "the Generalissimo in January threatened that the Government of China would not make any further material contribution to the war effort, including construction of military works, unless we agree to grant the loan, or alternatively, to purchase Chinese currency at the official rate of exchange for our military expenditures." This stance infuriated Morgenthau, who noted that the value of the Chinese yuan, which had been U.S.$0.30 before the war, had fallen to 5 cents in 1941, although the former was still the official rate. But at the time of the memo to FDR the black-market rate for the yuan was only one-half of one cent.[61] Morgenthau believed that Chiang was bluffing and that the United States should continue to deny the new loan. This stance by Chiang thus alienated two key leaders in Washington against the backdrop of the Stilwell issue, which had strained relations. Stilwell had been the highest American military representative in China but was recalled when Chiang demanded his removal.

Conclusion

The collapse of the *fabi* during the war was a major disaster for the Nationalist government. It undermined the morale of the military and government bureaucracy, those who were tied to fixed salaries. Corruption among military officers increased while ordinary soldiers suffered. Civilian officials could not live on their official salaries. Could this have been avoided or at least mitigated? Under wartime conditions perhaps the Chongqing government could not have maintained the stability of its currency; no policies could have been successful. Yet in retrospect it seems that many actions by the Nationalist government exacerbated the difficulties it faced. The attempt to keep the currency convertible in Shanghai when the city was an "isolated island" of neutrality surrounded by the Japanese was difficult and unlikely worth the cost. True, Chongqing found itself in a "currency war" with two other regimes (both controlled by the Japanese military). But, in fact, even though only the Chongqing government survived the war, all three regimes lost the currency war. None of them had sufficient revenue to cover expenses, and they printed money. All of the currencies suffered from rapidly deteriorating value.

Chiang Kai-shek seemed to have locked into maintaining an artificially high exchange value for the yuan, ignoring the difference between the official rate and the black-market rate. In the process he alienated many in the American government and society, including those who had been strong supporters of Chiang in the past. The United States was the only power capable of providing meaningful financial support to China after the war. But at war's end many in the American civilian and military leadership were angry with the Chiang government. Whatever the gains of a favorable exchange rate, they were more than offset by the loss of support in America. The large loans Chiang sought were generally not forthcoming until he had retreated to Taiwan and the Korean War changed the political climate in the United States. The defeat of the *fabi* thus contributed to the military and political demise of the Nationalist government.

Notes

1. Chang, *The Inflationary Spiral*, 49.

2. Young, *China's Wartime Finance and Inflation*, 12, 15. In her study Lin Meili gives slightly different figures: for 1943 the deficit was 41,943,703,152; for 1944, 138,726,128,798; and for 1945, 1, 202, 205, 543, 309. See Lin, *Kangzhan shiqi de huobi zhanzheng*, 38.

3. Young, *China's Wartime Finance and Inflation*, 152.

4. Coble, *China's War Reporters*, 106.

5. Adapted from Chang, *The Inflationary Spiral*, 372.

6. Ibid., 8.

7. Ibid.

8. Li, "An Alternative View on Occupation Policy," p. 90.

9. Ibid., 90–91; Chou, *The Chinese Inflation*, 119. See also Zhang, "'Ba-yi-san' Shiqi de Shanghai Yinhang Gonghui," 118–149.

10. Sherwood, *Fond Memories of a Young Man in Old China*, 191.

11. The definitive study of the "currency war" is Lin, *Kangzhan shiqi de huobi zhanzheng*.

12. Nakamura, "The Yen Bloc," 179.

13. Ibid., 171–179; Li, "An Alternative View on Occupation Policy," 138–145; *Tōa* 11, no. 3 (March 1938): 64–66. For details on the East Hebei regime, see Coble, *Facing Japan*, 272–273. See also Yang, "Guanyu wei Zhongguo lianhe junbei yinhang de jianwen."

14. Nakamura, "The Yen Bloc," 171–179, 190; Li, "An Alternative View on Occupation Policy," 138–145; Coble, "Chinese Bankers in the Crossfire," 164–165.

15. Boyle, *China and Japan at War*, 98; Tamagna, *Banking and Finance in China*, 309–311; Kimura, *Jihenka no Shina kin'yū oyobi kin'yū kikan*, 59–61; *Tōa* 11, no. 3 (March 1938): 66.

16. Ji, *A History of Modern Shanghai Banking*, 212.

17. Chongqing Shi Dang'an Guan, *Silian zhongchu shiliao*, 1:410–411.

18. Tamagna, *Banking and Finance in China*, 245–246; Nakamura, "The Yen Bloc," 190; Barnett, *Economic Shanghai*, 140; Shou, *Zhanshi Zhongguo de yinhang*, 74.

19. Tamagna, *Banking and Finance in China*, 317–319; Lieu, *The Silk Industry of China*, 419–420.

20. Tamagna, *Banking and Finance in China*, 324; Shou, *Zhanshi Zhongguo de yinhang*, 75–77; Barnett, *Economic Shanghai*, 25; Yao and Shen, "Wangwei Zhongyang chubei yinhang shimo," 240; Hu, "Wosuo zhidao de Wangwei Zhongyang chubei yinhang," 155. The new bank drew in and replaced the old Huaxing banknotes.

21. Young, *China's Wartime Finance and Inflation*, 153.

22. Qi, "Kangzhan shiqi da houfang yu lunxian qujian de fabi liudong," 137–169.

23. *Yinhang zhoubao* 22, no. 31 (August 9, 1938): 3.

24. Tamagna, *Banking and Finance in China*, 271–275; Nakamura, "The Yen Bloc," 178–181; Barnett, *Economic Shanghai*, 121, 142–143.

25. Chou, *The Chinese Inflation*, 13.

26. Barnett, *Economic Shanghai*, 112–113; Yin, "Waihui tongzhi xin zhengce zhi jiantao," 19.

27. Lin, *Kangzhan shiqi de huobi zhanzheng*, 65–69.

28. Li, "An Alternative View on Occupation Policy," 141–142; Ma, *Zhanshi jingji lunwen ji*, 197; *Foreign Relations of the United States*, "Re Currency Situation in North China," PRO.FO 371/23445 F/806/75/10; Arthur N. Young Papers, Hoover Institution, Box 68, Memo of March 31, 1941; Zhu, "Sannian lai di wo jian de huobi zhan," 485–488.

29. Lin, *Kangzhan shiqi de huobi zhanzheng*, 55.
30. Cited in *Foreign Relations of the United States*, 1938, 4:113.
31. Young, *China's Wartime Finance and Inflation*, 169.
32. Ibid., 235.
33. Ibid., 236.
34. Ibid., 238.
35. Lin, *Kangzhan shiqi de huobi zhanzheng*, 53.
36. Young, *China's Wartime Finance and Inflation*, 239.
37. Lin, *Kangzhan shiqi de huobi zhanzheng*, 108.
38. Young, *China and the Helping Hand*, 158; Nakamura, "The Yen Bloc," 181; Barnett, *Economic Shanghai*, 121–125, 133–135.
39. Shou, *Zhanshi Zhongguo de yinhang*, 78–79; Young, *China's Wartime Finance and Inflation*, 180.
40. Ke-wen Wang, "Collaborators and Capitalists," 47; Hinder, *Life and Labour in Shanghai*, 46.
41. Office of Strategic Services, *Programs of Japan in China*, 124–126.
42. Barnett, *Economic Shanghai*, 138; Tamagna, *Banking and Finance in China*, 324–326; Office of Strategic Services, *Programs of Japan in China*, 124; Young, *China's Wartime Finance and Inflation*, 183–186; 366; Yao and Shen, "Wangwei Zhongyang chubei yinhang shimo," 245–246, 253. Central Reserve Bank notes increased much faster than this during the same period.
43. An index of industrial output in Shanghai in 1939 (with 1936 equal to 100) shows cotton textile production at 104.5; silk textiles at 116.8; flour milling at 112.1; wool cloth at 164.8, rubber decreasing to 42.1; machinery at 121.1; and paper at 242.5. See Jiang, "Shanghai lunxian qianqi de 'gudao fanrong,'" 25. See also Lieu, *The Silk Industry of China*, 259; *Yinhang zhoubao* 22, no. 23 (June 14, 1938): 4, 22; no. 39 (October 4, 1938): 3; Tang Zhenchang, *Shanghai shi*, 800–803; Masuda, *Shina senso keizai no kenkyu*, 43.
44. Lu and Fang, *Minguo shehui jingji shi*, 693–698; Wei, "Shanghai 'gudao jingji fanrong' shimo," 109.
45. Barnett, *Economic Shanghai*, 129–130; Yuda Hua fangzhi ziben jituan shiliao bianji zu, *Yuda Hua fangzhi ziben jituan shiliao*, 337–343.
46. *Zhiye shenghuo* 1, no. 1 (April 15, 1939): 2.
47. Preston and Partridge, *British Documents on Foreign Affairs*, 7:365.
48. Lary, *The Chinese People at War*, 154–155.
49. Preston and Partridge, *British Documents on Foreign Affairs*, 7:468, 471, 489, 504–505; Zhongguo Renmin Kangri Zhanzheng Jinian Guan, *Kangzhan jishi*, 218–221.
50. Qisheng Wang, "The Battle for Hunan," 403.
51. Young, *China's Wartime Finance and Inflation*, 141.
52. Ibid., 152.
53. Ibid., 160–161.
54. Young, *Cycle of Cathay*, 241.
55. *Foreign Relations of the United States, 1944*, vol. 6: *China*, 843.
56. Perhaps the most famous example of Chiang Kai-shek's stubbornness was his detention under house arrest of General Zhang Xueliang, who had kidnapped Chiang in the Xi'an Incident of December 1936. Upon Zhang's return to Nanjing as an act of good faith, Chiang had him placed under house arrest. This continued after the war against Japan and later when Chiang retreated to Taiwan. Zhang was finally allowed to leave Taiwan in 1993 for Hawaii.
57. White and Jacoby, *Thunder out of China*, 115–116.

58. Young, *Cycle of Cathay*, 241.
59. *Foreign Relations of the United States, 1944*, vol. 6: *China*, 853.
60. Preston and Partridge, *British Documents on Foreign Affairs*, 7:284, 306.
61. *Foreign Relations of the United States, 1944*, vol. 6: *China*, 928–929.

Bibliography

Archives and Manuscript Collections

Arthur N. Young Papers, Hoover Institution on War, Revolution, and Peace, Stanford, Calif.
Public Records Office, Great Britain.

Newspapers and Periodicals Cited as Primary Sources

Tōa 東亜 (East Asia)
Yinhang zhoubao 銀行週報 (Bankers' weekly)
Zhiye shenghuo 職業生活 (Professional life)

References

Barnett, Robert W. *Economic Shanghai: Hostage to Politics, 1937–1941*. New York: Institute of Pacific Relations, 1941.

Boyle, John Hunter. *China and Japan at War: The Politics of Collaboration*. Stanford, Calif.: Stanford University Press, 1972.

Chang Kia-ngau. *The Inflationary Spiral: The Experience in China, 1939–1950*. Cambridge, Mass.: MIT Press, 1958.

Chongqing Shi Dang'an Guan 重慶市檔案館 (Chongqing Municipal Archives), Chongqing Shi Renmin Yinhang Jinrong Yanjiusuo 重慶市人民銀行金融研究所 (Finance Research Office of the Chongqing People's Bank of China), ed. *Silian zhongchu shiliao* 四聯總處史料 (Materials on the history of the Joint Four Banks General Office), vol. 1. Beijing: Dang'an chubanshe, 1993.

Chou, Shun-hsin. *The Chinese Inflation, 1937–1945*. New York: Columbia University Press, 1963.

Coble, Parks M. *China's War Reporters: The Legacy of Resistance against Japan*. Cambridge, Mass.: Harvard University Press, 2015.

———. "Chinese Bankers in the Crossfire, 1937–1945." In *China Reconstructs*, edited by Cindy Yik-Yi Chu and Ricardo K. S. Mak. Lanham, Md.: University Press of America, 2003.

———. *Facing Japan: Chinese Politics and Japanese Imperialism, 1931–1937*. Cambridge, Mass.: Council on East Asian Studies, 1991.

Foreign Relations of the United States: Diplomatic Papers. Great Britain: Public Records Office. PRO.FO 371/23445 F/806/75/10.

Hinder, Eleanor. *Life and Labour in Shanghai: A Decade of Labour and Social Administration in the International Settlement*. New York: Institute of Pacific Relations, 1944.

Hu Xuantong 胡宣同. "Wosuo zhidao de Wangwei Zhongyang chubei yinhang 我所知道的汪偽中央儲備銀行" (The Wang Jingwei puppet Central Reserve Bank that I knew). *Shanghai wenshi ziliao xuanji* 上海文史資料選集 (Shanghai literature and history), no. 33 (1980): 106–116.

Ji, Zhaojin. *A History of Modern Shanghai Banking: The Rise and Decline of China's Finance Capitalism*. Armonk, N.Y.: M. E. Sharpe, 2003.

Jiang Duo 姜鐸. "Shanghai lunxian qianqi de 'gudao fanrong' 上海淪陷前期的孤島繁榮" (The "flourishing isolated island" of the first period of occupied Shanghai). *Jingji xueshu ziliao* 經濟學術資料 (Materials on economic studies), no. 10 (1983): 25.

Kimura Masutaro 木村增太郎. *Jihenka no Shina kin'yū oyobi kin'yū kikan* 事變下の支那金融及び金融機關 (Finance and financial organizations in China since the incident). Tokyo: Kinyū Kenkyūkai, 1941.

Lary, Diana. *The Chinese People at War: Human Suffering and Social Transformation, 1937–1945*. Cambridge: Cambridge University Press, 2010.

Li, Lincoln. "An Alternative View on Occupation Policy: China's Resistance Potential." In *Resisting Japan: Mobilizing for War in Modern China, 1935–1945*, edited by David Pong, Norwalk, Conn.: East Bridge, 2008.

Lieu, D. K. *The Silk Industry of China*. Shanghai: Kelly and Walsh, 1940.

Lin Meili 林美莉. *Kangzhan shiqi de huobi zhanzheng* 抗戰時期的貨幣戰爭 (The currency war during the war of resistance period). Taibei: Guoli Taiwan shifan daxue lishi yanjiu suo, 1996.

Lu Yangyuan 陸仰淵 and Fang Qingqiu 方慶秋, eds. *Minguo shehui jingji shi* 民國社會經濟史 (A social and economic history of the Republican Period). Beijing: Zhongguo jingji chubanshe, 1991.

Ma Yinchu 馬寅初. *Zhanshi jingji lunwen ji* 戰時經濟論文集. (Collection of articles on the wartime economy). Shanghai: Zuojia shuwu, 1945.

Masuda Yoneji 增田米治. *Shina senso keizai no kenkyu* 支那戰爭經濟の研究 (Researches on China's wartime economy). Tokyo: Daiyamonda sha, 1944.

Nakamura, Takafusa. "The Yen Bloc, 1931–1941." In *The Japanese Wartime Empire, 1931–1945*, edited by Peter Duus, Ramon H. Myers, and Mark R. Peattie. Princeton, N.J.: Princeton University Press, 1996.

Office of Strategic Services, Research and Analysis Branch. *Programs of Japan in China: Extracts from FCC Intercepts of Short Wave Broadcasts from Radio Tokyo and Affiliated Stations from Dec. 1941 to January 1, 1945, and from OSS Sources*, vol. 1: *Central Coastal Provinces*. Honolulu, 1945.

Preston, Paul, and Michael Partridge, eds. *British Documents on Foreign Affairs: Reports and Papers from the Foreign Office Confidential Print*, part II, from 1940 to 1945, series E, Asia.

Qi Chunfeng 齊春風. "Kangzhan shiqi da houfang yu lunxian qujian de fabi liudong 抗戰時期大後方與淪陷區間的法幣流動" (The flow of Guomindang currency between Chinese-controlled and enemy-occupied areas during the resistance war against Japan). Jindai shi yanjiu 近代史研究 (Modern Chinese history studies), no. 5 (2003): 137–169.

Sherwood, Jack. *Fond Memories of a Young Man in Old China*. Bloomington, Ind.: AuthorHouse, 2009.

Shou Jinwen 壽進文. *Zhanshi Zhongguo de yinhang* 戰時中國的銀行 (China's banks in wartime). Chongqing, 1944. No publisher given.

Tamagna, Frank. *Banking and Finance in China*. New York: Institute of Pacific Relations, 1942.

Tang Zhenchang 唐振常, ed. *Shanghai shi* 上海史 (A history of Shanghai). Shanghai: Shanghai renmin, 1989.

Wang, Ke-wen. "Collaborators and Capitalists: The Politics of 'Material Control' in Wartime Shanghai." *Chinese Studies in History* 26, no. 1 (Fall 1992): 42–62.

Wang, Qisheng. "The Battle for Hunan." In *The Battle for China: Essays on the Military History of the Sino-Japanese War of 1937–1945*, edited by Mark R. Peattie, Edward J. Drea, and Hans J. Van de Ven. 403–420. Stanford, Calif.: Stanford University Press, 2011.

Wei Dazhi 魏達志. "Shanghai 'gudao jingji fanrong' shimo 上海 '孤島經濟繁榮' 始末" (Shanghai's economic flourishing during the isolated island period, from beginning to end). *Fudan xuebao* 復旦學報, no. 4 (August 12, 1985): 109–113.

White, Theodore, and Annalee Jacoby. *Thunder out of China*. New York: William Sloane, 1946.

Yang Jicheng 楊濟成. "Guanyu wei Zhongguo lianhe junbei yinhang de jianwen 關於偽中國聯合準備銀行的見聞" (On the puppet Federal Reserve Bank). *Wenshi ziliao xuanji* 文史資料選集, no. 10, 65–76.

Yao Shengxiang 姚盛祥 and Shen Jiazhen 深家振. "Wangwei Zhongyang chubei yinhang shimo 汪偽中央儲備銀行始末" (The puppet Wang government's Central Reserve Bank from beginning to end). *Jiangsu wenshi ziliao xuanji* 江蘇文史資料選集, no. 29 (1989): 236–253.

Yin Xiqi 殷錫琪. "Waihui tongzhi xin zhengce zhi jiantao 外匯統治新政策之檢討" (An examination of the new policy to control foreign exchange). *Dongfang zazhi* 東方雜誌 (The Eastern miscellany) 35, no. 3 (February 1, 1938): 19–22.

Young, Arthur N. *China and the Helping Hand, 1937–1945*. Cambridge, Mass.: Harvard University Press, 1963.

———. *China's Wartime Finance and Inflation*. Cambridge, Mass.: Harvard University Press, 1965.

———. *Cycle of Cathay: An Historical Perspective*. Vista, Calif.: Ibis, 1997.

Yuda Hua fangzhi ziben jituan shiliao Bianji Zu 裕大華紡織資本集團史料編輯組 (Editorial Group for Historical Materials on the Yuda Hua textile group), ed. *Yuda Hua fangzhi ziben jituan shiliao* 裕大華紡織資本集團史料 (Historical materials on the Yuda Hua textile capitalist group). Wuhan: Hubei renmin chubanshe, 1984.

Zhang Tianzheng 張天政. "'Ba-yi-san' Shiqi de Shanghai Yinhang Gonghui 八一三時期的上海銀行公會" (The Shanghai Bankers Association during the August 13 Battle of Shanghai). *Kangri zhanzheng yanjiu* 抗日戰爭研究 (Research on the Anti-Japanese War), no. 2 (2004): 118–149.

Zhongguo Renmin Kangri Zhanzheng Jinian Guan 中國人民抗日戰爭紀念館 (Museum of the War of Chinese People's Resistance against Japanese Aggression), ed. *Kangzhan jishi* 抗戰紀事 (Memoranda on the War of Resistance). Beijing: Zhongguo youyi chubanshe, 1989.

Zhu Chuxin 朱楚辛. "Sannian lai di wo jian de huobi zhan 三年來敵我間的貨幣戰" (The war of the enemy against our currency in the last three years). *Dushu yuebao* 讀書閱報 1, no. 11 (January 1, 1940): 485–488.

CHAPTER 7

When Urban Met Rural in the Japanese Occupation

Managing an Agricultural Research Station in North China

BRETT SHEEHAN

A child of privilege and technocrat by training, Shi Shaodong (石少東 1906–1983) was in the prime of his life when the Japanese invaded China in 1937. The need to find a livelihood in Japanese-occupied North China shaped Shi's life for the next eight years and left a lasting impression, such that he devoted a large portion of his memoir to the subject.[1] Even decades later, his emotions ran high when thinking about the occupation period. Yet his memoir is neither an anti-Japanese polemic nor a whitewashed story of the triumph of Chinese resistance. Shi expectedly condemned the Japanese, but he also portrayed sympathetic Japanese figures and often showed his own foibles and weaknesses.

Never published—in fact never finished—the manuscript of that memoir and archival sources together provide an unusually textured and full picture of Shi's life under Japanese occupation. Prior to the invasion, the technically trained Shi had devoted his life to modern industries such as railroads, which many hoped would provide China's salvation from its position of weakness in relation to Western and Japanese imperialism. Many in the Japanese occupation regime, however, had a different vision of China's future. Picturing China as backward and rural, they promoted an agenda in which China would be part of an autarkic sphere in Asia, producing commodities for the Japanese industrial machine.[2] This latter vision pushed the urban and urbane Shi into the business of agricultural development, a line of work he clearly had never imagined.

Shi ended up running an experimental agricultural research station and training institute for the Japanese military, one of twenty-two experimental agricultural stations in North China as of 1943, devoted to everything from wheat to soy beans.[3] The existence of these stations and their role in the occupation has been little studied in the English-language literature, and in retrospect they seem anomalous considering the damage wartime disruption brought to Chinese agriculture.[4] Through Shi Shaodong we can understand the origins and functions of one of them and see what happened in a forced marriage between urban expertise and rural production.

Shi's experiences during the war showed many of the contradictions of the occupation. Shi's avowed Chinese patriotism contrasted with his role as part of Japanese development schemes in China. The importance of agricultural development to the regime contrasted with the astounding shallowness of the commitment to this goal of many members of the Japanese military and Chinese occupation government. The banality of agricultural development contrasted both with the venality of the regime and the danger of agricultural work in the midst of armed Chinese guerilla resistance. The expertise and hard work of technocrats contrasted with a violent and arbitrary decision-making process. Most important, for both Chinese and Japanese participants, the need to pursue a livelihood, to get on with one's life, contrasted with the urgency and purpose of fighting a war. Shi's experience shows a regime remarkably incompetent at harnessing individual goals to state-building purposes. In the end, the Japanese occupation regime proved unable to link the supply lines of rural development and urban production. In fact, the occupation pushed the already distant urban and rural realms of China even farther apart.

As with all memoirs, Shi's story needs careful reading, but the level of detail and emotion provides valuable insights usually lacking in documentary sources. In order to preserve these benefits, I will tell as much of Shi's story as possible in his own words.

The Plan: "Suffering Disgrace to Fulfill Responsibility"

Shi's story began in the interior of Shandong Province in North China at the turn of the twentieth century. His father owned a local cash shop in the seat of Qingzhou County in the center of Shandong Province, about half way between Qingdao on the coast and the provincial capital of Jinan. Qingzhou had been the site of late-nineteenth-century Protestant and Catholic missionary activity, and at some point, the Shi family converted to Catholicism. (Shi Shaodong was a devout follower his entire life.) The Qingdao-Jinan (Jiaoji 膠濟) Railroad brought new life to the sleepy town in 1904, two years before Shi Shaodong's birth.[5] The railroad and foreign missionaries together provided connections to the outside world unusual for inland county capitals in the early years of the twentieth century. The Shi family took full advantage of these connections, and many of the Shi children went to China's finest universities.[6]

Shi Shaodong started his education at university in Qingdao and then transferred to the business school of Communications University in Beijing, where he studied management. After graduation in 1931 he went to work for the Qingdao-Jinan Railway in Qingdao.[7] During the early phases of the Japanese invasion in

1937, the railroad transferred Shi first to "the military supply command at Zhengzhou and then to the Southern Second Army vehicle supply command at Jinan."[8] The trauma of the Japanese invasion left such a deep impression on Shi that one of the first memories he recounts in his memoir is his emotional reaction to a play performed in Jinan in honor of Chinese soldiers fighting the Japanese advance in 1937. He remembered that the "the applause was like thunder. It was the longest ovation I saw in my entire life." As the soldiers' representative recounted tales of battlefield hardship, "there was no one in the audience who was not crying." When Shi returned to the railway office in Qingdao and recounted this performance to his colleagues, "[he] could not keep from tearing up. Tragedy and anger were all mixed up."[9] Shi certainly used this story to help establish his own patriotic credentials for potential readers, but even if exaggerated in retrospect, it also represents the "tragedy and anger" of his own early experience of the war.

Shortly after Shi viewed this performance, he lost his position with the railway, perhaps because the quick rout of the Chinese military by the Japanese put him out of a job.[10] He became, in his words, "a refugee." After leaving the railroad, Shi taught school for about four years; then in 1941 he went to work for the Dongya Corporation in Tianjin.[11] Run by a Qingzhou native, Song Feiqing, the Dongya Corporation often hired Shandong compatriots, and Shi managed to get an introduction to the factory through his personal networks.[12] According to a cliché Shi used in his memoir, the two families had been friends "for generations."[13] At some point either before or after Shi began work at Dongya, the Shi and Song families became distantly tied by marriage. In addition, two of Shi's younger brothers, as well as an uncle, would eventually go to work for Dongya.[14] Descendants of the Shi (Shek) and Song (Sung) families maintain contact to this day, even those who now live in the United States.

In spite of this closeness, Shi later wrote about his mixed feelings working for the Dongya Corporation: "At first when I entered Dongya, I was a refugee. I had previously been cultivated by the country [presumably on government scholarship to Communications University], and in principle I should be loyal and pay my debt back to the country, and I should not change and enter a commercial enterprise and work for private interests, but I met Feiqing like this, and he knew me and loved me." Song Feiqing impressed Shi with the attention he paid to the "health and happiness of dependents that lubricated human feelings."[15] Once when work pressure had given Shi insomnia, Song Feiqing required Shi to meet him every Monday, Wednesday, and Friday at eight in the morning at the company's badminton court for a game.[16] In the comfortable and paternalistic embrace of Song Feiqing and Dongya, Shi started his new life.

At the time Shi Shaodong went to work for the Dongya Corporation, the company was coming to the end of a wartime surge of prosperity.[17] The company had been founded to produce wool knitting yarn and other woolen goods, and wool had proved a valuable commodity during the early war period. Eventually, however, the war cut off the availability of Dongya's major raw material: high-quality wool imports from Australia. Without wool to spin, Dongya turned to the production of another textile: gunny sacks. Made with jute from India, gunny sacks were necessary for the transportation of rice, soy beans, cement, and other commodities. As such, gunny sacks became a vital product during the war, and Dongya made a fortune in the mid-war years by supplying both private parties and the Japanese Army.[18]

Safely ensconced within the safety of the "island" British Concession of Tianjin, Dongya had successfully taken advantage of wartime shortages and military needs while avoiding confiscation or threats from the occupation regime. With this success Dongya provided a sphere of comfort and care in spite of wartime shortages and deprivations. Most important, Dongya used its strong financial position to maintain scarce supplies for its employees. As Shi remembered, "At the time of the Anti-Japanese War, when every place had mixed grain flours, Dongya did not have a single employee without a few bags of 'foreign' [machine milled wheat] flour! Of course I am not saying that Dongya employees ate foreign flour every day during the time of the nation's troubles, but Dongya certainly distributed this from time to time. After it was received, it was treasured and wouldn't be eaten all at once, so it would accumulate."[19]

The gap between relative comfort at Dongya and deprivation in the rest of China, especially in rural areas, came home to Shi Shaodong when a former teacher came to Tianjin on business and stayed with Shi. During the Anti-Japanese War this teacher had left the railway bureau in Qingdao and went to work in the interior, where he took over responsibility for the Xinjiang Railway Bureau. Prior to this visit, the two had not seen each other for several years, and Shi noted his teacher was now shorter and thinner. When Shi served white-flour steamed bread (*mantou* 饅頭), his teacher "was very happy and ate [it] by the mouthful," saying, "For several years I have not eaten such good *mantou*." In fact, the teacher "ate only *mantou* and did not touch the dishes that had been prepared for him. … He returned the food, saying, 'Our friends and family in the interior cannot see even good *mantou;* I can only enjoy the *mantou* and can't stand to enjoy anything more.' "[20]

In December 1941, the outbreak of the "Pacific War" phase of the Sino-Japanese conflict threatened Dongya's relatively protected position. On the one hand, it cut off supplies of the jute from India needed to make quality gunny sacks. On the other hand, the Japanese occupied the British Concession, and Dongya came under the direct rule of the occupation government for the first time. In dramatic detail, Shi recounted the day he realized the factory was in danger of confiscation by the Japanese:

> [Song Feiqing said,] "Our factory is in a very dangerous position. Perhaps tomorrow or the day after, we will have to hand it over to someone else." His low and grief-stricken voice was still quite firm. On the surface he was retreating, but in his bones, he was attacking. At the time, I was at a loss. I could not imagine [such a thing]. After the Japanese had occupied the British Concession, they had not touched Dongya. People had already relaxed, thinking that for some reason [the Japanese] would not enter privately managed factories. We had even been congratulating ourselves on our good fortune. Who knew that we still would not be able to escape from this disaster?[21]

Song explained his plan to Shi Shaodong. Dongya planned to convince the Japanese authorities to leave the company alone in return for company sponsorship of an agricultural research project to promote domestic jute cultivation needed for gunny sack production. Flabbergasted, Shi reluctantly accepted the job of drafting the plan on which the entire future of the company depended. As he remembered later, "As a staff member I had to accept this new responsibility. I could not decline just because I was facing difficulty … but I am a so-called city slicker [can't distinguish between the five grains (*wu gu bufen de* 五谷不分的)]. I am a complete outsider when it comes to agriculture, especially in regard to the newly cultivated strain of 'foreign jute' 洋麻. I virtually had not even heard of it. Where to even begin to draft a development plan?"

The "foreign jute" (*yangma*) referred to here was a new variety that, though still inferior to Indian Jute, could be grown in China. As Shi noted elsewhere, it was better than nothing. Different kinds of jute produced gunny sacks of different qualities. Shi noted, "They used iron hooks to move gunny sacks on the wharves and loading docks. Once hooked, there would be a big hole and … things inside of the bags would leak out and there was no way to repair [them]. Gunny sacks made with [Indian] jute could be used ten times, but those made with domestic jute three times if you were lucky."

The executives of the Dongya Corporation had good knowledge of the seriousness of the jute shortage in North China, and perhaps that gave them hope that the regime would eventually take up Dongya's offer. The company's production of gunny sacks had nosedived after outbreak of the Pacific phase of the war by declining from 150,000 bags per month to only 50,000.[22] Eventually, the company sent representatives all over North China in a desperate attempt to locate domestic sources of jute as a poor substitute for Indian jute.[23] The Japanese regime was equally concerned. A top secret Mantetsu (South Manchurian Railway) report in 1941 had already noted an alarming reduction in Chinese jute crops in North China due to the flood in 1939.[24] In early 1942 Mantetsu published a secret report on gunny sack production and followed it up with a supplemental report a few months later. This second report stated that "North China needs twenty plus thousand tons [of gunny sacks] per year."[25] The author blamed lack of domestic cultivation of appropriate types of jute for shortages of gunny sacks.[26]

Shi's account of drafting a plan to grow this foreign jute for gunny sack production continued:

> I went home and ate dinner and then went to the Commercial Press Bookstore and Zhonghua Bookstore, opened by Beijing University in the French Concession, to buy some books on agriculture and farm management. [The Japanese had not taken over the French Concession because of their relationship with the Vichy government.] As a result I brought back seven or eight books of various sizes to be references for me as I hung in the air with nothing to stand on. When those agriculture experts wrote these books, it was originally to promote the education of those that came after. They never dreamed that I would use them as a weapon to protect Dongya.[27]

In this rather endearing description, we see Shi's (that is, the urban technocrat's) natural reaction to any new problem: buy a book or several books. We also see the seriousness with which Shi approached the task. He and his copyist worked for twenty hours before resting. Then they went to work again the next day. Shi notes, "The plan was fifty pages long. On the outside it looked good. As for what was inside, only heaven knows. … I gave the original to the president through the window of the first class car on the 4:00 p.m. train [to Beijing] at Tianjin's East Station. He took it laughing and shook my hand, saying I should go home and rest. I said to myself, 'I will go back and begin the work of starting the agricultural department.' He knew what I thought and nodded to me."[28]

The train pulled out of the station bound for Beijing, where Song used the plan to negotiate for the survival of the Dongya Corporation. Although Shi has emphasized the drama of the events in his memoir, the audacity of the plan did indeed provide cause for concern. Dongya was a well-to-do but only a medium-sized company. Taking responsibility for solving the regime's jute production problems in North China was an ambitious task, especially when lack of jute supplies had endangered the company's main line of business and source of income. Shi wrote that the cost estimates in the plan were probably faulty, so he simply added a note that Dongya "will absolutely have the ability to pay all the expenses of the proposed agriculture department. … Dongya's principle is not to take note of profit and loss, but to develop the supplies needed for the production of gunny sacks."[29] At the same time, the plan had more than a tinge of collaboration new to Dongya. The production and sale of gunny sacks in the previous year and a half could conveniently be portrayed as normal commercial activity, even if sold to the Japanese Army. Now, however, the company proposed a direct subsidy of the operations of the occupation regime. As Shi wrote, "The company's first priority was to make it inconvenient for the Japanese military to take a step into Dongya. [Song Feiqing] was willing to suffer disgrace in order to fulfill this heavy responsibility [*renwu fuzhong* 忍辱负重]. … No one knows to whom the president showed the agriculture department plan or to which government organ he gave it. The next day in the afternoon, he held a meeting back in Tianjin to discuss the matter."

Shi's manuscript is a little cryptic here, but reactions at this meeting the next day indicate there was a serious problem. Either the Japanese military had not accepted the plan or it had imposed conditions unacceptable to Dongya.

> Wang Xinsan [one Dongya executive] looked as if his blood was about ready to boil. … He walked up to president Song Feiqing, bowed at the waist, and spoke indignantly, familiarly, in a low voice and with strength, saying "President! It won't work!" This "won't" was forced out as his tightly clenched lips kept half the sound in. Finally, he said "It won't work" again and sat on a couch. The atmosphere in the room was very tense, and it was completely quiet.
>
> [Song Feiqing responded,] "The other side is very arrogant. We have said everything we could and raised as many reasons as we could possibly think of. No matter what reason you use, they don't listen. They don't use reason; they are in the military. …" As his last words that night [he added,] "Xinsan, go and try once more. Shaodong, you go together with Xinsan."

Shi Shaodong and Wang Xinsan decided to go to Beijing the next day. As they parted that night, the excited Wang shook Shi's hand, saying, "We need to fight like cornered beasts and pull wild waves to overturn them." As for Shi, he "thought that to take on a responsibility at the time of enemy soldiers, to take orders during crisis, this is very arduous work and not at all easy." In Beijing they went to see Wang Fuwu (王福五), a man Shi describes as "the real traitor." According to Shi, Wang had studied in Japan in his youth and then drifted along in Manchuria, a part of China occupied by Japan in 1931. Shi adds that Wang did not speak Japanese well, but the Japanese liked him and installed him in Beijing doing economic work. The description of the meeting with Wang Fuwu shows many of the contradictions of war, as Wang lived in protected luxury:

> Wang's office had a big door painted red. Above the door there was a small iron model of a Pekinese. … The main room in the front courtyard was for receiving visitors. It was broad and ornately decorated. There was a [blank in original] landscape painting on the wall. It wouldn't be convenient to ask where it came from, but it was truly top quality. … Coming in here, you wouldn't know it was a time of chaos and war in China. In the middle, the most fashionable short-legged Japanese coffee table sat in front of a screen. … We sat there and spoke with him. … It was like jumping into an abyss.
>
> [Wang Fuwu] smoked Sanbaotai cigarettes, though during the war they were very rare. It was the height of summer. Ash often dropped on the front of his gown. When brushed with his hand, it fell like snow on the Tianjin carpet. He did not care at all. I felt bad for the carpet.
>
> "Old Wang [Fuwu]" Xinsan looked at me and then turned back; he imploringly said, "I've spoken. Do you agree?"
>
> "Why don't you go back," after a long time Old Wang [Fuwu] said, looking at Xinsan. "Go back and tell Mr. Song to forget it. He's the one who told you to come? Yesterday we had arranged everything well. One day later, [he] goes back on his word. [He] doesn't know it's a matter of life and death."[30]

In his account of this rather surreal conversation, Shi never divulges what had been agreed on the day before or why that agreement had now become a matter of "life and death." Later in his memoir he implies that lots of people made money personally on the project, so it is reasonable to conclude that bribery was involved. If so, then the conversation with Wang Fuwu recounted above was simply a discussion of the amount of bribes to be paid. In any case, the two sides did come to agreement, and by June 1942, Dongya had established an agriculture department to promote jute cultivation in North China. The Japanese military did not take over Dongya.[31]

The Agricultural Research Station

At about the same time Japanese military representatives in Beijing adopted Dongya's plan for the promotion of jute cultivation, the Kōa Institute (Kōain 興亜院), the organization responsible for Japan's overall policy direction in occupied China, had drafted its plan for gunny sack production in North China.[32] It is unclear if the Kōa Institute drafted its plan independently or if it simply adopted Dongya's plan for cultivation of foreign jute as part of the overall project. Dongya became one of six designated jute purchasers in the Tianjin area, and it became the primary producer of gunny sacks needed by the Japanese military.[33] By dint of mixing different kinds of domestic jute (not including the still experimental foreign jute), Dongya had become the only Chinese company to successfully produce gunny sacks without supplies of jute from India.[34] Eventually the occupation regime would have three experimental agricultural research stations in North China devoted to different varieties of jute cultivation, and one of these was Dongya's.[35]

At Dongya, the minutes of the board of directors meeting that approved the founding of the agriculture department make no mention of the Japanese military or a quid pro quo. They only state that the growing of jute "has a close relationship to society and our company, and it should be aggressively pursued." When told that the plan would cost at least six or seven hundred thousand yuan, an enormous sum at the time, the board meekly approved the proposal with only the admonition that "the president and vice president(s) are to make a detailed investigation and handle the matter carefully."[36]

Dongya established the administrative offices of its agriculture department in a quiet courtyard in Beijing. Shi remembered that "the courtyard was large, but few people went in and out. It was quiet as death and without the breath of life. ... It was especially suited to finding quiet amid noise, truly the best place to evade eyes and ears." The need for discretion was obvious to Shi. According to him, "The establishment of the agriculture department was Dongya's [version] of national shame [*dongya de guochi* 東亞的國恥]," a phrase frequently used at the time to describe Chinese humiliation at the hands of foreigners.[37]

Shi Shaodong ran the agriculture department, but the Japanese military assigned his second in command, a Japanese man named Tsujihara Yafumi (辻原八二三), who "had studied at university in Beijing prior to the war. ... He had an authentic Beijing accent, and he could write passably in Chinese. [He] could even use vocabulary and literary phrases appropriately."[38] Shi remained wary of Tsujihara at first, but gradually came to trust him:

> We talked about everything, including occasionally exchanging opinions about the Sino-Japanese political situation. … Slowly we became intimate acquaintances [*zhiji* 知己], and when he could think on behalf of Dongya, his opinions were never far from mine. He had a responsibility to the Japanese military, but because he was trusted by the military, when we encountered difficult problems, he would find a way around them. … He was the same as the [other] Japanese who worked at Dongya during the war. He earned a lot of money from Dongya, but at the same time Dongya saved not a small amount of bribes.[39]

As proof of Tsujihara's reliability, Shi recounted a story about a business trip the two took to Baoding to meet with the Hebei provincial government about publicizing jute growing. On the road to Baoding, they became suspects in anti-Japanese guerilla activity. This story illuminates both the danger and banality of life in wartime China, and I present Shi's account almost in full.

> We heard that [Chinese] guerilla forces had killed a traitor [helping Japan] in the city that morning. The military and the military police had declared martial law and arrested the killer. Transport had been disrupted, and it was impossible to purchase food. Fortunately, we had eaten an evening meal on the train. Also we had brought some crackers and snacks as gifts, so we just ate some of those and went to sleep. Unexpectedly, not long after we had lain down, the Japanese military police came to check out the hotel.[40]

At the hotel, the military police entered Shi and Tsujihara's room.

> One military policeman was armed with guns and bullets. Another was a plainclothesman wearing the outfit of a Chinese ruffian with white cuffs folded back half a foot and clasps made out of strips of cloth. Around his waste a bulge stuck out. It was certainly a gun. It seems that they [the police] came because of us. After coming in the door, [they] read our names from a book. Tsujihara didn't dare get up. I also lay there not moving. It was Tsujihara who first complained to the military police saying, "This man's surname is "Seki" but you read it as "Ishi."[41] … [I worried] if it kept going like this it would be really bad.
>
> MP: "The military police are investigating this place. You didn't even move. This is not the way to show respect to the Imperial Army!"
>
> Tsujihara: "Standing up doesn't count as showing respect!" But he still sat up. He sat up, and I twisted my body. He stopped me with his

hand, telling me not to move. Using Chinese he said, "You sleep; it has nothing to do with you."

MP: "What does he do?"

Tsujihara: "Head of the Beijing Agriculture Department; his tone implied that the department was most important. He did not bring up the relationship with Dongya. The MP was suspicious. Tsujihara lit a cigarette in a very relaxed manner because the MP still hadn't thought what he should say. Taking advantage of the pause, [he asked,] "Who did the guerillas kill today?"

MP: "This is a secret. How do you know?"

Tsujihara: "Everyone knows, and you still say it is a secret." He laughed through his nose.

MP: "Laugh! Why do you laugh?" The MP was very unhappy.

Tsujihara: "Do the military police have the right to prohibit people laughing?" I closed my eyes and pretended to sleep. I thought [the policeman] was probably looking askance at him.

MP: "We should be a little more serious about this matter."

Tsujihara: "I agree."

MP: "I ask you honorable [sir], what are you doing here?"

Tsujihara: "Don't be so polite. We came at the invitation of the province to investigate a plan to expand the growing of foreign jute." This was something of a lie.

MP: "Tell me the details."

Tsujihara: "This is a secret. I'm sorry I can't obey"

MP: "[I will] trouble you to come to down to the military police office!" His tone of voice was not too tactful. I suddenly became frightened. At the same time I blamed Tsujihara. … Bothering the military police is not worth the trouble.

Tsujihara: "Promoting jute violates military police code. That's truly laughable!" His tone was also not too polite.

MP: "You have probably misunderstood. No matter what, I must report back to my superior." This sentence was much more relaxed.

Tsujihara: "How do your superiors know we are here? Is it possible that it's connected to the assassination?"

MP: "You can't say that. We still need to report to our superiors. We don't dare speak directly; we can only use this method."

Tsujihara: "Just report me to your superiors. I think that's enough." Tsujihara was a little tired; he was thinking if he could make them back down, he could rest.

MP: "Thanks for the cigarette; it's great." I was thinking Tsujihara must have handed him a cigarette and lit it for him. After the MP enjoyed the cigarette, he expressed his thanks. Both sides' expressions [improved]. It was impossible to guess how it would end, but I was relaxing a little.

Tsujihara: "It's late. You have been working hard all day. Go back and get some rest! I bid you goodnight."

MP: "How much did you have to drink tonight?"

Tsujihara: "There was nothing to eat here because of the martial law. [I] could only drink. I bid you goodnight!"

MP: "I also bid you goodnight." There was the noise of the door to the room opening and then closing. Without doubt the MP had left. I slowly opened my eyes. ... [Tsujihara] said, "It's true that they have had something to drink. They were just looking for trouble." I nodded and the two of us laughed. Victory was written all over his face [as he was] blinking his eyes up at the ceiling.

I lay down, thinking that Tsujihara's future with the military wouldn't be worth much. Although he was an employee of the military department, in his gut something hard to describe had given him a devil-may-care personality.

This story contains many expected elements of wartime life. The assassination, the closing of the city, unreliable food supplies, and declaration of martial law all point to the ongoing Sino-Japanese conflict. On top of these, the half-drunk belligerent Japanese military policeman and plainclothes Chinese tough with a gun bulging from under his clothes seem almost too cliché, as if from a bad movie about the war. Other elements seem more surprising. For example, Tsujihara first established his authority by correcting the policeman's pronunciation of a Chinese name. Perhaps his status as a Japanese "China hand" indicated a certain position in the occupation period. Tsujihara took responsibility for protecting his boss, the Chinese Shi, while adopting a combination of hostility and camaraderie with the military policeman. Any bystander would need a program to keep track of the roles the players in this little drama took up and then discarded within the space of a few minutes. Ambiguity, arbitrariness, and serendipity perhaps best describe Chinese and Japanese relations during this encounter and during the war in general.

In any case the incident passed. Shi and Tsujihara concluded their business with the Hebei provincial government, represented by a Japanese military man who endorsed the jute-growing plan. Shi's most vivid memory of the meeting involved the fact that the Hebei provincial authorities submitted a falsified and exaggerated receipt for reimbursement of lunch expenses, claiming a simple business lunch as a dinner banquet.[42] Shi's experiences indicate that this kind of day-to-day venality was common under the occupation regime. After the meeting, Shi and Tsujihara returned to Beijing and reported to their contact with the Japanese military, the Sanbaotai cigarette-smoking Chinese Wang Fuwu, with whom Dongya had negotiated in the beginning.

In Beijing, in addition to its office in the quiet neighborhood, the Dongya agriculture department established a training academy at a Japanese military experimental farm in the Beijing suburbs. On this farm, the Dongya agriculture department moved into a spacious building formerly used as a military brothel. Shi Shaodong had heard that all the comfort women had come from Korea, and the price list was still on the wall when Shi took possession of the premises. He was suitably sickened by the thought.[43]

The training academy recruited students from middle school graduates for two types of course: intensive and regular. Students in the intensive program undertook a three-month crash course, after which they worked at assigned jobs for three months before returning to the training school for advanced study. Students in the regular course studied for six months and then left to work on the outside. Shi notes, "During school besides free room and board, students received a monthly stipend. In North China during the occupation this kind of treatment was very attractive."[44] The academy had no problem in quickly recruiting one hundred students.

The more than twenty teachers who ended up at the Dongya agriculture department were a motley lot. Almost all were Japanese. Of them, "Some were college teachers and some were graduates of higher vocational schools, and some couldn't even read. [We] had a little of everything. ... In addition, there were two Chinese from the Northeast." Shi recalled frequently treating the teachers to Japanese food, when they would "toast each other as if it was worth their lives."[45] Dongya, of course, paid the bills. Shi's biggest conflict with the teachers came when they drew up a plan for jute promotion different from that agreed to by the military, a plan Shi was certain would bankrupt Dongya.

> If [the plan] was completely implemented, then even three Dongyas could not afford it. Although we had made a promise to the military in regard to taking on the entire burden, we could only propose a different opinion. I separately met with the different teachers, using the strategy of divide and conquer, raising vegetables by pouring wine. ... Tsujihara found out I was worried about meeting expenses and calmly told me it was not necessary to be overly conscientious. He said [the teachers] had just arrived and needed to show off to the military. After a while, there would be a way to solve the problem. ... [Unconsoled,] I was anxious to the end.

> [Dongya proposed a compromise that the Japanese military and some teachers accepted.] Tsujihara and I gave gifts and invited military officials in charge to dinner, so they agreed to change [the plan]. ... There was the cost of the gifts, but in comparison to the bottomless pit [of the teachers' plan], it was much cheaper.
>
> A rather young instructor, Fujita, who had drafted the teachers' plan ... was very disappointed when he had to revise [it in accordance with the compromise]. Because of this his mood darkened, and he was mad at everything. He made trouble daily.[46]

In one example of that trouble, Fujita once requested the purchase of an expensive brand of graph paper, but Shi refused to approve the expenditure because the agriculture department had other supplies to use. Fujita ran into Shi's office "like an arrow, and pounded his fist on the table, using his whole body like a declaration of war." Shi protested in his limited Japanese by scolding him for being unreasonable: "Grabbing hold of his arm, I pulled him out. I said, 'I will report you to the military department; you can be impolite to your superiors!' "[47] Without saying a word, Shi walked into the courtyard and ordered his driver to bring the car. Shi drove directly to Wang Fuwu's place, where he ran into a Japanese military officer named Andō Shigeru, whom Shi had known before the war in Shandong.

> After I explained the details, [Andō] immediately took up the phone to ask the head teacher to tell [teacher] Fujita to come to the military department. After he arrived, he made a 90 degree bow to Andō. Andō yelled at him like a dog. [Fujita] only said, "Yes, yes, yes." He didn't even dare fart. Andō even blamed him with great significance, saying that we should be frugal with goods during the time of the "sacred" war. [Also] politeness should be emphasized in the cooperation between Japanese and Chinese. The head of the agriculture department is your superior. Insulting superiors is a serious mistake. [Andō] ordered him to apologize to me and ask for punishment. He did it very respectfully.

The other teachers at the institute sympathized with Fujita and blamed Shi Shaodong for going over their heads directly to the military department. They planned to strike in protest. In order to ameliorate their feelings, Shi did the following: "[I] bought an eight treasures rice. Also carrying a steamer tray of meat dumplings, I took a three-wheeler toward the teachers' building. ... having seen the gifts I was giving, they were very welcoming. ... A whiff of the delicious aroma brought happiness to the heart. ... [Food] eaten in the mouth brings sweetness to the stomach. ... The next day teacher Fujita arrived [for work] especially early. ... Everybody worked as usual."

Three elements stand out in the story of this conflict with this teacher. First, Wang Fuwu continued to serve as superintendent and liaison to the Japanese military for the Dongya agriculture department. In spite of Shi's disdain for the man, he played a pivotal role in mediating Chinese and Japanese interests. Second, resolution of the incident did not even reach Wang Fuwu, but instead derived from Shi's previous networks with Japanese military officers. Though often hostile, Sino-Japanese contact had been long and deep in North China. Third, under normal circumstances, the story of the conflict between Shi and the teachers would not warrant much attention. Under military occupation, however, the conflict became charged with issues of nationalism such that it might have even become a matter of life and death. Shi's story of a later conflict with another teacher shows how dangerous small personal conflicts could become during occupation.

> Teacher Kunō was the only teacher among them who could speak Chinese. ... His family had been in the military for three generations. His grandfather had participated in the Russo-Japanese War, his father, in the Manchurian Incident. He himself was an officer in the puppet Manchurian army. He came to North China to work on foreign jute with the idea of promoting jute growth in puppet Manchuria. He often wore a military uniform to work. At his waist he hung a sword that he often used to show off for villagers and colleagues.
>
> Once, he came from the countryside to Beijing to report on his work. He spent the night at the agriculture department office. ... (Kunō, like many teachers, was upset that we made them live in the office because hotels were too expensive.) That evening when he came back to the office, it was already past midnight. He used his sword to bang on the gate. The gatekeeper, seeing that [Kunō] was drunk as a skunk, did not dare to open the door, afraid that he would get cut by the sword with a result too terrible to consider. Then we all got up, and one person picked up a chair in preparation to resist the attack. After the gate was opened, he came at us with the sword. There were many of us, and he didn't know who was who. There were a few moments of confusion, and he stumbled back and forth as if he wanted to go to bed. Who would have thought, but the German shepherd ... saw that Kunō was being disorderly and attacked him. Under attack, he took his sword and killed the German shepherd. A weapon belonging to three generations was used, and he finally was able to expend his anger.

The next day they showed the dog's corpse to Tsujihara, who scolded Kunō but also asked the military to be lenient because Kunō had been drunk. In the end, the military prohibited Kunō from wearing a sword, and he took it back to his station in the countryside, ignominiously wrapped in newspaper rather than hanging from his waist.[48]

In this story we see a much different occupation than that of the first few months after the invasion, portrayed by Timothy Brook, when Japanese soldiers wielded their swords with abandon and virtual impunity.[49] Four years into the occupation, even using a sword against a dog could be grounds for censure. Nonetheless, the story reminds us that these were not normal times. This was an armed occupation in which Chinese might run afoul of their occupiers at any time and for no particular reason. The unequal power relations of the occupation created tensions at every turn. In the harsh light of day the self-important Kunō appears a buffoon to be scolded by his superiors. In a drunken altercation at night, however, he was an armed member of an occupying force against whom defense could not really go beyond blocking his blows with a chair.

The Countryside: "When You Perform, You have to Exaggerate"

If life at the Dongya agriculture department's Beijing offices was fraught with potentially dangerous petty squabbling, life in the countryside was no better. In addition to training cultivators and sending agricultural experts to the countryside, the Dongya agriculture department also supervised experimental fields. Shi's recollections of this operation show the extent to which the whole effort was doomed by incompetence, negligence, and not a little "weapons of the weak" sabotage by Dongya. As an example of the incompetence, Shi recalls a Japanese expert who spent a great deal of time and effort testing soil to determine alkaline content, but Shi concluded that he was a charlatan whose tests never showed any reactions at all. In Shi's words, "The Japanese deceive themselves and others without shame."[50] Yet the Dongya agriculture department did its part in deception, as shown in the visit of representatives of the Japanese military to an experimental farm: "In all there were more than ten people. Some of them carried hand guns. … That day, Dongya [first] hosted lunch at a Cantonese restaurant … in Tianjin's French Concession. When the Japanese saw the wine, they drank and ate [together] from twelve noon until three in the afternoon until they were finally finished. By the time we got to the farm, it was almost five o'clock."[51]

Shi's description of the model farm they visited on this trip shows the extent of the deception in which he and Dongya engaged. At this farm, the agriculture department rented its office from the township head. In the office they hung up a map of the "spread of acres of jute and a chart showing statistics on the spreading acreage. These statistics were for show and far from reality. When you perform, you should exaggerate anyway." Shi continues:

> I have completely forgotten how many acres of foreign jute were grown [by the agriculture department in total], how much jute was harvested, how much product Dongya received, and how many gunny sacks Dongya was able to make [as a result] of the attempt to promote the growing of foreign jute. Even if there were records to check now, those records can't be reliable evidence. My records were never the same as the records of the company in Tianjin. And the records of the military department were often empty figures. ... I never heard that gunny sacks were actually made from the program to promote foreign jute cultivation. ... Machine production cannot work with a small amount of material. All of the sample products shown to the military department were from production in Manchuria brought by the teachers as examples.[52]

Shi's description of the experimental farm also shows the breadth of the gap between the urbanized agriculture department and its erstwhile constituency: peasants. At the experimental farm, Shi visited with the Japanese delegation, he describes the hardships faced by agriculture department employees who lived at the farm: "The office was a peasant's residence, and the bathroom could only be used by the women of the landlord's family. All the men went out to the latrine in the fields. When it rained, it was necessary to take an umbrella to the bathroom. Afterward [one would] use a sorghum stalk split in two to wipe. Drinking water was an even bigger problem. All of it was muddy water from the irrigation channels; it was like yellow mud; there was only this to cook rice and make tea."[53]

Unlike the Dongya agriculture department, some of the local peasants benefited greatly from the model farm, and Shi heard rumors that all of the fertilizer provided by Dongya went on the personal fields of the local township head.[54] At another Dongya experimental farm, in a remote area poorly served by roads, "Peasant families undertook the growing of foreign jute very enthusiastically, but fertilizer was sold for cash to divide up. ... [The peasants] all appeared welcoming. At the time of harvest, however, none of them could be seen. We were worried about the lack of safety [because of guerillas], so it was not convenient to go to the villages to follow up. As a result, we didn't even see the shadow of a jute plant. I heard that the guerillas took [the jute] and sold it cheaply."[55] In yet another rural location, an unexpected water release from a reservoir flooded fields and destroyed the jute crop, causing one peasant family to request compensation from Dongya. This particular farm is notable in Shi's memory because he remembers one day riding a bicycle there from Tianjin and getting soaked and muddy in the rain. The village had no restaurant or store, so Shi looked forward to a good meal at the peasant's house for comfort, but "Grandma Ma herself went to the kitchen to prepare a four-plate and one-bowl egg feast: one plate of salted eggs, one of cold tossed eggs, one of scrambled eggs, one of fried eggs, and a bowl of river eggs."[56] Shi's sarcasm at the poor treatment from the peasants drips from every word but does not obviate the fact that at every turn the city slicker Shi found himself out of place in the countryside while peasants proved adept at using Dongya's agriculture department for their own purposes. Likewise, the urbanites sent by Dongya to grow jute may have been unused to defecating in fields and wiping themselves with sorghum stalks, but this must have been common for rural folk. These city people would have had a hard time in the countryside even during peacetime, though war, not peace, forced this particular connection between Chinese city and village.

Conclusion

From the beginning Song Feiqing and Shi Shaodong had thought that "Failure for the agricultural station was success for Dongya," but "Planning for failure was not easy. ... Inside [Dongya] many hard-core types complained about the costs of the agriculture department. [But] in the end, failure did come." As the war dragged on, "[The Japanese] teachers were all sent to the front to sacrifice their lives." As a result they suspended classes and sent the remaining students directly to the countryside to begin jute cultivation. Many of them died or were hurt in guerilla attacks. "One fourth of the personnel fled while others did not work hard and were cut from the roles. Some became frightened and resigned on their own. ... The personnel for expansion [of foreign jute production] scattered to the winds, defeated and broken up."[57]

With disappointing results from both the experimental farms and the student training program, the Japanese military took jute cultivation back into its own hands. Shi states, "From any vantage point, the military department had truly no reason to express satisfaction with Dongya's work spreading the growing of jute." Amazingly, the Japanese military, which had threatened to confiscate Dongya two and a half years earlier, now apologized for taking back operations. "[The military] extolled the work Dongya had already done in promoting the growing of jute and volunteered to compensate Dongya for any losses incurred because it was taking back the 'rights.' We thanked heaven and earth and happily handed over this work, allowing us to relax a little." Shi explained the soft treatment as a result of official venality: "Because they had privately been eating too many sweets [taking benefit], they did not raise the fact that they had threatened us with the confiscation of Dongya in order to force us to undertake the promotion of jute growing. It was as if it was forgotten, a clean slate." As Shi remembered, "Everyone involved from the top to the bottom got a share."[58]

In order to hand over operations to the Japanese military, Shi drafted a long report on Dongya's expenses. "It was all accounted for. Dongya's total losses for two and one half years were to be paid back, although in truth how much of this figure actually was received is difficult to say. I think this was another way for the military department to put money in private pockets."[59] Dissolution of the agriculture department freed Shi to go back to Dongya to work. It left Tsujihara Yafumi without a job as well, and Dongya hired Tsujihara, both to thank him for running interference with the occupation regime during his time with the agriculture department and to use him as a "shield to ward off the enemy" for the remainder of the war. Like Shi, Tsujihara found himself in the relative wartime comfort of a private company that had found a niche in the occupation military-industrial complex. There they waited out the war. After Japanese surrender, Tsujihara disappeared from the historical record while Shi had a chance to go back to the railroad, but he remembers, "I had already become connected to [Song] Feiqing through thick and thin and could not bring myself to say I was leaving, so I stayed at Dongya, bowing to the end and using my life to repay one who knew me. There were a lot like me at Dongya."[60] After the war, Shi Shaodong, Song Feiqing, and the Dongya Corporation all managed to avoid serious accusations of collaboration. Shi went to work for a business Song set up in Hong Kong and eventually made his way to the United States.[61]

Shi's account of Dongya's agricultural research station portrays the unlikely characters who came together under wartime occupation. Perhaps Shi's most surprising revelations involve the Japanese military. Rapacious soldiers appeared mostly as specters, such as those who threatened to take over Dongya but never actually arrived, or the clients at the military brothel so recently departed. Other Japanese soldiers were less frightening. Andō, the military officer, actually helped Shi Shaodong discipline the belligerent Japanese teacher Fujita, and Tsujihara, sent by the military, became Shi's biggest ally. The military policeman who questioned Shi and Tsujihara in Baoding came off as more bluster than bite, though still potentially dangerous. Rather than from Japanese soldiers, most of Shi's references to threats involve those from Chinese. On the one hand, he makes frequent reference to the Chinese guerillas who kept him from visiting remote experimental farms or who threatened or killed students in the countryside.

Without a doubt, though, Shi reserves his greatest approbation for the Chinese "real traitor" Wang Fuwu, who used his connections with the Japanese military to achieve a high position in the occupation government and live a life of luxury.

Many of the figures in Shi's wartime story, however, are simply middling figures using the Dongya research station to get ahead or perhaps just get by. There are the Chinese students at the training academy who leaped at the chance of regular meals and a stipend but who later ran afoul of guerillas and rough rural life. The carpetbagging Japanese and Chinese teachers who came south from Manchuria to teach the North Chinese how to grow foreign jute do not appear particularly competent nor are they horribly threatening. Even the sword-wearing teacher Kunō seemed more a buffoon than a threat in the harsh light of day. Likewise, peasants and local officials rented buildings to Dongya, stole fertilizer for themselves, sold jute to the guerillas, and apparently laughed at the city slickers forced to go out in the rain to relieve themselves.

Although the dissolution of the agriculture department had been amicable and Shi could take credit for coming to Dongya's rescue at a key moment of wartime danger, even decades latter he emotionally referred to this episode as "an attack on our spirits from this humiliating life [from which] our hearts could never be washed clean. It led to a lifetime of regret." He continues:

> Originally I entered Dongya, this leading institution of patriotism and principle, temporarily hiding and waiting for the water to clear, to again try to devote myself to the nation. Who would have thought that [like] a fish that has swallowed a hook regrets not enduring his hunger, it's already too late. ... From then on, I could only raise my guard and do my utmost to protect the interests of the company and do nothing to help the enemy. There was no certainty of victory, but [we] could at least continue fighting in spite of setbacks, do one's duty as a citizen during the tragic time of war.[62]

The logic here is a little slippery, but essentially Shi Shaodong portrays himself as at heart a patriot who, in the absence of the ability to help his country, placed his loyalty in the corporation for which he worked. As with millions of other Chinese in the occupation period, he ended up cooperating with the regime just by keeping his job. This was not the loyalty described by Wen-hsin Yeh of security agents who imagined "brotherhood" fashioned in the manner of swashbuckling novels.[63] It was instead the loyalty of the technocrat to his professional role within the business firm and to his personal relationship with his boss. Thus Shi's experience with the agriculture department became both a job well done and a lifetime of regret. In fact this odd combination of technocratic expertise and nationalist conflict characterizes much of Shi's experience of working in wartime China.

In Shi's story and in the initial plans for jute cultivation and gunny sack production drafted back in 1941, readers can perceive two different narratives of the war. On the one hand, technocrats at Mantetsu and the Kōa Institute, Shi Shaodong himself, and the board of directors at Dongya produced reams of rational-sounding surveys and plans full of charts and figures, trying to present scientific solutions to economic problems without direct mention of the wartime needs driving the allocation of resources. On the other hand, through Shi's memoir, we see the "traitor" Wang Fuwu, sitting in his Beijing compound with priceless works of Chinese art hanging on the wall and expensive cigarette ash dropping on an even more expensive Tianjin carpet, demanding compliance with the occupation regime—compliance that most likely involved bribery and certainly involved a Dongya subsidy for agricultural development in China for manufacturing needs. Shi's memoir, melodramatic as it is, serves as an important reminder that technocrats may have staffed the mid-levels of both the Japanese and Chinese bureaucracies but that their careful plans coexisted with the reality of a messy, venal, and often violent political and military process.[64]

The technocrats continued to function, keeping Dongya, and at some level the Japanese occupation regime, alive. At the same time, technocrats like Shi were singularly unprepared to deal with the realities of the Chinese countryside. Under the peculiar contingencies of the culture and economy of wartime China, the gulf between urban and rural grew larger, and the problems of future state building thus became harder.

Notes

1. Shi drafted the manuscript in the United States, probably in the 1970s, as part of a project to eulogize Song Feiqing, Shi's boss. When I examined the manuscript, it was divided into two sections. The first is seventy-four handwritten pages, and the second, forty-four. I have arbitrarily labeled them Shi Shaodong, "Memoir" 1 and "Memoir" 2. Passages quoted here were translated by me from the original Chinese. I am grateful to members of the Sung (Song) family for sharing Shi's manuscript and the notes of Song Feiqing's widow, Li Jingfang, with me. I am also grateful to Shi Shaodong's widow and son, Zhang Donglian and Frances Shek (Shi), for meeting with me and sharing their reminiscences and photographs. Finally, thanks to Jiang Xiling and Zhang Peiwen for helping me decipher Shi's script. This research was made possible in part by assistance from the Sung family, the University of Wisconsin Graduate School, the Fulbright Foundation, the Chiang-ching Kuo Foundation, and the University of Southern California.

2. On Japan's drive for autarky, see Barnhart, *Japan Prepares for Total War*, especially the introduction and ch. 8.

3. *Huabei nongshi shiyanchang yaolan.*

4. On the war's impact on agriculture, see Kirby, "The Chinese War Economy," 186, and Muscolino in this volume.

5. On Qingzhou during this period, see Sheehan, *Industrial Eden*, ch. 1.

6. Interview with Zhang Donglian and Frances Shek.

7. A capsule biography of Shi can be found in Dongya Maoni Fangzhi Gufen Youxian Gongsi, *Fushe huaxue chang gongzuo gaikuang.*

8. Shi, "Memoir" 1.

9. Ibid.

10. Ibid., and interview with Zhang Donglian and Frances Shek.

11. Dongya Maoni Fangzhi Gufen Youxian Gongsi, *Fushe huaxue chang gongzuo gaikuang.*

12. Interview with Zhang Donglian and Frances Shek.

13. Shi, "Memoir" 1.

14. Interview with Zhang Donglian and Frances Shek.

15. Shi, "Memoir" 2.

16. Ibid.

17. On a similar boom from 1938 to 1940 in Shanghai, see Henriot, "Shanghai Industries under Japanese Occupation."

18. "Minutes of the Meeting of the Board of Directors," May 23, 1940; and Sheehan, *Industrial Eden*, ch. 4.

19. Shi, "Memoir" 2.

20. Ibid.

21. Excerpts and quotes in the next several paragraphs are from Shi, "Memoir" 1.

22. "Minutes of the Meeting of the Board of Directors," January 2, 1942, and June 7, 1942.

23. "Minutes of the Meeting of the Board of Directors," September 20, 1942.

24. Mantetsu Hokushi Keizai Chōsa Jo, "Shōwa jūkonendo hokushi shuyō jukyuu busshi jukyū chōsa sankō shiryō."

25. Hashimoto, *Hokushi okeru masabukuro gaisetsu*, 1, 2. This later report refers to the earlier work in its preface.

26. Ibid., 2.

27. Shi, Memoir" 1.

28. Ibid. I have rearranged the paragraphs in this account to put them in chronological order.

29. Quotes and excerpts in the next several paragraphs are from ibid.

30. Ibid.

31. Dongya did place one or two Japanese individuals on salary, though their actual role at the company is unclear; see Sheehan, *Industrial Eden*, ch. 4.

32. Hashimoto, *Hokushi okeru masabukuro gaisetsu*, 4. On the Kōa Institute, see Kubo, "The Koa-in"; Wu, "Contending Political Forces during the War of Resistance"; and Imura, *Jyūgonen Sensō Jyūyō Bunken Shirīzu*, 17.

33. Hashimoto, *Hokushi okeru masabukuro gaisetsu*, 13, 15.

34. Ibid., 22.

35. *Huabei nongshi shiyanchang yaolan.*

36. "Minutes of the Meeting of the Board of Directors," June 7, 1942.

37. Shi, "Memoir" 1.

38. Ibid. Tsujihara was likely the author of a two-volume textbook on the Chinese language published in 1935 and 1936 called *Kago kyoohon*. For Romanization of Tsujihara's name, I follow the catalogue entry for this textbook in the foreign studies library of Osaka University, http://webcatplus-equal.nii.ac.jp/libportal/DocDetail?txt_docid=NCID%3ABA65214772; accessed September 28, 2009. Thanks to Michelle Damien for finding this entry for me.

39. Shi, "Memoir" 1.

40. This and the following excerpts are from ibid.

41. "Shi" (石) is commonly read "Ishi" in Japanese names, which Shi transliterates into Chinese as "Yixi 意稀," but apparently the Japanese reading for "Shi" as a Chinese name was Seki, which Shi writes as "Saiqi 塞奇."

42. Ibid.

43. Ibid. The 1943 survey of North China experimental farms notes that a jute cultivation farm was located on a military base in the Beijing suburbs. See *Huabei nongshi shiyanchang yaolan*.

44. Shi, "Memoir" 1.

45. Ibid.

46. Ibid.

47. Quotes and excerpts in the next several paragraphs are from ibid.

48. Ibid.

49. Brook, *Collaboration*.

50. Shi, "Memoir" 1.

51. Ibid.

52. Ibid.

53. Ibid.

54. Ibid.

55. Ibid.

56. Ibid.

57. Ibid.

58. Ibid.

59. Ibid.

60. Shi, "Memoir" 2.

61. Sheehan, *Industrial Eden*, chs. 6 and 7.

62. Shi, "Memoir" 1.

63. Yeh, "Urban Warfare and Underground Resistance," 111–132.

64. Wang Fuwu here reminds me of "Jimmy" Wang, the "fixer," portrayed in Timothy Brook's description of Nanjing in the immediate aftermath of occupation; see Brook, *Collaboration*, ch. 5.

Bibliography

Archives and Manuscript Collections

Archives of the Dongya Corporation, Tianjin, China.

Beijing Municipal Archives.

Interview with Zhang Donglian and Frances Shek, widow and son of Shi Shaodong, New Jersey, July 2000.

Shi Shaodong 石少東. Untitled memoir manuscript, papers of the Sung family, Berkeley California, original divided into two sections. Cited in notes as Shi, "Memoir" 1, and Shi, "Memoir" 2.

References

Barnhart, Michael A. *Japan Prepares for Total War: The Search for Economic Security, 1919–1941.* Ithaca and London: Cornell University Press, 1987.

Brook, Timothy. *Collaboration: Japanese Agents and Local Elites in Wartime China*. Cambridge, Mass. and London: Harvard University Press, 2005.

Dongya Maoni Fangzhi Gufen Youxian Gongsi 東亞毛呢紡織股份有限公司 (Dongya Woolen Spinning and Weaving Limited Shareholding Corporation). *Fushe huaxue chang gongzuo gaikuang* 附設化學廠工作概況 (General situation of the subsidiary chemical factory). Tianjin: Dongya Corporation, 1944.

Hashimoto Masayasu 橋本正保. *Hokushi okeru masabukuro gaisetsu* 北支ニ於ける麻袋概説 (Gunny sacks in North China). Mantetsu Research Department, n.p., 1942.

Henriot, Christian. "Shanghai Industries under Japanese Occupation: Bombs, Boom, and Bust (1937–1945)." In *In the Shadow of the Rising Sun: Shanghai under Japanese Occupation*, edited by Christian Henriot and Wen-hsin Yeh, 17–45. Cambridge: Cambridge University Press, 2004.

Huabei nongshi shiyanchang yaolan 華北農事試驗場要覽 (Survey of experimental farms in North China). Archives of the Agricultural Department of the North China Political Commission, Beijing Municipal Archives, J25-1-156.

Imura Tetsuo 井村哲郎, ed. *Jyūgonen Sensō Jyūyō Bunken Shirīzu*, 17 十五年戰爭重要文献シリーズ 17 (Documents from Fifteen Years of War Series, 17). Kōain kankō, toshyo, zasshi mokuroku 興亜院刊行図書雑誌目録 (Catalogue of Kōain periodicals, books, and, magazines). Tokyo: Fuji, 1994.

Kirby, William. "The Chinese War Economy." In *China's Bitter Victory: The War with Japan, 1937–1945*, edited by James C. Hsiung and Steven I. Levine, 185–212. Armonk, N.Y.: M. E. Sharpe, 1992.

Kubo, Toru. "The Koa-in." In *China at War: Regions of China, 1937–1945*, edited by Stephen R. Mackinnon, Diana Lary, and Ezra Vogel, 44–64. Stanford: Stanford University Press, 2007.

Mantetsu Hokushi Keizai Chōsa Jo 満鉄北支経済調査所 (Economic Research Department of the South Manchurian Railway). "Shōwa jūkonendo hokushi shuyō jukyuu busshi jukyū chōsa sankō shiryō 昭和十五年度北支主要物資需給調査参考資料" (Reference materials on commodity supply and demand in North China for 1940). Beijing: Mantetsu, 1940.

"Minutes of the Meeting of the Board of Directors," January 2, 1942. Archives of the Dongya Corporation, Tianjin, 1-38-5-01.

"Minutes of the Meeting of the Board of Directors," June 7, 1942. Archives of the Dongya Corporation, 1-38-5-02.

"Minutes of the Meeting of the Board of Directors," May 23, 1940. Archives of the Dongya Corporation, 1-27-3-02.

"Minutes of the Meeting of the Board of Directors," September 20, 1942. Archives of the Dongya Corporation, 1-38-5-03.
Sheehan, Brett. *Industrial Eden: A Chinese Capitalist Vision*. Cambridge, Mass: Harvard University Press, 2015.
Tsujihara Yafumi 辻原八二三. *Kago kyōhon* 華語教本 (Chinese language textbook). No place mentioned. Shunmei shojo, 1935–1936.
Wu, Tien-wei. "Contending Political Forces during the War of Resistance." In *China's Bitter Victory: The War with Japan 1937–1945*, edited by James C. Hsiung and Steven I. Levine, 51–78. Armonk, N.Y.: M. E. Sharpe, 1992.
Yeh, Wen-hsin. "Urban Warfare and Underground Resistance: Heroism in the Chinese Secret Service during the War of Resistance." In *Wartime Shanghai*, edited by Wen-hsin Yeh, 111–132. London: Routledge, 1998.

CHAPTER 8

Salt Wars

MAN BUN KWAN

> Few people understand the basic and vital importance of salt in the Sino-Japanese War economy. ... Japan ... holds the whip-hand in her control of salt. ... If the Japanese are determined to close the China war this year, a strict blockade of the coastal salt-works area would break down resistance and morale in the provinces of Central China inside of three months.
>
> Confidential Situation Report No. 11
> Far Eastern Section, Office of Strategic Services, June 17, 1942

The situation seemed dire indeed. While Sichuan, Yunnan, and the northwest were relatively self-sufficient, much of the country's production capacity was lost with the fall of major salt fields in the northeast, Shanxi (Hedong 河東), Hebei (Changlu 長蘆), and Jiangsu (Haizhou 海州) to the Japanese invaders. Those remaining in Zhejiang, Fujian, and Guangdong were under constant threat, and Zigong (自貢), long renowned for its deep-drilling brine wells in the interior, was bombed repeatedly. Supplies to non-salt producing Henan, Hubei (except Yingcheng), Hunan (except Xiangtan), Anhui, and Jiangxi were thus severely disrupted.[1] By June 1940, Japanese control of the Yangzi denied Sichuan salt access to markets downstream beyond Yichang (宜昌). The report quoted above further warned of how rising gabelle (salt taxes) and prices, hoarding, salt famine in Free China, and the depressing effect of a bountiful supply in Japanese-occupied territory would erode public confidence in the Nationalist government.

How could the Office of Strategic Services be wrong? This chapter analyzes the war of salt among areas under Japanese (and puppet regime) occupation and under Free China held by both the Nationalists and the Communists.[2] Waging total war, all used salt as part of their arsenals and pursued a broadly similar strategy.[3] Initially, prewar institutional restrictions were lifted, and each area imposed an embargo on salt against the other areas. As the war entered a protracted phase, each implemented controlled economies; developed plans and invested heavily to expand production; monopolized the trade; increased taxes; and imposed rationing and levies for revenues while promoting "exports" through smuggling, bartering for supplies and otherwise contraband items with each other, as well as supporting its own currency.[4] When the tide of war began to change in 1943 (if not earlier or later, depending on the theater), the battle lines also began to blur. The Japanese, the puppet regimes, and the Nationalists legitimized smuggling with each other while the Communists, with their control of transport routes and grain supply, evolved a more varied strategy among their various base areas.[5] Salt famines, bland eating (*danshi* 淡食), rationing, blockades, smuggling, black markets, rising prices, and gabelle amid a supply glut and exports to Japan and Korea thus reigned over daily life in wartime China.

Nationalist China

The Nationalist government prepared for war as best it could. Officials and scholars had been discussing the need to control the salt industry (*tongzhi yanye* 統制鹽業) as part of the drive toward a planned economy (*tongzhi jingji* 統制經濟) and gabelle reform.[6] In late 1935, the government required salt merchants to hold a strategic reserve of six million *dan*, or one year's supply in the interior provinces, collecting in the process over ¥10 million in gabelle. With so much of their capital committed, merchants lobbied successfully for permission to sell a portion of the shipments upon arrival.[7] When war did break out, the merchants could neither pay the requisite gabelle for the immediate release of all the salt stockpiled in the government depots on the coast, nor organize emergency evacuation of this strategic material into the interior. The task of removing, organizing, and financing the transportation fell on the government, along with a drastic overhaul of divisional boundaries to supply the territory still under its control and, where feasible, the lifting of all prewar limits on production.[8] Sichuan would expand to support Hunan, Hubei, Guizhou, Shaanxi, and Henan. What remained of Zhejiang production was redirected to cover Hunan, Jiangxi, and Southern Anhui. Guangdong would also ship to Hunan, Jiangxi, and Guangxi, with Fujian supplementing Hunan and Jiangxi.[9] These emergency measures became the first steps to nationalize the salt trade.

Sichuan, the only major salt division still intact, was the centerpiece in the Nationalist plan. Miao Qiujie (繆秋杰), a career salt technocrat, had been posted to the province to solve the problem of over-production in 1936. Under his "state-controlled free marketing" (*tongzhi ziyou* 統制自由) policy, each salt yard would still enjoy a designated market area, but any duly registered salt merchants would be allowed, at least nominally, to participate in the production, transportation, and pooled sale of salt in Sichuan and Guizhou.[10] As the salt-producing coastal provinces fell, however, Miao and his superiors reversed course. Production in Sichuan would have to be increased from seven million to twelve million *dan* to supply the designated provinces and make up for the lost gabelle.[11] Shuttered brine wells and evaporation pans were reopened throughout the province.[12] Daningchang in Eastern Sichuan, bordering Hubei, came to life again, producing salt that was carried on the back of couriers to the upper reaches of Duhe, then put on small crafts to Yunyang for Northwestern Hubei.[13] By way of Wujiang and Yuanjiang, Sichuan shipments could bypass the Yangzi River to reach Hunan.[14] New salt wells, collieries, and transportation routes were developed, with the effort coordinated by state control and planning. Production was promoted through subsidies to compensate for brine of low salinity, in addition to bonuses, loans, and advances.[15] However, even with tons of steel cable airlifted over the Hump each year for deep well drilling and other technical innovations by Fan Xudong's 范旭東 model salt refinery, the attempt to increase supply failed to overcome bottlenecks in gas, coal, and brine supply.[16] Between 1937 and 1945, annual Sichuan salt production never exceeded ten million *dan*.[17] Indeed, after reaching 9.8 million *dan* in 1941, production began to decline. (See table 8.1 for the production statistics.) Transportation difficulties caused an inventory glut in 1942 while costs remained high, forcing a retrenchment.[18] Elsewhere, success was also modest. With increased production in Yunnan, the province remained relatively self-sufficient, although that did not prevent hoarding and rising prices.[19] The northwest (Gansu and Shaanxi) also experienced growth, with part of their output supplying Henan, despite a high transport cost.[20] Overcoming constant threats of invasion and a loss of salt fields, Fujian and Eastern Guangdong also managed modest gains to support Hunan and Jiangxi.[21]

To solve bottlenecks in production, transportation, and distribution, as well as to stabilize prices and revenues, the Nationalist government implemented a plan to nationalize the salt industry.[22] In July 1937, Harvard- and Wharton-trained MBAs at the Salt Administration began planning for state financing of private salt making, state collection, transportation, and wholesaling, with state distribution depots supplemented by registered outlets and cooperatives.[23] The war and the people's livelihood—supply was the issue, not price or revenue—justified the centralized control of salt and other strategic resources. In the first phase, private merchants would still be allowed to participate in distribution, but they would be phased out as the state perfected the system. To finance the production, purchase, and transportation of twenty million *dan* of salt, officials budgeted a state capitalization of ¥3 billion in *fabi* (法幣 nationalist currency), although 1.5 billion was actually required, assuming a turnover rate of twice a year and zero inflation. The annual gabelle yield of ¥80 million would be incorporated into the state-set selling price, with a projected profit of ¥300 million. The Nationalist Party Central Committee plenary meeting approved the plan in 1939.[24] It would serve the purposes of adjusting "production and consumption of salt as the needs of national defense warrant," stabilize salt prices, rationalize distribution, minimize merchants' windfall profits, and simplify gabelle collection.[25] A committee of five—with three Harvard graduates (Chen Changheng, Ma Taijun, and Wei Tingsheng) among the members—was charged with designing the regulations to implement the plan.[26]

The foreign staff at the Salt Administration opposed the plan for a variety of reasons, including personal animosity.[27] O. C. Lockhart, the American associate director, dismissed the "ostensible purpose(s)" of the plan as a mere cover to fund the mounting budget deficit. He warned that aside from inefficiencies and the Salt Administration's inability to supervise a new sprawling bureaucracy, financing the government's investment would "seriously affect the budget and … further … unsettle prices rather than stabilize them." Furthermore, salt revenues would "become a variable commercial profit" that would raise significant legal issues. Since 1914, the gabelle had been collateralized for repayment of foreign loans, and the plan would be "in clear contravention of the assurances heretofore given to foreign governments, [and] to interested banking groups, and would therefore tend to affect unfavorably the sympathetic attitude of lending interest toward China's financial difficulties during the existing war." It was a "peculiarly inopportune" undertaking at a time of war.[28] After Lockhart's resignation, R. D. Wolcott, another American, continued the campaign as acting associate director. Writing to Manuel Cox at the Currency Stabilization Board, he complained that the Nationalist government was depriving the salt merchants of their "age-old rights." He predicted that the state's borrowings would double under the plan and contribute to a "vicious circle" of inflation with "grave consequences to the national currency and to the livelihood of the people."[29]

To Chongqing, however, the timing could not be more opportune. Revenue farmers had long stymied attempts at reforming the gabelle system through lobbying, underwriting bond issues, and contributing from their deep pockets. Displaced by the Japanese occupation, their hereditary privilege as sole purveyors of salt could be withdrawn without any compensation from the government and their monopolist profits absorbed as state revenues. To supervise and manage the production, collection, transportation, and distribution of salt would also require an army of bureaucrats. Suspicious that China's civil service was being used as "hunting grounds" by foreign adventurers, the Nationalists dismissed the objections of its foreign staff.[30]

Lockhart's and Wolcott's warnings, however, proved prescient. The implementation of the plan in 1941 with ¥100 million budgeted by the Finance Ministry and a ¥400 million loan from the Joint Office of Four State Banks proved woefully inadequate, necessitating an additional ¥400 million loan from the banks.[31] Even after the state changed its tri-annual price adjustment to monthly audits, producers soon complained of losses as wartime inflation eroded the official profit margin of 15 percent.[32] Aggravated by transportation problems and material and capital shortages, production slowed, and as a result, the portion collected by the state also began to decline (see table 8.1).

To make up for the supply shortfall while keeping revenues flowing, the Nationalist government adjusted its policy of total embargo to accommodate, if not encourage, smuggling as a more nuanced form of economic warfare.[33] In April 1941, the Finance Ministry filed a plan for "legitimate" merchants in Henan to import salt from the coast into Nationalist territory through designated crossings, an arrangement to which the Japanese acquiesced.[34] Six months later, the government also revised the gabelle assessment method. Consistent with the principle that consumption should be taxed by value (*congjia jizheng* 從價計徵) instead of by weight, henceforth salt would be taxed *ad valorem*, assessed at the time of release from the yard and then upon sales at 30–40 percent of local price. As a result, revenues from salt doubled for the year.[35]

The Salt Administration also addressed the problems of capital shortage and transportation by promoting joint public-private enterprises through transport tenders (*daiyun* 代運) and agents (*weituo* 委托). Tenders would be reimbursed only for insurance and cost of transportation plus interest and a wastage allowance. Agents would pay all taxes and levies before release of the salt, as well as costs en route, to be reimbursed with interest after a shipment was sold.[36] In addition, private banks were encouraged to finance shipments and tax payments through document billing, with tenders' costs of borrowing partially reimbursed (calculated at half the difference between the state bank's interest rate and market rate) by the Salt Administration.[37] Making the arrangement ever more enticing, agents' costs were reimbursed at market rate (as reported by the banks at the point of sale) to keep pace with inflation. In addition to state and provincial banks, well-connected private banks, such as Shanghai Commercial and Savings and Jincheng, joined the trade with their own salt companies. Providing financing, they also served as local repositories of salt revenues. These revenues were interest-free until the deposits were due at the Salt Administration, so the private banks could draw on the extra liquidity to make more loans and profits.[38] Despite "nationalization," the production and transportation of salt thus remained partially in private hands, with banks increasingly active in the trade. Similarly, salt was retailed through a mixed system of official outlets, franchised retailers, cooperatives, and private merchants, in addition to rationing (*jikou shouyan* 計口授鹽) enforced in Henan, Jiangxi, Hunan, Zhejiang, Fujian, and Eastern Guangdong, where supply was particularly tight.[39] Beginning in 1941, the system was extended to urban areas in Guizhou, Shaanxi, Sichuan, and Yunnan.

Such a complex program inevitably generated contradictions and problems. Imperfect supervision of the sprawling production facilities bred smuggling, stringent gabelle collection drove away merchants, and price controls discouraged their participation.[40] Matching supply and demand through rationing was difficult under the best of circumstances. Even when and where salt was plentiful, profiteering by merchants continued, and it was impossible to collect accurate population data with the country at war.[41] In Southern Jiangxi, where a pocket of "free trade" in salt persisted, spot shortages continued despite the Herculean efforts of pole bearers, including thousands of Hakka women, who made the two-week round trip from Fengshun in Guangdong to Anyuan in Southern Jiangxi, a distance of over two hundred miles on rugged terrain, balancing 80–100 *jin* of salt on their shoulders.[42] Yiyang, in Northeastern Jiangxi, similarly struggled over shortages as local officials pleaded for supply from Zhejiang; a ration standard of nine *liang* per person per month, reduced from eleven (average prewar consumption was estimated at 1.5–2 *jin*) was inadequate.[43] In Hunan, Xue Yue, the provincial governor, negotiated a barter arrangement with Li Hanyun, his counterpart in Guangdong. Hunan would supply rice to Guangdong at the rate of one *dan* of salt to 1.5 *dan* of rice, allegedly generating a handsome profit for the provincial trade bureau, as well as Xue's relatives and associates.[44] In Sichuan, some private dealers hoarded their stock to drive up prices. Local governments were then charged with the responsibility of wholesaling and distribution (*tonggou tongxiao* 統購統銷) in 1940, but they too became mired in graft and short supply. By late 1941, private merchants again handled the distribution of salt.[45] Smuggling, charges of corruption, and waste spread as the black market price of salt, fed by inflation, continued to climb.[46] Even Beipei, a "model" district outside Chongqing, was not immune to long lines of anxious citizens waiting for their purchase.[47]

One solution was legitimized smuggling. Visiting Chongqing as coordinator of the Office of Strategic Services (under cover as special assistant to the U.S. ambassador), Esson Gale observed "ample stocks of textiles, shoes, dress goods, thermos bottles, etc., obviously much of the material coming in from occupied China. This sort of smuggling is more or less winked at by the government, which has actually got the customs now collecting duties on such goods, thus giving them a quasi-legitimate charter. As they *will* come into Free China, the government apparently feels it might as well derive a much needed revenue."[48]

On June 26, 1942, the Nationalist government promulgated the "General Guidelines for Wartime Matériel Procurement" (Zhanshi Zhengqu Wuzi Banfa Dagang 戰時爭取物資辦法大綱) to legitimize, if not encourage, the importation of salt, metals, gasoline, and other commodities from occupied areas.[49] Seizing the opportunity, Shouning merchants transported salt from Eastern Fujian to Taishun, Zhejiang, and hence to Jiangxi via Qingyuan, which quickly became a boomtown for smugglers.[50] Smuggling continued along the Yangzi via Wuhu, Anqing, and Jiujiang into Anhui and Jiangxi. Another coastal route ran from Shanghai to Wenzhou, then transshipped for the journey up to Jinhua deep inside Zhejiang, where supplies could then be transported overland to Jieshou (Anhui), which became another boomtown.[51] Merchants in Hunan also worked with puppet forces to bring in salt and other supplies.[52] Xinxiang district in Henan became a "free market" for salt and other products, serving both the Japanese and the Nationalist areas.[53]

Nevertheless, the Nationalist government's salt policies during the war accomplished much. (See tables 8.1 and 8.2 for production and sales statistics.) The "age-old rights" of revenue farmers were officially abolished on January 2, 1942, an achievement that had been denied to generations of gabelle reformers.[54] Employing smuggling and anti-smuggling in economic warfare, the government secured salt and other supplies. The Nationalists also enjoyed a measure of success with salt from Sichuan, competing against the Shaan-Gan-Ning base area, leading the Communists to complain about "a lot of salt unsold" and deteriorating barter terms, which dropped from 4.1 bolts of cloth for one hundred catties or one dan of salt in 1940 to 1.4 in 1944.[55] Above all, the nationalization of salt proved a boon to the depleted national treasury. In addition to the gabelle, monopoly profits, wastage, and other surcharges, local, provincial, and national levies, such as a "military alimental subsidy" (*guojun fushifei* 國軍副食費), were collected.[56] The result was a massive increase of salt-derived revenues.[57] Between 1942 and 1945, salt-derived revenues from the new system generated over ¥80 billion, accounting for almost half of the central government's tax revenues for the period, and generated the bulk of its income from state-run monopolies.[58] However, after adjusting for inflation, the sum was only a fraction (approximately 5 percent) of the yuan's 1937 purchasing power as the price of salt rose, albeit more slowly than for other commodities.[59] Furthermore, as borrowing, deficit spending, and inflation exploded, the contribution of salt-related revenues as a percentage of total government income declined. Indeed, supply and transportation were the issues, not revenue or price (at least after 1942).

Table 8.1. Salt production by jurisdiction, 1937–1945 (thousands of *dan*)

Year	*Nationalist*	*State-collected*	*Communist*	*Occupied*	*Total*	*Adjusted Total*[a]
1937	42,663			20,498	63,160	(63,244)
1938	22,576			18,003	40,570	(40,654)
1939	20,665			35,027	55,682	(55,766)
1940	24,441			35,056	59,497	(62,485)
1941	19,179			47,065	66,244	(69,288)
1942	21,768	8,853	6,845	58,036	86,649	(89,275)
1943	25,080	16,126	2,508[b]	66,288	93,876[b]	(96,572)
1944	16,605	15,251	3,340	51,300	71,245	(74,363)
1945	13,235	11,643	3,690	46,330	63,255	(65,846)

Sources: Caizhengbu Yanwushu Yanwu Jihezongsuo, *Zhongguo yanzheng shilu*, vol. 1, tables 14 and 22; Nankai Daxue, *Zhongguo jindai yanwushi ziliao xuanji*, vol. 4, statistical tables 1 and 2; Ding and Tang, *Zhongguo yanyeshi*, jindai/dangdai (Modern/contemporary), 333.

[a]Figures in this column, enclosed in parentheses, are totals from the preceding column combined with available statistics from Shaan-Gan-Ning Bianqu Caizheng Jingjishi Bianxiezu, *Kangri zhanzheng shiqi Shaan-Gan-Ning bianqu caizheng jingji shiliao zhaibian* (converted at 1 *tai* = 1.2 *dan*); Shandong and Central China base areas.

[b]Xue Muqiao, *Kangri zhanzheng shiqi he jiefang zhanzheng shiqi Shandong jiefangqu de jingji gongzuo*, 246.

Table 8.2. Salt sales by jurisdiction, 1937–1945 (thousands of *dan*)

	Jurisdiction				
Year	*Nationalist*	*State-transported*	*Communist*	*Occupied*	*Total*
1937	40,366			17,249	57,615
1938	23,973			19,442	43,415
1939	21,143			22,560	43,703
1940	22,236			35,825	58,061
1941	20,984			33,145	54,129
1942	20,202	25,325		38,337	58,539
1943	22,270	27,768		45,808	68,078
1944	16,035	18,687		35,793	51,828
1945	15,150	13,647	4,270	18,190	37,610

Sources: Caizhengbu Yanwushu Yanwu Jihezongsuo, *Zhongguo Yanzheng shilu*, vol. 1, tables 14 and 22; Nankai Daxue, *Zhongguo jindai yanwushi ziliao xuanji*, vol. 4, statistical tables 1 and 2; Ding and Tang, *Zhongguo yanyeshi*, jindai/dangdai (Modern/contemporary), 333.

Communist Base Areas

The Chinese Communist Party (CCP) had eaten bland before, a lesson from its Jiangxi soviet period (1931–1934). It survived the Nationalist blockade and extermination campaigns—allowing "not a grain of rice, or a pinch of salt, or a ladle of water" through—by smuggling, working with private merchants, encouraging local production, and developing new transportation routes.[60] With the outbreak of full-scale war with the Japanese, the CCP also evolved a trade and tax policy, which included salt, as part of its controlled economy to solve the interlinked problems of securing war supplies, civilian consumption, and revenue and supporting base-area currencies as it expanded its guerilla warfare to nineteen major base areas.[61] At Shaan-Gan-Ning, where it was headquartered, salt was one of the three "treasures" (licorice and animal hair and felt being the other two). Capable of producing as much as 300,000 loads (*tuo* 馱, 150 *jin* each or 1.2 *dan*, approximately) in a good year before the war, the base area needed 70,000 loads for self-sufficiency. From 1931 to 1939, production from over five thousand *mu* of salt fields (one *mu* approximately 1/6 acre) and trade remained in private hands as the party paid little attention to gabelle collection or the trade.[62] Following a poor season in 1939, the base area established a salt bureau in 1940 and deployed over four thousand troops and militia to work on existing fields and developed approximately four thousand *mu* of new fields.[63] In the aftermath of the Southern Anhui Incident in January 1941, when the Nationalists imposed a total embargo on both imports and exports, as well as a termination of subsidies, the border region developed its salt production, transportation, and trade with both Nationalist and Japanese-occupied territories in Shanxi, Shaanxi, and Gansu in exchange for much needed cash and necessities, such as cotton cloth, through a government-managed and controlled trade.

Salt thus became one of the principal articles of trade. An ambitious production target of two million *tuo* was set for 1941, but as production expanded, transportation became a problem, and Lin Boqu, chairman of the Shan-Gan-Ning base area government, was finally persuaded that transportation of the sixty thousand *tuo* produced, the so-called public salt (*gongyan* 公鹽), should become part of the peasant corvée duties to support the Eighth Route Army.[64] Against the Nationalist blockade, the base area established a salt company in September 1942 (folded into the Guanghua Salt Company in June 1943 as the business front for the base area's trade bureau and bank). Once the gabelle was paid, salt was traded freely within the border region. However, the company held a monopoly for all salt exports in exchange for needed imports and *fabi* to help bolster the border region's own currency, underwrite "national salvation bonds" (*jiuguo gongzhai* 救國公債), and stabilize prices. Coordinating with private salt traders and transportation teams (whether public, private, joint, or cooperative), Guanghua sent salt into neighboring base areas such as Jin-Sui and Nationalist-held territory in Henan, Southern Shaanxi, and Shanxi, as well as Japanese-occupied Henan and Shanxi.[65]

Despite problems of coordination and smuggling, the operation proved a boon (if not a propaganda success) to the border region as a learning process. Rather than simply issuing orders, the party learned how to mobilize peasants as it overcame its initial reluctance by offering economic incentives for refugee settlement, salt production, and transportation.[66] After soldiers and militia withdrew from production in 1943, bonuses, interest-free loans, and advances encouraged peasant participation, as did raising the purchase price of salt and improvements in the transport network.[67] In lieu of their corvée service, peasants could pay a fee (*gongyan daijin* 公鹽代金) that financed the operation of transport cooperatives.[68] A propaganda campaign centered on Lu Zhongcai and other salt transport heroes became part of the Yan'an heritage.[69] It was also a fiscal success for the base area.[70]

As the single largest "export" item by weight (if not by value), salt helped finance importation of cotton cloth and other needed supplies, in addition to generating a sizable portion of the base area's revenues, income for various salt transport cooperatives, and exchange earnings.[71] The gabelle rate for salt sold and consumed inside the border region remained a relatively low ¥1.5–2 per *tuo* between 1937 and 1939, increasing to 400 *juanbi* (券幣) by 1943, averaging 5–6 percent of cost. Initially, exports were taxed at 5 percent, *ad valorem*, whereas matériel such as gasoline (30 percent) and "luxuries" such as wine (60 percent) were charged a higher rate, and opium was reportedly banned altogether.[72]

Learning about economic work, Mao and his colleagues thus evolved a salt policy. As nature's bounty and an alimental necessity, salt should be a public good.[73] To ensure supply and self-sufficiency for the border region, the gabelle must be light and the price cheap, and the masses must be mobilized through various forms of joint public-private enterprises for production, collection, and transportation—interest-free loans and advances, with the participation of private shareholders in cooperatives organized by peasants, the military, educational institutions, and even the law courts. However, as part of the border region's economic warfare strategy, salt exported to Nationalist and Japanese-occupied territory came under government control through the Guanghua Salt Company, with judicious taxing and pricing in exchange for cotton, cotton cloth, medicine, and other much needed supplies, as well as currencies to stabilize Shaan-Gan-Ning's prices and currency.

Various Communist base areas applied this salt policy and evolved additional strategies to adapt to local conditions. As the first base area established behind enemy lines in 1938, Shanxi, Chahar, and Hebei (the Jin-Cha-Ji base area) combined several guerilla areas, necessitating a more decentralized but coordinated trade strategy. Efforts to promote the production of earth salt leached from saline soil to supply the entire base area fell short.[74] Supplies (salt and grain) for Northern Hebei and Suiyuan (Taiyue) had had to be smuggled in from Japanese-occupied Shanxi through Dingxiang and Yingxian by merchants in exchange for mountain products (*shanhuo* 山貨) such as dates and almonds. In Eastern Hebei, the Communists developed a guerilla area along the coast and organized salt workers into the Salt Workers' National Protection Team (Yanmin Baoguodui 鹽民報國隊) as part of the resistance effort. Salt pans developed by the Japanese were sabotaged, depots raided, and inventory seized.[75] While Western Hebei remained dependent on smuggled Changlu salt, the area produced cotton and cotton cloth that could be traded with iron from Shanxi and Central Hebei, a trade that the Communists promoted.[76] Unlike Shaan-Gan-Ning's Guanghua Company, however, Yumin (established in 1938) was abolished as Jin-Cha-Ji's trading company in 1939. Instead, district commercial bureaus conducted trade through firms with government investment, as well as with private shareholders. In this precursor to the joint public-private enterprise system, merchants and companies who preferred to remain private were encouraged to form trade alliances. Responsibility for the conduct of trade was local, and profits were distributed according to local business customs.[77] Following the practice in Shaan-Gan-Ning, participation of private merchants and investors, as well as government organizations (including universities and the Eighth Route Army), were encouraged.[78] Peasants or cooperatives or the trade company handled the transportation, while distribution too could be performed by private merchants or cooperatives, with dividends declared in kind.

Similarly, the Jin-Ji-Lu-Yu base area, seat of the North China Bureau and command post of the Eighth Route Army, underwent a learning process. Straddling the four provinces of Shanxi, Hebei, Henan, and Shandong, initial policy was a total embargo against both imports and exports. Organized production of earth salt, whether by private merchants, the rich, and the enlightened gentry, was promoted for self-sufficiency.[79] In non-salt producing areas such as Eastern Henan (Taihang), where shortages were particularly acute, taxation was imposed, but otherwise trade was left to private merchants and cooperatives. The result was not merely an unstable supply and exchange rate, but also the importation of luxuries, cosmetics, and even opium. Imposing an embargo against such "undesirable goods" only stimulated smuggling, which could not be contained. From 1940, the base area government began to control trade through "firms" under a Trade and Industry Bureau. Smuggling of Changlu salt was encouraged through a low gabelle and higher price, in addition to the offering of mountain goods such as almonds, fodder, and foodstuffs to barter for cotton cloth, medicine, paper, and even matériel through "flash" merchants (*shandian shangren* 閃電商人). By 1942, "free trade" within the base area, encouragement of smuggled exports, controlled imports, and a managed exchange rate became the new policy under the Trade and Industry Bureau. It was finally recognized that total embargo against occupied areas was not only impossible, but also detrimental to the base area, serving only to reinforce the enemy. For better coordination, the tax and trade bureaus were combined, sharing offices with the base area's bank.[80] Cadres posing as merchants were posted at Tianjin, Shanghai, and Beijing to conduct "business" directly. To supply the base area, volunteer peasant women would steal from the Changlu salt fields, while guerilla forces organized raids of salt depots and provided protection.[81] Cooperatives again handled salt transportation and distribution, facilitating a quick delivery to Shanxi. By 1943, an articulated policy of controlled trade emerged. To ensure supply within the base area, the government was to trade fairly with private merchants, even if at a loss. The base area was to strive for advantageous terms of trade, but monetary profit was only a part of the equation. Indeed, the pursuit of short-term profits might jeopardize the long-term security of the base area and could be detrimental to the national resistance effort. Toward that goal, the trade of grains, almonds, dried peaches, pepper, and other mountain goods had to be managed judiciously by the base area government in exchange for salt and cotton.[82]

Also established in 1938, the Shandong base, divided into five areas, similarly evolved its own solution to the interlinked problems of currency warfare, revenue needs, price stability, and supplying the war effort. At the Bohai area in the north, Communist guerillas began to assert control by 1940 and developed new fields through loans in cash and grain, producing by 1942 over 100,000 *dan* of salt while exporting some 4,000 *dan*. The recovery and development of the Yangjiaogou and Tuowang salt fields to 64,000 *mu* produced over 2.4 million *dan* of salt in 1944, permitting the base area to become self-sufficient, with a transport, storage, and inventory system to regulate supply and prices.[83] Trade within the area was free before 1942, after which it became a government monopoly.[84] For the Binhai area south of Qingdao, the traditional revenue farming and distribution system by private merchants was replaced by salt exchanges (*yanye jiaoyisuo* 鹽業交易所), with peasants encouraged to participate and develop salt fields through low-interest loans.[85] From an initial total embargo on imports and exports, followed by bartering, the *fabi* became acceptable as legal tender to help maintain the base area's "foreign exchange" reserves and to finance needed imports of industrial goods and military supplies. However, as relations with the Nationalists soured, merchants had to use the base area's currency to purchase salt. In 1943, over one million *dan* of salt were "exported" via Northern Jiangsu (Huaibei) and Northwestern Anhui to Henan and Hubei, as well as to Nationalist and Japanese-occupied territory. The judicious management of this trade (and other agricultural surplus), with the adjustment of prices as necessary and relatively light gabelle charges to promote shipments to Nationalist and Japanese-held territories, allowed the base area to manipulate its currency against both the Nationalist *fabi* and puppet currencies, finally driving them out while still generating a sizable revenue.[86] Toward the end of the war, salt trade and profit-sharing between North China (Hebei and Shandong) and Central China (Subei) helped integrate the various base areas.[87]

In other parts of China, where the Communists fought for tenuous control, they evolved a different policy mix on production, the gabelle, pricing, and trade. The Central China (Huazhong) base area, with eight bases scattered over Anhui, Henan, Hunan, Hubei, Jiangsu, Jiangxi, and Zhejiang Provinces, had partial control of the Fu'ning and Yancheng (Fudong) salt fields in Huainan and Huaibei.[88] In addition to salt smuggled in from Japanese- and puppet-controlled areas, as well as Shandong base areas, salt production in Fudong grew with private investors and the settlement of refugees, averaging 800,000 *dan* annually between 1941 and 1945, with over 100,000 *dan* shipped to Northern Anhui, Eastern and Southern Henan, and Northern Hubei.[89] For the non-salt producing Henan-Hubei (Yu-E) border region founded in 1938, salt was gabelle-free to attract shipment.[90] Elsewhere, a light gabelle combined with an export tax of 15 percent *ad valorem* was adopted to compete against supply from the occupied areas, generating over ¥30 million in salt-related revenues for the base area in 1942.[91] Although not the single largest source of tax revenue, salt consistently came in second, behind transit taxes on goods among the various base areas in the region.[92] By late 1943, the base area government began to assert its control over salt production and trade, insisting that salt must be bartered at advantageous terms for supplies in kind instead of puppet regime currency.[93] Where control by the Japanese and Nationalists' anti-smuggling forces remained strong, as in Eastern Zhejiang (Zhedong), wedged between Shanghai and Ningbo, Communist guerillas fought for partial control of the production fields around Andong on the coast by mobilizing salt workers to facilitate smuggling and collecting the gabelle indirectly from village heads as their major source of revenue.[94]

The non-salt-producing Huaibei-Su-Yuan base area, founded in March 1940 and covering parts of Northern Anhui and Jiangsu, was also vital to the transport of salt for Northeastern Anhui, Central Hubei, and Southwestern Henan. While acknowledging that controlled imports and exports were critical to economic warfare, the base area government also recognized that obsession with profits and monopoly could be harmful to the base area. A light gabelle and transit taxes were designated as regular revenues for government and military expenses. To attract trade, private merchants, duly registered and subject to targets set by the government, remained the mainstay of commerce.[95]

Private merchants performed other services elsewhere. In the neighboring Central Anhui base area, the trade bureau, using the Jicheng Company as a front, bartered with the Japanese and elements of the puppet regime. With the cooperation of Yang Taiyan, owner of a fleet of private junks based at Wuhu, arrangements were made with Zhou Yunhai, a major dealer of salt and cotton, with offices in Shanghai and Wuhu. Zhou's company, Haiji, would smuggle salt from Haizhou, with transportation provided by Yang in exchange for rice.[96] Other trade was conducted through the China Commodity Company (Zhonghua Wuzi Gongsi) in Shanghai with the puppet regime's Navy Department. With the blessing of its Japanese adviser, Zhonghua bartered with Jicheng, shipping supplies to the base area on a navy bottom, thus evading Japanese inspection, and sending rice back to Shanghai. Through a network of mutual friends, Shi Yuangao, plant manager of a Xianhecaosu herbal medicine factory, established the Anyuan Company. Through this company, the Yuanjiang base area bartered rice, tobacco, and other agricultural products for salt, cotton cloth, yarn, medicine, and paper for printing money with Mitsubishi (Shanghai).[97] Transported by guerillas and peasants organized as a "resistance cart society" (*chekanghui* 車抗會), the system eventually enabled the Communists to supply salt to base areas in Anhui, Central Hubei, and Southwestern Henan, with prices at least 10 percent below competing supplies from Japanese- and puppet-controlled areas.[98] By 1944, capitalizing on food shortages in the occupied Lower Yangzi, representatives of the base area were confident enough to negotiate directly with Wang Zidong, head of the Wuhu chamber of commerce, and his Japanese adviser. The Communists offered grain, foodstuffs, and even opium in a barter formula that included 30 percent in matériel (explosives, fuses, machine guns, and telegraph equipment), 30 percent in controlled supplies (steel, copper, tools, and lathes), and the remainder in salt, matches, batteries, medicine, and sundries.[99]

In guerilla areas in South China, yet a different mix of strategies was pursued. At the Central Guangdong base area, the borrowing of salt from merchants was supplemented by the imposition of a transit tax, ranging from twenty cents per one hundred *jin* to ¥2 per ten thousand *jin*, or it was waived where necessary (¥1 = 100 cents).[100] In Hainan Island, after Nationalist subsidies ended in 1940, the Communists relied increasingly on the gabelle and operated periodic salt markets to raise revenues and supplies for themselves and the population. Salt was also a mobilization tool: to enjoy salt, one must join the resistance.[101]

Embargos, barter, controlled and free trade, gabelle-free or taxed directly or indirectly, as well as other local ad hoc policies, thus reveal considerable variations in policies pursued by the Communists without a centralized salt administration. While the various policies generated sizable revenues for the base areas, problems remained. In Shaan-Gan-Ning, among the issues identified in party documents were government-run hostels that forced peasant transports to stop and pay high prices. Local branches of the salt company imposed their own fees (such as taking two bowls of salt from every load, purchasing salt at a depressed price, or cheating at the weighing scales). All these practices in the pursuit of profits not merely discouraged peasants from participating in the trade, but also encouraged smuggling.[102] In 1942, at least 100,000 *tuo* of salt, worth 500 million base area currency (*bianbi* 邊幣), were smuggled by merchants and the military into Nationalist-held territory amid clashes between the Communists' own anti-smuggling forces and the Eighth Route Army.[103] The participation of various public institutions (including the courts and universities) in salt trading and transportation further aggravated problems of coordination.[104] While Mao Zedong extolled his policy of controlled exports as a delicate balance between public and private (*gongsi jian gu* 公私兼顧) interests, some of his subordinates complained of his having conceded too much, while in practice private merchants were often denied opportunities.[105] Similarly, Mao's calls for valuing economic work equally with bravery in battle, vigilance against wasteful spending and (worse) corruption, and coordination among the various base areas often went unheeded. Competition against Sichuan salt and a Nationalist blockade left a lot of Shaan-Gan-Ning production unsold, while smuggling by crafty merchants (*jianshang* 奸商) also proved difficult, if not impossible, to contain.[106]

Occupied China

Japanese designs for salt began well before the outbreak of full-scale conflict. The invasion of the northeastern provinces in 1931 was followed by the seizure of salt revenues and the Revenue Inspectorate.[107] After considerable debate and wavering, the Nanjing government countered by requiring the placement of its own officials to supervise salt production and shipments, effectively shutting down the salt trade from the provinces, resulting in the bankruptcy of private Chinese producers and merchants there.[108] However, negotiations to continue exports from Qingdao and "surplus" Changlu and Haizhou salt to Japan and Korea continued, finally yielding an agreement between Tokyo and Nanjing in 1936.[109] Henceforth, salt for industrial use was exported at a gabelle rate of ¥1 per ton. On the other hand, the Japanese puppet regime in the northeast also encouraged sales of refined salt to North China and Shanghai by lowering its export duty and by smuggling.[110]

When full-scale war broke out in 1937, the Japanese identified several objectives. The Ministry of Finance in Tokyo ordered that occupied China must supply two million tons of salt to Japan by 1942 and 3.5 million tons by 1945.[111] While the Japanese military gladly shared the revenue and profits, a blockade would have to be implemented to starve the resistance effort. Production should be expanded to feed growing industrial demands at home and provide a cheap supply for Japan's occupied subjects while raising revenues for the puppet regimes.[112] To achieve these goals, the military, Japanese *zaibatsu*, private investors, and the puppet regimes joined forces.[113] There were debates at times over how these objectives should be prioritized, but all agreed on direct government control and reform of the salt industry with modern technology and the removal of traditional revenue farmers.[114] With the start of the world war, Japan seized the Salt Revenue Inspectorate and conducted surveys to identify industries and resources deemed crucial for its war effort, with smuggling to areas outside of the occupation playing a supplemental role in acquiring Nationalist *fabi* for conversion into American dollars and pounds sterling (part of the currency war discussed by Parks Coble in this volume).[115] To ensure a cheap supply, embargo and anti-smuggling efforts should be vigilant, and consumption in China should be curbed through rationing.[116] Included in a five-year plan to develop resources in China, salt production would be expanded to feed Japan's domestic demand (both alimental and industrial) and wean the country from dependence upon Egyptian, Indian, Mediterranean, and American imports.[117] Elaborate plans were made to expand production in China through various regional development corporations with the support of the Japanese military and capital from Japanese companies, puppet regimes, and collaborators.

In the northeast, the Manchurian Salt Company (Manshū Engyō Kabushiki Kaisha) was established in 1936 with a capital of ¥5 million from a group of Japanese companies; it was to take over and develop the production facilities of bankrupted Chinese merchants.[118] Planned export targets ranged from 400,000 to 800,000 tons per year. Actual exports ranged from 17,000 to 508,000 tons.[119]

The same policy was implemented in North China, an area including the salt production centers of Changlu (Hebei), Qingdao (Shandong), and Hedong (Shanxi).[120] Soon after the war began, the China Development Corporation (Kōchū Kōshi 興中公司), a subsidiary of the Southern Manchurian Railroad Company, made a one million yen loan to the Changlu Salt Administration to improve and develop salt fields for exports to Japan.[121] With another investment of ¥18.75 million from the North China Development Corporation (Kita Shina

Kaihatsu Kaisha 北支那開発会社), the puppet regime in North China, Mitsui, and Mitsubishi, the North China Salt Company (Kita Shina Engyō Kabushiki Kaisha 北支那塩業株式会社) was established in 1939 to expand production capacity in Changlu, with 600,000 tons planned for export to Japan by 1940.[122] Through loans and Chinese fronts such as the Bohai Salt Company, 94,804 *mu* of salt pans were developed at Han'gu and 2,296,000 tons of Changlu salt shipped to Japan during the war years.[123] Separately, Japanese companies organized the Shandong Salt Company (Santō Engyō Kabushiki Kaisha 山東塩業株式会社) in 1937 to develop salt fields in Shandong. They were joined by the North China Development Corporation, Mitsui, and Mitsubishi in 1938, bringing capitalization of the company to ¥10 million, with 600,000 tons targeted for export to Japan and Korea.[124] The transportation, wholesaling, and distribution of salt in Hebei and Henan remained in the hands of revenue farmers in partnerships (such as Dexing) led by collaborators, with rampant smuggling to Free China tacitly approved by the Japanese military or distributed through programs requiring peasants to barter salt for grain or cotton.[125]

In Central China, the Japanese occupation seized control of the salt fields as the Japanese military and *zaibatsu* capital initially displaced Chinese merchants, not merely in salt production, but also in distribution.[126] Haizhou (Huaibei), the major salt field in the region, was held by the North China Military Command. After a protracted negotiation, the Central China Command assumed jurisdiction in 1939, eventually passing control to the Central China Salt Company (Kachū Engyō Kohin Yūgen Kōshi 華中塩業股份有限公司), a subsidiary of the Central China Development Corporation (Chūshina Shinkō Kabushiki Kaisha 中支那振興株式会社).[127] The distribution and export of salt were entrusted initially to the Tongyuan Company. Capitalized at five million yen, the company was jointly held through Tongyuan (18 percent); collaborators at Haizhou (12 percent); Deyuan Shiye Gongsi, a secret partnership of the puppet regime (30 percent); Central China Salt (10 percent); and Japanese *zaibatsu*, including Mitsui, Mitsubishi, and Okura (9 percent each).[128] In addition to handling all salt exports, Tongyuan also collected the gabelle on behalf of the Japanese Army. After the military kept its share, the puppet regime received the remainder, which constituted one-third of its revenues for 1938.[129] Through improvements to the fields, modern technology, and the removal of "exploitative" capitalists, Japanese planners believed that production could easily be expanded, making as much as 900,000 tons available for export to Japan annually. Unfortunately, natural disasters repeatedly disrupted the plan. It took over a year for production to recover to the prewar level of 600,000 tons, with over ¥1 million in loans to repair the salt fields. Henceforth, the rebuilding and rejuvenation of existing fields preoccupied the regime.[130] In 1943, a five-year contract was signed by the Nanjing puppet regime for an annual export of 150,000 tons to Japan.[131]

The Tongyuan Company also monopolized salt distribution in occupied Jiangsu, Zhejiang, Anhui, and Jiangxi, replacing the preexisting network of revenue farmers.[132] Under a stringent system of transport permits and an extensive list of controlled commodities, military approval, inspection, and rationing were enforced.[133] Pacification campaigns were supplemented by economic warfare: military-issued currency (*junpiao* 軍票) to collect raw materials and foodstuffs or using the company's control of salt to barter for supplies such as rice, vegetable oil, hemp, and cotton.[134] However, as the war dragged on, smuggling became even more rampant. As much as 80 percent of the supplies intended for Anhui south of the Yangzi (Bangbu and Wuhu under Japanese occupation) reportedly were shipped west instead to Tongcheng and Qianshan into Free China. Taizhou, Huaiyin, and Danyang also served as transshipment points.[135] Even with the "assistance" of the Japanese Army, it was impossible to contain the traffic, just as the Communists too shared the same predicament with "treacherous" merchants bribing their troops to facilitate the traffic.[136]

In South China, the same strategy of military control, rationing, and planning to develop production for export was pursued, although smuggling, feuding Japanese companies, and disagreements between the army and the navy again hampered the effort.[137] Finally, Japanese military intelligence conducted surveys and approved a plan for new salt fields.[138] Burying their feud, Mitsui Bussan and Dai Nippon Engyō formed the Tōa Engyō Kabushiki Kaisha 東亜塩業株式会社 (East Asia Salt Company) in 1941 to double Hainan Island's salt production to 600,000 tons per year for export to Japan.[139] However, guerilla activities and labor and supply shortages prevented implementation of the plan.

Exports of salt to Japan from occupied China during the war years thus came primarily from the northeast and North China, made possible with Japanese investment and requisitioned land and labor in those regions. However, the acreage of salt fields developed to supply Japan fell far short of the planned targets.[140] Demands and needs of the Japanese empire nevertheless must be fulfilled. Exports to Japan and Korea during the period thus accounted for at least half of the production.[141] With at least half a million tons requisitioned by the Japanese military and over ten million tons (approximately 16.8 *dan* per ton) shipped to Japan and Korea for the period, salt supplies became strained as production capacity failed to keep pace.

Export demand and gabelle-free requisition taxed not merely the salt supply, but also the puppet regimes. Shipments to Japan and Korea generated little revenue as the duty remained at ¥0.05 per *dan* during the period amid rising inflation. The struggling puppet regimes resorted to successive gabelle increases and additional levies to raise revenues. The result was a thirty-eightfold increase in revenues from salt between 1937 and 1945.[142] As Nanjing was forced to lower the per capita ration standard from 1.5 *jin* to 0.7 *jin* per month, actual supply was even lower or none at all.[143] The salt companies also increased their prices to maintain their profits. In 1941, Nanjing, nominal capital of the puppet regimes, reported shortages and bland eating.[144] By 1944, amid Allied bombings of railroad links in North China, even salt shipments that did go through were used to barter for food and other supplies with the Communists rather than being used for rationing.[145] There was little reason for the people in Free China to envy their compatriots in occupied China.

War and Daily Life: "Three Days without Salt, We Feel Weak"

In the decade before the war, China's annual salt consumption hovered at 40–60 million *dan*, with production restricted to contain oversupply. From 1937 to 1945, in comparison, total production averaged over 66 million *dan*, reaching a high of over 93 million in 1943, while sales averaged 53 million *dan*. Except for 1938, when less than 24 million *dan* of current-year production was left after exports to Japan and Korea, an average of over 50 million *dan* was theoretically available each year to feed the country between 1937 and 1945. Shortages of salt were thus as much a problem of production, supply, wartime disruption of transportation, and economic warfare, aggravated by exports to Japan and Korea.[146] As total war engulfed the country, a war of salt was waged through government planning, rationing, embargoes, blockades, and smuggling, transforming the basic and common commodity into a strategic matériel.

The results were mixed. None of the plans came to full fruition. Despite heavy government and *zaibatsu* investment, Japanese targets for new fields and exports remained unfulfilled. For the Nationalists and the Communists, promotion of the salt industry through government loans, advances, and even the direct involvement of the military (as in the case of the Communists in Shaan-Gan-Ning and Shandong) also achieved modest growth without reaching the planned targets. Embargoes came and went as strategies and battle lines shifted. Smuggling, illegal on one side but perfectly legitimate on the others, proved impossible to contain. Meanwhile, all the regimes derived a significant portion of their revenues from salt through ever-higher gabelle, levies, and monopoly profits.

Few were left unaffected by this aspect of the total war. Workers toiled to increase production, whether as a matter of survival under the Japanese or as a patriotic duty in Free China. Mule teams and couriers struggled with sacks of salt on their backs over rugged terrain, and boatmen risked their lives (and cargo) navigating treacherous rapids to make their deliveries. Revenue farmers who had controlled the trade before the war found their hereditary privilege abolished, while advocates of gabelle reforms celebrated as smugglers, hoarders, well-connected merchants, bankers, and bureaucrats profited. Instead of a product of free trade, however, salt became primarily a government monopoly, a transformation that presaged the nationalization of the industry in 1952. Ultimately, it was the populace who had had to eat bland food and suffer under an increasingly regressive tax.

Notes

1. U.S. Office of Strategic Services, Joint Chiefs of Staff; held at Library of Congress; Caizhengbu Yanwu Zongju, *Yanzheng gailun*, 60–63. The author would like to thank the Charles P. Taft Memorial Fund for support of this project.

2. For a convenient survey of the literature, see Huang Jian, Cheng Longgang, and Zhou Jing, *Kangzhan shiqi de Zhongguo yanye*, passim, and Zhang Lijie, "Kangzhan shiqi."

3. For a succinct summary of the phases in this aspect of the war, see Qi, "Kangzhan shiqi."

4. Wang Shihua, *Kaifa yu lueduo*, ch. 1, and Chen Lei and Dai Jianbing, "Tongzhi jingji yu kangri zhanzheng."

5. On smuggling, see Qi, *Zhongri jingji*, passim, esp. ch. 4 on the shifting routes.

6. Minutes of Salt Administration meeting, April 19, 1935; JD, 700189; and Huang Lingjun, "30–40 niandai Zhongguo sixiangjie de jihua jingji sichao."

7. "Archives of the National Board for Refined Salt"; JD, 200572.

8. Dong, "1937–1941 nian Guomin zhengfu."

9. Caizhengbu Yanwu Zongju, *Yanwu faling huibian*, 14–16, 24–26, 35–40; "Zhanshi yan zhi yunxiao gaikuang." On Zhejiang production, see Hou Qiang, *Ningbo yanyeshi*, 72–75. Eastern Guangdong supplied Hunan and Jiangxi, while Western Guangdong supplied Guangxi. For supply to Guangxi and Hunan from Guangdong and Hainan via Yu'nan, see http://www.yunfudaily.com/zt/200906230023.htm; accessed September 14, 2009. For the route to Jiangxi from Western Fujian, see www.wenhuazz.com/showArticle.asp?ArticleID=1902; accessed September 14, 2009; and Pan Rongyang, "Kangri zhanzheng shiqi Fujian yanye jingji guanli yanjiu," 47–48.

10. The evolution of Sichuan's salt administration is too complex a story to tell here. See Lin, *Chuanyan gaiyao*, 33–62; Caizhengbu Yanwu zongju et al., vol. 2: "Chuannan," 1–128, and "Chuanbei," 1–112; Miao et al., *Chuancuo gailue*, passim.; Li Han, *Miao Qiujie*, 104–111; Zigongshi Yanwu Guanliju, 234–236; and Zelin, passim.

11. Dong, *Kangzhan shiqi*, 164. By 1941, the gabelle collected had fallen to ¥100 million from the prewar high of ¥240 million. Letter from Wolcott to Cox, June 19, 1941, in Box 74, Arthur N. Young Papers. The official return was a shade over ¥125 million. See Caizhengbu Yanwushu Yanwu Jihezongsuo, *Zhongguo yanzheng shilu*, 1:27. 16 *liang* = 1 *jin;* 100 *jin* = 1 *dan;* 1.2 *dan* = 1 *tuo.*

12. Ren, "Kangri zhanzheng shiqi de Sanxia yanye."

13. http://www.syiptv.net/travel/ShowArticle.asp?Article ID=18683&Page=2; accessed September 26, 2009.

14. Li Zhancai and Zhang Jing, *Chaozai*, 229–230.

15. Caizhengbu Yanwu Zongju, *Yanzheng gailun*, 56–60.

16. Zhang Xiaomei, *Chuanyan shi kuang ji zengchan wenti*, passim. On the Jiuda salt refinery, see Kwan, *Beyond Market and Hierarchy*, 121.

17. *ZGJDYWSZLXJ*, 4:252–253, and Caizhengbu Yanwu Zongju, *Yanzheng gailun*, 56. Miao, however, reported to Chiang Kai-shek that Sichuan production reached 10.27 million *dan* in 1939. See Liu Jinghua, "Kangzhan shiqi Guomin zhengfu yanwu guanli tizhi de bianqian," 8–17, esp. 13.

18. Caizhengbu Yanwu Zongju, *Yanzheng gailun*, 60.

19. Shishi wenti yanjiuhui, *Kangzhanzhong de Zhongguo jingji*, 417.

20. Tian and Zhou, *Zhonghua yanyeshi*, 497–498; Li Han, *Miao Qiujie yu Min'guo yanwu*, 179.

21. Zhang Xiaohui and Pan Deng, "1942–1945 nianjian Yuedongqu de shiyan yunxiao"; Pan, "Kangri zhanzheng shiqi Fujian yanye jingji guanli yanjiu," 46.

22. Dong, *Kangzhan shiqi*, 129–140. Beginning in 1939, the sale of tobacco and alcohol came under state control, followed by salt, sugar, matches, antimony, tungsten, and tea. See He, *Kangzhan shiqi zhuanmai shiliao*, passim.

23. Zhu Tingqi, director of the administration, was Song Ziwen's classmate at Harvard; Bei Gongyi, a chief secretary under Zhu, was trained at Wharton. For the influence of other Western-trained "technocrats," see Kirby, "Engineering China."

24. "Outlines of Plan for the Introduction of Alimentary Salt Monopoly in China: Translation"; Salt Administration memo to the Finance Ministry, December 1940; in Arthur N. Young Papers, Box 74; and Guojia Shuiwu Zongju, *Zhonghua min'guo gongshang shuishoushi*, 188–192.

25. Salt Administration confidential memo to the Finance Ministry, December 1940; in Arthur N. Young Papers, Box 74.

26. "Yanzhuanmai fang'an fagui cao'an huibian."

27. Zhu Tingqi and O. C. Lockhart were "at complete logger-heads." See R. D. Wolcott's letter, May 13, 1938, R. D. Wolcott Papers, Bentley Historical Library, University of Michigan, Ann Arbor.

28. O. C. Lockhart's draft, February 27, 1941, and revised memo to Song Ziwen, March 14, 1941; in Arthur N. Young Papers, Box 74.

29. Wolcott's confidential letter to Cox, June 19, 1941; in Arthur N. Young Papers, Box 74.

30. Wolcott, too, resigned in February 1942, bringing an end to the "synarchy" of the Salt Administration. See his letter to L. C. Wolcott, August 6, 1927, in R. D. Wolcott Papers. He also offered his services to the U.S. Navy intelligence. See Box 1, File 48, L. C. Yarnell Papers.

31. Chongqingshi Dang'anguan, *Silian zongchu shiliao*, 2:461. Subsequent loans for the purpose of financing the purchase and transportation of salt were ¥387 million for 1942 (January–November); ¥478 million for 1943 (January–November); and ¥4.69 billion for 1944. Revolving lines of credit and loans to the divisional and provincial salt administrations amounted to ¥2.243 billion in 1945.

32. JD, 300567, 300645; Song Shangze and Wang Zhenhua, "Kangzhan shiqi Chuanyan de jiage guanli," esp. 67. Miao Qiujie, one of the architects of the monopoly plan, was dismissed

after he ordered a salt price increase to alleviate producer losses. See Li Han, *Miao Qiujie*, 149–150.

33. Weng, *Kangzhan yilai de jingji*, 80–84.

34. Caizhengbu Yanwu Zongju, *Yanwu faling huibian*, 114–115; Qi, *Zhongri jingji*, 94–116, 135–136; and Liu Xudong: "Riwei shiqi de Henan yanwuju," and *Tianjin wenshi ziliao xuanji*, 211.

35. Zhang Bofeng and Zhuang Jianping, *Kangri zhanzheng*, 5:184.

36. See Caizhengbu Yanwu Zongju: *Yanwu faling huibian*, 55, and *Yanzheng gailun*, 55, 120–121, 130, 140; Yang Xingqin, *Zhongguo zhanshi yanwu*, 72–76.

37. Luo and Huang, "Zigong yanye yingyun zhong de yahui," 96.

38. Li Jianchang, *Guanliao ziben yu yanye*, 86–90.

39. Tian and Zhou, *Zhonghua yanyeshi*, 517. See also Huang Yunhua, "Jikou shouyan yu jikou shouliang," 26–27, and Hou Fangkui, "Zhanshi E'xi shiyan gouxiao qingkuang."

40. Caizhengbu Yuedong Yanwu Guanliju et al., *Yanwu gaiyao*, 3:62.

41. "Cong pubian shishi jikou shouyan suoqi," 68.

42. www.kjwhsky.net/old/topic.asp?topic_id=20453 14K 2009-5-6; accessed September 16, 2009; http://www.hakkaw.com/xw07/2007-8-28/2007828211147_3.html; accessed October 3, 2009.

43. Dong Zhenping, "Kangzhan qianqi," 197–204.

44. Xiao, "Xue Yue chouban Hunansheng maoyiju neimu." Only 7,000 *dan* of salt were shipped. See Ye, "'Zhongweiyan' yu Yue-Xiang yanliang huihuan."

45. Caizhengbu Yanwu Zongju, *Yanzheng gailun*, 123.

46. Salt Administration report, May 22, 1944; in Zhongguo Di'er Lishi Dang'anguan, *Zhonghua minguoshi dang'an ziliao huibian*, series 5, part 1, vol. 14, 153–156; Caizhengbu Yanwu Zongju, *Yanzheng gailun*, 123; *ZGJDYWSZLXJ*, 4:71–83; and Guojia Shuiwu Zongju, *Zhonghua min'guo gongshang shuishoushi*, 214–216.

47. For the problem in 1941, see JD, 800351 and 800349. For 1943, see Zhongguo Di'er Lishi Dang'anguan, *Zhonghua minguoshi dang'an ziliao huibian*, 2:993–994.

48. "Letters from Chungking," July 19, 1942; in Esson M. Gale Papers, Box 1; emphasis in original. Gale served in the Salt Revenue Inspectorate from 1914 to 1927.

49. *Jingjibu gongbao*, May 17–18, 1942, 431–432.

50. "Kangri zhanzhen qijian Qingyuan yanshi de xingshuai."

51. Huang Meizhen et al., *Riwei*, 537–538, and Dong, "Zhejiang." On smuggling routes, see "Gesheng huoyun diaocha baogao," passim, and Qi, *Zhongri jingji*, 227–229.

52. Qi, *Zhongri jingji*, 121.

53. Liu Xudong, "Riwei shiqi de Henan yanwuju," 206–208.

54. *ZGJDYWSZLXJ*, 4:47.

55. "General Feature of Salt Production in Shaan-Gan-Ning Border Region," Arthur N. Young Papers, Box 74; SGN, *Kangri zhanzheng shiqi Shaan-Gan-Ning bianqu caizheng jingji shiliao zhaibian*, 6:222; and Schran, *Guerilla Economy*, 137.

56. For the myriad of levies and surcharges, see Zhang Bofeng and Zhuang Jianping, vol. V, 184–202; and Guojia Shuiwu Zongju, *Zhonghua min'guo gongshang shuishoushi*, 243–263.

57. Caizhengbu Yanwushu Yanwu Jihezongsuo, *Zhongguo yanzheng shilu*, 1:27; Ding et al., *Minguo yanwu shigao*, 407; Dong, *Kangzhan shiqi;* Guojia Shuiwu Zongju, *Zhonghua min'guo gongshang shuishoushi*, 225; Zhang Bofeng and Zhuang Jianping, vol V, 165.

58. Guojia Shuiwu Zongju, *Zhonghua min'guo gongshang shuishoushi*, 227, 238–239.

59. Zhang Lijie, "Kangzhan houqi."

60. Zhou Li and Gong Dandan, "Zhongyang suqu shiqi queyan wenti yanjiu," 94–102. See also Jiangxisheng Dang'anguan et. al., *Min Zhe Gan geming genjudi caizheng jingji shiliao xuanbi*, 414–418.

61. "Zhonggong zhongyang guanyu muqian fabi wenti ge genjudi ying caishu de zhengce," 18–20; Seldon, *China in Revolution*, 145.

62. Mao Zedong (drafted by Li Fuchun), "Jingji wenti yu caizheng wenti"; SGN, *Kangri zhanzheng shiqi Shaan-Gan-Ning bianqu caizheng jingji shiliao zhaibian*, 3:292–296.

63. Mu, "Kangri zhanzheng shiqi Shaanbei diqu yanwu." A small number of "bad elements" (*erliuzi* 二流子) were also deployed. See SGN, *Kangri zhanzheng shiqi Shaan-Gan-Ning bianqu caizheng jingji shiliao zhaibian*, 8:745.

64. Letters to Xie Juezai, August 6, 1941, and August 22, 1941; "Bianqu caizheng jingji zhengce," 247; *Mao Zedong ji*, 8:250–259; Zhongyang Dang'anguan et. al., *Shaan-Gan-Ning*, 2:346–348; and SGN, *Kangri zhanzheng shiqi Shaan-Gan-Ning bianqu caizheng jingji shiliao zhaibian*, 3:292–313; 4:127–150, 193–207, 375–378; 6:16.

65. Song Jinshou, *Kangzhan shiqi de Shaan-Gan-Ning bianqu*, 458–461, and Shangyebu Shangye Zengce Yanjiuhui, *Jianguo qianhou shangye gongzuo shilu*, 82. On the evolution of these companies, see SGN, *Kangri zhanzheng shiqi Shaan-Gan-Ning bianqu caizheng jingji shiliao zhaibian*, 4:408–419; Chen Zhijie, "Kangzhan shiqi Shaan-Gan-Ning bianqu gongying shangye de goucheng yu jingying." On the transportation system, see Li Jianguo, "Shaan-Gan-Ning," and Tong, "Kangzhan shiqi Shaan-Gan-Ning bianqu shiyan yunshu yanjiu," passim.

66. Liu Yanping, "Shaan-Gan-Ning."

67. Including the resettlement of refugees. See Mu, "Kangri zhanzheng shiqi Shaanbei diqu yanwu," esp. 5.

68. SGN, *Kangri zhanzheng shiqi Shaan-Gan-Ning bianqu caizheng jingji shiliao zhaibian*, 3:301–306, 744–813; 6:73, 439–541.

69. *Mao Zedong ji*, 8:254–259, and Zhonggong Xibei Zhongyangju Diaocha Yanjiu Shi, *Zhang Qingfeng yun yan qijia*, passim.

70. "General Feature of Salt Production in Shaan-Gan-Ning Border Region," Arthur N. Young Papers, Box 74; SGN, *Kangri zhanzheng shiqi Shaan-Gan-Ning bianqu caizheng jingji shiliao zhaibian*, 3:296–297 and 311–312; Shaanxisheng Dang'anguan and Shaanxisheng Shehui Kexueyuan, *Shaan-Gan-Ning;* Schran, *Guerilla Economy*, 133 and table 6.5; Mu, "Kangri zhanzheng shiqi Shaanbei diqu yanwu," 5; Wang Jianguo, "Lun Huazhong kangri genjudi gongshang shuishou ji dui huazhong kangzhan de zuoyong," 174; Lü, "Shaan-Gan-Ning," 11, 13; Ding and Tang, *Zhongguo yanyeshi*, 310.

71. Ding and Tang, *Zhongguo yanyeshi*, 312; SGN, *Kangri zhanzheng shiqi Shaan-Gan-Ning bianqu caizheng jingji shiliao zhaibian*, 6:48, 59, 65, 77, 82, 89, 236–237, 367, 374–375, 427, 426–427, 566–569; Seldon, *China in Revolution*, 146; Yung-fa Chen, "The Blooming Poppy."

72. On opium, see Yung-fa Chen, "The Blooming Poppy."

73. SGN, *Kangri zhanzheng shiqi Shaan-Gan-Ning bianqu caizheng jingji shiliao zhaibian*, 1:125.

74. On the Communist effort in this area, see Thaxton, *Salt of the Earth*, passim.

75. Hong and Xie, "Jidong jiefangqu yanwu gongzuo lueshu."

76. On the three trade routes between Southeastern Shanxi and Central Hebei, see Chen Tingxuan, *Kangri genjudi jingjishi*, 216–217 and 440. See also Kangri Zhanzheng Shiqi Jin-Cha-Ji Bianqu Caizheng Jingjishi Ziliao Xuanbian Bianxiezuet al., *Kangri zhanzheng shiqi*

Jin-Cha-Ji bianqu caizheng jingjishi ziliao xuanbian: "Zhonglun," 335, 437, and "Gongshang hezuo," 453.

77. "Zhonglun," 255, in Kangri Zhanzheng Shiqi Jin-Cha-Ji Bianqu Caizheng Jingjishi Ziliao Xuanbian Bianxiezu et al., *Kangri zhanzheng shiqi Jin-Cha-Ji bianqu caizheng jingjishi ziliao xuanbian.*

78. Ibid., 356–357; *gongshang hezuo*, 495–512. Private investors were limited to ¥500 per person/company. See Li Gongpo, *Huabei dihou*, 120.

79. Kangri Zhanzheng Shiqi Jin-Ji-Lu-Yu Bianqu Caizheng Jingjishi Ziliao Xuanbian Bianjizu, *Kangri zhanzheng shiqi Jin-Cha-Ji bianqu caizheng jingjishi ziliao xuanbian*, 2:242–243.

80. Henansheng Caizhengting et al., *Jin-Ji-Lu-Yu*, 1:95, 237 and 2:465–468, 528–530; Caizhengbu Caizheng Kexue Yanjiusuo, *Kangri genjudi de caizheng jingji*, 132–150; Shangyebu Shangye Zhengce Yanjiuhui, *Jianguo qianhou shangye gongzuo shilu*, 40; and Shangyebu Shangye Jingji Yanjiusuo, *Geming genjudi shangye huiyilu*, 171–191.

81. Jia and Liu, "Gaozhuang funü beiyandui"; Henansheng Caizhengting et al., *Jin-Ji-Lu-Yu*, 2:510–518.

82. Ibid., 237–238, and Kangri Zhanzheng Shiqi Jin-Ji-Lu-Yu Bianqu Caizheng Jingjishi Ziliao Xuanbian Bianjizu, *Kangri zhanzheng shiqi Jin-Ji-Lu-Yu bianqu caizheng jingjishi ziliao xuanbian*, 2:1216.

83. It came with military assistance. See Xue, *Xue Muqiao huiyilu*, 123, and http:www.fyjs.cn/bbs/htm_data/158/0909/207091; accessed September 26, 2009.

84. Wang Aimin, "Bohai geminqu yanzheng guanli shuping."

85. Shandongsheng Caizheng Kexue Yanjiusuo and Shandongsheng Dang'anguan, *Shandong geming genjudi caizheng shiliao xuanbian*, 1:199–200 and 5:303–307; Zhongguo Renmin Yinhang Jinrong Yanjiusuo, *Zhongguo geming genjudi Beihai yinhang shiliao*, 1:456, 486–487; and Liu Dake, "Shandong jiefangqu yanwu gongzuo jilue."

86. Xue, *Kangri zhanzheng*, 5–6 and 246. For the first half of 1941, the gabelle constituted 12 percent of the base area's revenue, and for 1944 and 1945, 11 and 10 percent, respectively.

87. Integration came after considerable haggling over the terms. Ibid., 246–247.

88. Huazhong Kangri Genjudi He Jiefangqu Gongshang Shuishoushi Bianxiezu, *Huazhong kangri genjudi he jiefangqu gongshang shuishou shiliao xuanbian*, 1:494–501.

89. Jiangsusheng Caizhengting et al., *Huazhong kangri genjudi caizheng jingji shiliao xuanbian*, 3:183–184, and Zhonggong Henan Shengwei, *Yu-Wan-Su*, 2:218.

90. Jiangsusheng Dang'anguan et al., *Huazhong kangri genjudi caijing shiliao xuanbian*, 432.

91. Zhan and Cheng, "Huazhong kangri genjudi yanye shulue," 24–26.

92. Wang Jianguo, "Lun Huazhong kangri genjudi gongshang shuishou ji dui huazhong kangzhan de zuoyong." Goods were tax-free if in transit through Southern Jiangsu. See Jiangsusheng Dang'anguan et al., *Su'nan kangri genjudi*, 126–128.

93. Jiangsusheng Dang'anguan et al., *Suzhong kangri genjudi*, 235–237; 322–336.

94. Zhejiangsheng Dang'anguan et al., *Zhedong kangri genjudi*, 247–248, 345–346, and Hou Qiang, "Kangri zhanzheng shiqi," 111–114.

95. That also led to widespread smuggling. See Anhuisheng Caizhengting et al., *Anhui geming genjudi caijing shiliao xuan*, 1:55–68, 468–472.

96. Shen and Wu, "Zai teshu huanjing zhong de teshu maoyi," 349–351.

97. Ying et al., *Wanjiang kangri genjudi caijing shigao*, 96–98.

98. Jiangsusheng Dang'anguan et al., *Suzhong kangri genjudi*, 1:58 and 3:464; Ying et al., *Wanjiang kangri genjudi caijing shigao*, 100–101; Anhuisheng Caizhengting et al., 2:56; Shangyebu Shangye Jingji Yanjiusuo, *Geming genjudi shangye huiyilu*, 261–262.

99. Ying et al., *Wanjiang kangri genjudi caijing shigao*, 112–113; Shen and Wu, "Zai teshu huanjing zhong de teshu maoyi," 351.

100. Foshanshi Shuiwuju et al., *Zhujiang, Yuezhong geming genjudi caizheng shuishou shiliao xuanbian*, 166, 283, 298.

101. Hainan Xingzhengqu Dang'anguan et al., *Qiongya geming genjudi caijing shuishou shiliao xuanbian*, 2:48–49, 68–69.

102. Zhongyang Dang'anguan et. al., *Shaan-Gan-Ning*, 2:348–352.

103. SGN, *Kangri zhanzheng shiqi Shaan-Gan-Ning bianqu caizheng jingji shiliao zhaibian*, 4:129, 136, 561–563 and 6:401–406. Elsewhere, attempts to ban the military from salt and other trading proved futile. See Jiangsusheng Dang'anguan et al., *Huazhong kangri genjudi caizheng jingji shiliao xuanbian*, 3:371, and Jiangsusheng Dang'anguan et al., *Suzhong kangri genjudi*, 169.

104. SGN, *Kangri zhanzheng shiqi Shaan-Gan-Ning bianqu caizheng jingji shiliao zhaibian*, 8:384, 451, 510, 556, 635; Chen Zhijie, "Kangzhan shiqi Shaan-Gan-Ning bianqu gongying shangye de goucheng yu jingying," 114–116; and Song Jinshou, *Kangzhan shiqi de Shaan-Gan-Ning bianqu*, 489.

105. SGN, *Kangri zhanzheng shiqi Shaan-Gan-Ning bianqu caizheng jingji shiliao zhaibian*, 4:571, and Liao, "Su-Wan bianqu de caijing gongzuo," esp. 67.

106. Liu Ruilong, Report, April 19, 1945. On the same problem in Northern Jiangsu, see Kōain Kachū Renrakubu, *Sohoku kyōsan chiku jitsujō chōsa hōkokusho*, 211–212.

107. Kantōgun sanbōbu, *Manshū jihen choku kisaki no Tosansho ensei nikansuru shōhō*, 63–67.

108. On the debate and lobbying, see Kwan, *Beyond Market and Hierarchy*, 102–108.

109. Beginning with Shigemitsu Mamoru's cable to Tokyo, dated June 17, 1931, JACAR, B09042269700. Even before that agreement, Chiang Kai-shek had already approved a 70,000 ton shipment from Changlu. See Jiang, Cable to Kong Xiangxi, August 17, 1935; Ju and Zhang, *Riben zai huabei jingji tongzhi lueduoshi*, 206.

110. Keizai Chōsakai Dainibu Daisanhan, *Manshūkoku enmu gyōsei seido kaikakuan*, passim.; Zhang Lijie, "Kangzhan quanmian."

111. Ding et al., *Minguo yanwu shigao*, 296.

112. Kōain Kachū Renrakubu, Report, December 10, 1941, JACAR, B006050552399.

113. On the participation of *zaibatsu* (financial combines, trust or corporate groups), especially Mitsui bussan, in the war, see Sakamoto, *Zaibatsu to teikoku shugi*, passim., esp. 378–379, for a list of its investments in various companies.

114. "Riben zhengfu suoyi guanyu Zhongguo yanwu xingzheng gaige zhi fang'an."

115. For these surveys, see Kyōji Asada et al., *Nihon teikoku shugika no Chūgoku*, 17–25, and below. On the evolution of Japanese policies in different parts of occupied China, see Qi Chunfeng, *Zhongri jingji*, 60–61; Jiang Pei, "1937–1941 nianjian Riben tongzhi huabei celue tiaozheng shulun"; and Dai, *Zuie de zhanzheng zhizhai*, 94.

116. Nakamura, *Senji Nihon no Kahoku keizai shihai*, 242–256, and Shanghaishi Dang'anguan, *Riben zai huazhong jingji lueduo shiliao*, 196–209.

117. For Japan's domestic production and import statistics, see *Senzen senchūno seifu kankei shuppanbutsu*, tables.

118. Suzuki, *Manshū kigyōshi kenkyū*, 610–615.

119. "Ri'man jingji tongzhi fangce yaogang"; "Manzhouguo jiben guoce dagang," 38, 70, 90–95, 287, and 298; Kōgyō Kagakukai Manshū Shibu, *Manshū no shigen to kagaku kōgyō*, 282.

120. Kōain Kahoku Renrakubu, *Kahoku engyō ritchi jōken chōsa hōkokusho*, passim. See also Liu Hongjuan, "Erci shijie dazhan qijian Riben dui Tianjin Changluyan de tongzhi he lueduo," 153–161, and Yang Caidan, "Kangri zhanzheng shiqi riben dui Hedong yanchi de lueduo," 46–49.

121. Contract, August 21, 1937, JACAR, B02130155100, and unpublished materials from *ZGJDYWSZLXJ*. On the China Development Corporation, see Jie Xueshi, ed., *Mantie yu Huabei kaifa huishe*, passim.

122. Minami Manshū Tetsudō Kabushiki Kaisha: *Kita Shina engyō*, 109–117, and *Kita Shina en*, 73; Bao, "Riben qinhua shiqi Changlu yanye kaifa." The goal for 1945 was 1.01 million tons. See Kita Shina Engyō Kabushiki Kaisha, "Kaisha."

123. Kita Shina Engyō Kabushiki Kaisha, "Dai ni-kai." See also Yan, "Wo suo zhidao de Bohai yanye gongsi," and Jin, "Riben zhanling qijian de kaitan he lueyan."

124. Kōain [Kahoku Renrakubu] Chintao Shutchōjo, *Santō-shō ni okeru engyō*, 49–50; Santō Engyō Kabushiki Kaisha, "Dai jū ichi eigyō hōkokusho"; *ZGJDYWSZLXJ*, 3:26–30, 86; Kobayashi et al., *Shina senryōchi keizai no hatten*, 211–214. For a list of Japanese companies receiving such shipments, see Japanese consul (Tianjin), Letter to the Changlu District Salt Administration, September 8, 1938.

125. Cheng, "Changlu Dexing yanwu zonggongsi shimoji"; Liu Xudong, "Riwei shiqi de Henan yanwuju," 199–202; Wou, "Food Shortage," 187.

126. Liu Hongqian, "Jiangsusheng he Lianghuai yanqu de kangri douzheng"; Tao, "Kangri zhanzheng shiqi de Huainan yanchang."

127. Shingo Sumiyoshi et al., *Chūka engyō jijō*, 438–439, and Kōain Kachū Renrakubu Reizai Dai 2-Kyoku, *Kachū engyō kohin yūgen kōshi ni tsuite*, 3–4. In 1943, the company was "sold" to Zhonghua Yanye Gufen Youxian Gongsi, a company with the Ministry of Finance of the Nanjing puppet regime as the biggest shareholder. See Ding and Tang, *Zhongguo yanyeshi*, 183.

128. *ZGJDYWSZLXJ*, 3:143–160. Tongyuan also received approval and capital from the Japanese military. See Chūshi kakengun Shanhai Ishūdan, Cable to the Army Ministry.

129. Shanghaishi Dang'anguan, *Riben zai huazhong jingji lueduo shiliao*, 264.

130. Kōain Kachū Renrakubu, *Kaishu engyō chōshashu*, 70–72; Haizhouqu Yanwu Guanliju, *Haizhouqu Yanwu Guanliju nianbao*, 51–54; and Huang Meizhen et al., *Riwei dui Huazhong lunxianqu jingji de lueduo yu tongzhi*, 340.

131. Nanjing to Tokyo cable, August 4, 1943, JACAR, B09042270500.

132. On the evolution of the company, see Ding and Tang, *Zhongguo yanyeshi*, 180–183. After considerable debate between the puppet regime and the Japanese, Tongyuan was replaced by the Yuhua Company. See Kōain Kachū Renrakubu, Report, December 16, 1941, JACAR, B06050552300; and Caizhengbu Yanwushu Xu Zhongguo Yanzheng Shilu Weiyuanhui, *Xu zhongguo yanzheng shilu*, 5–6.

133. Huang Meizhen, "Riwei dui yi Shanghai wei zhongxin de huazhong lunxianqu de wuzi tongzhi."

134. Shanghaishi Dang'anguan, *Riben zai huazhong jingji lueduo shiliao*, 190. See also Report on salt smuggling via Anqing, April 30, 1941, JACAR, B06050552700.

135. Kōain Seimubu, *Chūshi shio no kokka haikyū kankei chōsa hōkoku*, 152–153, 180–181.

136. Kōain Kachū Renrakubu, *Ryōsetsu*, 20, 60–65, and Yang Huizhuang, "Zenyang zhankai duidi jingji fan qinluezhan," 469–474.

137. Lai, "Kangzhan shiqi Riben dui huanan diqu jingji lueduo yu tongzhi de tiedian."

138. Minami shina hōmengun Nami shūdan shireibu, "Nanshi engan ni okeru enjō chosa yōzu."

139. Kasahara, "Saikin ni okeru Kainantō seien jōkyō."

140. *ZGJDYWSZLXJ* 3:14; Ding and Tang, *Zhongguo yanyeshi*, 180, 186; Jie, *Mantie yu Huabei jingji*, 234 and table 3-30; Kōain Kachū Renrakubu Reizai Dai 2-Kyoku, *Kachū engyō kohin yūgen kōshi ni tsuite*, 7; Pan Jian, "Wangwei zhengfu yanzheng yanjiu"; Guangdongsheng Dang'anguan, "Riben 'Dongya yanye zhushi huishe,'" 12–16.

141. *ZGJDYWSZLXJ*, 3:312–313; 316–317; Ding et. al., 328–329.

142. For a list of the increases and salt-related revenues, see Ding and Tang, *Zhongguo yanyeshi*, 195–199, and *ZGJDYWSZLXJ*, 3:314–315.

143. Ibid., 297–303.

144. *Nanjing xinbao*, March 1, 1941, as cited in Pan Jian, "Wangwei zhengfu yanzheng yanjiu," 23; Huang Meizhen et al., *Riwei dui Huazhong lunxianqu jingji de lueduo yu tongzhi*, 401. For reports from other areas, see *ZGJDYWSZLXJ*, 3:303–311.

145. Kangri Zhanzhen Shiqi Jin-Ji-Lu-Yu Bianqu Caizheng Jingjishi Ziliao Xuanbian Bianjizu, *Kangri zhanzheng shiqi Jin-Cha-Ji bianqu caizheng jingjishi ziliao xuanbian*, 2:1282.

146. Caizhengbu Yanwu Zongju, *Yanzheng gailun*, 109–110.

Bibliography

Archives and Manuscript Collections

Archives of the Jiuda salt refinery (JD)

Bentley Historical Library, University of Michigan, Ann Arbor

Arthur N. Young Papers, Hoover Institution on War, Revolution, and Peace, Stanford, Calif.

Institute of Modern History Archives, Academia Sinica

L. C. Yarnell Papers, East Asian Library, University of Southern California

Esson M. Gale Papers, Bentley Historical Library, University of Michigan, Ann Arbor

Japan Center for Asian Historical Records, National Archives of Japan (JACAR)

Kangri zhanzheng yu jindai Zhong Ri guanxi wenxian shuju pingtai 抗日戰爭與近代中日關係文獻數據平台 (Database of documents on the Anti-Japanese War and modern Sino-Japanese relations), http://www.modernhistory.org.cn

R. D. Wolcott Papers, Bentley Historical Library, University of Michigan, Ann Arbor

"Zhongguo jindai yanwushi ziliao xuanji bianyu" 中國近代鹽務史資料選辑編餘 (Selected materials on the history of salt in modern China). Unpublished material, Institute of Economics, Nankai University (ZGJDYWSZLBY)

Newspapers and Periodicals Cited as Primary Sources

Jingjibu gongbao 經濟部公報 (Ministry of economic affairs gazette)

Periodical and Documentary Publication Abbreviations

KZYJ: *Kangri zhanzheng yanjiu* 抗日戰爭研究 (Studies on the Anti-Japanese War of Resistance)

SGN: Shaan-Gan-Ning Bianqu Caizheng Jingjishi Bianxiezu 陝甘寧邊區財政經濟史編寫組 (Editorial Committee for the Selected Materials on the History of Finance and Economy of the Shaan-Gan-Ning Base Area during the Anti-Japanese War) et al., eds. *Kangri zhanzheng shiqi Shaan-Gan-Ning bianqu caizheng jingji shiliao zhaibian* 抗日戰爭時期陝甘寧邊區財政經濟史料摘編 (Selected materials on the history of finance and economy of the Shaan-Gan-Ning base area during the Anti-Japanese War), 9 vols. Xi'an: Renmin chubanshe, 1981

YYSYJ: *Yanyeshi yanjiu* 鹽業史研究 (Studies in the history of salt)

ZGJDYWSZLXJ: Nankai daxue Jingji yanjiusuo jingjishi yanjiushi 南開大學經濟研究所經濟史研究室 (Nankai University). *Zhongguo jindai yanwushi ziliao xuanji* 中國近代鹽務史資料選辑 (Selected materials on the history of salt in modern China), 4 vols. Tianjin: Nankai daxue, 1985–1991)

References

Anhuisheng Caizhengting 安徽省財政廳 (Anhui Provincial Finance Bureau) et al., eds. *Anhui geming genjudi caijing shiliao xuan* 安徽革命根據地財經史料選 (Selected materials on the fiscal and economic history of the Anhui revolutionary base area), 3 vols. Hefei: Anhui renmin chubanshe, 1983.

Bao Lianhe 鮑連和. "Riben qinhua shiqi Changlu yanye kaifa 日本侵華時期長蘆鹽業開發" (Development of the Changlu salt industry during the Japanese invasion of China). *YYSYJ*, no. 2 (1995): 46–47, 53.

"Bianqu caizheng jingji zhengce 邊區財政經濟政策" (Fiscal and economic policy of the border region). In *Lin Boqu wenji* 林伯渠文集 (Collected writings of Lin Boqu). Beijing: Huayi chubanshe, 1996.

Caizhengbu Caizheng Kexue Yanjiusuo 財政部財政科學研究所 (Fiscal Research Institute of the Finance Ministry), ed. *Kangri genjudi de caizheng jingji* 抗日根據地的財政經濟 (Finance and economy of the anti-Japanese base areas). Beijing: Zhongguo caizheng jingji chubanshe, 1987.

Caizhengbu Yanwu Zongju 財政部鹽務總局 (Finance Ministry Salt Bureau), comp. *Yanwu faling huibian* 鹽務法令彙編 (Compendium of salt laws and regulations). Chongqing: Caizhengbu Yanwu zongju, 1942.

———. *Yanzheng gailun* 鹽政概論 (A general treatise on salt administration). Chongqing: Yanwu zongju, 1944.

Caizhengbu Yanwu Zongju 財政部鹽務總局 (Finance Ministry Salt Bureau) et al. *Zhongguo yanzheng shilu* 中國鹽政實錄 (A veritable record of salt administration, third compilation), 4 vols. 1933. No publisher given.

Caizhengbu Yanwushu xu Zhongguo Yanzheng Shilu Weiyuanhui 財政部鹽務署續中國鹽政實錄委員會 (Finance Ministry Salt Administration, Committee for the Compilation of the Veritable Record of Salt Administration, sequel), comp. *Xu zhongguo yanzheng shilu* 續中國鹽政實錄 (A veritable record of salt administration, sequel) Nanjing: Caizhengbu yanwushu, 1945.

Caizhengbu Yanwushu Yanwu Jihezongsuo 財政部鹽務署鹽務稽核總所 (Salt Auditing Department of the Salt Office of the Finance Ministry), comp. *Zhongguo yanzheng shilu* 中國鹽政實錄 (A veritable record of salt administration, fourth compilation), 2 vols. Nanjing: Caizhengbu, 1948.

Caizhengbu Yuedong Yanwu Guanliju 財政部粵東鹽務管理局 (East Guangdong Management Department of the Finance Ministry) et al. *Yanwu gaiyao* 鹽務概要 (Essentials of salt work), 3 vols. 1940. No publisher given.

Chen Lei 陳雷 and Dai Jianbing 戴建兵. "Tongzhi jingji yu kangri zhanzheng, 統制經濟與抗日戰爭" (Controlled economy and the Anti-Japanese War of Resistance). *KZYJ*, no. 2 (2007): 175–195.

Chen Tingxuan 陳廷煊. *Kangri genjudi jingjishi* 抗日根據地經濟史 (An economic history of the anti-Japanese base areas). Beijing: Shehui kexueyuan chubanshe, 2007.

Chen, Yung-fa. "The Blooming Poppy under the Red Sun." In *New Perspectives on the Chinese Communist Revolution*, edited by Tony Saich and Hans van de Ven, 263–298. Armonk, N.Y.: M. E. Sharpe, 2015.

Chen Zhijie 陳志杰. "Kangzhan shiqi Shaan-Gan-Ning bianqu gongying shangye de goucheng yu jingying 抗戰時期陝甘寧邊區公營商業的構成與經營" (The structure and operation of public trade companies in the Shaan-Gan-Ning border region during the Anti-Japanese War of Resistance). *KZYJ* no. 2 (2004): 100–117.

Cheng Haiou 程海鷗. "Changlu Dexing yanwu zonggongsi shimoji 長蘆德興鹽務總公司始末記" (The beginning and end of Changlu Dexing salt company). *Wenshi ziliao xuanji* 文史資料選輯 (Selected materials on literature and history), no. 44 (1963): 164–173.

Chongqingshi Dang'anguan 重慶市檔案館, et al., eds. *Silian zongchu shiliao* 四聯總處史料 (Historical materials of the joint office of four banks), 3 vols. Beijing: Dang'an chubanshe, 1993.

Chūshi kakengun Shanhai Ishūdan 中支派遣军上海伊集团 (Shanghai corps of the Japanese Army sent to China). Cable to the Army Ministry, December 19, 1938. JACAR, C04120698600.

"Cong pubian shishi jikou shouyan suoqi 從普遍實施計口授鹽說起" (Start talking about general salt rationing). *Zhejiang chao* 浙江潮 (Zhejiang tide), no. 121 (1940): 68.

Contract. August 21, 1937. JACAR, B02130155100.

Dai Jianbing 戴建兵. *Zuie de zhanzheng zhizhai* 罪惡的戰爭之債 (Criminal debts of war). Beijing: Shehui kexue wenxian chubanshe, 2005.

Ding Changqing 丁長清 and Tang Renyue 唐仁粵, eds., *Zhongguo yanyeshi* 中國鹽業史 (A history of the salt industry in China), 3 vols. Beijing: Renmin chubanshe, 1997.

Ding Changqing 丁長青 et al. *Minguo yanwu shigao* 民國鹽務史稿 (A draft history of salt affairs during the Republican period). Beijing: Renmin chubanshe, 1990.

Dong Zhenping 董振平. "1937–1941 nian Guomin zhengfu shiyan yunshu zidu shulun 國民政府食鹽運輸制度述論" (A review of the Nationalist government's alimental salt transport system, 1937–1941). *YYSYJ*, no. 1 (2002): 18–25.

———. "Kangzhan qianqi Jiangxi shiyan gongxiao wenti shulun 抗戰前期江西食鹽供銷問題述論" (Salt supply and sales in Jiangxi Province early in the War of Resistance). *Yanwenhua yanjiu luncong* 鹽文化研究論叢 (Anthology of studies on salt culture), no. 1 (2005): 197–204.

———. *Kangzhan shiqi guomin zhengfu yanwu zhengce yanjiu* 抗戰時期國民政府鹽務政策研究 (A study of Nationalist salt policy during the War of Resistance). Ji'nan: Qilu shushe, 2004.

———. "Zhejiang zhanshi shiyan shouyunchu shouyun shuping 浙江戰時食鹽收運區收運述評" (A review of the alimental salt collection and transport system in Zhejiang during the war). *YYSYJ*, no. 1 (1999): 18–23.

Foshanshi Shuiwuju 佛山稅務局 (Foshan Tax Bureau) et al., eds. *Zhujiang, Yuezhong geming genjudi caizheng shuishou shiliao xuanbian* 珠江粵中革命根據地財政稅收史料選編 (Selected historical materials on fiscal and tax revenue of Pearl River and Central Guangdong revolutionary base area). 1985. No publisher given.

"Gesheng huoyun diaocha baogao 各省貨運調查報告" (Provincial surveys of goods transport). Ca. 1941. No publisher given. Accessed online 5/27/2020 May 27, 2020, through Kangri zhanzheng yu jindai Zhong Ri guanxi wenxian shuju pingtai.

Guangdongsheng Dang'anguan 廣東省檔案館 (Guangdong Provincial Archives). "Riben 'Dongya yanye zhushi huishe' luejian Yinggehai yantian gongcheng gaikuang 日本'東亞鹽業株式會社' 掠建鶯歌海鹽田工程概況" (Construction of Yinggehai salt fields by the Japanese East Asia Salt Co.). *Minguo Dang'an* 民國檔案 (Republican Archives), no. 3 (1998): 12–16.

Guojia Shuiwu Zongju 國家稅務總局 (National Tax Bureau), comp. *Zhonghua min'guo gongshang shuishoushi - yanshui juan* 中華民國工商稅收史 – 鹽稅卷 (A history of commercial and industrial taxation during the Republican period: Gabelle). Beijing: Zhongguo caizheng jingji chubanshe, 1999.

Hainan Xingzhengqu Dang'anguan 海南行政區檔案館 (Hainan Administrative Area Archives) et al., eds. *Qiongya geming genjudi caijing shuishou shiliao xuanbian* 瓊崖革命根據地財經稅收史料選編 (Selected fiscal, economic, and taxation materials on the Qiongya revolutionary base area), 2 vols. No place of publication listed: Hainan renmin chubanshe, 1984.

Haizhouqu Yanwu Guanliju 海州鹽務管理局 (Haizhou Salt Bureau), comp. *Haizhouqu Yanwu Guanliju nianbao* 海州區鹽務管理局年報 (Annual report of Haizhou Salt Bureau). Nanjing: Haizhouqu Yanwu Guanliju, 1943.

He Simi 何思眯. *Kangzhan shiqi zhuanmai shiliao* 抗戰時期專賣史料 (Historical materials on state monopolies during the War of Resistance). Taibei: Academia Historica, 1992.

Henansheng Caizhengting 河南省財政廳 (Finance Bureau of Henan Province) et al., eds. *Jin-Ji-Lu-Yu kangri genjudi caijing shiliao xuanbian (Henan bufen)* 晉冀魯豫抗日根據地財經史料選編 (河南部分) (Selected materials on the fiscal and economic history of the Henan part of the Jin-Ji-Lu-Yu anti-Japanese base area (Hunan area), 4 vols. Beijing: Dang'an chubanshe, 1985.

Hong Sheng 洪升 and Xie Jia 謝嘉. "Jidong jiefangqu yanwu gongzuo lueshu" 冀東解放區鹽務工作略述 (Salt work in the Eastern Hebei liberated area) *Yanzhao wenhua* 燕趙文化 (Culture in Hebei), no. 1 (2006); http://www.hebsky.gov.cn/explib/library; accessed December 27, 2009.

Hou Fangkui 侯方奎. "Zhanshi E'xi shiyan gouxiao qingkuang 戰時鄂西食鹽購銷情況" (Salt supply in wartime western Hubei). *Hubei wenshi ziliao* 湖北文史資料 (Historical materials of Hubei), no. 14 (1986): 201–205.

Hou Qiang 侯強. "Kangri zhanzheng shiqi Ningbo de yanchanpin zousi yu jisi 抗日戰爭時期寧波的鹽產品走私與缉私" (Smuggling and anti-smuggling of salt products in Ningbo during the Anti-Japanese War of Resistance). *Zhonggong Ningbo shiwei dangxiao xuebao* 中共寧波市委黨校學報 (Bulletin of the Ningbo municipal party school), no. 1 (2011): 111–114.

———. *Ningbo yanyeshi yanjiu* 寧波鹽業史研究 (A history of Ningbo's salt industry). Hangzhou: Zhejiang daxue chubanshe, 2011.

Huang Jian 黄健, Cheng Longgang 程龍剛, and Zhou Jing 周勁, eds. *Kangzhan shiqi de Zhongguo yanye* 抗戰時期的中國鹽業 (The salt industry during the War of Resistance). Chengdu: Bashu shuhe, 2011.

Huang Lingjun 黃岭峻. "30–40 niandai Zhongguo sixiangjie de jihua jingji sichao 30–40 年代中國思想界的計劃經濟思潮" (Planned economy among Chinese thinkers during the 1930s and 1940s). *Jindaishi yanjiu* 近代史研究 (Studies in modern history) 2 (2002): 150–176.

Huang Meizhen 黃美真. "Riwei dui yi Shanghai wei zhongxin de huazhong lunxianqu de wuzi tongzhi" (Shanghai-centered control of materials in occupied Central China under the Japanese puppet regime). In *Qiewenji* 切問集 (Inquiries), 2 vols., edited by Fudan Daxue Lishixi 復旦大學歷史系 (History Department of Fudan University), 1:568–587. Shanghai: Fudan daxue chubanshe.

Huang Meizhen 黃美真 et al., eds. *Riwei dui Huazhong lunxianqu jingji de lueduo yu tongzhi* 日偽對華中淪陷區經濟的掠奪與統制 (Plundering and economic control of occupied Central China under the Japanese and puppet regime). Beijing: Shehui kexue wenxian chubanshe, 2005.

Huang Yunhua 黃蘊華. "Jikou shouyan yu jikou shouliang 計口授鹽與計口授糧" (Rationing salt and grain). *Mandihong* 滿地紅 (Red all over the land) 1, no. 6 (1939): 26–28.

Huazhong Kangri Genjudi He Jiefangqu Gongshang Shuishoushi Bianxiezu 華中抗日根據地和解放區工商稅收史編寫組 (Editorial Committee for the History of Commerce and Industry in the Central China anti-Japanese Base Area and Liberated Region), ed. *Huazhong kangri genjudi he jiefangqu gongshang shuishou shiliao xuanbian* 華中抗日根據地和解放區工商稅收史料選編 (Selected historical materials on commerce and industry in the Central China anti-Japanese base area and liberated region), 2 vols. Hefei: Anhui renmin chubanshe, 1986.

Hubeisheng Caizhengting 湖北省財政廳 (Finance Bureau of Hubei Province) et al., eds. *Huazhong kangri genjudi caijing shiliao xuanbian* 華中抗日根據地財經史料選編 (Selected materials on the fiscal and economic history of the Central China anti-Japanese base area). Wuhan: Hubei renmin chubanshe, 1985.

Japanese consul (Tianjin). Letter to the Changlu District Salt Administration, September 8, 1938. In ZGJDYWSZLBY.

Jia Shuzhen 賈淑珍 and Liu Xudong 劉旭東. "Gaozhuang funü beiyandui 高莊婦女背鹽隊" (Female salt carriers of Gaozhuang). *Han'gu wenshi ziliao* 漢沽文史資料 (Historical materials of Han'gu), no. 3 (1990): 84–85.

Jiang Jieshi (Chiang Kai-shek). Cable to Kong Xiangxi, August 17, 1935. In *Zhonghua min'guoshi dang'an ziliao huibian* 中華民國史檔案資料彙編 (Collected archival materials on Republican China), edited by Zhongguo Dier Lishi Dang'anguan 中國

第二歷史檔案館 (Second Historical Archives of China), series. 5, part 1, vol. 14, 217. Suzhou: Jiangsu Guji shudian, 2000.

Jiang Pei 江沛. "1937–1941 nianjian Riben tongzhi huabei celue tiaozheng shulun 1937–1941 年間日本統治華北策略調整述論" (An analysis of Japanese policy adjustments in governing North China, 1937–1941). *Jianghai xuekan* 江海學刊, no. 1 (2004): 166–170.

Jiangsusheng Dang'anguan 江蘇省檔案館 (Jiangsu Provincial Archives) et al., eds. *Huazhong kangri genjudi caizheng jingji shiliao xuanbian* 華中抗日根據地財政經濟史料選編 (Selected materials on the fiscal and economic history of the Central China anti-Japanese base area), 4 vols. Beijing: Dang'an chubanshe, 1984.

———. *Su'nan kangri genjudi* 蘇南抗日根據地 (Southern Jiangsu anti-Japanese base area). Beijing: Zhonggong dangshi ziliao chubanshe, 1987.

———. *Suzhong kangri genjudi* 蘇中抗日根據地 (Central Jiangsu anti-Japanese base area). Beijing: Zhonggong dangshi ziliao chubanshe, 1990.

Jiangxisheng Dang'anguan 江西省檔案館 (Jiangxi Provincial Archives) et al., eds. *Min Zhe Gan geming genjudi caizheng jingji shiliao xuanbian* 閩浙贛革命根據地財政經濟史料選編 (Selected historical materials on the finance and economy of Fujian-Zhejiang-Jiangxi revolutionary base area). Xiamen: Xiamen daxue chubanshe, 1988.

Jie Xueshi 解學詩 ed. *Mantie yu Huabei jingji* 滿鐵與華北經濟 (The Southern Manchurian Railway Co. and the economy of North China). Beijing: Sheke wenxian chubanshe, 2007.

———. *Mantie yu Huabei kaifa huishe* 滿鐵與華北開發會社 (The South Manchurian Railway Co. and the North China Development Co.). Beijing: Shehui kexue wenxian chubanshe, 2011.

Jin Huaiyi 靳懷義. "Riben zhanling qijian de kaitan he lueyan 日本佔領期間的開灘和掠鹽" (Development of salt fields and plundering of salt during the Japanese occupation). *Han'gu wenshi ziliao* 漢沽文史資料 (Historical materials of Han'gu), no. 3 (1990): 156–157.

Ju Zhifen 居之芬 and Zhang Limin 張利民. *Riben zai huabei jingji tongzhi lueduoshi* 日本在華北經濟統制掠奪史 (Japanese economic control and plunder in North China: A history). Tianjin: Guzhi chubanshe, 1997.

"Kangri zhanzheng qijian Qingyuan yanshi de xingshuai 抗日戰爭期間慶元鹽市的興衰" (The rise and decline of Qingyuan salt mart during the Anti-Japanese War), http://www.chinafoods.cn/news/html/2008-01/196647.htm; accessed September 14, 2009.

Kangri Zhanzheng Shiqi Jin-Cha-Ji Bianqu Caizheng Jingjishi Ziliao Xuanbian Bianxiezu 抗日戰爭時期晉察冀邊區財政經濟史資料選編編寫組 (Editorial Committee for the Selected Materials on the Fiscal and Economic History of he Shaanxi-Chahar-Hebei Border Region during the Anti-Japanese War) et al., eds. *Kangri zhanzheng shiqi Jin-Cha-Ji bianqu caizheng jingjishi ziliao xuanbian* 抗日戰爭時期晉察冀邊區財政經濟史資料選編 (Selected materials on the fiscal and economic history of the Shanxi-Chahar-Hebei border region during the Anti-Japanese War), 4 vols. Tianjin: Nankai daxue chubanshe, 1984.

Kangri Zhanzheng Shiqi Jin-Ji-Lu-Yu Bianqu Caizheng Jingjishi Ziliao Xuanbian Bianjizu 抗日戰爭時期晉冀魯豫編區財政經濟史選編編輯組 (Editorial Committee for

Selected Materials on the Fiscal and Economic History of the Shanxi-Hebei-Shandong-Henan Border Region during the Anti-Japanese War), ed. *Kangri zhanzheng shiqi Jin-Ji-Lu-Yu bianqu caizheng jingjishi ziliao xuanbian* 抗日戰爭時期晉冀魯豫編區財政經濟史資料選編 (Selected materials on the fiscal and economic history of the Shanxi-Hebei-Shandong-Henan border region during the Anti-Japanese War of Resistance), 2 vols. Beijing: Zhongguo caijing chubanshe, 1990.

Kantōgun sanbōbu 関東軍参謀部 (Kwantung army command), comp. *Manshū jihen choku kisaki no Tosansho ensei nikansuru shōhō* 満州事変直接后の東三省塩政に関する詳報 (Comprehensive report on the handling of salt in the northeastern provinces of China after 1931). 1932. JACAR, C01002785400.

Kasahara Taro 笠原太郎. "Saikin ni okeru Kainantō seien jōkyō 最近に於ける海南島製塩調査" (Recent situation of salt production in Hainan Island). 1942. JACAR, B09042273300.

Keizai Chōsakai Dainibu Daisanhan 経済調査会第二部第三班 (Economic Research Association, Section Two, Subsection Three). *Manshūkoku enmu gyōsei seido kaikakuan* 滿洲國鹽務行政制度改革案 (Draft reform plan for salt administration in Manchuko). Shenyang: Minami Manshū tetsudō kabushiki kaisha, 1932.

Kirby, William C. "Engineering China: Birth of the Developmental State, 1928–1937." In *Becoming Chinese*, edited by Wen-hsin Yeh, 137–160. Berkeley: University of California Press, 2000.

Kita Shina Engyō Kabushiki Kaisha 華北塩業株式会社 (North China Salt Corp.). "Dai ni-kai eigyō hōkokusho 第二回営業報告書" (Second company report, 1939–1940). JACAR, B08061243900.

———. "Kaisha shisan, shihon kōsei eigyō shūnshi jōkyō chosho 会社資産、資本構成及営業収支状況調書" (Record of company assets, capital, and operations, 1944). JACAR, B06050422900.

Kōain Kachū Renrakubu 興亜院華中連絡部 (Kōa Institute, Central China Department). *Kaishu engyō chōshashu* 海州鹽業調查書 (Survey report on the Haizhou salt industry). Shanghai: Kōain Kachū Renrakubu, 1939.

———. Report, December 10, 1941. JACAR, B006050552399.

———. Report, December 16, 1941. JACAR, B06050552300.

———. *Ryōsetsu shōkō enjō chōsa* 兩浙松江鹽場調査 (Survey of salt fields in Zhejiang and Songjiang). Shanghai: Kōain Kachū Renrakubu, 1940.

———. *Sohoku kyōsan chiku jitsujō chōsa hōkokusho* 蘇北共産地区実情調査報告書 (Survey report on condition in Subei Communist area). Shanghai: Kōain Kachū Renrakubu, 1941.

Kōain Kachū Renrakubu Reizai Dai 2-Kyoku 興亞院華中連絡部經濟第 2 局 (Kōa Institute Central China Department, Second Economics Division). *Kachū engyō kohin yūgen kōshi ni tsuite* 華中塩業股份有限公司ニ就テ (Central China Salt Industry Co.). Nanjing, 1941. No publisher given.

Kōain Kahoku Renrakubu 興亜院華北連絡部 (Kōa Institute, North China Liaison Office), *Kahoku engyō ritchi jōken chōsa hōkokusho* 華北塩業立地条件調査報告書 (Survey report of production conditions of salt in North China). 1941. No publisher given.

Kōain [Kahoku Renrakubu] Chintao Shutchōjo 興亜院 [華北連絡部] 青島出張所 (Kōa Institute [North China Liaison Office] Qingdao Branch), *Santō-shō ni okeru engyō* 山東省に於ける塩業 (Salt industry in Shandong Province). Qingdao: Kōain [Kahoku Renrakubu] Chintao Shutchōjo, 1940.

Kōain Seimubu 興亜院政務部 (Kōa Institute, Political Department). *Chūshi shio no kokka haikyū kankei chōsa hōkoku* 中支鹽ノ國家配給關係調查報告 (Survey report of salt rationing in Central China). Tokyo: Kōain seimubu. No date given.

Kobayashi Yoshio 小林義雄 et al. *Shina senryōchi keizai no hatten* 支那占領地経済の発展 (Economic development in occupied China). Tokyo: Tōa kenkyujo, 1944.

Kōgyō Kagakukai Manshū Shibu 工業化学会満州支部 (Industrial Chemical Society, Manchukuo branch), comp. *Manshū no shigen to kagaku kōgyō* 満州の資源と化学工業 (Resources and chemical industries in Manchuria). Tokyo: Maruzen kabushiki kaisha, 1943.

Kwan, Man Bun. *Beyond Market and Hierarchy*. New York: Palgrave Macmillan, 2014.

Kyōji Asada 浅田喬二 et al. *Nihon teikoku shugika no Chūgoku: Chūgoku senryōchi keizai no kenkyū* 日本帝国主義下の中国: 中国占領地経済の研究 (China under Japanese imperialism: A study of occupied China's economy). Tokyo: Rakuyū shobō, 1981.

Lai Zhengxiong 賴正雄. "Kangzhan shiqi Riben dui huanan diqu jingji lueduo yu tongzhi de tıedıan 抗戰時期日本對華南地區經濟掠奪與統制的特點" (Characteristics of Japanese plundering and economic control of southern China during the War of Resistance). *Jianghai xuekan* 江海學刊, no. 1 (2004): 176–179.

Letters to Xie Juezai 謝覺哉. August 6, 1941, and August 22, 1941. In Mao Zedong 毛澤東, *Mao Zedong shuxin xuanji* 毛澤東書信選集 (Mao Zedong's selected letters), 176–178 and 187–188. Beijing: Renmin chubanshe, 1983.

Li Gongpo 李公朴. *Huabei dihou* 華北敵後 (Behind enemy lines in North China). Beijing: Sanlian shudian, 1979.

Li Han 李涵. *Miao Qiujie yu Min'guo yanwu* 繆秋杰與民國鹽務 (Miao Qiujie and salt administration during the Republican period). Beijing: Zhongguo kexue jishu chubanshe, 1990.

Li Jianchang 李建昌. *Guanliao ziben yu yanye* 官僚資本與鹽業 (Bureaucratic capital and the salt industry). Beijing: Sanlian shudian, 1963.

Li Jianguo 李建國. "Shaan-Gan-Ning bianqu de shiyan yunxiao ji dui bianqu de yingxiang 陝甘寧邊區的食鹽運銷及對邊區的影響" (The transportation and sales of alimental salt in the Shaan-Gan-Ning border region and its effects). *KZYJ*, no. 3 (2004): 163–180.

Li Zhancai 李占才 and Zhang Jing 張勁. *Chaozai: Kangzhan yu jiaotong* 超載: 抗戰與交通 (Overload: Communications and the Anti-Japanese War). Guilin: Guangxi shifan daxue chubanshe, 1996.

Liao Yuan 廖原. "Su-Wan bianqu de caijing gongzuo 蘇皖邊區的財經工作" (Fiscal and economic work of the Jiangsu Anhui border region), November 16, 1941. In Anhuissheng Caizhengting et al., *Anhui geming genjudi caijing shiliao xuan*, 1:55–68.

Lin Zhenhan 林振翰. *Chuanyan gaiyao* 川鹽概要 (Essentials of Sichuan salt), rev. ed. Shangwu yinshuguan, 1919. No place given.

Liu Dake 劉大可. "Shandong jiefangqu yanwu gongzuo jilue 山東解放區鹽務工作紀略" (A brief history of salt work in the Shandong liberated area). *YYSYJ*, no. 2 (1992): 69–77.

Liu Hongjuan 劉紅娟. "Erci shijie dazhan qijian Riben dui Tianjin Changluyan de tongzhi he lueduo 二次世界大戰期間日本對天津長蘆鹽的統制和掠奪" (Japanese control and plundering of Changlu salt during World War II). *Chengshishi yanjiu* 城市史研究 (Urban history research), nos. 11/12 (1996): 153–161.

Liu Hongqian 劉洪乾. "Jiangsusheng he Lianghuai yanqu de kangri douzheng 江蘇省和兩淮鹽區的抗日鬥爭" (Struggles during the War of Resistance against Japan in Jiangsu Province and Lianghuai salt division). *YYSYJ*, no. 3 (1995): 63–69.

Liu Jinghua 劉經華. "Kangzhan shiqi Guomin zhengfu yanwu guanli tizhi de bianqian 抗戰時期國民政府鹽務管理體制的變遷" (Institutional changes of the Nationalist government's Salt Administration during the War of Resistance). *YYSYJ*, no. 3 (2005): 1–32.

Liu Ruilong. Report, April 19, 1945. In Anhuisheng Caizhengting et al. *Anhui geming genjudi caijing shiliao xuan*, 1:195–203.

Liu Xudong 劉序東. "Riwei shiqi de Henan yanwuju 日偽時期的河南鹽務局" (The Henan provincial salt bureau under the Japanese puppet regime). *Tianjin wenshi ziliao xuanji* 天津文史資料選輯 (Historical materials of Tianjin), no. 3 (2002): 199–212.

Liu Yanping 劉艷苹. "Shaan-Gan-Ning bianqu yanye wenti yanjiu 陝甘寧邊區鹽業問題研究" (A study of the salt problem in the Shaanxi-Gansu-Ningxia border region). *Yan'an Daxue Xuebao* 延安大學學報 (Journal of Yan'an University) 41, no. 6 (2019): 58–61.

Lü Yangju 呂揚炬. "Shaan-Gan-Ning bianqu shangye gongzuo gaishu 陝甘寧邊區商業工作概述" (On commercial work in the Shaan-Gan-Ning border region). In *Geming genjudi shangye huiyilu* 革命根據地商業回憶錄 (Memoirs on commerce in the revolutionary base areas), edited by Shangyebu Shangye Jingji Yanjiusuo 商業部商業經濟研究所 (Commercial Economics Research Institute of the Commerce Department). Beijing: Zhongguo shangye chubanshe, 1984.

Luo Deming 羅德明 and Huang Yuetang 黃躍棠. "Zigong yanye yingyun zhong de yahui, chengdui huipiao he yanyun baoxian 自貢鹽業營運中的押匯, 承兌匯票和鹽運保險" (Document billing, remittance and insurance in Zigong's salt trade). *Zigong wenshi ziliao xuanji* 自貢文史資料選輯, no. 18 (1986): 93–97.

"Manzhouguo jiben guoce dagang 滿州國基本國策大綱" (Basic principles of Manchuria), December 8, 1942. In *Dongbei jingji lueduo* 東北經濟掠奪 (Plundering of economic resources in the Northeast), edited by Zhongyang Dang'anguan 中央檔案館 (Central Archives) et al. Beijing: Zhonghua shuju, 1991.

Mao Zedong 毛澤東 (drafted by Li Fuchun 李富春). "Jingji wenti yu caizheng wenti 經濟問題與財政問題" (Economic and fiscal problems). In *Mao Zedong ji*, 3:292.

Mao Zedong ji 毛澤東集 (Collected writings of Mao Zedong), 10 vols. Hong Kong: Yishan chubanshe. No date given.

Miao Qiujie 繆秋杰 et al. *Chuancuo gailue* 川鹺概略 (Brief overview of Sichuan salt). 1939. No publisher given.

Minami Manshū Tetsudō Kabushiki Kaisha 南満州鉄道株式会社 (South Manchurian Railway Company). *Kita Shina engyō kaihatsu hōsaku narabini chōsa shiryō* 北支那塩業開発方策並調査資料 (Feasibility study on the development of the salt industry in North China). 1937. No publisher given.

———. *Kita Shina en oyobi sōdagyō kaihatsu keikaku* 北支那塩及曹達業開発計画 (Plan for development of the salt and soda industry in North China). Dairen: Minami Manshū Tetsudō Kabushiki Kaisha chōsabu, 1940.

Minami shina hōmengun Nami shūdan shireibu 南支那方面軍集団司令部 (South China military headquarters), comp. "Nanshi engan ni okeru enjō chosa yōzu 南支沿岸ニ於ケル塩場調査要図" (Classified map of coastal salt fields in South China). 1941. JACAR, C04123316900.

Mu Ren 牧人. "Kangri zhanzheng shiqi Shaanbei diqu yanwu 抗日戰爭時期陝北地區鹽務" (Salt affairs in Northern Shaanxi during the Anti-Japanese War of Resistance). *YYSYJ*, no. 5 (2005): 3–7.

Nakamura Takafusa 中村隆英. *Senji Nihon no Kahoku keizai shihai* 戦時日本の華北経済支配 (Japan's economic control of North China during the war). Tokyo: Yamakawa shuppansha, 1983.

Nanjing to Tokyo cable. August 4, 1943. JACAR, B09042270500.

Nankai Daxue 南開大學 (Nankai University). *Zhongguo jindai yanwushi ziliao xuanji* 中國近代鹽務史資料選輯 (Selected materials on the history of salt in modern China), 4 vols. Tianjin: Nankai Daxue, 1985–1991.

Pan Jian 潘健. "Wangwei zhengfu yanzheng yanjiu 汪偽政府鹽政研究" (Salt administration under Wang Jingwei's puppet regime). *YYSYJ*, no. 4 (2008): 19–25.

Pan Rongyang 潘榮陽. "Kangri zhanzheng shiqi Fujian yanye jingji guanli yanjiu 抗日戰爭時期福建經濟管理研究" (A study of Fujian salt industry during the Anti-Japanese War period). PhD dissertation, Fujian Shifan Daxue, 2009.

Qi Chunfeng 齊春風. "Kangzhan shiqi Zhong Ri jingji fengsuo yu fan fensuo douzheng 抗戰時期中日經濟封鎖與反封鎖鬥爭" (On economic blockade and counter-blockade struggles between China and Japan during the War of Resistance). *Lishi Dang'an* 歷史檔案 (Historical Archives) 3 (1999): 123–128.

———. *Zhongri jingji zhan zhong de zousi huodong, 1937–1945* 中日經濟戰中爭的走私活動, 1937–1945 (Smuggling activities in Sino-Japanese economic warfare, 1937–1945). Beijing: Renmin chubanshe, 2002.

Ren Guiyuan 任桂園. "Kangri zhanzheng shiqi de Sanxia yanye" 抗日戰爭時期的三峽鹽業 (The salt industry in the Three Gorges during the Anti-Japanese War); http://www.studa.net/Profession/060421/08403678-2.html; accessed September 14, 2009.

Report on salt smuggling via Anqing. April 30, 1941. JACAR, B06050552700.

"Riben zhengfu suoyi guanyu Zhongguo yanwu xingzheng gaige zhi fang'an 日本政府所以關於中國鹽務行政改革之方案" (Proposal for the reform of China's salt administration by the Japanese government). October 11, 1938. In *ZGJDYWSZLXJ*, 3:18–20.

"Ri'man jingji tongzhi fangce yaogang 日滿經濟統制方策要綱" (General principles of controlled economy in Japanese occupied Manchuria). March 30, 1934. In *Dongbei jingji lueduo* 東北經濟掠奪 (Plundering of economic resources in the Northeast), edited by Zhongyang Dang'anguan 中央檔案館 (Central Archives) et al. Beijing: Zhonghua shuju, 1991.

Sakamoto Masako 坂本雅子. *Zaibatsu to teikoku shugi* 財閥と帝国主義 (Zaibatsu and [Japanese] imperialism). Kyōto: Mineruva shobō, 2003.

Santō Engyō Kabushiki Kaisha 山東塩業株式会社 (Shandong Salt Corp.). "Dai jū ichi eigyō hōkokusho 第十一営業報告書" (Eleventh company report). 1943. JACAR, B0806262000.

Schran, Peter. *Guerilla Economy*. Albany, N.Y.: SUNY Press, 1975.

Seldon, Mark. *China in Revolution*. Armonk, N.Y.: M. E. Sharpe, 1995.

Senzen senchūno seifu kankei shuppanbutsu: Engyō narabini ensei 戦前戦中の政府関係出版物: 塩業並塩制 (Government publications before and during the war: Salt industry and salt control). 1922–1943. No publisher given.

Shaan-Gan-Ning Bianqu Caizheng Jingjishi Bianxiezu 陝甘寧邊區財政經濟史編寫組 (Editorial Committee for the Selected Materials on the History of Finance and Economy of the Shaan-Gan-Ning Base Area during the Anti-Japanese War) (SGN) et al., eds. *Kangri zhanzheng shiqi Shaan-Gan-Ning bianqu caizheng jingji shiliao zhaibian* 抗日戰爭時期陝甘寧邊區財政經濟史料摘編 (Selected materials on the history of finance and economy of the Shaan-Gan-Ning base area during the Anti-Japanese War), 9 vols. Xi'an: Renmin chubanshe, 1981.

Shaanxisheng Dang'anguan 陝西省檔案館 (Shaanxi Provincial Archives) and Shaanxisheng Shehui Kexueyuan 陝西省社會科學院 (Shaanxi Institute of Social Sciences), eds. *Shaan-Gan-Ning bianqu zhengfu wenjian xuanbian* 陝甘寧邊區政府文件選編 (Selected documents of the Shaan-Gan-Ning border region government). Beijing: Dang'an chubanshe, 1991.

Shandongsheng Caizheng Kexue Yanjiusuo 山東省財政科學研究所 (Shandong Institute of Finance) and Shandongsheng Dang'anguan 山東省檔案館 (Shandong Provincial Archives), eds. *Shandong geming genjudi caizheng shiliao xuanbian* 山東革命根據地財政史料選編 (Selected materials on the fiscal history of the Shandong revolutionary base area), 6 vols. Jinan: Shandongsheng caizheng yanjiusuo, 1985.

Shanghaishi Dang'anguan 上海市檔案館 (Shanghai Municipal Archives), ed. *Riben zai huazhong jingji lueduo shiliao* 日本在華中經濟掠奪史料 (Historical materials of Japanese economic plunder in Central China). Shanghai: Shanghai shudian, 2005.

Shangyebu Shangye Jingji Yanjiusuo 商業部商業經濟研究所 (Commercial Economics Research Institute of the Commerce Ministry), ed. *Geming genjudi shangye huiyilu* 革命根據地商業回憶錄 (Memoirs on commerce in the revolutionary base areas). Beijing: Zhongguo shangye chubanshe, 1984.

Shangyebu Shangye Zhengce Yanjiuhui 商業部商業政策研究會 (Commerce Ministry Commercial Policy Research Group), ed. *Jianguo qianhou shangye gongzuo shilu* 建國前後商業工作實錄 (A veritable record of commercial work before and after 1949). Beijing: Zhongguo shangye chubanshe, 1988.

Shen Junchang 沈君常 and Wu Jinzhang 吳錦章. "Zai teshu huanjing zhong de teshu maoyi 在特殊環境中的特殊貿易 (Special trade under special circumstances). In *Wanjiang kangri genjudi* 皖江抗日根據地" (Wanjiang anti-Japanese base area), edited by Wanjiang Kangri Genjudi Bianshen Weiyuanhui 皖江抗日根據地編審委員會

(Editorial Committee for the Wanjiang anti-Japanese Base Area), 347–353. Beijing: Zhonggong dangshi chubanshe, 1990.

Shingo Sumiyoshi 住吉信吾 et al. *Chūka engyō jijō* 中華鹽業事情 (China's salt industry). Kawasaki: Ryūshuku sanbō, 1943.

Shishi wenti yanjiuhui 時事問題研究會, ed. *Kangzhanzhong de Zhongguo jingji* 抗戰中的中國經濟 (China's economy in the War of Resistance). No location given. Kangzhan shudian, 1940; repr. 1957.

Song Jinshou 宋金壽. *Kangzhan shiqi de Shaan-Gan-Ning bianqu* 抗戰時期的陝甘寧邊區 (Shaan-Gan-Ning border region during the Anti-Japanese War of Resistance). Beijing: Beijing chubanshe, 1995.

Song Shangze 宋尚澤 and Wang Zhenhua 王振華. "Kangzhan shiqi Chuanyan de jiage guanli 抗戰時期川鹽的價格管理" (Management of Sichuan salt prices during the War of Resistance). *Zigong wenshi ziliao* 自貢文史資料 (Selected historical sources of Zigong), no. 16 (1986): 52–70.

Suzuki Kunio 鈴木邦夫. *Manshū kigyōshi kenkyū* 滿州企業史研究 (Business history of Manchuria). Tokyo: Nihon keizai hyōronsha, 2007.

Tao Gong 陶巩. "Kangri zhanzheng shiqi de Huainan yanchang 抗日戰爭時期的淮南鹽場" (Huainan salt fields during the Anti-Japanese War of Resistance). *YYSYJ*, no. 3 (1995): 72–74.

Thaxton, Ralph. *Salt of the Earth*. Berkeley: University of California Press, 1997.

Tian Qiuye 田秋野 and Zhou Weiliang 周維亮. *Zhonghua yanyeshi* 中華鹽業史 (A history of salt in China). Taibei: Taiwan shangwu yinshuguan, 1979.

Tong Xin 童欣. "Kangzhan shiqi Shaan-Gan-Ning bianqu shiyan yunshu yanjiu 抗戰時期陝甘寧邊區食鹽運輸研究" (A study of alimental salt transportation in the Shaan-Gan-Ning border region during the War of Resistance). MA thesis, Yan'an Daxue, 2019.

Wang Aimin 王愛民. "Bohai geminqu yanzheng guanli shuping, 1937–1949 渤海革命區鹽政管理述評" (A review of salt administration in Bohai revolutionary region, 1937–1949). *Liaocheng daxue xuebao* 聊城大學學報 (Bulletin of Liaocheng University), no. 3 (2019): 10–17, 72.

Wang Jianguo 王建國. "Lun Huazhong kangri genjudi gongshang shuishou ji dui huazhong kangzhan de zuoyong 論華中抗日根據地工商稅收及對華中抗戰的作用" (On commercial and industrial taxes in the Central China anti-Japanese base area and their contribution to the War of Resistance). *Jianghai xuekan* 江海學刊 (Academic journal of Jiangsu and Shanghai), no. 1 (2004): 145–149.

Wang Shihua 王士花. *Kaifa yu lueduo* 開發與掠奪: 抗日戰爭時期日本在華北華中淪陷區的經濟統制 (Development and plunder: Economic control in North and Central China during the Anti-Japanese War). Beijing: Zhongguo shehui kexue chubanshe, 1998.

Weng Wenhao 翁文灝. *Kangzhan yilai de jingji* 抗戰以來的經濟 (The economy in the War of Resistance). Chongqing: Shengli chubanshe, 1942.

Wou, Ordoric. "Food Shortage and Japanese Grain Extraction in Henan." In *China at War*, edited by Stephen R. Mackinnon, Diana Lary, and Erza Vogel, 175–206. Stanford, Calif.: Stanford University Press, 2007.

Wu Dingchang 吳鼎昌. *Huaxi xianbi* 花谿閒筆 (Miscellaneous notes of a flowery brook). No publisher or date given.

Xiao Bolin 肖伯麟. "Xue Yue chouban Hunansheng maoyiju neimu 薛岳籌辦湖南省貿易局內幕" (Inside story of Xue Yue's Hunan provincial trade company). *Hunan wenshi ziliao* 湖南文史資料 (Historical materials of Hunan), no. 29 (1988): 113–117.

Xue Muqiao 薛暮橋. *Kangri zhanzheng shiqi he jiefang zhanzheng shiqi Shandong jiefangqu de jingji gongzuo* 抗日戰爭時期和解放戰爭時期山東解放區的經濟工作 (Economic work in Shandong during the anti-Japanese and liberation wars). Jinan: Shandong renmin chubanshe, 1984.

———. *Xue Muqiao huiyilu* 薛暮橋回憶錄 (Memoirs of Xue Muqiao). Tianjin: Renmin chubanshe, 2006.

Yan Cheng 嚴成. "Wo suo zhidao de Bohai yanye gongsi 我所知道的渤海鹽業公司" (The Bohai salt company that I knew). *Han'gu wenshi ziliao* 漢沽文史資料 (Historical materials of Han'gu), no 2 (1988): 82–85.

Yang Caidan 楊彩丹. "Kangri zhanzheng shiqi riben dui Hedong yanchi de lueduo 抗日戰爭時期日本對河東鹽池的掠奪" (The plundering of Hedong salt pans by Japan during the Anti-Japanese War). *YYSYJ*, no. 3 (2005): 46–49.

Yang Huizhuang 楊惠莊. "Zenyang zhankai duidi jingji fan qinluezhan 怎樣展開對敵經濟反侵略戰" (How to wage economic warfare against the enemy). August 13, 1940. In Anhuisheng Caizhengting et al., *Anhui geming genjudi caijing shiliao xuan*, 2:467–477.

Yang Xingqin 楊興勤. *Zhongguo zhanshi yanwu* 中國戰時鹽務 (Salt affairs in wartime China). Guomin chubanshe, 1943. No place of publication given.

"Yanzhuanmai fang'an fagui cao'an huibian 鹽專賣方案法規草案彙編" (Draft regulations on state salt monopolization). S-02-14 (1). Dated October 1941. Held at the Institute of Modern History Archives, Academia Sinica.

Ye Shaohua 葉少華. "'Zhongweiyan' yu Yue-Xiang yanliang huihuan 中委鹽與粵湘鹽糧會還" (Nationalist Central Committee member salt and the barter of Guangdong salt with Hunan rice). *Guangzhou wenshi ziliao* 廣州文史資料 (Historical materials of Canton), no. 8 (1963): 23–30.

Ying Zhaolin 應兆麟 et al. *Wanjiang kangri genjudi caijing shigao* 皖江抗日根據地財經史稿 (An economic and fiscal history of the Wanjiang anti-Japanese base area). Hefei: Anhui renmin chubanshe, 1985.

Zelin, Madeleine. *The Merchants of Zigong*. New York: Columbia University Press, 2005.

Zhan Ling 詹玲 and Cheng Longgang 程龍剛. "Huazhong kangri genjudi yanye shulue 華中抗日根據地鹽業述略" (A brief history of the salt industry in the Central China anti-Japanese base area). *Sichuan ligong xueyuan xuebao* 四川理工學院學報 (Journal of Sichuan University of Science and Engineering, social sciences ed.) 25, no. 6 (2010): 24–26.

Zhang Bofeng 章伯锋 and Zhuang Jianping 庄建平, eds. *Kangri zhanzheng* 抗日戰爭 (Anti-Japanese war), 7 vols. Chengdu: Sichuan daxue chubanshe, 1997.

Zhang Lijie 張立杰. "Kangzhan houqi Guotongqu de yanzheng gaizhi 抗戰後期國統區的鹽政改制" (Institutional change of salt administration in Nationalist-controlled areas during the latter part of the War of Resistance). *KZYJ*, no. 3 (2004): 141–162.

———. "Kangzhan quanmian baofaqian Riben dui Zhongguo yanzheng de pohuai yu guomin zhengfu de duice 抗戰全面爆發前日本對中國鹽政的破壞與國民政府的對策" (Japanese encroachment on China's salt administration before 1937 and the Republican government's response). *YYSYJ*, no. 1 (2008): 20–26.

———. "Kangzhan shiqi Zhongguo yanye chanxiao gaikuang yanjiu 抗戰時期中國鹽業產銷概況研究" (On salt production and sales during the War of Resistance). *YYSYJ*, no. 3 (2015): 88–96.

Zhang Xiaohui 張曉輝 and Pan Deng 潘燈. "1942–1945 nianjian Yuedongqu de shiyan yunxiao 1942–1945 年間粵東區的食鹽運銷" (Transport and sales of alimental salt in eastern Guangdong, 1942–1945). *Min'guo dang'an* 民國檔案 (Republican Archives), no. 1 (2010): 130–135.

Zhang Xiaomei 張肖梅. *Chuanyan shi kuang ji zengchan wenti* 川鹽實況及增產問題 (Current situation of Sichuan salt and problems in increasing production). Chongqing: Zhongguo guomin jingji yanjiusuo, 1939).

"Zhanshi yan zhi yunxiao gaikuang 戰時鹽之運銷概況" (Wartime salt transportation and distribution). Dated December 3, 1941. In *Zhonghua min'guo gongshang shuishou shiliao xuanbian* 中華民國工商稅收史料選編 (Selected historical materials on industrial and commercial taxation from the Republic of China), 2 vols., edited by Di'er Dang'anguan 中國第二歷史檔案館 (Second Historical Archives of China), 2nd comp. Nanjing: Nanjing daxue chubanshe, 1995.

Zhejiangsheng Dang'anguan 浙江省檔案館 (Zhejiang Provincial Archives) et al., eds. *Zhedong kangri genjudi* 浙東抗日根據地 (Eastern Zhejiang anti-Japanese base area). Beijing: Zhonggong dangshi ziliao chubanshe, 1987.

Zhonggong Henan Shengwei Dangshi Ziliao Zhengji Bianzuan Weiyuanhui 中共河南省委黨史資料徵集編纂委員會 (Henan Provincial Committee for the Collection and Editing of Historical Materials on Party History), ed. *Yu-Wan-Su kangri genjudi* 豫皖蘇抗日根據地 (Henan-Anhui-Jiangsu border region), 2 vols. Zhengzhou: Henan renmin chubanshe, 1990.

Zhonggong Xibei Zhongyangju Diaocha Yanjiu Shi 中共西北中央局調查研究室 (Research Office of the Northwestern Central Bureau of the Chinese Communist Party). *Zhang Qingfeng yun yan qijia* 張慶豐運鹽起家 (Zhang Qingfeng prospering from salt transport). 1944. No publisher given.

"Zhonggong Zhongyang guanyu muqian fabi wenti ge genjudi ying caiqu de zhengce 中共中央關於目前法幣問題各根據地應採取的政策" (Central Committee's directive on the *fabi* problem in various base areas). January 5, 1942. In *Huazhong genjudi caijing shiliao xuanbian* 華中根據地財經史料選編 (Selected historical materials on fiscal and economic matters of the anti-Japanese base areas in Central China), edited by Hubeisheng Dang'anguan 湖北省檔案館 (Hubei Provincial Archives) et al. Wuhan: Hubei renmin chubanshe, 1989.

"Zhonggong Xibei zhongyangju guanyu yunxiao shiyan de jueding 中共西北中央局關於運銷食鹽的決定" (Northwestern bureau central committee's decision on salt transportation and sales). May 18, 1941. In *Shaan-Gan-Ning bianqu kangri minzhu genjudi* 陝甘寧邊區抗日民主根據地 (Shaan-Gan-Ning anti-Japanese democratic base area), 2 vols., edited by Zhongyang Dang'anguan 中央檔案館 et al. Beijing: Zhonggong dangshi chubanshe, 1990.

Zhongguo Di'er Lishi Dang'anguan 中國第二歷史檔案館 (Second Historical Archives of China), ed. *Zhonghua minguoshi dang'an ziliao huibian* 中華民國史檔案資料彙編 (Collected archival materials of the Republic of China). Nanjing: Jiangsu guzhi chubanshe, 2000.

Zhongguo Renmin Yinhang Jinrong Yanjiusuo 中國人民銀行金融研究所 (Finance Research Institute of the People's Bank of China), ed. *Zhongguo geming genjudi Beihai yinhang shiliao* 中國革命根據地北海銀行史料 (Historical materials of the North Sea Bank in the Chinese revolutionary base area), 4 vols. Jinan: Shandong renmin chubanshe, 1986.

Zhongyang Dang'anguan 中央檔案館 (Central Archives) et al., eds. *Dongbei jingji lueduo* 東北經濟掠奪 (Plundering of economic resources in the northeast). Beijing: Zhonghua shuju, 1991.

———. *Shaan-Gan-Ning bianqu kangri minzhu genjudi* 陝甘寧邊區抗日民主根據地 (Shaan-Gan-Ning anti-Japanese democratic base area), 2 vols. Beijing: Zhonggong dangshi chubanshe, 1990.

Zhou Li 周琍 and Gong Dandan 龔丹丹. "Zhongyang suqu shiqi queyan wenti yanjiu 中央蘇區時期缺鹽問題研究" (Study on the scarcity of salt in the central soviet area). *YYSYJ*, no. 3 (2014): 94–102.

Zigongshi Yanwu Guanliju 自貢市鹽務管理局 (Zigong Municipal Salt Bureau), comp. *Zigongshi yanyezhi* 自貢市鹽業志 (A gazetteer of Zigong salt industry). Chengdu: Sichuan renmin chubanshe, 1995.

PART IV

Living and Working on the New Frontiers

CHAPTER 9

Chasing Images Amid Clouds of War

New Visual Evidence for Republican-Era Frontier Mobilization and Local Development

MATTHEW D. JOHNSON

On March 18, 2003, the discovery of a startling cache of films was announced by the *China Broadcast Media Report* (*Zhongguo guangbo yingshi bao* 中國廣播影視報), a professional journal published by the state-owned China Media Group. Contained in canisters labeled only "Jinling University" (Jinling Daxue 金陵大學), the decades-old collection revealed more than twenty years of documentary filmmaking by the little-known Chinese educational cinematographer Sun Mingjing (孫明經, 1911–1992), a Republican-era figure whose career had taken him throughout China on journeys that yielded image after stunning image of an earlier time.[1] Described as a "traveler with a camera" (*dai sheyingji de lüren* 帶攝影機的旅人), Sun documented university life, industry, physical culture, and scientific discovery in prewar China. From 1937 onward, his subjects included border defense in Suiyuan, salt mines in Sichuan, and state building in Xikang Province.

Sun Mingjing was born in Nanjing and trained as an educational cinematographer at the University of Nanking, an affiliation that bolstered his career during the 1930s and 1940s even as it haunted him after 1949, when he was labeled a Rightist and reduced to teaching English at the Beijing Film Academy for much of the remainder of his professional life.[2] This chapter is devoted to those educational and photojournalistic activities that Sun carried out under the auspices of the Nanjing government's Ministry of Education and the reformist China Educational Cinematography Society, both of which were later relocated to Sichuan during the War of Resistance to Japan (1937–1945). Through these activities, it is possible to understand Sun not only as a documentary filmmaker, but also as a patriotic "nationalist professional" whose particular profession, education, became a vehicle for state mass mobilization efforts from the period of the mid-1930s "national emergency" (*guo nan* 國難) through the war itself.[3] As a photojournalist and participant in several scientific survey expeditions along China's ethnic frontiers, Sun provides historians with a wide-angle perspective on state-building and mobilization efforts taking place under the guidance of provincial governments yet far from the central government strongholds of Nanjing and Chongqing.

Using Sun Mingjing's career as both an organizational and analytic lens through which to focus on the problem of "total war" more generally, I argue the following: (1) prewar Republican initiatives in the areas of educational cinematography and "electrified education" (*dianhua jiaoyu* 電化教育) provided the technological and institutional foundation for civil mobilization following 1937; (2) likewise, for China's coastal and northern fronts military mobilization began prior to the conventionally accepted July 7, 1937, start date of the War of Resistance; and (3) provincial development programs continued throughout the war years, as did mass and primary education efforts aimed at acculturating China's ethnic "minority" populations.[4] If total war from 1937 onward did not make mass mobilization a ubiquitous feature of state-society relations, it did intensify and expand ongoing efforts that were already under way throughout the Republic.

Mobilization Nationalized

Sun Mingjing entered the Christian missionary-founded University of Nanking in 1927.[5] A bright student who attracted the attention of both university president Chen Yuguang and College of Sciences dean Wei Xueren, he advanced rapidly through the recently introduced educational filmmaking curriculum and by 1934 was producing his own educational films under Wei's direction.[6] During the time of Sun's enrollment, the University of Nanking was one of several private institutions then being reshaped by central government efforts to restore national sovereignty in higher education, resulting in the secularization of college curricula and increasing emphasis on the social and political sciences, in keeping with the new party-state's emphasis on national reconstruction.[7] The University of Nanking soon became a hub of Chinese and foreign academic inquiry, famously hosting the National Agricultural Research Bureau, from which the first studies of the Nanjing Government Land Committee were conducted.[8]

Sun's first direct contact with the central government occurred in 1934, when he and mentor Wei Xueren were recruited by the Ministry of Education to produce a short film on the topic of "national conditions" (*guo qing* 國情) for use by the Educational Film Production and Popularization Commission. The resulting *Famous Sites of Suzhou* (*Suzhou ming sheng* 蘇州名勝), shot in the vicinity of Nanjing, was shown for free as part of early state mass education efforts aimed at promoting citizenship, physical fitness, and hygiene.[9] In 1936 Sun was made assistant director of the University of Nanking Educational Cinematography Department, whereupon he became an active participant in the recently established

China Educational Cinematography Society (Zhongguo Jiaoyu Dianying Xiehui 中國教育電影協會; also known as the National Educational Cinematographic Association of China; hereafter ZJDX) under the tutelage of renowned educational reformer Cai Yuanpei. Closely connected to the League of Nations International Educational Cinematographic Institute (IECI), this organization was a Ministry of Education creation that represented one of several conduits for international assistance established following the arrival of the league's Mission of Educational Experts in 1931.[10] Educational cinematography, as practiced by Sun and others associated with the ZJDX and University of Nanking, was at least partly understood according to V. I. Lenin's dictum that cinema represented the "most important art" for influencing mass opinion—a view quoted during IECI member Baron Alessandro Sardi's visit to China in 1932, during which the Italian aristocrat also described how Mussolini's Fascist Party had harnessed this new technology in the service of national education.[11]

By 1933, Sun was not only involved in the production of film for domestic use, but also sent several titles concerning family hygiene, student life, economic development, rural reconstruction, and traditional Chinese handicrafts to other League of Nations members as part of a wider effort to promote China's image abroad.[12] The majority of films made by Sun Mingjing as a young professional were thus educational in the sense that they promoted public awareness of China's national conditions, industries, and government. Others extolled the process of modernization itself or served to promote hygiene, physical culture, and general knowledge (*chang shi* 常識) for citizens. Dividing his time between Nanking University and the ZJDX, Sun was involved in filming a variety of subjects, including Chinese manufactures (*Ceramics* and *Jingdezhen*); geographic landmarks and travel sites (*Lao Mountain, Scenes of Wuxi,* and *Scenes of West Lake*); and technological innovations (*Creation of the Light Bulb*).[13] Sun also produced instructional materials for university classroom use, such as *Solar Eclipse,* a 1936 scientific film shot in Hokkaido, Japan, using color Kodak film. Within the university's Educational Cinematography Department, Sun also instructed students in the use of media technology, including both motion pictures and radio broadcasts, for the purposes of mass mobilization or "arousal" (*huanqi* 喚起).[14] A related project included the organization of a projector-bearing "rural service team" (*nongcun fuwu dui* 農村服務隊) for the popularization of scientific agricultural methods.[15]

From National Reconstruction to National Emergency

In all, Sun Mingjing's early cinematic output consisted of approximately ten films describing industrial conditions in China and other countries and twenty-six films on traditional Chinese handicrafts and local products. Sun also produced scientific films—visual records of scientific expeditions and experiments intended for university classroom instruction or reference use. Other works concerned general knowledge of hygiene, geography, and local history. Sun was thus simultaneously educator and propagandist, a national intellectual and an agent of the state. Devoting his professional career to the understanding, improvement, and representation of national conditions—the subject matter of his first work as a filmmaker—Sun's concern with development was reflected through the various uses to which he attempted to put his skills as an audiovisual expert. More obviously, the time that he spent in the orbit of national institutions such as the Ministry of Education and its affiliated organizations positioned him at a crossroads between internationally established and funded institutions, such as the University of Nanking, and the state-building agendas of the Nationalist party-state.

As demonstrated by the context in which Sun Mingjing pursued filmmaking as a tool of education and national salvation, audiovisual or "electrified" education was frequently paired with other developmental activities while also playing a role in the representation of China as a modernizing, progressive country at home and abroad. In 1922 American scholar J. B. Griffing had visited the University of Nanking Rural Studies Institute, bringing with him educational films concerning cotton growing that had been produced by the U.S. Department of Agriculture. Nearly a decade later J. C. Thompson, head of the university's Chemistry Department, purchased instructional materials from Shanghai Kodak to add to the departmental curriculum.[16] In 1932 English instructor W. Reginald Wheeler produced a short informational film to promote the University of Nanking and its activities for overseas audiences.[17] Gradually, educational filmmaking was moving from the classroom toward the public as educators became increasingly involved in social reform. Noted educator Tao Xingzhi, having first advocated the importance of electrified education in 1923, later published *A Discussion of China's Programs to Popularize Education* (*Zhongguo puji jiaoyu fang'an shangtao* 中國普及教育方案商討, 1935), in which he proposed the establishment of a government science film production bureau, rural education projection teams, and a wireless radio communications network for the purpose of revitalizing China's economy.[18] Similar proposals were made by other members of the ZJDX, including cinematic theorists Xu Gongmei and Chen Yousong.

Sun Mingjing's participation in the growing mass education movement—in reality a number of separate initiatives melding citizenship education with rural and economic reform—was exemplified by his production of a lengthy publicity film depicting James Yen's Ding County pilot program.[19] During the 1930s, however, Japanese invasion to the north and famine within the interior plunged China into a state of emergency that subsequently intensified the use of motion pictures as a tool of mass education and mobilization at the national level. Between 1932 and 1938, more than three hundred students were enrolled in the University of Nanking Educational Cinematography Department (later the Motion Picture Department), some to train as mass education personnel.[20] Additional measures followed. The Ministry of Education soon established an Electrified Education Committee (Dianhua Jiaoyu Weiyuanhui 電化教育委員會), led by University of Nanking professor Pan Chenghou, and an electrified education training course charged with preparing motion picture projectionists and radio technicians for work in provincial educational institutions, including those in Hu'nan, Guangxi, Jiangsu, and Shandong. These measures, authorized under the March 25, 1936, "National Hardship Period Education Program" promulgated by the Executive Council, were the result of central government emphasis on making "the expansion of broadcast education and promotion of film education" matters of national policy.[21]

Nanjing to Beiping, June 1937: Modernization and National Defense along the Long-Hai and Jin-Pu Railways

In June 1937, Sun Mingjing left Nanjing by train, equipped with photographic equipment and an internal passport issued by the Ministry of Education. His mission, as he would write a year later from the Republican government's wartime capital of Chongqing, was to "produce films concerning domestic geography, resources, industry, and living conditions" for distribution to educational institutions.[22] Professionally, this was an important task for Sun as he had recently become head of the Educational Cinematography Department of Nanjing University. In addition to the journey's educational significance, Sun published several photographs and dispatches written from the field, both from Chongqing and on the eve of the war itself. Taken together, they described in detail local efforts toward modernization and economic development, as well as mobilization for national defense.

The first leg of Sun's extensive trip along China's coastline and inland borders took him from Nanjing to Beiping via Xuzhou, Xinpu, Lianyungang, Tai'erzhuang, Zaozhuang (site of the Chung Hsing [Zhongxing] Coal Mining Company), and Tianjin. In Xinpu, he described how this "very small city" possessed hotels, bathhouses, stores, electric lights, and long-distance telephone lines.[23] Xinpu's prosperity was a direct result of its proximity to the Huaibei salt fields and the residences of Salt Gabelle administrators responsible for oversight and taxation of salt production who, as Sun observed, enjoyed making weekend trips to the region, which boasted large parks and an ancient well.[24] (On the importance of salt provisioning during this period, see Kwan Man Bun's chapter in this volume.) Sun visited the Huaibei salt fields personally while riding in an old Studebaker along a highway constructed by the local reconstruction committee (*jianshe weiyuanhui* 建設委員會) and repaired with black salt deemed unfit for sale by the Salt Affairs Bureau.[25] At Lianyungang's harbor, a major transshipment point for cotton grown in the northwest and coal mined from nearby Zaozhuang, an even wider range of economic activity was in evidence: local investors experimenting with cotton production, a provincial aquaculture school, and construction of a new reservoir.[26] After passing through Japanese-controlled Tai'erzhuang, Sun arrived at the site of the Chung Hsing Coal Mining Company, "the most modernized mine operated by Chinese investment within China," he noted.[27] Indeed, the mine operated three shafts; produced more than six thousand *dan* of coal a day; and had built its own middle school, hospital, library, and cultural institutions. Its chief engineer was German, and it employed four hundred technicians and seven thousand manual laborers, making it a "modernized, large scale-enterprise."[28] Sun's final stop before reaching Beijing was in Tianjin, where he paid a brief visit to observe additional fish cultivation and a cannery.[29]

Throughout this part of the journey, Sun encountered clear signals that despite such evidence of economic activity and modernization, China was very much a country on the brink of war. In Xuzhou, where he had stopped to photograph the city's famous gardens, he was picked up and questioned by the police, whose suspicions had been raised by another recent wave of photographic activity carried out by Japanese agents.[30] War preparations were evident everywhere, including at the Xuzhou Girls' Normal School, where two hundred students were enrolled in training classes for entry into the youth corps; Sun himself gave vent to a bit of patriotic spleen by likening the invading Japanese forces to recent locust infestations in the region.[31] At Lianyungang, Sun was introduced to officials at the Tax Police Bureau and Finance Ministry, who commanded twenty-six hundred and thirty thousand armed regulars respectively.[32] Sun photographed Tax Police regimental soldiers carrying out exercises with a Gatling gun, as well as the rearmament of the old Ming dynasty seawall in preparation for Japanese marine assault. Japan's military presence was notable at key train stations along the Jin-Pu Railway, and conspicuously so in Tai'erzhuang and Tianjin. Departing Tianjin for Beiping on June 21, 1937, Sun missed by roughly one week the Japanese military attack on Langfang and subsequent occupation of Tianjin on July 29.

The specter of invasion, however, was not all that disturbed Sun Mingjing during his journey. In one dispatch posted from Lianyungang, he wrote, "China is actually very large and possesses rich resources. But although development is getting on track [*zou shang guidao* 走上軌道], the lives of ordinary people have not yet improved."[33] Photographs taken by Sun in Xuzhou indicate that despite the fact that the city's historic gate, the Jiangbei Yi Lou, was now covered in commercial advertising and a large "national products company" (*guo huo gongsi* 國貨公司) displayed Chinese-manufactured goods in its windows, rural "backwardness" was also evident in the form of old-style agricultural equipment (e.g., a wood-and-stone rice husker) and elderly peasant women with bound feet. Xinpu, although a popular destination for weekend tourists, lacked a reliable supply of drinking water. Nonetheless, Sun's photography and writings also demonstrate a palpable sense of national pride, as when he described how even the poorest of his countrymen were uniformly "polite and welcoming," or in the care with which he documented historical sites such as Xuzhou's gardens, Xinpu's ancient well (now dry), and Ming dynasty seawalls.[34]

Although ostensibly traveling for educational purposes, during the course of his journey Sun became something of an itinerant expert and surveyor for many of the government functionaries and institutions he encountered. In Xinpu he met with local state officials, briefing them on educational conditions in Nanjing and conducting a photographic survey of the Huaibei Salt Fields for Salt Affairs Bureau use.[35] His dual roles as educator and national government envoy gained him access to numerous sites and offices of localized reconstruction efforts, private corporations, and schools, revealing a complex web of plans for economic expansion despite the fact that the outbreak of war already seemed a near certainty. Sun gathered considerable information about these plans, both for his own educational purposes and, it seems, with the intent of reporting back to Nanjing on the results of his investigations. As he would do several times during his career thereafter, Sun shifted easily from his educational and state duties into the role of photojournalist. His reporting, however, touched upon subjects and regions of considerable interest to, as well as distance from, officials in the national capital—among them the turbulent northern frontier.

Mobilization Militarized

Sun Mingjing reached Beijing in late June, apparently unaware that the Japanese military was preparing to wrest the city from Nanjing's control. Touring the centuries-old imperial city, Sun noted signs of its recent "improvement," an image reinforced by special visits to the former Imperial Palace, Summer Palace, and National Library.[36] After participating in Yenching University's annual graduation ceremony, he then filmed a special performance of "Luanzhou shadowplay," a type of traditional puppet show that had supposedly originated during the reign of Emperor Han Wudi (141–86 BC). The performance would have been of special significance to Sun, who would later claim that he saw in its use of light and shadow a Chinese antecedent to Western invention of the cinema. Shortly following these more leisurely pursuits and after a brief inspection of the Fragrant Hills Ciyou Academy, he took part in the first meeting of the Northwest Survey Expedition (Xibei Kaocha Tuan 西北考察團), held in Zhongnanhai's Huairentang hall and chaired by Beiping mayor Qin Dechun.[37]

The Northwest Survey Expedition was part of a more general effort to open China's northwest regions to national development during the 1930s. This period had witnessed the growth of considerable political and intellectual support for transforming the "borderland" to a "heartland" in line with broader policies of territorial reintegration.[38] Despite such support, however, the region proved difficult to integrate, whether ethnically, politically, or militarily.[39] Local power holders opposed to the national government of Chiang Kai-shek included Sun Dianying, Feng Yuxiang, and the Muslim warlords of the "Ma clan"—Ma Bufang, Ma Hongkui, Ma Hongbin, and Ma Buqing. Nonetheless, the National Economic Council had opened a branch office in the region in 1933, and even avowed socialists like the Soviet enthusiast Zhang Junmai (Carsun Chang) had articulated visions for linking the northwest to the interior: "[We can] designate large areas as experimental farms [*shiyan suo* 試驗所] and use machine cultivation. At the same time, [we can] map out transportation routes between the interior and the northwest or [the territory] beyond the Great Wall, so we can take what we have reaped by cultivating pastures and ship it to the interior in order to resist importation of rice from abroad. This is what our country should immediately undertake."[40]

Yet planning development remained an ongoing process, despite the fact that Han expansion into the region had been under way since at least the eighteenth and nineteenth centuries.[41] The Northwest Survey Expedition was thus part of a longer lineage of "frontier studies" (*bianjiang xue* 邊疆學) related to solving problems of both economic self-sufficiency and national defense "beyond the Great Wall" and pioneered by the Qing dynasty scholar Gu Yanwu.[42] Support for the endeavor came from Yenching University, the National Academy of Beiping, the Popular Reading Publishing Company, the Hebei Migration Society, and the Northwest Migration and Cultivation Advancement Society.[43] Prominent historian, ethnographer, and folklorist Gu Jiegang served as the expedition's titular head, having received sponsorship from the Sino-British Cultural and Educational Endowment Fund.[44] Another key backer, however, was Duan Chengze (a.k.a. Duan Shengwu), who had founded both the Hebei Migration Society and the Northwest Migration and Cultivation Advancement Society, appointing Gu as head. Duan, a former division commander in the army of former Zhejiang and Jiangsu military governor Sun Chuanfang, had left Sun's defeated forces following the Northern Expedition and traveled to Suiyuan Province, where he became involved in local efforts to "set up industry and commerce" (*xingban shiye* 興辦事業).[45] The Hebei Migration Society, in which Duan held the position of general secretary, was subsequently established for the sake of transferring disaster-struck inhabitants of Hebei, Shandong, and He'nan to Suiyuan to serve as farmer-cultivators, first in Baotou and then, when the initial venture proved unsuccessful, in Wuyuan.

In short, the Northwest Survey Expedition emerged from a thick institutional matrix of overlapping scholarly, national, and regional networks that coalesced around the larger issue of Chinese nation-state survival—an issue seen, in turn, as hinging on the opening (through settler relocation and cultivation of northwest "wastelands") of Mongol-occupied territories originally subjugated during the former Qing dynasty.[46] By joining the expedition, Sun Mingjing committed to working alongside a group of thirty-five university and pre-collegiate educators, fifty-eight students, fifteen representatives of "social organizations" (*shehui tuanti* 社會團體), six industrial and commercial figures, four individuals of "unknown profession," and one government official all of whom, together, planned to conduct surveys of social, educational, agricultural, hygienic, geographic, and other conditions in Suiyuan and Ningxia Provinces. Duan, who addressed the preparatory meeting alongside Beiping mayor Qin Dechun, noted that while the expedition was already "too late" in terms of bringing development to the northwest, it could hope to make a "future contribution toward the [region's] economic development."[47] Following a group photograph to conclude the event, expedition members boarded a train heading west on the Beiping-Suiyuan Railway, bound for Datong.

Beiping to Suiyuan, June–July 1937: The Northwest Survey Expedition

> We are inspecting the northwest, putting the hot summer to use;
> We are seeking questions, seeking answers;
> We will open and develop the northwest and try hard to contribute;
> Opening productive land, reporting on our national territory, and reviving the nation!
>
> ("Song of the Northwest Survey Expedition")[48]

As Sun Mingjing and the other members of the Northwest Survey Expedition left Beiping, spirits quickly ran from high to low. The sight of the Great Wall moved Sun to write glowingly of his awaited encounter with the "Great Northwest of [our] ancestral homeland" (*zuguo de da Xiebei* 祖國的大西北) and to praise the mighty Beiping-Suiyuan railway for making such a journey possible.[49] By the time that the party reached Datong, however, the sight of Japanese troops positioned at Zhangjiakou Station had already served to remind its members that Chaha'er Province, the gateway to Suiyuan and Northern Shanxi, was on the brink of falling into foreign hands. The title of Sun's Datong dispatch expressed this shift in mood succinctly: "The [Beiping-Suiyuan] railroad radiates national glory—the Great Wall lacks national defense."[50] With the supervisor of forestry and land reclamation (*lin-ken duban* 林墾督辦) now apparently departed from Chaha'er, any territory beyond Badaling and Juyongguan ("the gateway to Beiping") appeared vulnerable to further invasion. Only a statue erected to deceased national hero and railroad engineer Zhan Tianyou (the "national glory" of Sun's title) still indicated that Zhangjiakou had once been a symbol of Chinese pride.

By contrast, the situation in Suiyuan remained cautiously hopeful. In 1933 Minister of Home Affairs Huang Shaohong had responded to the Japanese invasion of northern Rehe Province by attempting to woo pro-autonomy Mongols in the Suiyuan region to the cause of border defense.[51] While the effort was not an immediate success, Huang's conciliatory overture was followed by a rapid militarization of the entire northwest on Chiang Kai-shek's personal orders. The Xinjiang Construction and Planning Commission, established in Nanjing after January 1934, played a key role in this strategic plan, which included the deployment of foreign-made armored vehicles along a new roadway connecting Xi'an and Lanzhou.[52] While the position of the Nanjing-based central government steadily eroded in North China after 1935, culminating in the signing of the He-Umezu Agreement by Beijing Military Commission chairman He Yingqin, Suiyuan governor and Seventh Army Group commander Fu Zuoyi successfully defeated a Japanese-coordinated invasion force in December 1936, supported by forces provided by Chiang and Shanxi governor Yan Xishan.[53]

During the early part of the journey into Suiyuan, much of the Northwest Survey Expedition's energy was consequently spent reporting conditions related to the province's security. The first stop was Jining—Suiyuan's primary grain storage point, the province's eastern entrance by rail, an important crossroads between China and the Soviet Union, and headquarters of the Thirteenth Army, commanded by Tang Enbo. Here Sun Mingjing and the other members, accompanied by Tang's officers, inspected military facilities, barracks, and the surrounding countryside.[54] Although the dirt roads of Jining remained muddy from a recent rain, Sun observed, children were seen hard at work digging trenches.

Following a military review, during which the Thirteenth Army had proudly displayed its "German style equipment," Tang gave a speech expressing his hope that the expedition would bring additional development to the northwest. Sun dutifully commemorated the event by photographing Tang together with Duan Chengze; the expedition then decamped for Guisui, Suiyuan's capital.

Chairman of Suiyuan's provincial government and battle-seasoned North China military commander Fu Zuoyi—who did not greet the expedition members—can probably be credited with having presided over this rapid militarization of Guisui's local economy and society. Repeated Japanese and Inner Mongolian incursions into the region, later repulsed by a coalition of forces directed by Fu, Shanxi provincial governor Yan Xishan, and Chiang Kai-shek, had left a landscape dotted with "martyr's parks" (*lieshi gongyuan* 烈士公園), graves, and memorial stele (including one inscribed by Hu Shi) commemorating those who had died during combat. In Fu's place, the expedition was greeted instead by Prince Pan, who presented Sun and the other members with a yurt.[55] Interviews with lower-ranking provincial officials were accompanied by tours of the local electrical station and flower mill, the provincial library, and a detailed introduction to the "citizens' army" (*guomin jun* 國民軍) system. Based on a model adapted from adjacent Shanxi Province, this method of soldier training combined daily political and cultural education, military exercises, and economic production organized around units of soldier-homesteaders.[56] Other evidence of modernizing activity included ongoing highway and hydraulic construction; a factory that produced rugs (using antiquated technology imported from coastal Tianjin); a recently established middle school and technical school; a hospital (originally constructed by missionaries); and a vigorous local trade in wool, hair, and skins.[57]

To an assembled group of provincial officials and educators, Sun Mingjing gave a lecture on the topic of educational cinematography, later conferring with the head of the Education Department on the topics of audiovisual education and mobile projection. As during his railway trek from Nanjing to Beiping, he also recorded photographic evidence of deep cracks in the region's modernizing potential, particularly in the area of political and social control. Another Mongol noble serving on the Mongol Autonomous Political Affairs Committee, Prince Kang, was suspected of collusion with the Japanese and would later be executed. The Minsheng (or "People's Livelihood") Canal, a primary source of water for the region, was popularly known as the "People's Death" Canal due to its state of general disrepair and tendency to flood.[58] What appeared to Sun as poverty and backwardness, though less evident within Guisui proper, could easily be viewed along the roadside in the form of ramshackle hotels, migrant seasonal laborers, and human-pulled carts.[59] As he noted, the "nicest car in Guisui" belonged to Japanese secret agents who openly operated in the vicinity of the provincial capital.[60]

A more sobering perspective on the limits of military government came when the Northwest Survey Expedition, traveling further west, decamped from Guisui for Baotou. Here the group discovered an uncooperative government, whose lack of assistance effectively spelled the end of the journey. Having finally received word of the Japanese invasion on July 7, 1937, the group began to break up, with Sun and several other members, including Duan Chengze, remaining to survey provincial institutions and local land reclamation efforts. (On land reclamation efforts, see Micah Muscolino's chapter in this volume.) Sun described a city overrun by opium—a trade worth more than ¥1.5 million per year in taxes to the city's government offices—and prostitution. There were, he observed, few real "locals" in Baotou but mainly adventurers and itinerant tradespeople.[61] In adjacent Jining, a population of twenty thousand was able to support approximately one thousand licensed sex workers, and Sun noted demurely that other members of the expedition had been bombarded with solicitations during their stay. In Salaqi County Sun discovered the real cause behind the "People's Death" Canal's dysfunction: a poorly constructed, and periodically jammed, sluice. Opium cultivation was common in the region, and Sun's photographs capture fields of poppies being harvested by Shanxi migrants. Beyond Baotou's south gate the group also encountered the offices of the Sui-Xi (Western Suiyuan) Cultivation Office (Sui-Xi Tunken Chu 綏遠屯墾處), a structure with larger and newer buildings than the provincial government and whose success could be attributed to the lucrative business of selling recently "opened" land to migrants from other, more populous inland provinces.

As attested to by the presence of Mongol banner government offices, lamaseries, primary schools, and herders, Han cultivation had not completely displaced pastoral nomadism and princely power along the northern frontier. Yet a letter sent by Sun from the Dalat Banner official compound, home to the ill-fated Prince Kang, also describes the construction of village-level (*xiang* 鄉) institutions and "supervisory committees" (*jiancha weiyuanhui*) that rivaled banner institutions for local authority and control.[62] Despite the comparatively freewheeling atmosphere of Baotou, by 1937 much of this non-Mongol state expansion, nominally tied to Nanjing, had fallen under the sponsorship and oversight of provincial military governors like Yan Xishan. Traveling from Baotou to Wuyuan (a city positioned on the fertile "River's Bend" region of the Yellow River), Sun and the remaining expedition members were briefed and entertained by a number of officials representing the Suiyuan Cultivation Superintendency

Office, created by Yan in 1931 to promote economic development and military control over the northwest region.[63] Settlers in the areas opened by Yan were exclusively soldier-cultivators, former members of Yan's Shanxi Army, reorganized into thirty-one separate production teams.[64] Approximately three thousand men were, in the governor's own words, to "build production and save the nation" (*zao chan jiu guo* 造產救國).[65] According to a 1934 report given to Sun by office head Guo Weifan, these soldiers—models for Fu Zuoyi's forces in adjacent Guisui—had opened 77,000 *mu* of land to cultivation, including 4,000 *mu* for "special cropping," 20,000 *mu* for broom corn millet, 13,000 *mu* for wheat, and 12,000 *mu* for peas.

Suiyuan Cultivation Superintendency Office personnel repeatedly stressed the importance of their endeavor, which had been carried out with no support or investment from the central government, to national defense. Such military-economic development schemes, promoted by provincial military governors like Fu Zuoyi and Yan Xishan, do not appear to have been uncommon by the late 1930s, nor were they unsuccessful in linking the northwest region to coastal economies (in Sun's photos Longxing township, the county seat of Wuyuan, appears bedecked with advertising for Hong Kong products). County officials of the newly opened areas were, as Sun Mingjing described them, "indistinguishable from any other Nationalist Party official."[66] Although infrastructure between Baotou and Wuyuan remained comparatively undeveloped—the canals poorly dredged, the highways bumpy and cratered—in regional terms, the northwest mode of military cultivation represented an important innovation, albeit one that owed a great deal to previous, private efforts to irrigate the Upper Yellow River zone, dating back to the earlier part of the century. In villages surrounding Wuyuan, Sun recorded further evidence that cultivation and cooperative farming were providing the frontier state with a viable economic and defensive base. In Hebei County, villagers had received military training and together owned more than two hundred rifles.[67] They were garrisoned by a "military cultivation center" (*jun ken zhongxin* 軍墾中心)—actually an adjacent fortified village—with its own cooperative, in which each soldier owned a share worth ¥80. Sun also toured "Hebei New Village," a model community established by Duan Chengze following his forays into Suiyuan local development and Heibei (Province) migrant relocation. Every morning Hebei men and boys were convened for a "spiritual lecture" (*jingshen jianghua* 精神講話) and participated in armed drilling. The village maintained its own Wu Xun Memorial Hall (named after the Qing dynasty educator of the poor), which provided regular lectures on topics related to cultivation, defense, and self-improvement. New Village women enrolled in literacy classes; its cadres included coastal intellectuals as well as soldiers and farmers. Near Wuyuan, Sun also witnessed another "new" event—the collective marriage of twenty women from the Beiping Relief Institute (Beiping Jiuji Yuan 北平救女院) to bachelors from three surrounding villages. These young brides (Sun observed that only one of their number had previously been a prostitute) had accompanied the Northeast Survey Expedition during the entirety of its journey, bringing with them their own clothes for the ceremony, which culminated with a communal exchange of vows in front of the Republican flag.

Mobilization Provincialized

Following the return journey from Wuyuan to Shijiazhuang, Sun Mingjing was detained and questioned by Shijiazhuang police on suspicion of being a traitor and internal spy—a testament to the unusual amount of maps, reports, and photographic equipment that he had accumulated since starting out from Nanjing more than a month earlier. War was raging, and loyalties were suspect. And yet Sun remained outwardly optimistic that the Nanjing government would prevail, writing in his published record of the "ten-thousand *li*" journey along China's coastal and northern frontier that "the Chinese are a people who do not gladly suffer insult—the great people's war of resistance has finally begun!"[68]

Despite this bellicose rhetoric, during the early years of the war Sun's own activities remained essentially unchanged. His forward to the collection of letters and photographs published as *Hunting Images over Thousands of Miles* (*Wan li lie ying ji*), written in Chongqing on July 7, 1938, listed him as head of the Nanking University Department of Educational Cinematography, where he supervised "production of films concerning the geography, natural resources, industry, and society of the interior."[69] After returning to Nanjing in 1937, Sun had supervised the shooting and editing of two widely distributed "national defense" (*guo fang* 國防) films: *Defense against Air Attack* (*Fang kong* 防空, 1937) and *Defense against Poison Gas* (*Fang du* 防毒, 1937). At the request of the China Educational Cinematography Society he also traveled to the famous salt-producing city of Zigong, where he shot and released a short promotional reel, *Salt from the Mines of Zigong* (*Zigong jing yan* 自貢井鹽, 1938), which was praised by eminent geographer Huang Guozhang as a "model of geographic and industrial scientific investigation." Such surveys not only played an important role in central government industrial planning, but were also important for convincing coastal industries to relocate their facilities to Sichuan, Guizhou, and the western Xiang (Hubei and Hu'nan) region as the Nationalists retreated from Japanese invasion.[70] Later, Sun recorded part of this massive relocation process when he photographed the removal of an electric plant to Yunnan.[71]

In Sichuan, Sun's work continued under the auspices of West China Union University, located in Chengdu and comprised of émigré students and faculty from the Nanking, Ginling, Shantung (Cheeloo), and Yenching missionary-founded universities and colleges. During the war, film production in the hinterland areas was primarily directed by institutions that succeeded the Central Film Industries Guidance Commission and the Ministry of Education.[72] Sun and Guo Youshou thus aided the war effort by overseeing the training of new mobile film technicians and projectionists through the China Educational Cinematography Society Electrified Education Training Section and the Nanking University Motion Picture Department. In 1939, Sun joined yet another major frontier survey, the Sichuan-Xikang Scientific Expedition (Chuan-Kang Kexue Kaochatuan 川康考察團), directed by Huang Guozhang and sponsored by the Chongqing wartime government of Chiang Kai-shek.

Comprised of faculty from more than ten universities, the Sichuan-Xikang Scientific Expedition is probably best understood as an attempt by the Chongqing government to increase its knowledge of, and control over, Xikang Province—a poorly mapped frontier region whose provincial government had only been established since January 1, 1939. Provincial chairman Liu Wenhui was a National Revolutionary Army general and former Sichuan provincial leader whose relations with Chiang were frequently tense, as the two vied for control over China's strategically crucial western region, now a lifeline to the outside world as Japan's military forces consolidated their control over the national railway system and eastern coastline. Prior to the outbreak of war over the control of China's heartland, central government control over Sichuan itself had been variable: Nanjing lacked a "free hand" but remained influential at the level of provincial politics.[73] Since the last years of the Qing dynasty, centralized authority within Xikang (Tibetan "Kham," claimed by Lhasa as part of eastern Tibet), had been built up between 1908 and 1911 as a counter to British influence in Tibetan affairs, which had increased alarmingly following the 1904 Younghusband expedition.[74] Conflict between Tibetan armies and Chinese garrison troops were frequent until 1931, when the Nanjing government reached an agreement with Tibet to grant Lhasa control over Kanze (Ganzi) and Nyarong (Xinlong) districts.

By the early 1930s, Nanjing was already rapidly losing control of its frontier regions and their provincial governments. The northeast was dominated by Japan, with the Japan-sponsored state of Manchukuo occupying much of the ancestral Manchu homeland and provinces in North China (Rehe and Chaha'er) succumbing to Japanese military encroachment thereafter. The Inner Mongolia Autonomy Movement, led by Prince Demchuk-donggrub (Prince De), and a coup led by Xinjiang warlord Sheng Shicai had moved the northwest further out of Nanjing's orbit, necessitating rapid militarization of the region under generals Fu Zuoyi and Song Zheyuan. Likewise, conflict in Xikang remained endemic, including sporadic clashes between Lhasa's armies and regional Kham forces.[75] The Twenty-Fourth Army of National Revolutionary Army general Liu Wenhui had first occupied Xikang in 1927; in 1928 Chiang Kai-shek appointed Liu governor of Sichuan and commander-in-chief of Sichuan-Xikang border defense.[76] A Xikang Political Affairs Commission was established in the city of Kangding under Liu's direction later that year.[77] Provincial planning, which coincided with renewed Chinese efforts to consolidate control over the region, began in 1934.[78] However, mutual suspicion and political self-interest consistently placed Liu Wenhui and Chiang Kai-shek at loggerheads, with the result that Chiang's forces and appointees were essentially shut out of the region by Liu's Twenty-Fourth Army.[79] Despite having been appointed provincial chairman by Chiang personally, Liu maintained the firm belief that central government intrigues lay behind local Khamba opposition to his rule.[80] He was not mistaken, and more obvious challenges from Chiang in subsequent years included the establishment of a field headquarters in Xichang and several military intelligence stations in Kangding, Xichang, and Ya'an.[81]

Within this embattled context, Liu oversaw a program of provincial development that, though primarily centered around the capital of Kangding, recalled earlier attempts by Qing-appointed official Zhao Erfang (the "butcher of monks" to many Khambas) to reform the region by introducing provincial and county political institutions, Han colonization, and intensified resource extraction.[82] Although the central government Mongolian and Tibetan Affairs Commission had drawn up plans for the development of regional communication and transportation infrastructure in 1930, Liu Wenhui retained control of the region's institutions and resources.[83] Liu's power further expanded in 1940, when the Xikang provincial government was given administration of two additional border regions formerly incorporated into Sichuan. Khamba-occupied regions (*Kham shu diqu* 康屬地區), populated primarily by monastic clergy and seminomadic herders (and occasional slavers), remained virtually ungovernable. During the Sino-Japanese War, Chiang Kai-shek sought to bring China's southwestern provinces under the control of the Chongqing-based central government, beginning with a 1941 attempt to build a highway linking China and India. Two survey teams were dispatched in preparation for the project, which was ultimately suspended due to the Tibetan government's refusal to allow further Chinese encroachment in Xikang.[84] Throughout 1942 Lhasa officials continued to reject Chiang's attempts to station "technical experts" along the existing India-China pack route, and in general the shipment of both military and non-military goods into Chongqing continued to be stymied by Tibetan non-cooperation well into 1943.

Chengdu to Xikang, June–December 1939: The Sichuan-Xikang Scientific Expedition

Although the fact that factionalism and war made Xikang, and Southwest China more generally, into strategic headaches for Chiang Kai-shek, scientific surveys of the region were carried out frequently by a number of institutions with connections to local governments as well as to Nanjing and, later, Chongqing. Three years prior to Sun Mingjing's 1938 trip to Zigong, the China Engineering Society, Western Academy of Sciences, Chongqing University, National Military Commission, Three Gorges Defense Bureau, and National Resources Commission had all carried out geological surveys of the region for the purpose of developing China's metallurgical industries and resources in conjunction with mobilization for war.[85] More localized efforts to map West China also emerged as China-Japan conflict mounted. Together with Sichuanese "patriotic industrialist" Lu Zuofu, Liu Wenhui archrival (and relative) Liu Xiang supported the establishment of regional survey and development initiatives such as the West China Industrial Development Corporation and Sichuan Geological Survey Office. Finally, although Liu Wenhui's posthumous reputation as a frontier "warlord" and opponent of Khamba autonomy suggests a peripatetic political figure with only spurious ties to Xikang and its people, there is ample evidence to suggest that, as in the case of Suiyuan, semi-autonomous provincial governments also played an important role in transforming state-society relations during the post-1937 period.

Departing for Xikang in June 1939, the Sichuan-Xikang Scientific Expedition thus represented a relatively early attempt by Chongqing to effectively survey the regions under Liu's dominion and tie the Xikang periphery more closely to the hinterland center thereby.[86] As part of his personal effects, Sun Mingjing carried with him a notebook in which he had written, in Tibetan: "I have come on this trip on official business of Nanking Ginling University, [and] I am one of the leaders of the Nanking Ginling University Motion Picture Department. My duties are specifically to make films. I have come to Xikang with orders from the central government. Please provide direction and any needed assistance. Thank you."[87] Yet in the end, Sun's second major frontier journey produced a record of the complexities of provincial administration and Khamba-Han tensions, the latter still smoldering in Ganzi and other regions only recently brought under Kangding's control.

Sun filmed eight separate educational films depicting Xikang and its inhabitants. It is, however, his photographs of the province, later reprinted as *The Year*

1939: Into Xikang (*1939 nian: Zoujin Xikang*), that capture much of the diversity of the province, as well as the steady creep of Kangding's political authority. As recorded by Sun, the expedition's point of entry into Xikang was Ya'an city. Ya'an's main street, Zhongzheng Road, was named after Chiang Kai-shek, while its security was maintained by the pragmatically named Patrol and Protection Office, located in a former ancestral temple.[88] As a testament to Liu Wenhui's "self development" (*zishen jianshe* 自身建設) initiatives, Ya'an boasted two middle schools, one provincial and one private. Local industries were largely devoted to processing raw materials mined and harvested from the Xikang interior—a "tea brick" factory, paper-making facility, and government-built nitrate plant. Local roads and bridges facilitated commerce and transportation; a rice transshipment station provided rationed foodstuffs for workers.

This first, western leg of the Expedition's trek took the members first to Kangding, via the Hanyuan Passage—a major corridor connecting Sichuan and Tibet, but whose treacherous terrain excluded mechanized vehicles. Notable sights encountered along the way included the town of Tianquan, and a primary school nestled deep in the mountains. Reaching the ancient city of Xingjing, then called Linqiong, Sun paused to photograph a former temple converted into a middle school the Nationalist Party Xingjing county headquarters and Taihu Temple, whose wooden carvings could be dated back to at least the Tang dynasty. Here, between Ya'an and Luding, the Expedition passed charcoal- and rice-bearing porters, small-scale iron mining and smelting facilities, and ceramics manufacturers.[89] While the scale of such industries remained small, their existence testified to the tenuous connections linking Xikang's economy to that of adjacent Sichuan via the Sichuan-Xikang Road. Reaching Luding, Sun photographed the famous Luding Bridge (later immortalized by Chinese Communist Party histories of the Long March), as well as horse markets where highland tea growers traded their crop for steeds.

In Luding Sun also photographed a structure that represented Liu Wenhui's most recent efforts to provincialize (if not nationalize) the people of newly established Xikang—the Mass Education Hall (Minzhong Jiaoyu Guan 民眾教育館).[90] The presence of provincial institutions devoted to popular suasion was, perhaps unsurprisingly, particularly evident in Kangding itself. Here, in the provincial capital, Khamba inhabitants moved along streets over which presided the new offices and public assemblies of the Xikang provincial government: the government headquarters, Xikang Reconstruction Department, Provincial Tibetan People's Primary School, military garrison, electrical generating facility, and Provincial Government Nursery School.[91] As Sun noted, Liu personally addressed his constituents every month by convening a "citizens' assembly" (*guomin jihui* 國民集會). Soldiers took part in similar state rituals, including flag-raising ceremonies and a "Sun Yat-sen remembrance week." (On the use of holidays to support regime legitimacy, see Maruta Takashi's chapter in this volume.) Equally evident were the limitations of Liu's institutionalizing and homogenizing initiatives. Provincial wealth was controlled primarily by merchants, pawnbrokers, bankers, and transport companies with external ties to Sichuan, Shaanxi, and Tibet. For Khamba people, Buddhist iconography, monasteries, and religious figures denoted local ethno-political identities not yet assimilated by either Lhasa or the Xikang government. Sun's camera captured Kangding's Khamba communities eating, working, celebrating, and marrying in spaces controlled by local leaders (*tusi* 土司) with whom Liu Wenhui maintained uneasy alliances throughout his tenure as provincial chairman. In both geographical and ethnic terms, Kangding represented Xikang's frontier rather than its center.

Pushing on north and west toward Ganzi, the expedition entered a region where a tense military standoff was unfolding between Liu Wenhui's forces and the military guard of the Ninth Panchan Lama, whose remains had been interred in Ganzi Temple since 1937.[92] Discouraged from traveling further by county officials, the expedition disbanded, with many of its members returning to Chengdu. Sun, however, remained, filming a shamanic ritual (*tiao shen* 跳神)—the footage would later be released as part of *The Life of Lamas* (*Lama shenghuo* 喇嘛生活 1939). Other photographs taken in Ganzi depict county officials and their families, the compound of a Khamba *tusi* lineage (the Khangsar family, whose twenty-two-year-old leader Liu had recently been placed under house arrest), the monthly citizens' assembly, and a military review conducted by Liu's Twenty-Fourth Army.[93] Plunging deeper into the Xikang highlands, Sun reached Dege and Baiyu, traveling ancient pathways and camping in the mountains along the way. As in Ganzi, this foray into the Kham heartland yielded proof that Kangding's influence was fast approaching the limits of the China-Tibet frontier. A Han-Tibetan primary school had recently been established by Dege's county government; in Baiyu, a provincial school and part-time primary school (for children of nomadic families), as well as the familiar citizens' assembly, served as reminders of the homogenizing ambitions of the provincial state.[94]

The presence of children and young men in Republican school uniforms, however, did not signify that these ambitions had been fully realized. Whereas in Baiyu the county's Han officials posed for Sun flanked by their Tibetan bodyguards, in Dege—a Khamba stronghold—*tusi* chieftains and monasteries dominated the landscape. Provincial power, in other words, remained primarily confined to eastern Xikang and was manifested in military, political, educational, economic, and cultural forms at the county level. These included officialdom, state-owned pastures, and schoolteachers—a network of human and exchange relationships reaching westward from Kangding. Yet Sun's camera also captured a considerable range of exceptions to this totalizing image: weapons allegedly left by the CCP Chinese Red Army near Daofu; Buddhist temples and Khamba herders; Han Chinese priest Li Guoguang and his Tibetan wife; foreign-educated county teacher Liu Wenguang, the baseball enthusiast.[95] Sun Mingjing's Xikang was not simply an ethnic frontier—rather, it was a region divided by competing identities and loyalties among which province, and perhaps nation, were perhaps becoming the most dominant. That the development process reflected the priority of local (or simply different) events, rather than a distant war with Japan, speaks to the fact that in Western China, competition for human resources had preceded even the period of "national hardship" by a considerable margin.

Economy, Education, and Provincial State Building

The example of Xikang thus suggests that pre-1937 development of human and natural resources continued during the war years but was not solely the outgrowth of mobilization under total war conditions. Nonetheless, state expansion into frontier economies and strategic industries was accelerated by war and the threat of Japanese invasion, as in the case of metallurgy in West China or extraction of raw materials from the Himalayan foothills beyond.[96] For Liu Wenhui's Xikang provincial government, another overarching goal of local development was political, economic, and military control, as Liu sought to consolidate his own dominance over the region at the expense of central authority. Results were mixed. As observed in a report during a Chongqing-authorized inspection mission to Xikang in 1943, the province's primary industries included wool and weaving, hide processing, alcohol, paper, timber, chemicals, and tea.[97] Yet provincial government attempts to increase economic profitability through investment had incurred large losses. Part of the problem was related to an increase in cross-Himalayan transshipment, which had introduced tea from India as a direct competitor with local highland tea—a severe disruption to an industry formerly based on commerce via ancient "tea roads."[98]

In other areas, particularly those related to social control, the provincial government appeared more successful when measured in its own assimilating terms. Attempted acculturation of Khamba people by Xikang statebuilders had begun in earnest in 1934, signaled by the publication of special issue of *Xikang-Tibet Vanguard* (*Kang-Zang qianfeng* 康藏前鋒), devoted to primary schooling and mass indoctrination in the values of national citizenship.[99] Promoters of "border education" (*bianjiang jiaoyu* 邊疆教育) envisioned that within ten years, at least 50 percent of all Khamba "compatriots" would have received some form of state-sponsored education and that all religious practitioners—primarily Buddhists—would benefit from equal access to primary schooling.[100] Plans for "implementing a Mongol and Tibetan education plan," developed at the national Second Educational Conference, targeted Xikang, Tibet, Qinghai, Mongolia, and Xinjiang. Educators in the Sichuan-Xikang Border Defense Army compiled instructional materials for dissemination in primary schools attended by Khambas, emphasizing Chinese-language learning and citizen training.[101] Such initiatives were not entirely new. The late Qing dynasty government of Zhao Erfang, for example, had established temple schools from 1907 onward and more than thirty Mandarin-language schools at the county level prior to Zhao's assassination by Sichuanese revolutionaries in 1911.[102]

Although these county-level institutions diminished in importance for nearly two decades thereafter, the revitalization of provincial and county government under Liu Wenhui once again brought education to the fore. Education above the primary level also expanded, accelerating slightly during the 1930s, as provincial planning intensified, spreading from the Sichuan-bordering east to the more heavily Khamba-populated west.[103] This method of border consolidation thus sought to bring highlanders into the orbit of state control through the provincial Education Department, which between 1943 and 1945 went on to establish an experimental school for the "border people" of Xikang, of which Liu was the nominal head and which offered a curriculum including courses in industry and agriculture.[104] Liu also attempted to establish himself as a patron of Buddhist schools and academies.[105] In general, however, educational initiatives remained confined to provincial strongholds Kangding and Luding, where the 1937 Mass Education Annual Plan (later revised in 1939) called for more robust acculturating institutions.[106] Chief among these, as Sun Mingjing also observed, were the "mass education halls," in which lectures and performances drew audiences of hundreds. A typical monthly performance in Kangding—this one the third of 1941—included a lecture titled "How Will We Save the Nation?," report on "The Lives of Rural Khamba People," and an entertainment program that included performances of "Aviation Saves the Nation" and "The Mysterious Little Spy."[107] Public culture, coupled with political suasion, thus represented another side to wartime education and blended with preexisting efforts to create a homogenous (or "equal") provincial populace through mass educational efforts, as evidenced by the inclusion of both under the broader institutional mantle of "education" or "instruction." To be sure, education also revealed numerous limitations to the reach of the Xikang provincial government. In addition to

Buddhist monasteries, Christian missionary groups also remained active in the region, with the Border Service Department Church of Christ in China perhaps the most notable example.[108] Nor did mass educational efforts ever fully supersede existing inter-ethnic and cultural differences. As reported back by Chongqing's inspector, the region between Xikang, Tibet, and India remained "inhabited by numerous races and religions, its politics, education, and culture 'backward'" (i.e., beyond the reach of the state). Most inhabitants were still nomadic pastoralists. Transportation through the region was extremely difficult, as was the "improvement of Tibetans," among whom old customs remained. Government orders for the establishment of county-level institutions remained difficult to carry out, and "national sentiment … [was] weak."[109]

Changes in Xikang observed by Sun Mingjing and other members of the expedition, though not uniform throughout the province, pointed to the significance of sub-national, prewar development efforts as an important foundation on which the total mobilization of human and strategic resources was based. As the Xikang example suggests, part of this process included attempts to acculturate and mobilize "border peoples" through contact with the Han-dominated state. For the central government in Chongqing, the war years of 1937–1945 were also a time of intensified ethnopolitics. The Western Academy of Sciences, co-founded by Lu Zuofu, had for years devoted part of its resources to a study of the Yi people; when Sun visited Sichuan's Yi regions in 1940, after returning from Xikang, his photographs and films provided evidence of ongoing Nationalist Party efforts at readying non-Han societies for war.[110] Despite poor research conditions, ethnographic or anthropological studies provided one of the principal lenses through which state agents focused their attention on China's comparatively untapped internal border regions.[111] In other words, the Sichuan-Xikang Scientific Expedition represented just one instance of a series of studies carried out by institutions such as the West China Border Research Society, or other members of China's sociological community, that focused on Xikang alongside Gansu, Yunnan, and Sichuan as regions of growing national significance.[112] Sun himself returned to Xikang at least once during the war years, taking with him a group of students, as well as an amplified public address system—the latter a gift to Liu Wenhui, for whom Sun seems to have become a sporadic consultant on issues related to "electrified mass education." Following his initial Xikang journey, Sun also encouraged former University of Nanking classmate Li Wanjun to invest money in a hydroelectric station built in Dajianlu County, following which a grateful Liu is supposed to have donated a building to West China Union University as a token of his appreciation for Sun's support.[113]

Conclusion: Frontier State Making, Security, and Total War

This chapter has described the significance of local civil-military officials, provincial governors, quasi-private institutions and firms, and international development agencies as proponents of overlooked developmental projects throughout the 1930s and 1940s—groups that closely mirrored the wartime state in appearance and function. The resemblances were not accidental. For Duan Chengze, Fu Zuoyi, and Liu Wenhui, the experience of "war" referred to civil conflict, frontier security, and cycles of ethnic violence—all of which emerged prior to 1937 amid the ruins of the Qing empire. Sovereignty and territorial control, rather than total war per se, were the goals that drove these local, or sub-national, developmental initiatives forward. As Sun Mingjing traveled from frontier to frontier during his sojourns as educational filmmaker and state agent, he recorded numerous examples of mobilization efforts carried out in the name of the republic but presided over instead by provincial leaders and generals whose names are rarely recorded in contemporary discussions of modern social organization—bureaucratization, mass mobilization and conscription, coordinated redistribution of populations and resources—as they arose in twentieth-century China. Because war and contested sovereignty were endemic features of the Chinese political landscape after 1911 (and well before), it is perhaps unsurprising that a variety of actors, national and sub-national alike, would have adopted new strategies of human and resource mobilization in their attempts to secure significant portions of that landscape against external threats. This dynamic was particularly visible along China's territorial and ethnic frontiers; however, because of scholarly fixation on the rise and fall of national governments, it has gone largely overlooked.[114]

The limited nature of Nationalist-led local reconstruction efforts, along with their apparent postwar failure, has tended to overshadow other evidence for education, development, and mobilization strategies carried out by sub-national actors and in regions whose names are either forgotten—neither Suiyuan nor Xikang survived provincial reorganization after 1949—or confined to histories of the national periphery. From this perspective, the principal impact of total war on Chinese state-society relations can be understood in terms of the aggrandizement of state and military power vis-à-vis local structures of organization or competing "ethnic" forms. Ongoing processes of frontier expansion, militarization, and development were accelerated by the war effort but not created by it. Just as China's coastal defenses had been steadily constructed in advance of the events of 1937, these frontier state-building activities were carried out to secure

China against possible security threats arising from activities of other Eurasian states, empires, and non-Han ethnic groups. Sun Mingjing's filmmaking and photography captured the complex nature of this ongoing national project—the networks of media, education, markets, and military power on which it rested, coupled with the localized, politically fragmented, and contested reality of its history.

Notes

1. See Zhang Tongdao and Li Yu, "Bei yiwang de huihuang," 99.

2. Sun's Rightist verdict was reversed in 1978; in 1991 he received a national commendation for his professional achievements and service to the state.

3. The case for Sun as documentary filmmaker is made most cogently in Zhang Tongdao and Zhu Ying, "Sun Mingjing yu Geli'erxun," 68–73. Zhang and Zhu compare Sun to the British filmmaker John Grierson, another figure identified with documentary film history but whose career was spent equally—as was Sun's—in the service of state and commercial propaganda agencies (e.g., the British Empire Marketing Board). On nationalism and professionalism in Republican China, see Zuoyue Wang, "Saving China through Science"; Xiaoqun Xu, *Chinese Professionals and the Republican State.*

4. The concept of electrified education has its roots in 1920s and 1930s progressive visions of social—especially rural—improvement. By the postwar period, however, the use of hardware and technology to enhance classroom teaching and improve instruction more generally would be referred to as "audiovisual education," a shift also denoted in Sun's writings through introduction of the *ying-yin* binomial. On the audiovisual education concept particularly, see Januszewski, *Educational Technology.*

5. Sun's father, Sun Xisheng, and mother, Sui Xinzi, were both graduates of the Dengzhou School in Shandong; Sun Xisheng was an early student of optics who may have been one of the first in China to translate the word "cinema" as "electric image" (*dian ying* 電影). See Huo, "Sun Mingjing he ta de Xikang bijiben," 76.

6. Chen Yuguang (1893–1989) had received part of his education in the United States, during which he had also studied educational cinematography and its uses within American universities.

7. Wang Dezi, *Nanjing Daxue bainian shi,* 596–600. See also Yeh, *The Alienated Academy,* 62–63.

8. See Esherick, "Numbers Games," 387–411.

9. Sun Jiansan, "20 shiji 30 niandai," 52. Other films shot by Sun, depicting female athletics classes at Ginling Women's College, were supposedly used by Guo's organization to discourage female foot binding. (Guo Youshou 郭有守, 1901–1978 was an official of the Republic of China's Ministry of Education and educational cinematographer, propagandist, and censor.)

10. See League of Nations Mission of Educational Experts, *The Reorganization of Education in China.* Principal members of the league mission included C. H. Becker (Germany), M. Falski (Poland), P. Langevin (France), and R. H. Tawney (Britain). See also Hayhoe and Bastid, *China's Education and the Industrialized World.*

11. Zhang Li, *Guoji hezuo zai Zhongguo,* 54.

12. Cited in ibid., 55. Original source: *Shen bao,* May 20, 1933, 15.

13. Another 1936 production, *Silk* (*Chunsi*), was given English-language intertitles and exported to the United States for use in educational institutions. See Li Jinping and Xin Xianming, "Jiaoyu dianyinghua de xianqu," 89.

14. Sun Jiansan, "20 shiji 30 niandai," 49.

15. Zhang Tongdao, "Yige shidai de suxie," 23.

16. Zhao and Yang, Jinling Daxue de san wei Lianhe guo Zhongguo weiyuan, guwen yu jiaoyu dianying," 108. Shanghai Kodak was established in 1928.

17. Li Jinping and Xin Xianming, "Jiaoyu dianyinghua de xianqu," 89.

18. Li Ning and Huang Qiuxiao, "Jindai Zhongguo dianhua jiaoyu de fazhan lichen shulun," 154.

19. See Buck, *Tell the People;* Kiang, *Dr. Y. C. James Yen;* and Hayford, *To the People.* The mass education movement promoted by James Yen and Tao Xingzhi was one important example of pre-1928 initiatives for hygienic modernization (the First National Conference of the Mass Education Movement was held in Beijing in August 1923); the Council on Health Education, established in 1920, was another.

20. Zhu, Xin, and Sang, "Jiedu Sun Mingjing jiaoshou," 70; Zhang Tongdao and Li Yu, "Bei yiwang de huihuang," 99.

21. Sun Jiansan, "1936 nian dianhua jiaoyu," 112–113.

22. Sun Mingjing, *Wan li lie ying ji.* The English-language translation of this publication, *Filming as War Clouds Loom in 1937,* appeared in 2006 on Foreign Languages Press (Beijing). All translations appearing here are the author's own and are based on the original 2003 reprint.

23. Sun Mingjing, *Wan li lie ying ji,* 11–12, letter dated June 10, 1937.

24. During the war, the Salt Gabelle would be replaced by the Central China Salt Industry Company (Hua Zhong Yan ye Gufen Youxian Gongsi), established in 1938 by the Japanese-planned and -directed Central China Development Company. Coble, "Japan's New Order and the Shanghai Capitalist," 147.

25. Sun Mingjing, *Wan li lie ying ji,* 14–16, letter sent on day of the Dragon Boat Festival (fifth day of the fifth lunar month), 1937

26. Ibid., letter dated June 1937.

27. Ibid., 40, letter dated June 20, 1937. Economic historian Timothy Wright has described how mines in China during the Republican period were often prey to Nationalist Party extortion. However, in the case of Chung Hsing, connections to northern warlords and politicians, including the heads of major railroads (e.g., the Long-Hai and Jin-Pu), had allowed the mine to flourish during the 1910s and 1920s. Wright, *Coal Mining in China's Economy and Society,* 159.

28. Sun Mingjing, *Wan li lie ying ji,* 37, letter dated June 17, 1937.

29. Ibid., 41, letter dated June 21, 1937.

30. Ibid., letter dated June 9, 1937.

31. Locusts were a common source of famine in Asia and Africa during the 1930s. It is perhaps not an accident that they became a crucial plot device in the cinematic version of Pearl S. Buck's *The Good Earth,* also released in 1937.

32. The "tax police" were a military force established in 1931–1932 by T. V. Soong (Song Ziwen, then minister of finance); their initial function was to ensure revenue collection. After

1932 their ranks were supplemented with cadets from Zhang Xueliang's Northeast Army, and in time they became a force—largely ineffective—for resisting the Japanese invasion of Shanghai. Wakeman, *Spymaster*, 322.

33. Sun Mingjing, *Wan li lie ying ji*, 22–23, letter dated June 15, 1937.

34. Ibid.

35. Ibid., 14–16, 22–23.

36. Ibid., 42–43, 44–46, letters dated June 25 and 27, 1937.

37. Ibid., 47–48, letter dated June 30, 1937. The Ciyou (Nurturing Youth) Academy was a philanthropic institution established in 1920 by the late Qing dynasty and Republican scholar-official Xiong Xiling. Devoted to the "education, nurture, and protection" (*jiao, yang, wei*, as described in Sun's dispatch) of orphaned children and serving as a college preparatory school for the disadvantaged, it was funded solely by private donations. See also Zhou Qiuguang, "Modern Chinese Educational Philanthropy," 51–83.

38. Tighe, "From Borderland to Heartland," 54–74.

39. Lipman, "Ethnicity and Politics in Republican China," 285–316; Hsiao-ting Lin, "Nationalists," 121–142.

40. Quoted in Jeans, *Democracy and Socialism in Republican China*, 162. A concise overview of the National Economic Council and its branch offices appears in Kirby, *State and Economy in Republican China*, 64.

41. Millward, "New Perspectives on the Qing Frontier," 113.

42. Ibid., 116.

43. See Wang Longsheng, "Shuqi Xibei kaocha tuan zai Suiyuan."

44. Lipman, *Familiar Strangers*, 6. Gu's own account of the expedition is reprinted in Gu, *Kaocha Xibei riji*. Schneider, *Ku Chieh-kang and China's New History*, remains the definitive English-language overview of Gu Jiegang's life and career prior to 1949.

45. Sun Mingjing, *Wan li lie ying ji*, 47–48.

46. Johnson, "Race for Real Estate," 26–28. Tighe, *Constructing Suiyuan*, provides a systematic account of provincial political and economic institution building.

47. Sun Mingjing, *Wan li lie ying ji*, 47–48.

48. Ibid., 53–55, letter dated July 1, 1937. Original lyrics: 我们考察西北，利用伏暑；我们寻找问题，寻求答案；我们开发西北，努力建树；开地利，报国土，复兴民族!

49. Ibid.

50. Ibid.

51. Hsiao-ting Lin, *Modern China's Ethnic Frontiers*, 43.

52. Ibid., 45.

53. Boyd, "In Pursuit of an Obsession"; Jowett, *Rays of the Rising Sun*.

54. Sun Mingjing, *Wan li lie ying ji*, 69–70, letter dated July 2, 1937.

55. Ibid., 79–80, letter July 3, 1937.

56. Ibid., 93–94, letter dated July 5, 1937.

57. Ibid., 100–102, letter dated July 5, 1937.

58. Ibid., 128–129, letter dated July 9, 1937. This gloomy moniker derived from a play on words: 民死 (*min-si*) for 民生 (*min-sheng*). Original canal architect Wang Tongchun (d. 1924) had developed plans to irrigate the region with Beijing's support and succeeded in creating a network of canals that made cultivation surrounding the Yellow River cities of Anbei, Wuyuan, and Linhe possible by the time of his death.

59. Sun Mingjing, *Wan li lie ying ji*, 115–119, letter dated July 8, 1937.

60. Ibid., 100–102.
61. Ibid., 133–134, letter dated July 10, 1937.
62. Ibid., 137–138, letter dated July 13, 1937.
63. Ibid., 152–155, letter dated July 17, 1937.
64. Also included were soldiers from the Shanxi Army 409th and 419th regiments.
65. Sun Mingjing, *Wan li lie ying ji,* 152–155, letter dated July 17, 1937.
66. Ibid.
67. Ibid., 166–168, letter dated July 20, 1937.
68. Ibid., 182–185, letter dated July 30, 1937.
69. Ibid., author's forward.
70. Huang Guozhang quoted in ibid.; Chu, "Kang zhan qijian Xi'nan," 102. Organization for relocation began on August 10, 1937; a proclamation that the government would be relocated to Chongqing was made on November 20. Relocation of the central government took place from August 4, 1938, onward, while industrial relocation committees were set up from March 1938 onward.
71. Zhang Tongdao and Li Yu, "Bei yiwang de huihuang," 100.
72. Guo, "Jiyi zhong de Zhongguo jiaoyu dianying yundong," 108.
73. "Significant Developments," 173.
74. Hsiao-ting Lin, "The 1934 Chinese Mission to Tibet," 328.
75. Dong, "Xikang jian sheng shi-mo ji," 21–23; Wang Yan, "Qian xi di san ci Kang-Zang jiufen," 105–108.
76. Prior to the occupation, Liu had been appointed Sichuan-Xikang land reclamation envoy.
77. Zhou Weizhou, "1930–1933 nian Xizang yu Kang, Qing zhanzheng zhiyanjiu," 1.
78. Fan, "1939–1944 nian Xikang sheng Kang shu ge xian zongjiao yangtai de shehui fenxi," 32. Liu was subsequently made chairman of the Xikang Provincial Construction Commission.
79. During the 1920s, Liu had received Chiang's backing as a counterweight to other Sichuan-based military officials, including Liu Xiang (a Liu Wenhui relation), Deng Xihou, and Tian Songyao. Having vied unsuccessfully with Liu Xiang's armies for provincial control, Liu Wenhui found himself essentially exiled to Xikang.
80. Wang Haibin, "Xikang sheng zhihua jincheng zhong de quanli boyi (1927–1939)," 123.
81. Li Dianyuan, "Lun Liu Wenhui fan Jiang," 115. See also Liu Wenhui, *Zoudao renmin zhenying de lishi daolu.*
82. See Peng, "Frontier Policies," 61; Wang Chuan, "Qing mo, Minguo shiqi Xikang diqu de nongye gaijn jiqi shiji chengxiao," 54–59.
83. See "Meng-Zang Weiyuanhui jueyi tongguo Kang-Zang gonglu youzheng dianzheng hangzheng san qi jihua," 2–5.
84. Hsiao-ting Lin, "War or Stratagem?," 449.
85. Chu Ming, "Kang zhan qijian Xi'nan," 101.
86. Hsiao-ting Lin, "War or Stratagem?," 456.
87. Quoted in Huo, "Sun Mingjing he ta de Xikang bijiben," 77.
88. Sun Mingjing, *1939 nian,* 1–22.
89. Ibid., 34–55.
90. Ibid., 56–59.

91. Ibid., 60–127.

92. At the time, Ganzi Temple was the largest ritual center of Yellow Sect Lamaism in northern Xikang and also served as the temporary "field headquarters" of the Ninth Panchan Lama—the location of his ninth incarnation's interment. In 1925 the Ninth Panchan Lama had been expelled from Tibet, after which he traveled through Gansu and Inner Mongolia. In 1931 his title was recognized by the Nationalist government, and he attempted to return to Tibet under the protection of a retinue that included three hundred armed guards. In 1937 he died in Yushu, Qinghai Province.

93. Sun Mingjing, *1939 nian,* 169–191. Sun arrived in Ganzi in August 1939. In October 1939 the Khangsar family, allied with Liu Jiaju, took the Ganzi military commander and magistrate prisoner. In December 1939 Liu Wenhui launched a counterattack, chasing the Khangsar chieftain (Ch. *deqinwangmu*) and remaining Office of the Panchan Lama retinue back to Yushu.

94. Sun Mingjing, *1939 nian,* 192–218.

95. Ibid., 219–238.

96. Chu, "Kang zhan qijian Xi'nan," 101–102.

97. Report from Lin Rulin.

98. Ibid. Another competitor, also introduced to the region via infrastructure constructed following the central government's relocation to Chongqing, was tea from Yunnan.

99. Wang Qilong and Deng Xiaoyong, "1949 nian yiqian Zang qu jiaoyu yanjiu shuping," 43.

100. Ibid.

101. Wang Qilong and Deng Xiaoyong, "1949 nian yiqian Zang qu jiaoyu," 46.

102. Lin Junhua, "Ganzi Zang qu xuexiao jiaoyu fazhan shi gaisuo," 39.

103. Ibid.; Wu and Zhang, "Sishi nian dai Xichang minzu jiaoyu de huigu."

104. Ibid.," 46.

105. Wang Chuan, "Liu Wenhui yu Xizang diqu Zang chuan Fojiao jie guanxi shulun," 78–84.

106. Liu Xianqiang and Zhao Xingmin, "Minguo shiqi Kang qu minzhong jiaoyu de fazhan," 123.

107. Ibid., 125.

108. Deng, "'Shehui fuyin' yu biandi shehui gailiang," 196–202.

109. Report from Lin Rulin.

110. This expedition, the Yi Nationality Region Scientific Survey, took place in April 1949 and reached four counties in Sichuan: Leibo, Mabian, Pingshan, and E'bian.

111. See Rodriguez, *China's Frontier Enterprise.*

112. "The West China Border Research Society," 65–66; Li Hanlin, Fang Ming, Wang Ying, Sun Bingyao, and Qi Wang, "Chinese Sociology," 612–640. In the film and documentary world, this interest was reflected by titles such as *Moving Genghis Khan's Relics* (*Chengjisihan yiling* 成吉思汗移陵, 1939), *Tibetan Pilgrimage* (*Xizang xunli* 西藏巡禮, 1940), *Long Live the Nation* (*Minzu wansui* 民族萬歲, 1940), and *Scenes of Xinjiang* (*Xinjiang fengguang* 新疆風光, 1940). See Xu Suling, "Guanyu 'Xizang xunli,'" 556–558.

113. Zhu, Xin, and Sang, "Jiedu Sun Mingjing jiaoshou," 71.

114. Significant exceptions to this general rule would include not only frontier studies, but also studies of Chinese cities during the first half of the twentieth century. See, for example, Esherick, *Remaking the Modern Chinese City.*

Bibliography

Newspapers and Periodicals Cited as Primary Sources

Man

Far Eastern Survey

References

Boyd, James. "In Pursuit of an Obsession: Japan in Inner Mongolia." *Japanese Studies* 22, no. 3 (December 2002): 289–303.

Buck, Pearl Sydenstricker. *Tell the People: Talks with James Yen about the Mass Education Movement.* New York: John Day, 1945.

Chu Ming 初明. "Kang zhan qijian Xi'nan houfang ye jin gongye jianshu" 抗戰期間西南後方冶金工業簡述 (A brief discussion of the metallurgy industry in the southwest during the Anti-Japanese War). *Minguo dang'an* 民國檔案 (Republican archives), no. 2 (1988): 101–107.

Coble, Parks M. "Japan's New Order and the Shanghai Capitalist: Conflict and Collaboration, 1937–1945." In *Chinese Collaboration with Japan, 1932–1945,* edited by David P. Barrett and Lawrence N. Shyu. Stanford, Calif.: Stanford University Press.

Deng Jie 鄧杰. "'Shehui fuyin' yu biandi shehui gailiang-Zhonghua jidu jiaohui bianjiang fuwu yundong zhong de funv shigong" 社會福音與邊地社會改良中華基督教會邊疆服務運動中的婦女事工 (The social gospel and the reform of frontier society: The women's ministry of the Chinese Christian association frontier service movement). *Zongjiao xue yanjiu* 宗教學研究 (Religious studies), no. 2 (2006): 196–202.

Dong Enqiang 董恩強. "Xikang jian sheng shi-mo ji" 西康建省始末記 (The establishment of Xikang as a province from beginning to end). *Minguo chunqiu* 民國春秋 (Republican spring and fall), no. 2 (1996): 21–23.

Esherick, Joseph W. "Numbers Games: A Note on Land Distribution in Prerevolutionary China." *Modern China,* 4, no. 1 (October 1981): 387–411.

———, ed. *Remaking the Modern Chinese City: Modernity and National Identity.* Honolulu: University of Hawai'i Press, 2000.

Fan Zhaoquan 范召全. "1939–1944 nian Xikang sheng Kang shu ge xian zongjiao yangtai de shehui fenxi 1939–1944 年西康省康屬各縣宗教樣態的社會分析" (Social analysis of the state of religion in counties in Xikang, 1939–1944). *Xizang yanjiu* 西藏研究 (Tibetan research), no. 4 (August 2009): 32–40.

Gu Jiegang 顧頡剛. *Kaocha Xibei riji* 考察西北日記 (Diary of an investigation in the northwest). Lanzhou: Lanzhou guji shudian, 1983 [1938].

Guo Youshou 郭有守. "Jiyi zhong de Zhongguo jiaoyu dianying yundong" 記憶中的中國教育電影運動 (Memories of the movement for Chinese educational films). *Dianying yu boyin* 電影與播音 (Film and broadcast) 4, no. 5 (June 1945): 108.

Hayford, Charles. *To the People: James Yen and Village China.* New York: Columbia University Press, 1990.

Hayhoe, Ruth, and Marianne Bastid, eds. *China's Education and the Industrialized World: Studies in Cultural Transfer.* Armonk, N.Y.: M. E. Sharpe, 1987.

Huo Shui 活水. "Sun Mingjing he ta de Xikang bijiben 孫明經和他的西康筆記本" (Sun Mingjing and his Xikang notebook). *Xikang ren-wen dili* 西康人文地理 (Xikang humanities and geography), no. 1 (2005): 76.

Januszewski, Alan. *Educational Technology: The Development of a Concept*. Englewood, Colo.: Libraries Unlimited, 2001.

Jeans, Roger B. *Democracy and Socialism in Republican China: The Politics of Zhang Junmai (Carsun Chang), 1906–1941*. Lanham, Md.: Rowman and Littlefield, 1997.

Johnson, Matthew D. "Race for Real Estate: Constructing Ethno-National Borders in Western Inner Mongolia, 1636–1934." Unpublished paper, 2002.

Jowett, Phillip S. *Rays of the Rising Sun, Armed Forces of Japan's Asian Allies, 1931–1945*, vol. 1: *China and Manchuria*. Solihull, UK: Helion, 2004.

Kiang, John C. K., ed. *Dr. Y. C. James Yen: His Movement for Mass Education and Rural Reconstruction*. South Bend, Ind., 1976. No publisher given.

Kirby, William C. *State and Economy in Republican China: A Handbook for Scholars*, vol. 1. Cambridge, Mass.: Harvard University Asia Center, 2001.

League of Nations Mission of Educational Experts. *The Reorganization of Education in China*. Paris: League of Nations Institute of Intellectual Co-operation, 1932.

Li Dianyuan 李殿元. "Lun Liu Wenhui fan Jiang 論劉文輝反蔣" (On Liu Wenhui's opposition to Chiang [Kai-shek]). *Shehui kexue yanjiu* 社會科學研究 (Social science research), no. 1 (1994): 112–116.

Li Hanlin, Fang Ming, Wang Ying, Sun Bingyao, and Qi Wang. "Chinese Sociology, 1898–1986." *Social Forces* 65, no. 3 (March 1987): 612–640.

Li Jinping 李金萍 and Xin Xianming 辛顯銘, "Jiaoyu dianyinghua de xianqu: Jinling Daxue dianjiao ruanjian bianzhi yu tuiguang shiye jishi 教育電影化先驅—金陵大學電教軟件編制與推廣事業紀實" (Pioneer of electrification of education: Jinling [Nanjing] University's production and distribution of electrified educational film materials). *Dianying jiaoyu yanjiu* 電影教育研究 (Research on film education), no. 4 (2007): 88–96.

Li Ning 李寧 and Huang Qiuxiao 黃秋嘯. "Jindai Zhongguo dianhua jiaoyu de fazhan lichen shulun 近代中國電化教育的發展歷程述論" (The development of electrified education in modern China). *Heilongjiang shi zhi* 黑龍江史志 (Record of Heilongjiang history), no. 4 (2009): 154–156.

Lin, Hsiao-ting. *Modern China's Ethnic Frontiers: A Journey to the West*. New York: Routledge, 2011.

———. "Nationalists, Muslim Warlords, and the 'Great Northwestern Development.'" *China and Eurasia Forum Quarterly* 5, no. 1 (2007): 121–142.

———. "The 1934 Chinese Mission to Tibet: A Re-Examination." *Journal of the Royal Asiatic Society*, 3rd series, 12, no. 3 (November 2002): 328.

———. "War or Stratagem? Reassessing China's Military Advance towards Tibet, 1942–1943." *China Quarterly*, no. 186 (2006): 446–462.

Lin Junhua 林俊華. "Ganzi Zang qu xuexiao jiaoyu fazhan shi gaisuo 甘孜藏區學校教育發展史概索" (Ganzi Tibetan area education development). *Xizang yanjiu* 西藏研究 (Tibetan research) 2 (1993): 39–46.

Lipman, Jonathan N. "Ethnicity and Politics in Republican China: The Ma Family Warlords of Gansu." *Modern China* 10, no. 3 (July 1984): 285–316.

———. *Familiar Strangers: A History of Muslims in Northwest China.* Seattle: University of Washington Press, 1997.

Liu Wenhui 劉文輝. *Zoudao renmin zhenying de lishi daolu* 走到人民陣營的歷史道路 (Walking on the road to the people's side). Zhongyang wenshi chubanshe, n.d. No place given.

Liu Xianqiang 劉先強 and Zhao Xingmin 趙興民. "Minguo shiqi Kang qu minzhong jiaoyu de fazhan 民國時期康區民眾教育的發展" (The development of mass education in Xikang during the Republican period). *Jiaoyu pinglun* 教育評論 (Critical religion), no. 1 (2008): 123–126.

"Meng-Zang Weiyuanhui jueyi tongguo kaifa Kang-Zang gonglu youzheng dianzheng hangzheng san qi jihua 蒙藏委員會決議通過開發康藏公路郵政電政航政三期計畫" (The Mongolian and Tibetan Affairs Commission decides on plans for three stage policies for public roads, mail, electricity, and travel between Tibet and Xikang). March 27, 1930. Reprinted in *Minguo dang'an* 民國檔案 (Republican archives), no. 3 (1992): 2–5.

Millward, James A. "New Perspectives on the Qing Frontier." In *Remapping China: Fissures in Historical Terrain,* edited by Gail Hershatter, Emily Honig, Jonathan N. Lipman, and Randall Stross, 113–129. Stanford, Calif.: Stanford University Press, 1996.

Peng Wangbin. "Frontier Policies, Provincial Politics, and Movements for Khampa Autonomy during the Republican Period." In *Khamps Pa Histories: Visions of People, Place, and Authority,* edited by Lawrence Epstein, 58–80. Leiden: Brill, 2000.

Pepper, Suzanne. *Radicalism and Education Reform in 20th-Century China: The Search for an Ideal Development Model.* Cambridge: Cambridge University Press, 1996.

Report from Lin Rulin, inspector, Xi-chuan/Xikang, to Ministry of Finance. November 2, 1943. Reprinted in *Minguo dang'an* 民國檔案 (Republican archives), no. 3 (1993): 25–28.

Rodriguez, Andres. "China's Frontier Enterprise: Frontier Studies and Nation Building during the Republican Period (1912–1949)." PhD dissertation, University of Oxford, 2009.

Schneider, Lawrence. *Ku Chieh-kang and China's New History: Nationalism and the Quest for Alternative Traditions.* Berkeley: University of California Press, 1971.

"Significant Developments—Nanking Extends Control in Harassed Szechwan." *Far Eastern Survey* 6, no. 15 (July 21, 1937): 173.

Sun Jiansan 孫建三. "20 shiji 30 niandai de Zhongguo tiyu dianying yu kang-Ri jiuwang yundong 20世紀30年代的中國體育電影與抗日" (Chinese physical education films and resistance to Japan in the 1930s). *Yishu pinglun* 藝術評論 (Art criticism) 8 (2008): 52.

———. "1936 nian dianhua jiaoyu zai Zhongguo dansheng de jingguo yu xiangguan wenxian shiliao 1936 年電化教育在中國誕生的經過與相關文獻史料" (Documents related to the birth and process of electrified education in China in 1936). *Dianhua jiaoyu yanjiu,* no. 2 (2009): 112–113.

Sun Mingjing 孫明經 (Zhang Ming 張鳴, ed.). *1939 nian: Zoujin Xikang* 1939 年走進西康 (The year 1939: Into Xikang). Jinan: Shandong huabao chubanshe, 2003.

———. *Wan li lie ying ji* 萬里獵影記 (Record of chasing images over ten thousand miles). Reprinted in Sun Mingjing 孫明經, *1937 nian: Zhan yun bianshang de lie ying* 1937 年: 戰雲邊上的獵影 (1937: Images captured amid clouds of war). Ji'nan: Huabao chubanshe, 2003.

Sun Mingjing 孫明經 and Sun Jiansan 孫建三. *Dingge Xikang: Kekao sheyingjia jingtouli de kangzhan houfang* 定格西康: 科考攝影家鏡頭裡的抗戰後方 (Framing Xikang: The rear areas during the Anti-Japanese War through the lens of an experimental photographer). Guilin: Guangxi shifan daxue chubanshe, 2010.

Tighe, Justin. *Constructing Suiyuan: The Politics of Northwestern Territory and Development in Twentieth Century China*. Leiden: Brill, 2005.

———. "From Borderland to Heartland: The Discourse of the North-West in Early Republican China." *Twentieth-Century China* 35, no. 1 (November 2009): 54–74.

Wakeman, Frederic E., Jr. *Spymaster: Dai Li and the Chinese Secret Service.* Berkeley: University of California Press, 2003.

Wang Chuan 王川. "Liu Wenhui yu Xizang diqu Zang chuan Fojiao jie guanxi shulun 劉文輝與西藏地區藏傳佛教界關係述論" (On the relationship between Liu Wenhui and Tibetan spread of Buddhism). *Zhongguo Zang xue* 中國藏學 (China Tibetan studies), no. 3 (2006): 78–84.

———. "Qing mo Minguo shiqi Xikang diqu de nongye gaijn jiqi shiji chengxiao 清末民國時期西康地區的農業改進及其實際成效" (Agricultural reforms and their effectiveness in Xikang during the end of the Qing and Republican periods). *Minguo dang'an* 民國檔案 (Republican archives), no. 4 (2004): 54–59.

Wang Dezi 王德滋, ed. *Nanjing Daxue bainian shi* 南京大學百年史 (The abundant history of Nanjing University). Nanjing: Nanjing Daxue chubanshe, 2002.

Wang Haibin 王海兵. "Xikang sheng zhihua jincheng zhong de quanli boyi (1927–1939) 西康省制化進程權力博弈" (The game of power in the making of Xikang Province). *Zhongguo bianjiang shi di yanjiu* 中國邊疆史地研究 (Research on the history and geography of China's frontiers), 18, no. 3 (September 2008): 19–26, 143.

Wang Longsheng 王龍勝. "Shuqi Xibei kaocha tuan zai Suiyuan 暑期西北考察團在綏遠" (The summer Northwest survey expedition in Suiyuan). *Dang'an yu shehui* 檔案與社會 (Archives and society), no. 6 (2004): 3.

Wang Qilong 王啟龍 and Deng Xiaoyong 鄧小咏. "1949 nian yiqian Zang qu jiaoyu yanjiu shuping 1949 年以前藏區教育研究述評" (Review of research on education in Tibet before 1949). *Xizang Daxue xuebao* 西藏大學學報 (University of Tibet journal) 16, no. 4 (December 2001): 43–49.

Wang Yan 王燕. "Qian xi di san ci Kang-Zang jiufen 淺析第三次康藏糾紛" (Analysis of the third conflict between Xikang and Tibet). *Minguo dang'an* 民國檔案 (Republican archives), no. 2 (2003): 105–108.

Wang, Zuoyue. "Saving China through Science: The Science Society of China, Scientific Nationalism, and Civil Society in Republican China." *Osiris,* 2nd series, 17 (2002): 291–322.

"The West China Border Research Society." *Man* 46 (May–June 1946): 65–66.

Wright, Timothy. *Coal Mining in China's Economy and Society, 1895–1937.* Cambridge: Cambridge University Press, 1984.

Wu Liucun 伍柳村 and Zhang Zhiying 張志英. "Sishi nian dai Xichang minzu jiaoyu de huigu 四十年代西昌民族教育的回顧" (Memories of Xichang minorities' education in the 1940s). *Wenshi zazhi* 文史雜誌 (Literature and history journal), no. 3 (1992): 46.

Xu Suling 徐蘇靈. "Guanyu 'Xizang xunli' 關於西藏巡禮" (Tibetan pilgrimages). *Zhongyang ribao* 中央日報 (), February 15, 1941. Reprinted in *Kang-Ri zhanzheng shiqi de Chongqing dianying* 抗日戰爭時期的重慶電影 (Chongqing movies during the Anti-Japanese War), edited by Chongqing Shi Wenhua ju Dianying Chu 重慶市文化局電影處 (Film Office of the Chongqing Municipal Culture Bureau), 556–558. Chongqing: Chongqing chubanshe, 1991.

Xu, Xiaoqun. *Chinese Professionals and the Republican State: The Rise of Professional Associations in Shanghai, 1912–1937.* Cambridge: Cambridge University Press, 2010.

Yeh, Wen-hsin. *The Alienated Academy: Culture and Politics in Republican China.* Cambridge, Mass.: Council on East Asian Studies, Harvard University, 1990.

Zhang Li 張力. *Guoji hezuo zai Zhongguo: Guoji lianmeng juese de kaocha, 1919–1946* 國際合作在中國: 國際聯盟角色的考察 (International cooperation in China: An investigation of the role of the League of Nations, 1919–1946). Taipei: Zhongyang yanjiuyuan jindaishi yanjiusuo, 1999.

Zhang Tongdao 張同道. "Yige shidai de suxie: Sun Mingjing de yingxiang rensheng zhongguo sheyingjia 一個時代的速寫: 孫明經的影像人生" (A quick sketch of an era: Sun Mingjing's influential life). *Zhongguo zheyingjia* 中國攝影家 (China photographer), no. 4 (2007): 23.

Zhang Tongdao 張同道 and Li Yu 黎煜. "Bei yiwang de huihuang—lun Sun Mingjing yu Jinling Daxue jiaoyu dianying 被遺忘的輝煌論孫明經與金陵大學教育電影" (A forgotten splendor—on Sun Mingjing and Jingling University film education). *Beijing dianying xueyuan xuebao* 北京電影學院學報 (Beijing film institute journal), no. 4 (2005): 18–27.

Zhang Tongdao 張同道 and Zhu Ying 朱影. "Sun Mingjing yu Geli'erxun: Guannian, lilun, yu shijian 孫明經與各里爾遜: 觀念,理論,與實踐" (Sun Mingjing and [John] Greirson: Concept, theory, and practice) *Dianying yishu* 電影藝術 (Film art), no. 2 (2006): 68–73.

Zhao Huikang 趙惠康 and Yang Aihua 楊愛華. "Jinling Daxue de san wei Lianhe guo Zhongguo weiyuan, guwen yu jiaoyu dianying—chongdu *Huigu wo guo zaoqi de dianhua jiaoyu yougan* 金陵大學的三位聯合國中國委員顧問與教育電影—重讀回顧我國早期的電化教育有感" (Three Chinese United Nations delegates from Jinling [Nanjing] University—reaction on rereading "Remembering our country's early education electrification"). *Dianhua jiaoyu yanjiu* 電化教育研究 (Research on education electrification), no. 189 (January 2008): 108.

Zhou Qiuguang (Edward A. McCord, trans.). "Modern Chinese Educational Philanthropy: Xiong Xiling and the Xiangshan Children's Home." *Republican China* 19, no. 1 (November 1993): 51–83.

Zhou Weizhou 周偉洲. "1930–1933 nian Xizang yu Kang, Qing zhanzheng zhiyanjiu 1930–1933 年西藏與康青戰爭之研究" (Research on the 1930–1933 war between Tibet and Xikang/Qinghai). *Xizang minzu xueyuan xuebao (zhexue shehui kexue ban)* 西藏民族學院學保 [哲學社會科學版]) (Tibetan Institute journal [philosophy and social science edition]), 28, no. 1 (January 2007): 1–11.

Zhu Jing 朱敬, Xin Xianming 辛顯銘, and Sang Xinmin 桑新民. "Jiedu Sun Mingjing jiaoshou: Zhongguo dianhua jiaoyu de kaikuozhe yu dianjiren 解讀孫明經教授: 中國電化教育的開口者與奠基人" (Interpreting professor Sunmingjing: Originator and founder of electrified education in China). *Dianhua jiaoyu yanjiu* 電化教育研究 (Research on education electrification), no. 11 (2006): 70.

CHAPTER 10

Wartime Water and Soil Conservation in Gansu

MICAH S. MUSCOLINO

The Nationalist government's mobilization of all of China's resources—"each straw and each log," as Chiang Kai-shek put it—for the Anti-Japanese War of 1937–1945 wrought tremendous environmental destruction.[1] Yet, somewhat paradoxically, the imperative of rationally and efficiently exploiting resources for the war effort also lent impetus to a range of state-led conservation efforts in China's unoccupied territories. These initiatives included water and soil conservation programs based on globally circulating scientific principles that built upon prewar precedents. Beginning in the 1920s, Chinese agriculture, forestry, and water conservancy experts promoted globalized visions of soil erosion's causes and consequences that drew inspiration primarily from conservation efforts in the United States.[2] During World War II, influenced by American advisers to China, the Nationalist central government implemented its first comprehensive water and soil conservation programs in Northwest China's Loess Plateau (Huangtu Gaoyuan 黃土高原), a region that covers 640,000 square kilometers and suffers from high rates of erosion and acute water shortages.

For Chinese water and soil conservation specialists in wartime China's "great rear areas" (*da houfang* 大後方), resisting the Japanese and reconstructing the nation meant checking water and soil loss by rationalizing land use. Water and soil conservation assumed enormous importance after the Japanese occupied China's main economic centers and forced the Nationalist regime to focus on developing China's unoccupied western interior and efficiently developing its land and resources to support wartime economic mobilization.[3] Among the foremost initiatives taken in pursuit of these goals was the founding of the Tianshui Water and Soil Conservation Experiment Area (Tianshui Shuitu Baochi Shiyanqu 天水水土保持實驗區) in August 1942 by the Nationalist regime's Ministry of Agriculture and Forestry (Nonglinbu 農林部).[4]

The planning and implementation of wartime water and soil conservation programs in Northwest China fell to mid-level bureaucrats, most of whom had received training abroad during the prewar period. The conservation measures that these technical experts devised for Tianshui ran up against local landholders, who displayed nothing in the way of obedience toward the dictates of the Nationalist regime or willingness to sacrifice for its war effort. Not only did Chinese technocrats get around this opposition, however, but their transnational connections also proved instrumental in garnering financial support for wartime conservation programs and ensuring their success.

Fighting Erosion to Develop the Northwest

The wartime drive to develop the northwest set the stage for water and soil conservation programs. With the Japanese invasion of China's coastal provinces in 1937, as a high-ranking Gansu provincial official put it in 1940, "The Northwest suddenly emerged from an obscure border region into a vital base for prolonged resistance and national reconstruction." Among the provinces that comprised the northwest, Gansu "occupied a key position as the center of the region," particularly due to its place "on the path of direct communication with Soviet Russia" via Xinjiang to the west. This strategic position made Gansu not only a "great pulse of China," but also a "pivotal point linking Asia and Europe." Gansu possessed wide expanses of arable land and natural resources "of great value" to national defense, so it had "a significant role to play" in the War of Resistance and "good prospects for future economic development." In agriculture, Gansu had taken steps to increase production and feed its rapidly growing population. But due to "the ignorance of the peasants," farming methods remained "primitive" and output lagged. Much of Gansu was well suited for afforestation and animal husbandry, but these enterprises had been neglected in the past. Remedying these circumstances required state-initiated improvements.[5]

Water and soil conservation figured prominently among the measures that contemporaries advocated to improve agricultural production in the northwest. Forester Ling Daoyang 凌道揚 (1888–1993) and conservation expert Ren Chengtong 任承統 (1898–1973), in an article published in 1943, put forth a comprehensive argument for water and soil conservation's importance in China's wartime mobilization. These two authors and their ideas merit detailed discussion for the light that they shed on the origins of wartime conservation programs and their relationship with the larger goal of developing the northwest.

One of China's most renowned experts in agriculture and forestry, Ling Daoyang came from Baoan County, Guangdong Province. After graduating in 1909 from Saint John's University in Shanghai, Ling earned a BS in 1912 from Massachusetts Agricultural College and an MF in 1914 from Yale University's School of Forestry. After briefly investigating forestry in Germany, Ling returned to China in 1915 as head of the University of Nanking's (Nanjing's) Forestry

Department. In addition to his scientific credentials, he also had political connections. Ling helped Sun Yat-sen to compile forestry and agricultural data for his Three Principles of the People (Sanmin Zhuyi 三民主義) lectures in 1917 and held a slew of academic and official positions. Significantly for our purposes, in 1939 the Nationalist regime appointed Ling as executive commissioner of the Yellow River Conservancy Commission and chairman of its Forest and Soil Conservation Committee (Linken Weiyuanhui 林墾委員會), which oversaw the formulation of plans to limit water and soil loss.[6]

Through his service at the University of Nanking and in Nationalist government conservation agencies, Ling had forged close ties with Ren Chengtong. Ren was born in Shanxi Province's Xin County and attended Xinzhou Middle School (Xinzhou Zhongxue) until 1918, when he gained admission to the preparatory course at Shanxi University. Ren entered the University of Nanking in 1920, and after graduating in 1923 he joined the faculty of its School of Agriculture and Forestry until leaving in the mid-1930s to direct an agricultural experiment station in the northwestern province of Suiyuan. Following the outbreak of war with Japan, Ren surveyed possible sites for refugee land reclamation projects in Southwest China on behalf of the Nationalist regime. In 1939, along with Ling, Ren co-founded the Yellow River Conservancy Commission's Forest and Soil Conservation Committee. Ren and Ling conducted surveys of erosion conditions in Shaanxi and Gansu for the committee during the early 1940s, and these surveys impressed upon them the importance of water and soil conservation in the wartime reconstruction of the Northwest.[7]

Because China was still an agricultural nation, Ling and Ren emphasized, state and society had to pay attention to the food supply problem (*shiliang wenti* 食糧問題). Thus, "for the sake of the War of Resistance and for the sake of national reconstruction, forest reclamation and water control [*linken shuili* 林墾水利] [were] sectors of urgent importance in economic reconstruction." According to a popular proverb, "The common people cannot live without water and soil," and past sages also said that "where there is soil, there is wealth." But in the northwest, people had reclaimed loess hillsides all over, leading to severe water and soil loss and declining crop production. In the view of Ling and Ren, "Flood and drought problems, land problems, public safety problems, and ethnic problems are all produced by this."[8]

The practice of setting fires to clear land on mountain slopes for cultivation had destroyed "the rich forest resources" that Ling and Ren believed to have once existed in the northwest. During the annual rainy season, "the scarce amount of precious precipitation" ran off slopes and eroded the land's fragile loess soils. Not only did erosion decrease agricultural production, but by increasing the Yellow

River's sediment load, it also aggravated flood disasters downstream. For this reason, "The northwest's water and soil conservation problem is not only a problem of increasing production in rear areas, but [conservation] is also a fundamental method of controlling rivers."[9]

As soil and water loss grew more severe, cultivated area and productivity decreased with dire effects. Between 1927 and 1937, Ling and Ren estimated, Gansu's cultivated area had decreased by 33.3 percent due to degradation caused by erosion. Throughout the northwest, gully deluges replaced natural springs so that "the amount of beneficial water decrease[d], and the amount of harmful water increase[d]." Worse yet, "excess population" had turned into a problem, "leading to the horrible phenomenon that Malthus called human elimination [*renwei taotai* 人為淘汰]." Ling and Ren's investigations found that population growth and widespread cultivation of mountain slopes during the Tongzhi reign (1851–1875) coincided with the intense interethnic violence between Han and Hui that broke out in the northwest during the Tongzhi and Guangxu (1875–1908) periods. As a local saying in Gansu went, "When the iron oxen [i.e., plows] reach the tops of mountains, there will soon be a rebellion."[10] Therein, as they claimed, lay the origins of the northwest's land problems and ethnic problems.[11]

Households that had previously migrated into Gansu and cultivated mountain slopes had simply abandoned their land and moved elsewhere after soil fertility declined. Without forests to retain water resources, each summer and autumn flash floods occurred, and erosion grew more severe. "As a result, flood disasters increase[d], soil decrease[d], and people's lives [grew] more difficult." No wonder that "localities are unstable, bandits cause disturbances, and social problems have no way of being resolved." Fuel shortages too presented a serious problem. With forests cut down and shrubs cleared, poor people (*pinmin* 貧民) had to dig up saplings and grasses, activities that made water and soil loss even worse on denuded lands. Hence, as Ling and Ren stated, "The northwest's water and soil conservation problem is not only the core of economic reconstruction during the period of resistance and reconstruction, but it is also the only way to completely solve the social problems and ethnic problems of the northwest." Based on their investigations, Ling and Ren held that "water and soil conservation should be part of the basis for reconstruction in the northwest, and the path to its success is in vigorously remedying past ills and making detailed plans."[12]

To prevent the limited amount of available water and soil from decreasing further, in the loess highlands on the border between Shaanxi and Gansu "appropriate plans should be made as demonstration based on the principle that forests impede mud and flowing sands." Experience with river management showed that simply doing engineering projects downstream would not limit sedimentation and prevent breaches. Solving those problems also required forestry and conservation measures upstream. "Because water downstream all comes from upstream tributaries and water in upstream tributaries all comes from land on mountain slopes within the scope of watersheds, [we] must devise a method of managing these expansive mountain slopes, make rainwater permeate the ground to decrease surface runoff, devise methods to make upstream soil have greater water retention capacity, and make slopes on either side of gullies less vulnerable to scouring by flowing water to decrease erosion and decrease the flow volume downstream."[13]

Unlike in the United States, water and soil conservation in China was a new undertaking. Yet the Yellow River Conservancy Commission and the Ministry of Agriculture and Forestry had jointly launched water and soil conservation programs in Gansu.[14] Terracing in areas suitable for agriculture, the planting of grasses in areas designated for animal husbandry, and afforestation in areas set aside for forestry would rationalize land use and increase production.[15] The Nationalist regime would also establish water and soil conservation experiment stations in severely eroded territories in the northwest as research and demonstration projects.[16] The Tianshui Water and Soil Conservation Experiment Area was one of them.

Land Disputes

As one of wartime China's most prominent agricultural improvement projects, the Tianshui Water and Soil Conservation Experiment Area benefited from the foreign connections of technical experts, as well as support from wartime China's international partners. On behalf of the Nationalist government's Executive Yuan, Ling Daoyang and the Yellow River Conservancy Commission arranged for Walter C. Lowdermilk, assistant chief of the U.S. Soil Conservation Service, to come to China in 1942 as an agricultural adviser.[17] This wartime visit marked Lowdermilk's second stay in China. From 1922 to 1927, he had taught at the University of Nanking's School of Agriculture and Forestry. Ren Chengtong was among Lowdermilk's students at that time and collaborated with him on a series of field studies on deforestation, streamflow, and erosion in North China.[18] In addition to sharing their Nanking connection, Ling also helped Lowdermilk conduct runoff studies in Qingdao during the mid-1920s, when Ling served there as director of the city's Bureau of Agriculture and Forestry.[19]

In 1942–1943, Lowdermilk returned to China to "make a joint study of land use problems" in the northwest, where, in his words, "Erosion is most acute and affects decisively the problem of control of floodwaters in the Yellow River."[20] Along the way, Lowdermilk and a field staff of Chinese technicians would "designate a number of suitable areas for demonstration projects and put them on the land for technical men to see."[21] These agricultural development projects held critical importance in China's war effort. Food production, as Lowdermilk put it, was "the basis for efficient resistance of the people during war time and for rehabilitation, reconstruction and industrialisation [*sic*] during the post-war period."[22]

During their journey to the northwest, Lowdermilk and his Chinese staff visited Tianshui three times.[23] During his first stop at Tianshui in May 1943, Lowdermilk surveyed land at the mouth of a gully to the south of the town called Lüergou (呂二溝), which the Ministry of Agriculture and Forestry had initially selected for its conservation experiment station, but it proved unsuitable. When Lowdermilk returned in July, he and his staff identified nearly two thousand *mu* of inclined land on the eastern edge of Lüergou near the Li Guang Mausoleum (Li Guang Mu 李廣墓) as a site for water and soil conservation measures. Gansu Province and the Tianshui County government agreed to assist the Tianshui Water and Soil Conservation Experiment Area in arranging to purchase the land, but it proved far more difficult than anticipated.[24]

According to Lowdermilk, the Tianshui County magistrate initially "put through a condemnation proceeding" on behalf of the experiment area "to acquire certain lands for public purposes, for demonstration." But after taking this small tract of land and ousting the farmers, the experiment area grew vegetables for its staff on it instead of using it for conservation work, so farmers complained to the magistrate "that their land [had been] taken from them on false pretenses" and was not "being used for experimentation in the interests of the public." As a result, the magistrate grew far less sympathetic. When the experiment area asked him to "put through the purchase of more land at a low price" to the government, nothing happened.[25]

Regardless of whether vegetable growing was the reason, the magistrate held that the approximately two thousand *mu* of land that the experiment area sought to buy was "connected to the farmers' livelihoods [and] difficult to purchase in its entirety." After Lowdermilk visited Tianshui for the third time in September, the experiment area's attention focused on trying to acquire land at Liangjiaping (梁家坪) and Fenshanding (坋山頂) in the loess headlands south of Tianshui for its conservation measures.[26] The experiment area wanted to purchase this land before Lowdermilk (who had come back to Tianshui to spend a month "applying practical measures" to land "designated for experimental projects") departed for Chongqing before going back to the United States.[27] In his diaries and letters home, Lowdermilk voiced dissatisfaction at the experiment area's inability to

Figure 10.1. Walter C. Lowdermilk and his field party pausing in a field of buckwheat near the Tianshui Water and Soil Conservation Experiment Area. September 1943. Source (figures 10.1 through 10.3): W. C. Lowdermilk Papers, ca. 1912–1969. Bancroft Library, University of California, Berkeley. BANC MSS 72/206, container 5: Pictures taken in China by W. C. Lowdermilk, 1943.

purchase any land in the forty days since he had last passed through Tianshui in July and the fact that "all that was done was a map covering only a part of the research area—and that was done on request by some other bureau."[28] Yet Lowdermilk also expressed concern that his presence in Tianshui was "being used as a means of forcing action, which local people do not want to take."[29]

The Experiment Area had sent the Tianshui County government a chart of 220 *mu* of land that it hoped to acquire at Fenshanding and Liangjiaping, intending to buy another 213 *mu* of gullied land after conducting additional surveys.[30] But with the land purchase "stalled in the Magistrate's office," the experiment area's director had the Ministry of Agriculture and Forestry telegraph Gansu's provincial governor to instruct the Tianshui County magistrate to buy the land, but the county government did not take any action.[31] As result, the experiment Area failed to obtain any land before Lowdermilk left Tianshui in mid-October. The head of Gansu's Reconstruction Office, Zhang Xinyi (張心一 1897–1992), later came to Tianshui to conduct investigations; he recommended purchasing all of this land at once, so the experiment area requested the county government to acquire all 433 *mu*. But the landowners insisted on adhering to the originally stipulated 220 *mu*, and the government had to concede.[32]

Figure 10.2. Field planning in the Tianshui Water and Soil Conservation Experiment Area. October 1943.

Figure 10.3. Putting in a demonstration bank channel. October 1943.

Despite these setbacks, official connections with Zhang Xinyi proved indispensable for the experiment area. Born in Gansu's Yongjing County and a 1922 graduate of Tsinghua University, Zhang went to the United States to earn a second BS in animal husbandry from Iowa State College in 1925 and an MS in agricultural economics in 1926 from Cornell University. After returning to China, from 1927 to 1929 Zhang joined the faculty of the University of Nanking, where Lowdermilk and many of the Tianshui Water and Soil Conservation Experiment Area's top personnel had once studied and taught, as professor of agricultural economics. Zhang went on to hold posts within the Nationalist government as chief of agricultural statistics for the Bureau of Statistics of the Legislative Yuan from 1929 to 1932 and from 1934 to 1940 as director of rural credit for the Bank of China. Zhang later returned to Gansu, where he served from 1940 to 1946 as head of the provincial Reconstruction Bureau.[33] In that capacity, Zhang promoted several water and soil conservation projects near Lanzhou.[34]

That the Tianshui Water and Soil Conservation Experiment Area could develop as planned, according to the recollections of a member of its staff, "was inseparable from Zhang Xinyi's strong support." With Zhang's assistance, the experiment area "attracted widespread attention and support in society, and [Zhang] personally assisted in solving the problem of requisitioning and renting the land for use as the experiment area's offices and land for use as its experiment station. Without his support, it is difficult to say whether water and soil conservation enterprises could have gained a footing in Gansu."[35]

Following Zhang's intervention in the controversy, the Tianshui County magistrate came around and instructed the landowners about "water and soil conservation's meaning and the benefits of improving cultivation [*gailiang zhongzhi* 改良種植]." Yet the landowners objected that they came from poor households with hundreds of people who relied on this land for their livelihoods, so they had no intention of selling it. Exasperated county officials admitted that they did not know how to go about obtaining the land without arousing opposition from its owners. Eventually, the Gansu provincial government directed the county to simply requisition the land or make a compulsory purchase if difficulties persisted.[36]

Landowners responded with dismay at the possibly of the Tianshui Water and Soil Conservation Experiment Area's carrying out a "compulsory purchase" (*zhenggou shoumai* 徵購收買) of their land for "afforestation and water and soil conservation experiments." According to a petition from the landowners to the Nationalist government, the land in question contained "dozens of ancestral graves," so they met the news [of a compulsory purchase] with "extreme fear."[37] Along with appealing to traditional geomantic beliefs to protect their property rights, landowners also employed the rhetoric of China's War of Resistance to oppose state-led conservation initiatives. In the words of the petition, "Government reconstruction emphasizes the people's livelihood and vigorously promotes agricultural development to provide for the people's food [supply]." From that perspective, the government had no justification for purchasing several hundred *mu* of privately owned fields that people cultivated "as their source of livelihood" and leaving "well over a thousand men and women, old and young," for dead. As the petition stressed, "It totally goes against the various intentions of national reconstruction, protecting the soil [*baotu* 保土], increasing agricultural and forestry production, vigorously ensuring that the people's food [supply] is adequate, strengthening the power of the War of Resistance, and stabilizing the minds of people in rear areas." Moreover, "afforestation" should not be done near the Tianshui city walls, on cultivated farmland, or near gravesites. As the petitioners argued, soil and water conservation experiments should take place only on steep slopes near water sources.[38]

Instead, the landowners' petition recommended that personnel use over one hundred *mu* of land along the old course of the Lüer River, where the Tianshui Agricultural Experiment Office had already started to plant trees, and another one hundred *mu* of publicly owned land nearby at the original site of the Santaisi (三台寺) Temple. These areas had no connection to privately owned fields, and in the landowners' view that made them most suitable for conservation measures. "What is inappropriate," the petition asked, "about public land for public use?" By saving on government expenses and avoiding harm to the people, using these areas would be advantageous to both public and private interests. Given this option, they asked, "Why must over two hundred *mu* of the people's privately owned land be purchased for [experimentation] to be suitable?"[39]

In addition to the rhetoric of wartime reconstruction and appeals to the public interest, the landowners' petition also resorted to legal arguments. Article 767 of the Republic of China's Civil Code stipulated that property rights holders could request the return of wrongfully occupied or seized property, request the elimination of obstructions to their property rights, and request the prevention of any threats to their property rights. These stipulations intended to define property rights and "maintain mutual benefits." As the landowners argued, "Our land was legally acquired and should enjoy the Civil Code's protection. If the property rights holders are unwilling to sell, then other people should not be able to subject [the property] to seizure. The principle is clear. If this land is requisitioned it will not be in accordance with the laws and decrees." Article 352 of the Land Law, they went on to argue, ruled out requisitioning land used for one enterprise for another more important enterprise unless it was unavoidable. The

Tianshui Water and Soil Conservation Experiment Area's activities failed to meet this standard, the petition argued, so it should use publicly owned land instead. Since the old site of the Santaisi Temple was available, "Why must [it] be appropriate to purchase the fields that we currently cultivate as the only source of livelihood?" In the words of the landowners, the urgent need to "to avoid killing [their] entire families and destroying [their] ancestors' graves" had moved them to request that the experiment area find another location and refrain from purchasing their land.[40]

The Tianshui Water and Soil Conservation Experiment Area responded with skepticism toward these claims. Lowdermilk had noted that the land the experiment area wanted belonged to "a powerful man in the city," whom the county magistrate did not want to force to sell, and that put the area "up against a serious situation" with no prospect of implementing any of its measures.[41] He was not mistaken. Over one-third of the land in question belonged to "wealthy gentry landlords" (*fushen dizhu* 富紳地主), including men named Xiao Maotang (蕭茂堂) and Wan Zhengtie (萬正怗), who took the lead in the protests. The experiment area maintained that it had taken pains to carefully demarcate all gravesites and agreed not to lay claim to any of them. But Wan Zhengtie's "family trade" was fortunetelling (*jiaye fengjian* 家業風鑒), so he allegedly feared that water and soil conservation measures would "transform the nearby topography" and damage *fengshui*.[42]

Yet Lowdermilk identified another more fundamental economic factor behind the landowners' unwillingness to agree to the sale: China's wartime inflation.[43] Because the value of the Nationalist government's currency would most likely continue to plummet, as he put it, "If one can not [*sic*] immediately buy some material thing and keep his holdings in real property, he stands the chance of finding his money depreciating. So no one wants to sell land now! All these matters make preparation very slow."[44] As further explored by Parks Coble in this volume, nobody wanted to part with land in exchange for increasingly worthless cash, a fact that largely explained the experiment area's difficulties.

Between August and November 1943, county leaders met with the landowners five times and failed to make a deal with them, so no conservation measures went forward.[45] With the dispute persisting, the head of Gansu's Land Administration Bureau came to Tianshui to help the Tianshui Water and Soil Conservation Experiment Area purchase the land. After consulting local officials, he "ascertained that the landowners were stubborn and impervious to reason" and advocated moving ahead with requisitioning procedures (*zhengshou shouxu* 徵收手續) based on the Land Law to avoid further meetings about the purchase. Zhang Xinyi likewise believed that the experiment area needed to purchase or rent all the land for its experiments. In response to the landowners' objections, Zhang asserted that although their petition claimed that the government wanted to seize good farmland, in reality the land consisted of nothing but dry, barren slopes. Furthermore, as Zhang stated, purchasing 200–300 *mu* of land from "wealthy gentry" like Wan Zhengtie and Xiao Maotang would not harm their livelihoods. If investigators found any poor households among the landowners, the experiment area and county government would devise a solution for them. But claims that the land purchase placed several thousand people's lives in jeopardy were, in Zhang's estimation, "truly a bunch of nonsense" (*cheng wei yipian huyan* 誠為一片胡言).[46]

The experiment area had orders to carry out conservation work, but it also recognized that it had to obtain land and cooperate with farmers to realize its plans. Consequently, it had considered "the people's interests" and taken care to preserve them. The experiment area offered to pay market prices to purchase and rent the land and had given landowners considerable benefits. If farmers took part and cooperated with the experiment area's programs, it would plan improvements for their land, offer guidance, supply them with seedlings, and loan them tools. Yet the agency needed to purchase land for long-term experimental measures. If the experiment area could not reach an agreement to buy land for this purpose, it intended to petition the Administrative Yuan to make a compulsory purchase.[47]

With the landowners refusing to cooperate, Zhang Xinyi and other provincial leaders came to Tianshui yet again at the end of December 1943 and gathered them for another meeting. The Gansu authorities outlined the options of sale, rent, and cooperation—in which owners kept the land but the experiment area would use it for free—and set the end of the month as their deadline. If they could not come to an agreement by that time, the government would simply requisition the land. But this ultimatum did not have an immediate effect. Although some landowners signed an agreement, others insisted on land prices that the government considered unreasonably high. Officials believed that the "wealthy gentry landlord" Wan Zhengtie continued to orchestrate the opposition. At a meeting with county officials on January 8, 1944, landowners voted to elect a farmer named Huang Zhengzhong (黃正中) as "assessment commissioner" (*pingjia weiyuan* 評價委員). But Wan Zhengtie and a group of other landowners called for a reelection, in which Wan came away the victor. Nonetheless, at another meeting on February 12, the Tianshui Water and Soil Conservation Experiment Area, county government officials, and the landowners finalized a rental agreement, and on February 29 the experiment area finally started to put in conservation measures on this land.[48]

But even after the settlement of the land dispute, conservation projects had to avoid impinging upon the gravesites of local households. A report from May 1944 described the arrangements made to resolve this issue. The experiment area's designs for terrace embankments and ditches along the contour avoided originally existing graves. But the Han and Wan surname groups, "due to their geomantic beliefs" (*ganyu fengshui zhi shuo* 感輿風水之説), wanted to place new graves on the embankments and requested that they forego taking part in the demonstration work. The experiment area, fearing that similar problems would plague future conservation projects, convened a meeting with the Tianshui County government. County officials conducted a survey and decided that whenever field engineering projects encountered a gravesite, they would have to set aside one *zhang* (the equivalent of 3 1/3 meters) in front, two *zhang* behind, and one *zhang* five *chi* (one *chi* = 33 1/3 centimeters) to the left and right of the grave's position.[49] Even after the experiment area had acquired its land, it had to adjust is programs to appease influential local landowners.

Work Relief for Water and Soil Conservation

Despite this local friction, the Tianshui Water and Soil Conservation Experiment Area gained funding from some of wartime China's most well-known international relief initiatives. During an investigative tour of Northwest China on behalf of United China Relief, Ling Daoyang passed through Tianshui in winter 1944 with a fellow traveler named Xu Weilian (徐維廉, William Hsu, 1884–1966). Xu, who hailed from Suizhong County in Northeast China's Liaoning Province, grew up in a Christian household and went to missionary schools in his youth before attending Yenching University. After he had taught at Huiwen Middle School, a famous Methodist educational institution in Changli, Hebei Province, the church recommended Xu for study at the University of Michigan, where he obtained his MA in history. When Xu returned from the United States in 1925, he took over as principal of Huiwen Middle School.

Following the outbreak of the War of Resistance, in mid-1938 Xu Weilian left occupied Hebei for Hunan. While in the city of Hengyang, Xu encountered thousands of wounded soldiers, and in December 1938 this experience moved him to establish the first branch of China's Friends of the Wounded Society (Shangbing Zhi You She 傷兵之友社). The Friends of the Wounded Society soon attracted the interest of Soong Mei-ling, who promoted it as part of the New Life Movement. Beginning in early 1941, Xu Weilian also organized joint initiatives between his Friends of the Wounded Society and Chinese Industrial Cooperatives. Although the Friends of the Wounded Society had declined by 1942, Xu's involvement in Chinese Industrial Cooperatives grew, and in mid-1943 he accepted an appointment as Chinese Industrial Cooperatives' general secretary. In this capacity, Xu also cultivated extremely close relations with leading members of United China Relief.[50]

After observing the Tianshui Water and Soil Conservation Experiment Area's work, Ling Daoyang and Xu Weilian affirmed the importance of its efforts to halt water and soil loss in the northwest and proposed funding a work relief (*yi gong dai zhen* 以工代振) initiative to employ thirty refugees for conservation projects. To that end, in autumn 1945 the Gansu International Relief Committee transmitted funds from United China Relief, while the Tianshui representatives of the China Inland Mission (CIM), the Chinese Industrial Cooperatives Office, and the Child Welfare Institute organized the Tianshui Branch Committee of the Gansu International Relief Committee to administer them.[51] Lowdermilk often socialized with the CIM missionaries while staying in Tianshui and visited projects run by Chinese Industrial Cooperatives on his tour of Gansu.[52] Even though Lowdermilk had already gone back to the United States, these connections may have proven useful in arranging the work relief program.

The experiment area's provisional director, Ye Peizhong (葉培忠), served as the Tianshui Branch Committee's chairman, and his personal background further eased efforts to gain access to international relief funds.[53] A native of Jiangsu's Jiangyin County, Ye Peizhong graduated in 1927 from the Forestry Department at the University of Nanking, where he studied with Lowdermilk and Ling Daoyang. After working briefly at a forestry station in Guangxi, Ye returned to Nanjing in 1929 to assist in designing a botanical garden for the Sun Yat-sen Mausoleum. In preparation for that task, Ye traveled to the Royal Botanical Garden in Edinburgh in 1930 to study garden design and plant breeding. Upon returning to China with his M.Sc. in 1931, Ye became the Sun Yat-sen Mausoleum Botanical Garden's first director, but its operations came to a halt in 1937, when the Japanese brutally occupied Nanjing. Ye taught briefly at an agricultural school in Hunan before moving to Sichuan to become the director of the province's Emeishan Forestry Experiment Station, and from 1941 to 1943 he conducted research for the Nationalist government's Chongqing Tung Oil Research Institute. Ye later joined Lowdermilk's staff for his investigation of the northwest. When their trip concluded in 1943, Ye remained in Gansu to lend his expertise to the Tianshui Water and Soil Conservation Experiment Area and eventually became its director.[54]

Based on the funds available, the Gansu International Relief Committee's Tianshui Branch Committee, with Ye Peizhong as its chair, planned for the work relief project to last six months.[55] Employing refugees to build terraces and ditches would "decrease the slope length of inclined fields to improve farmland and, because the level ditches function to intercept flow, conserve runoff and sediment to maintain land fertility [*dili* 地力] and increase the soil's water content to meet the goals of increasing agricultural production and decreasing flood disasters during peak season [*hongfeng shuihuan* 洪峰水患]."[56] Furthermore, refugee laborers would construct small-scale earthen check dams (*xiaoxing lanshui tuba* 小型攔水土壩) to divert rainwater from roadways into level ditches to limit gully erosion.[57]

But the "refugees" employed for this work relief project did not come from a war zone. At the time of the Tianshui Branch Committee's founding, famine had struck Tongwei County to the northeast of Tianshui, so the Branch Committee decided to recruit famine victims from Tongwei as "refugee workers" (*nangong* 難工). While traveling to Lanzhou, a pastor from the CIM in Tianshui who acted as the Branch Committee's English-language secretary deputed colleagues from the CIM in Tongwei to recruit fifteen workers and give each of them ¥2,000 in travel expenses. After the workers from Tongwei arrived in Tianshui on August 27, the Tianshui Water and Soil Conservation Experiment Area assigned them work numbers; divided them into groups; and allocated shovels, hoes, pickaxes, and harrows, while the workers selected their own team leaders to look after food rations and other matters. When work began the next day, experienced laborers from the experiment area went along with the newly arrived refugees to provide training. Refugee laborers first built terraces and level ditches in Liangjiaping using techniques that "experiments had already proven simplest and most effective," so their work "gradually became more practiced [*chunshou* 醇熟] and attained the stipulated standards and work quotas." Ye Peizhong and other members of the Branch Committee periodically engaged in on-the-spot observations "so that each item of work was smoothly carried out."[58]

Thanks to the funding from United China Relief, as a report from the experiment area related, work was able to "develop quickly."[59] In mid-September, after the harvesting of hyacinth beans (*biandou* 扁豆) in Fenshanding, the highest point in the experiment area, the refugee laborers moved to the mountaintop to carry out work. Following the maize and sorghum harvest in October, the slack farming season arrived and land lay fallow, so the scope of their work expanded. That month, the Tongwei Inland Mission hired fourteen additional workers, along with fourteen more in November. The experiment station recruited another fourteen poor farmers from the outskirts of Tianshui, bringing the total to fifty-one, to complete as much work as possible before the ground froze in the winter. The labor force completed 7,812.9 *zhang* of terraces and level ditches, cleared 408 *zhang* of sediment from ditches, and constructed nine small check dams, accomplishing four-fifths of the planned work. If rain made it impossible to work in the fields, the workers transported gravel.[60]

When weather grew cold in late November, some workers from Tongwei returned home, with each of them given another ¥2,000 in traveling expenses. By December, the number of workers had dwindled to twenty-seven. On December 20, the ground at the worksite froze, and all laborers were dismissed. During the work period, the experiment area not only supplied the workers with cheap flour, but also showed them water and soil conservation lantern slides and newsreels from the United Nations Information Organization "to increase workers' knowledge and work enthusiasm [*gongzuo qingxu* 工作情緒]."[61] (On the use of film in education during the war, see Matthew Johnson's chapter in this volume.)

International relief efforts in China had employed work relief methods to dredge rivers and canals, build roads, and repair the Yellow River's dikes for decades. But water and soil conservation had only just begun. The experiment area trumpeted the effectiveness of using work relief for this purpose. Not only did the project administer relief, but "it was also able to train several dozen refugee workers as technical workers [*jishu gongren* 技術工人]." If widely implemented, the experiment area's report stated, work relief programs would "also have significance in terms of education and training." Given water and soil conservation's importance in China's northwest, it added, "in terms of agriculture, this can decrease water and soil loss to maintain land fertility, avoid drought, and increase agricultural production." In terms of water control, conservation techniques like afforestation, terraces, and ditches, which would "decrease the Yellow River's sediment load," presented "a method of fundamentally controlling flood disasters." To add further legitimacy, the report concluded that none other than Li Yizhi (李儀祉 1882–1938), the father of modern Chinese hydraulic engineering, had raised the possibility of using work relief in Yellow River management.[62]

No evidence exists that the work relief program resumed in early 1946 when the ground thawed. But unlike many other efforts launched by China's wartime technocrats, the Tianshui Water and Soil Conservation Experiment Area did not shut down when the conflict with Japan ended. Its research and extension programs expanded during the postwar years and into the PRC period. Today the agency still operates as the Yellow River Water and Soil Conservation Tianshui Management and Supervision Bureau/Tianshui Water and Soil Conservation Scientific Experiment Station (Huanghe Shuitu Baochi Tianshui Zhili Jiandu Ju 黃河水土保持天水治理監督局 / Tianshui Shuitu Baochi Kexue Shiyan Zhan 天水水土保持科學實驗站).

Conclusion

Tianshui did not see any combat during the Anti-Japanese War of Resistance, but the conflict profoundly influenced the conservation programs undertaken there. For Chinese water and soil conservation specialists, the interlocking goals of harnessing scarce resources to resist the Japanese invasion, develop the northwest, and strengthen the nation state required checking water and soil loss by rationalizing land use. Exploiting Northwest China's resources for military resistance and national reconstruction made water and soil conservation a priority as a means of increasing food production in unoccupied "rear areas" to fuel China's war effort.

Drawing on foreign connections formed prior to the war, mid-level bureaucrats and technical experts who served as the Tianshui Water and Soil Conservation Experiment Area's leaders obtained advice from Lowdermilk, as well as financial assistance from United China Relief and other wartime international relief initiatives. To be sure, implementing experimental water and soil conservation measures and carrying out demonstration projects at the local level did not always go smoothly. The landholders in Tianshui who frustrated the experiment area's work resorted to everything from geomantic beliefs to legal codes to avoid selling their land in exchange for China's devalued wartime currency. But these local elites also deployed the rhetoric of anti-Japanese resistance and national reconstruction to preserve their property rights against state efforts to procure their land for conservation projects. Their appropriation of such rhetoric to advance private interests indicates both the malleability of these discourses and the degree of friction that existed between wartime mobilization and the dynamics of local society far beyond the battlefield. It would take the Chinese Communist Party's program of land reform and collectivization during the 1950s to remove these entrenched obstacles, making it possible to implement water and soil conservation measures first formulated under the Nationalist regime during the wartime period on a wide scale.

Notes

1. Part of this destruction is recounted in Muscolino, *The Ecology of War in China*.
2. Muscolino, "Woodlands, Warlords, and Wasteful Nations."
3. Muscolino, "Refugees, Land Reclamation, and Militarized Landscapes in Wartime China."
4. Dong, "Jiefang qianhou Tianshui shuitu baochi keyan shiyan gongzuo"; Yang, "1940 niandai de Tianshui shuitu baochi shiyanqu shulun"; Mo, "Zhongguo shuitu baochi de faxiangdi."
5. Quotes are from "Cradle of China's Civilization." In autumn 1938, Gansu Province established an Agricultural Improvement Bureau charged with "effecting improvements in agricultural, forestry, and pastoral enterprises." All translations are mine.

6. Shandong Province appointed Ling its forestry commissioner in 1918, and in 1920 National Peking University made him dean of forestry. The city of Qingdao hired Ling to direct its Bureau of Agriculture and Forestry in 1922, but in 1928 he left to join National Central University as head of its Forestry Department. The Nationalist government made Ling director of the Ministry of Industry's Central Forestry Bureau in 1930, a post that he held until 1934, when he moved back to Guangdong as director of the province's Bureau of Agriculture and Forestry. China also nominated Ling as a delegate to the fifth Pacific Science Congress in Vancouver, British Columbia, and in 1933 the Pacific Science Council elected him chairman of its Forestry Section. Among his many other posts, Ling later served as chairman of the Water and Soil Conservation Association of China. *Who's Who in China,* 139–140. For more on Ling see Swislocki, "Seeing the Forest for the Village, Nation, and Province."

7. In late 1940, Ren attempted to found China's first water and soil conservation research organ, the Longnan Water and Soil Conservation Experiment Area (Longnan Shuitu Baochi Shiyanqu 隴南水土保持實驗區), based in Tianshui, on behalf of the Yellow River Conservancy Commission, but it soon folded due to a lack of funds and bureaucratic infighting. Ren Chunguang, "Pingzhi shuitu zaofu renlei."

8. Ling and Ren, "Xibei shuitu baochi shiye zhi sheji yu shishi," 85.

9. Ibid., 85–86.

10. Ibid., 86. On the violence between Han and Hui during the late Qing, see Lipman, *Familiar Strangers,* ch. 4.

11. Ling and Ren, "Xibei shuitu baochi shiye zhi sheji yu shishi," 86–87.

12. Ibid., 87.

13. Ibid., 88. Afforestation would take different forms in different regions. Lands on the border of Suiyuan, Shaanxi, and Ningxia, for instance, "had already reached high levels of abandonment because desert had gradually shifted south," so the government needed to plant "sand protection forests" along the Great Wall for demonstration purposes. Ibid.

14. Ibid., 89.

15. Based on "the U.S. Soil Conservation Bureau's regulations," Ling and Ren related, slopes with gradients under 15 percent should remain agricultural areas, those with gradients from 15 to 45 percent should become forestry and animal husbandry areas, while lands with gradients over 45 percent should be reserved for forestry. Ibid., 88.

16. Ibid., 90–91.

17. Lowdermilk: "Preliminary Report on Findings," 3, and Interview conducted by Malca Chall, 379–413.

18. Muscolino, "Woodlands, Warlords, and Wasteful Nations."

19. *Who's Who in China,* 139–140; Lowdermilk, "Factors Influencing the Surface Run-Off of Rain Waters."

20. Lowdermilk, "Preliminary Report on Findings," 4

21. Ibid., 6.

22. Ibid., 3.

23. Ibid., 7.

24. "Nonglinbu shuitu baochi shiyanqu kuaiyou daidian"; "Nonglinbu shuitu baochi shiyanqu cheng," February 25, 1944. See also Lowdermilk, "Preliminary Report on Findings," 12.

25. Letter dated September 28, 1943, in Lowdermilk, "Typed Transcripts of Handwritten Letters." See also Lowdermilk, "Diary, 1942–1943," September 28, 1943, 863.

26. "Gansu sheng zhengfu daidian"; "Nonglinbu shuitu baochi shiyanqu cheng."

27. Lowdermilk, "Preliminary Report on Findings," 12.

28. Lowdermilk, "Diary, 1942–1943," September 20, 1943, 834. See also letter dated September 20, 1943, in Lowdermilik, "Typed Transcripts of Handwritten Letters."

29. Lowdermilk, "Diary, 1942–1943," September 28, 1943, 863.

30. "Nonglinbu shuitu baochi shiyanqu cheng."

31. Lowdermilk, "Diary, 1942–1943," September 28, 1943, 864.

32. "Nonglinbu shuitu baochi shiyanqu cheng," February 25, 1944.

33. *Who's Who in China,* 8–9. See also Zhang Xinyi, "Liu nian lai Gansu shengchan jianshe"; Zhang Siwen: "Zhang Xinyi fangwen ji" and "Ji nongxuejia Zhang Xinyi"; and Liu, "Nongye jingjixuejia Zhang Xinyi."

34. Gao, "Zhongguo shuitu baochi shihua (caogao)," 62.

35. Ibid., 65.

36. "Gansu sheng zhengfu kuaiyou daidian"; "Nonglinbu shuitu baochi shiyanqu cheng," February 25, 1944.

37. "Chao yuan cheng."

38. Ibid.

39. Ibid.

40. Ibid.

41. Lowdermilk, "Diary, 1942–1943," September 28, 1943, 863.

42. "Nonglinbu shuitu baochi shiyanqu cheng," February 25, 1944.

43. Young, *China's Wartime Finance and Inflation;* Kia-ngau Chang, *The Inflationary Spiral.*

44. Letter dated September 27, 1943, in Lowdermilk, "Typed Transcripts of Handwritten Letters."

45. "Nonglinbu shuitu baochi shiyanqu cheng," February 25, 1944.

46. Ibid.

47. Ibid.

48. Ibid.

49. "Nonglinbu shuitu baochi shiyanqu sanshisan nian wu yuefen gongzuo jianbao biao."

50. Reynolds, "The Chinese Industrial Cooperative Movement," 399–408; Wang, "Xu Weilian yu kangzhan shiqi shangbing zhi you yundong chutan." On the New Life Movement, see Ferlanti, "The New Life Movement at War."

51. Two of Lowdermilk's acquaintances from the CIM served as the Branch Committee's English secretary and accountant; the director of the Chinese Industrial Cooperatives Office acted as its Chinese secretary; and the experiment area's provisional director, Ye Peizhong, was its chairman, while two others served as commissioners. "Mei yuan Hua hui gongzhen kuan bufen titian gouxu shigong jihua baogao"; "Mei yuan Hua hui gongzhen buzhu kuan gongzuo zong baogao." See also "Nonglinbu shuitu baochi shiyanqu cheng," September 1945.

52. See letters dated May 15, July 15, and September 25–October 14, 1943, in Lowdermilk, "Typed Transcripts of Handwritten Letters."

53. "Mei yuan Hua hui gongzhen kuan bufen titian gouxu shigong jihua baogao"; "Mei yuan Hua hui gongzhen buzhu kuan gongzuo zong baogao."

54. Zhongguo Kexue Jishu Xiehui, *Zhongguo kexue jishu zhuanjia zhuanlue, nongxue bian,* 199–214.

55. "Mei yuan Hua hui gongzhen kuan bufen titian gouxu shigong jihua baogao"; "Mei yuan Hua hui gongzhen buzhu kuan gongzuo zong baogao."

56. "Mei yuan Hua hui gongzhen buzhu kuan gongzuo zong baogao"; "Mei yuan Hua hui gongzhen kuan bufen titian gouxu shigong jihua baogao."

57. The funds allocated for hiring refugee workers were initially ¥15,000 per month, but after Japan's surrender in summer 1945 the price of materials declined for a time. Because goods were not as expensive, the experiment area could decrease its budget for wages to ¥12,000 per month. "Mei yuan Hua hui gongzhen buzhu kuan gongzuo zong baogao"; "Mei yuan Hua hui gongzhen kuan bufen titian gouxu shigong jihua baogao."

58. "Mei yuan Hua hui gongzhen buzhu kuan gongzuo zong baogao"; "Mei yuan Hua hui gongzhen kuan bufen titian gouxu shigong jihua baogao." See also "Nonglinbu shuitu baochi shiyanqu sanshisi nian ba yuefen gongzuo jianbao biao."

59. Ibid.

60. "Mei yuan Hua hui gongzhen buzhu kuan gongzuo zong baogao."

61. Ibid.

62. Ibid.

Bibliography

Archives and Manuscript Collections

Archives held at the Institute of Modern History, Academia Sinica, Taiwan
W. C. Lowdermilk Papers, Bancroft Library, University of California, Berkeley
Yellow River Conservancy Commission Archives

Newspapers and Periodicals Cited as Primary Sources

China Weekly Review
Linxue 林學

References

Chang, Kia-ngau. *The Inflationary Spiral: The Experience in China, 1939–1950.* Cambridge, Mass.: MIT Press, 1958.

"Chao yuan cheng 抄原呈" (Copy of original petition). Attached to notice from the Administrative Yuan, December 12, 1943. Institute of Modern History Archives, Academia Sinica, 20-59-003-05.

"Cradle of China's Civilization Caught up in Surge of North-west Provincial Development Movement." *China Weekly Review*, March 1, 1941, 452–453.

Dong Xianghua 董祥華. "Jiefang qianhou Tianshui shuitu baochi keyan shiyan gongzuo 解放前後天水水土保持科研實驗工作" (Water and soil conservation scientific research and experiment work in Tianshui before and after liberation). *Tianshui wenshi ziliao* 天水文史資料 (Tianshui literary and historical materials), no. 14 (2008): 376–384.

Ferlanti, Frederica. "The New Life Movement at War: Wartime Mobilisation and State Control in Chongqing and Chengdu." *European Journal of East Asian Studies* 11, no. 2 (2012): 187–212.

"Gansu sheng zhengfu kuaiyou daidian 甘肅省政府快郵代電" (Express mail in lieu of telegram from the Gansu provincial government). December 17, 1943. Institute of Modern History Archives, Academia Sinica, 20-59-003-05.

Gao Jishan 高繼善, "Zhongguo shuitu baochi shihua (caogao) 中國水土保持史話 (草稿)" (Brief history of water and soil conservation in China). In *Shuitu baochi zhi ziliao huibian, di yi ji* 水土保持志資料彙編第一輯 (Water and soil conservation gazetteer materials collection, part 1), edited by Huanghe shuitu baochi zhi bianweihui bianjishi 黃河水土保持志編委會編輯室 (Yellow River soil conservation gazetteer editing office) and Shaanxi sheng shuitu baochi zhi bianweihui bangongshi 陝西省水土志編委會辦公室 (Shanxi Province soil conservation gazetteer editing committee office). Xi'an: Shaanxi shuitu baochi bianjibu, 1988.

Ling Daoyang 凌道揚 and Ren Chengtong 任承統. "Xibei shuitu baochi shiye zhi sheji yu shishi 西北水土保持事業之設計與實施" (Planning and implementation of water and soil conservation measures in the northwest). *Linxue* 林學 (Forestry), no. 9 (1943): 85–93.

Lipman, Jonathan N. *Familiar Strangers: A History of Muslims in Northwest China*. Seattle: University of Washington Press, 1997.

Liu Feng 柳風. "Nongye jingjixuejia Zhang Xinyi 農業經濟學家張心一" (The agricultural economist Zhang Xinyi). In *Lanzhou renwu xuanbian* 蘭州人物選編 (Selected personages from Lanzhou), edited by Li Rongtang 李榮棠 et al., *Lanzhou wenshi ziliao xuanbian* 蘭州文史資料選編 (Lanzhou literary historical materials collection), no. 14 (1993): 211–213.

Lowdermilk, W. C., Adviser to the Executive Yuan. "Diary, 1942–1943." W. C. Lowdermilk Papers, Bancroft Library, University of California, Berkeley. BANC MSS 72/206, Carton 2: Diaries and notes.

———. "Factors Influencing the Surface Run-Off of Rain Waters." In *Proceedings of the Third Pan-Pacific Science Congress, Tokyo, October 30th–November 11th, 1926*, edited by National Research Council of Japan. Tokyo, 1929.

———. Interview conducted by Malca Chall, *Soil, Forest, and Water Conservation and Reclamation in China, Israel, Africa, and the United States*, vol. 2.

———. "Typed Transcripts of Handwritten Letters from Walter C. Lowdermilk, Agricultural Adviser to the Chinese Government, to his Wife and Family, October 1942–November 1943." W. C. Lowdermilk Papers, Bancroft Library, University of California, Berkeley. BANC MSS 72/206, Carton 8.

"Mei yuan Hua hui gongzhen buzhu kuan gongzuo zong baogao 美援華會工振補助款工作總報告" (Overall work report on United China Relief on relief supplementary funds for work relief). 1946. Institute of Modern History Archives, Academia Sinica, 20-59-013-04.

"Mei yuan Hua hui gongzhen kuan bufen titian gouxu shigong jihua baogao 美援華會工振款部分梯田溝洫施工計畫報告" (Report on plans for constructing terraces and ditches with portion of work relief funds from United China Relief). November 5, 1945. Institute of Modern History Archives, Academia Sinica, 20-59-011-10.

Mo Shiao 莫世鰲. "Zhongguo shuitu baochi de faxiangdi—Tianshui 天水中國水土保持的發祥地—天水" (The birthplace of Chinese water and soil conservation—Tianshui).

In *Huanghe wangshi* 黃河往事 (The Yellow River in the past), edited by Luo Xiangxin 駱向新. Zhengzhou: Huanghe shuili chubanshe, 2006.

Muscolino, Micah S. *The Ecology of War in China: Henan Province, the Yellow River, and Beyond*. New York: Cambridge University Press, 2015.

———. "Refugees, Land Reclamation, and Militarized Landscapes in Wartime China: Huanglongshan, Shaanxi, 1937–45." *Journal of Asian Studies* 69, no. 2 (2010): 453–478.

———. "Woodlands, Warlords, and Wasteful Nations: Transnational Networks and Conservation Science in 1920s China." *Comparative Studies in Society and History* 61, no. 3 (2019): 712–738.

"Nonglinbu shuitu baochi shiyanqu cheng 農林部水土保持實驗區呈" (Petition from the Ministry of Agriculture and Forestry water and soil conservation experiment area). February 25, 1944. Institute of Modern History Archives, Academia Sinica, 20-59-003-05.

"Nonglinbu shuitu baochi shiyanqu cheng 農林部水土保持實驗區呈" (Petition from the Ministry of Agriculture and Forestry water and soil conservation experiment area). September 1945. Institute of Modern History Archives, Academia Sinica, 20-59-011-10.

"Nonglinbu shuitu baochi shiyanqu kuaiyou daidian 農林部水土保持實驗區快郵代電" (Ministry of Agriculture and Forestry express mail in lieu of telegram). July 1943. Institute of Modern History Archives, Academia Sinica, 20-59-003-05.

"Nonglinbu shuitu baochi shiyanqu sanshisan nian wu yuefen gongzuo jianbao biao 農林部書圖寶石實驗區三十三年五月份工作簡報表" (Ministry of Agriculture and Forestry water and soil conservation experiment area; May 1944 brief work report). June 1944. Institute of Modern History Archives, Academia Sinica, 20-59-012-10.

"Nonglinbu shuitu baochi shiyanqu sanshisi nian shi yuefen gongzuo jianbao biao 農林部水土保持實驗區三十四年十月份工作簡報表" (Ministry of Agriculture and Forestry water and soil conservation experiment area; October 1945 brief work report). November 1945. Institute of Modern History Archives, Academia Sinica, 20-59-013-01.

"Nonglinbu shuitu baochi shiyanqu sanshisi nian ba yuefen gongzuo jianbao biao 农林部水土保持实验区三十四年八月份工作简报表" (Ministry of Agriculture and Forestry water and soil conservation experiment area; August 1945 brief work report). September 1945. Institute of Modern History Archives, Academia Sinica, 20-59-013-01.

Ren Chunguang 任春光. "Pingzhi shuitu zaofu renlei—Ji shuitu baochi zhuanjia Ren Chengtong 平治水土造福人類—記水土保持專家任承統" (Controlling water and soil and benefiting humanity—Remembering the water and soil conservation expert Ren Chengtong). In *Hou Ji chuanren: di yi ji* 後稷傳人: 第一輯 (Hou Ji's successors: Part 1), edited by Zhongguo Renmin Zhengzhi Xieshang Huiyi Shaanxi Sheng Xianyang Shi Weiyuanhui 中國人民政治協商會議陝西省咸楊市委員會 (Xianyang City Shaanxi Province People's Political Consultative Conference) and Yangling Qu Weiyuanhui Wenshi Ziliao Weiyuanhui 楊陵區委員會文史資料委員會 (Literature and History Committee of Yangling), 237–249. Xi'an: Sanqin chubanshe, 1996.

Reynolds, Douglas Robertson. "The Chinese Industrial Cooperative Movement and the Political Polarization of Wartime China, 1938–1945." PhD dissertation, Columbia University, 1975.

Swislocki, Mark. "Seeing the Forest for the Village, Nation, and Province: Forestry Policy and Environmental Management in Early-Twentieth-Century Yunnan." *Twentieth-Century China* 39, no. 3 (2014): 195–215.

Wang Miao 王淼. "Xu Weilian yu kangzhan shiqi Shangbing zhi You Yundong chutan 徐維廉與抗戰時期傷兵之友運動初探" (Preliminary investigation of Xu Weilian and the Friends of the Wounded Movement during the War of Resistance period). *Kangzhan shiliao yanjiu* 抗戰史料研究 (War of Resistance historical materials research), no. 1 (2016): 52–57.

Who's Who in China, 6th ed. Shanghai: China Weekly Review, 1950.

Yang Hongwei 楊紅偉. "1940 niandai de Tianshui shuitu baochi shiyanqu shulun 1940年代的天水水土保持實驗區述論" (A discussion of the Tianshui water and soil conservation experiment area during the 1940s). *Shuitu baochi yanjiu* 水土保持研究 (Water and soil conservation research) 18, no. 6 (2011): 277–282.

Young, Arthur N. *China's Wartime Finance and Inflation, 1937–1945*. Cambridge, Mass.: Harvard University Press, 1965.

Zhang Siwen 張思溫. "Ji nongxuejia Zhang Xinyi 記農學家張心一" (Remembering the agronomist Zhang Xinyi). *Gansu wenshi ziliao xuanji* 甘肅文史資料選輯 (Gansu literary and historical materials collection), no. 47 (1997): 1–37.

———. "Zhang Xinyi fangwen ji 張心一訪問記" (Record of an interview with Zhang Xinyi). *Linxia shi wenshi ziliao* 臨夏市文史資料 (Linxia municipality literary and historical materials), no. 3 (1987): 1–88.

Zhang Xinyi 張心一. "Liu nian lai Gansu shengchan jianshe (yijiusiyi nian zhi yijiusiliu nian) 六年來甘肅生產建設 (一九四一至一九四六年)" (Gansu's production reconstruction over the past six years). *Gansu wenshi ziliao xuanji* 甘肅文史資料選集 (Gansu literary and historical materials selection), no. 26 (1987): 1–14.

Zhongguo Kexue Jishu Xiehui 中國科學技術協會 (China Science and Technology Association), ed. *Zhongguo kexue jishu zhuanjia zhuanlue, nongxue bian: Linye juan (yi)* 中国科学技术专家传略中國科學技術專家傳略, 農學編:林業卷 (一) (Brief biographies of Chinese scientific and technical experts, agronomy section: Forestry [1]). Beijing: Zhongguo nongye chubanshe, 1991.

Contributors

Parks M. Coble is the James L. Sellers Professor of History at the University of Nebraska-Lincoln, where he is a specialist in modern East Asian history. He is the author of *China's War Reporters: The Legacy of Resistance against Japan* (2015); *Chinese Capitalists in Japan's New Order: The Occupied Lower Yangzi, 1937–1945* (2003); *Facing Japan: Chinese Politics and Japanese Imperialism, 1931–1937* (1991); and *The Shanghai Capitalists and the Nationalist Government, 1927–1937* (1986). His current research focuses on hyperinflation in civil war China.

Susan Glosser is associate professor of history at Lewis & Clark College in Portland, Oregon. Her research interests include family, gender, and political culture in nineteenth- and twentieth-century urban China. Her book, *Chinese Visions of Family and State,* 1915–1953, examined family reform ideals in the first half of the twentieth century and what they reveal about Chinese nation building. Current projects include material life in World War II Shanghai and Americans' changing perceptions of China during World War II. She also runs a desktop press, Opal Mogus Books, which publishes translated and annotated PRC pamphlets for classroom use.

Matthew D. Johnson is an independent consultant and associate fellow of the Global Diplomatic Forum. Previously he was Executive Dean of the Faculty of Arts and Social Sciences at Taylor's University, Malaysia, and served on the board of the Malaysian-American Commission on Educational Exchange. He is a cofounder and director of the PRC History Group (http://prchistory.org/) and board member (at large) of the Historical Society for Twentieth-Century China. His publications include *Visualizing Modern China: Image, History, and Memory, 1750–Present* (Lexington, 2014); *China's iGeneration: Cinema and Moving Image Culture for the Twenty-First Century* (Bloomsbury, 2014); and *Maoism at the Grassroots: Everyday Life in China's Era of High Socialism* (Harvard, 2015). A volume on propaganda in post-1949 China is forthcoming.

Kwan Man Bun teaches Chinese history at the University of Cincinnati. He is preparing a manuscript on the use of fertilizers in modern China.

Sophia Lee, before retirement, taught Chinese and Japanese history at California State University, East Bay. She is now writing a book about the print media, schools, and food security in Japanese-occupied Beijing, 1937–1945.

Maruta Takeshi is a professor at the Graduate School of Integrated Arts and Sciences of Hiroshima University. He researches the history of China, including topics such as political ceremonies and symbols, folk customs, and the Chinese Communist Party. He is the author of numerous articles and books.

Micah S. Muscolino is professor and Paul G. Pickowicz Endowed Chair in Modern Chinese History at the University of California, San Diego. He is the author of *Fishing Wars and Environmental Change in Late Imperial and Modern China* (2009) and *The Ecology of War in China: Henan Province, the Yellow River, and Beyond, 1938–1952* (2015).

Brett Sheehan is professor of Chinese History at the University of Southern California. His research focuses on the intersection of business and economy with social, political, and cultural phenomena. He is the author of *Trust in Troubled Times: Money, Banking and State-Society Relations in Republican Tianjin, 1916–1937* and *Industrial Eden: A Chinese Capitalist Vision,* as well as numerous articles and book chapters.

Di Wang is Distinguished Professor of History at University of Macau. He is the author of *Street Culture in Chengdu: Public Space, Urban Commoners, and Local Politics, 1870–1930* (2003); *The Teahouse: Small Business, Everyday Culture, and Public Politics in Chengdu, 1900–1950* (2008); *The Teahouse under Socialism: The Decline and Renewal of Public Life in Chengdu, 1950–2000* (2018); and *Violence and Order on the Chengdu Plain: The Story of a Secret Brotherhood in Rural China, 1939–1949* (2018). He has twice won the Best Book Award (Non-North American) from the Urban History Association (2005, 2020). He is a recipient of prestigious research grants from organizations such as the NEH, NHC, and Fulbright Program.

Wang Chaoguang is Director of the Institute of World History, Chinese Academy of Social Sciences. Among other positions, he acts as Vice General Secretary of the Chinese History Association and Vice President of the Modern Chinese

History Association. He is the author of *Peace or War?: Policies of the Nationalist Party in Northeast China after the Sino-Japanese War* (*He yu zhan de jueze: Zhanhou Guomindang de dongbei juece* 和與戰的抉擇：戰後國民黨的東北決策) and *The Politics of Film: Research on Film Censorship in Republican China* (*Yingyi de zhengzhi: Minguo dianying jiancha zhidu yanjiu* 影藝的政治: 民國電影檢查制度研究).

Wen-hsin Yeh is the Richard H. and Laurie C. Morrison Chair Professor in the Department of History at the University of California, Berkeley. She is a historian of culture, society, and politics in late imperial and modern China, including Taiwan, and is the author of *The Alienated Academy: Culture and Politics in Republican China, 1919–1937; Provincial Passages: Culture, Space, and the Origins of Chinese Communism, 1919–1927; and Shanghai Splendor: Economic Sentiments and the Making of Modern China, 1843–1949, along with numerous articles, book chapters, and edited volumes.*

Index